René Descartes (1596–1650) is well-known for his introspective turn away from sensible bodies and toward non-sensory ideas of mind, body, and God. Such a turn is appropriate, Descartes supposes, but only once in the course of life, and only to arrive at a more accurate picture of reality that we then incorporate in everyday embodied life.

In this clear and engaging book, David Cunning introduces and examines the full range of Descartes' philosophy. A central focus of the book is Descartes' view that embodied human beings become more perfect to the degree that they move in the direction of finite approximations of independence, activity, immutability, and increased knowledge. Beginning with an introduction and a chapter on Descartes' life and works, Cunning also addresses the following key topics:

- Descartes on the wonders of the material universe
- skepticism as epistemic garbage, and the easy dissolution of hyperbolic doubt
- Descartes' three arguments for the existence of God
- the ontology of possibility and necessity
- freedom and embodiment
- arguments for the immateriality of mind
- sensible bodies and the pragmatic certainty by which to navigate them
- Descartes' stoic view on how best to live.

Descartes is an outstanding introduction to one of the greatest of Western philosophers. Including a chronology, suggestions for further reading, and a glossary of key terms, it is essential reading for anyone studying Descartes and the history of modern philosophy.

David Cunning is Professor of Philosophy at the University of Iowa, USA.

The Routledge Philosophers

Edited by Brian Leiter

University of Chicago, USA

The Routledge Philosophers is a major series of introductions to the great Western philosophers. Each book places a major philosopher or thinker in historical context, explains and assesses their key arguments, and considers their legacy. Additional features include a chronology of major dates and events, chapter summaries, annotated suggestions for further reading, and a glossary of technical terms.

An ideal starting point for those new to philosophy, they are also essential reading for those interested in the subject at any level.

Also available:

Hobbes
A.P. Martinich

Darwin
Tim Lewens

Rawls
Samuel Freeman

Spinoza
Michael Della Rocca

Russell
Gregory Landini

Wittgenstein
William Child

Heidegger
John Richardson

Adorno
Brian O'Connor

Husserl, second edition
David Woodruff Smith

Aristotle, second edition
Christopher Shields

Kant, second edition
Paul Guyer

Hume
Don Garrett

Dewey
Steven Fesmire

Freud, second edition
Jonathan Lear

Habermas
Kenneth Baynes

Peirce
Albert Atkin

Plato
Constance Meinwald

Plotinus
Eyjólfur Emilsson

Einstein
Thomas Ryckman

Merleau-Ponty, second edition
Taylor Carman

Leibniz, second edition
Nicholas Jolley

Bergson
Mark Sinclair

Arendt
Dana Villa

Cassirer
Samantha Matherne

Adam Smith
Samuel Fleischacker

Descartes
David Cunning

For more information about this series, please visit: https://www.routledge.com/The-Routledge-Philosophers/book-series/ROUTPHIL

David Cunning

Descartes

Routledge
Taylor & Francis Group

LONDON AND NEW YORK

First published 2024
by Routledge
4 Park Square, Milton Park, Abingdon, Oxon OX14 4RN

and by Routledge
605 Third Avenue, New York, NY 10158

Routledge is an imprint of the Taylor & Francis Group, an informa business

British Library Cataloguing-in-Publication Data
A catalogue record for this book is available from the British Library

Library of Congress Cataloging-in-Publication Data
Names: Cunning, David, author.
Title: Descartes / David Cunning.
Description: Abingdon, Oxon; New York, NY: Routledge, 2023. |
Series: The Routledge philosophers |
Includes bibliographical references and index.
Identifiers: LCCN 2023002830 (print) | LCCN 2023002831 (ebook) |
ISBN 9780415775045 (hardback) | ISBN 9780415775052 (paperback) |
ISBN 9781351210522 (ebook)
Subjects: LCSH: Descartes, René, 1596–1650. | Philosophy,
Modern—17th century. | Philosophers—France—Biography.
Classification: LCC B1873 .C86 2023 (print) |
LCC B1873 (ebook) | DDC 194—dc23/eng/20230407
LC record available at https://lccn.loc.gov/2023002830
LC ebook record available at https://lccn.loc.gov/2023002831

ISBN: 978-0-415-77504-5 (hbk)
ISBN: 978-0-415-77505-2 (pbk)
ISBN: 978-1-351-21052-2 (ebk)

DOI: 10.4324/9781351210522

Typeset in Joanna
by codeMantra

Contents

Acknowledgments

I am extremely grateful to a number of scholars who provided invaluable comments on individual chapters of the manuscript: Deborah Brown, Colin Chamberlain, Andrea Christofidou, Daniel Garber, Don Garrett, Seth Jones, David Landy, Alan Nelson, Kristopher Phillips, Scott Ragland, and Marleen Rozemond.

I am also grateful to Kate Lohnes, who helped me as a research assistant in spring and summer of 2021. I benefited very much from our discussions of the Descartes texts and the secondary literature.

I also benefited from the fruitful discussions that took place in my graduate seminar on Descartes in fall 2022. The participants were Jan Forsman, Mansour Galpour, Michael Phillips, Farrow Ulven, Ziyu Wang, and Andy Williams.

I would also like to thank the larger community of scholars of early modern philosophy. The work that we do is very important. The debates and disagreements that arise in the literature and at conferences are extremely generative, and I am grateful to be part of the community that makes it all possible.

I am also extremely grateful to Nicholas Jolley, Ed McCann, Christia Mercer, and Alan Nelson for the many respects in which they have influenced my work as a philosopher and historian of philosophy.

I also want to thank Naomi Greyser and Mira Grey Cunning for levels of support that seem to come easily to them but that make a tremendous difference to me.

I am also grateful to Tony Bruce and Adam Johnson at Routledge for all of their assistance in bringing the manuscript to fruition. I also want to thank Ganesh Pawan Kumar Agoor for all of his work through the copy-editing process.

Finally, I would also like to thank two anonymous referees who provided me with extremely constructive feedback on the entire book. I especially want to note that there were cases in which the reviewers disagreed with my reading, but in which their comments were a remarkable combination of charitable and incisive.

Chronology

1596	Born on March 31 in La Haye (now Descartes), France.
1597	Mother (Jeanne) dies. Descartes is raised by his maternal grandmother, Jeanne Sain, with his older brother and older sister, in La Haye.
1600	Father (Joachim) remarries and leaves La Haye with new family.
1606	Enrolls at La Flèche.
1614 or 1615	Completes studies at La Flèche.
1616	Earns baccalaureate in civil and canon law at the University of Poitiers.
1616–1618	Likely resides in Paris.
1618	Travels to the Netherlands and joins the army of Prince Maurice of Nassau. Meets Isaac Beeckman. Completes Compendium Musicae and gives it to Beeckman as a gift.
1618–1619	Works on problems of mathematics and mechanics under the guidance of Beeckman.
1619	Leaves for (modern-day) Germany to join the army of Maximilian of Bavaria. Studies the mathematizable motions of geometrical projectiles with Johannes Faulhaber in Ulm.
1620	Begins working on Rules for the Direction of the Mind. Eventually abandons the project (probably in 1628).

1622–1628	Travel in France and Italy. Does research in optics, mathematics, and perceptual cognition.
1624	Public meeting held in Paris to critique the views of Aristotle; the organizers were exiled from the city on pain of death. (But Descartes was not present as far as is known.)
1625	Wrote to his father about the possibility of pursuing a career in civil service, but did not follow through.
1625 or 1626	Meets Mersenne, who becomes Descartes' chief correspondent.
1627	Meets Cardinal Bérulle, who encourages Descartes to continue his researches.
1628	Discovers the sine law of refraction. Initiates the anatomical study of animal bodies.
1629	Begins working on The World. Develops an interest in lens-grinding and in the geometry of lenses. Becomes so interested in the study of solar parahelia that he reports that he can hardly do anything else. Mersenne communicates to Descartes that Beeckman claimed some influence on Descartes' Compendium Musicae; in 1630 Descartes writes an angry letter to Beeckman and breaks off relations with him.
1629–1630	Settles in the Netherlands, where he would reside for the next twenty years.
1633	Galileo is condemned by the Catholic Church for the heliocentric view that he espouses in Dialogue Concerning the Two Chief World Systems. Descartes withholds publication of The World, which defends the same view.
1635	Daughter Francine is born to Hélène Jans.
1637	Publishes Discourse on Method, which includes Optics, Meteorology, and Geometry. The much more explicitly anti-Aristotelian Treatise on Man and The World would not be published until after Descartes' death. Grey hairs are beginning to appear on his head, and he reports that he needs to devote himself exclusively to the slowing down of their growth.

1640	Francine dies of scarlet fever at age 5. Descartes' father and sister die later that fall.
1641	Publishes *Meditations on First Philosophy* in Latin, along with six sets of objections and replies. Begins work on *Principles of Philosophy*.
1642	The teaching of anti-Aristotelian views banned in the city of Utrecht. Father Bourdin writes a set of (very critical) objections to the *Meditations*. A second edition of *Meditations on First Philosophy* is published, which adds Bourdin's objections (and Descartes' replies) and also a letter to Father Dinet that takes issue with both Bourdin and the rector of the University of Utrecht, Gisbert Voetius.
1643	*The Admirable Method of the New Philosophy of René Descartes* is published presumptively by Voetius but actually by Martinus Schoock, a professor at the University of Groningen. The book has nothing to say that is admirable about Descartes but instead is largely condemning. Descartes publishes an open and very hostile letter to Voetius, running some 200 pages.
1643–1649	Descartes engages a long and extremely fruitful correspondence with Princess Elisabeth of Bohemia.
1644	*Principles of Philosophy* is published, in part with the hope that it might be used as a textbook at Jesuit schools.
1645	Descartes reports that he will dedicate a year to the dissection of animals and the study of their anatomy. His friend Regius uses Cartesian principles to arrive at conclusions that Descartes rejects; soon thereafter Descartes ends their friendship.
1646	Descartes completes a draft of *The Passions of the Soul*. Queen Christina of Sweden initiates a correspondence with him.
1647	Descartes condemned by Revius and other theologians at the University of Leiden. French translations of *Meditations on First Philosophy* and *Principles of Philosophy* are published. Travels to Paris and meets Gassendi, Hobbes, and Pascal. Begins

work on *Description of the Human Body*, which he is not able to complete before his death.

1648 Returns to Paris upon the offer of a pension from the King to continue his researches, but political tumult has him returning to the Netherlands.

1649 Publication of *The Passions of the Soul*. Descartes moves to Sweden in October to be tutor to Queen Christina and a scholar in her court.

1650 Provides daily lessons to Queen Christina at 5:00 am and contracts pneumonia. Dies in Stockholm on 11 February.

One

Introduction

The very big picture

It is tempting to attribute to Descartes a single-minded focus on abstract metaphysical matters. In his *Meditations on First Philosophy*, he invites us on an epistemic journey in which we distance ourselves from sensible bodies and turn our attention inward toward non-sensory ideas of things like mind, body, God, and immutable essences. We then appeal to such ideas to ground a view of reality that is a far cry from the view of reality that we had before. Another reason that we might attribute to Descartes a focused interest on abstract reflection is that he uses negative language in describing embodiment – how it gets in the way of our ability to have and sustain veridical non-sensory perceptions, how it results in a continual bombardment of distracting sensations and passions, and how generally speaking it is an obstacle in the way of the grasp of truth.[1]

But Descartes also supposes that embodiment is the source of a significant number of benefits, so long as our relationship to it is optimized. Embodiment is our lot, he acknowledges, and that is not a bad thing. To be sure, we are wise to work through the

---

1 See for example *Second Replies*, AT 7:156–157, CSM 2:110–111, and *Principles of Philosophy* I.70–73, AT 8A:34–37, CSM 1:218–220. Note that the "AT" page references are to the twelve-volume collection of Descartes' work edited by Charles Adam and Paul Tannery. The "CSM" page references are to the widely used three-volume translation of Descartes' philosophical writings – the first two volumes by John Cottingham, Robert Stoothoff, and Dugald Murdoch, and the third volume (the correspondence) by Cottingham, Stoothoff, Murdoch, and Anthony Kenny.

DOI: 10.4324/9781351210522-1

Meditations and other metaphysical undertakings in order to arrive at non-sensory results that are unimpeachable. We arrive at a conception of self that provides us with an upgraded standard of evidence by which to identify the confusions that fall short of it. We arrive at a conception of God as the mark of supreme perfection, and we model our finite embodied lives accordingly: we recognize the goodness of qualities like independence, omniscience, activity, and immutability, and we approximate finite versions of these to the extent that is realistically possible.[2] We do metaphysics to understand the nature of God, and we do metaphysics to understand the kinds of creatures that there are and the kinds of features that they afford. Then we live and act. For example, we recognize that there exist bodies with features like size, shape, and motion, but not features like color or heat or *telos*,[3] and we experience and explain and predict material phenomena accordingly. We seek out and appreciate the immutable order is exhibited in such phenomena, and we uncover perfections in other aspects of the creaturely realm as well. We secure the small number of abstract metaphysical results that are available to us, and we incorporate those results in a way that is appropriate to our still embodied nature.

This chapter provides an outline of the book along with an initial discussion of some of the central tenets of Descartes' system. The second chapter addresses his life and works. Chapter 3 is an inventory of abstract metaphysical matters about which Descartes is largely silent. There is much that is beyond our tether, Descartes supposes, and rather than lament our limits, he will celebrate our reach. As Locke would later say,

---

2 This is a controversial interpretation; I defend it below. A more common view is that Descartes holds that standards of goodness are decided arbitrarily by God and hence that they are not pegged to the paradigm of divine perfection. That view is mistaken, I will argue, and it misleads us into thinking that the primary role of God in Descartes' system is epistemological.

3 This is roughly the purpose or goal toward which the activity of a thing is directed. Goal-directedness is a kind of mentality that is pervasive in nature, according to Descartes' Aristotelian opponent, even if it is very much unlike the reflective mentality that is exhibited in a human being. See also Skrbina (2005), 25–34, and Gotthelf (1976), 240–249.

It will be no excuse to an idle and untoward servant, who would not attend his business by candle-light, to plead that he had not broad sun-shine. The candle, that is set up in us, shines bright enough for all our purposes.[4]

Descartes agrees. There are some abstract metaphysical matters on which he takes a stand – for example, the existence and nature of God, the immateriality of mind, and the nature and existence of body – but there is much that he supposes to be beyond us. In numerous instances, he identifies a difficult metaphysical matter but exerts almost no effort to make sense of it. He leaves it alone in a way that is almost cavalier. In other cases, he engages a brief struggle, but he concludes that (for us at least) the matter admits of no resolution. The ideas from which we would garner the requisite information would appear to have too little content to do the work that we might expect of them. He does not despair of our epistemic situation, however, as there are other tasks that are more pressing.

The fourth chapter is a discussion of Descartes and skepticism. I argue that Descartes employs skeptical arguments to redirect the mind away from confused long-standing opinions – usually opinions that are grounded in a sense-based picture of reality. If we carefully entertain such arguments, we converge on axioms and premises that exhibit an unprecedented and (Descartes thinks) newfound level of evidence. We then marshal those axioms and premises in the service of deriving other results. The axioms and premises are so clear and evident that they leave in the dust the premises of the skeptical arguments themselves. That is to say, Descartes holds that his own skeptical argumentation is not particularly rigorous. In some cases, he will admit, it is incoherent. But it is indispensable. It enables us to arrive at non-sensory axioms and premises that dismantle confused conceptions of mind, body, and God. On the basis of emended conceptions of mind, body, and God, we arrive at a new picture of reality. We break a habit of affirming the longstanding opinions that we brought to inquiry, and we develop and benefit from cognitive habits that are more informed. We assemble the

---

4 Locke (1689), I.1, 45.

abstract metaphysical results that are within our grasp, and we apply them in our everyday embodied lives. Skepticism is indispensable, according to Descartes, but it is also in a way an afterthought. If we were not so confused, we would just grasp the rigorous picture of reality straightaway.

Chapter 5 addresses the arguments that Descartes offers for the existence and nature of God. Descartes offers three such arguments in total. I argue that contrary to appearances each of these is a free-standing argument and is entirely independent of the others. Across his writings Descartes is extremely sensitive to the epistemic position of his varying readers, and he is explicit that the reason why he offers the three different arguments is to reach as many minds as possible. I also attempt to interpret the three arguments charitably and to locate both their weaknesses and their strengths. The chapter then concludes with a discussion of similarities between the philosophical systems of Descartes and Spinoza.

The sixth chapter is about Descartes on human freedom. I argue that Descartes does not subscribe to a libertarian view according to which human action carries with it a two-way ability to do otherwise.[5] Descartes is instead a compatibilist; he holds that at any given moment our mental states cannot be other than they are, but our will is properly identified as free in circumstances in which it is not encumbered by the states of the body or other non-volitional factors. There are numerous passages in which Descartes reflects a compatibilist view of freedom. For example, he says in one passage that "now that we have come to know God, we perceive in him a power so immeasurable that we regard it as impious to suppose that we could ever do anything that was not already preordained by him."[6] He adds in another that the immutable and eternal will of God "is the *total* cause of everything."[7] But there are also passages

---

5 There are different ways of characterizing the view, but one is this: according to the libertarian, no matter what we end up choosing to do at a given moment, it was possible for us to make a different choice instead. See also Van Inwagen (1983). For a discussion of libertarian freedom in the context of Descartes, see Ragland (2006) and Wee (2006).

6 *Principles* I.40, AT 8A:20, CSM 1:206.

7 "To Princess Elizabeth, 6 October 1645," AT 4:314, CSMK 272, emphasis added.

in which he sounds more libertarian. I attempt to address all of the latter and argue that in the context of Descartes' larger system, they admit of a compatibilist reading as well. The second half of Chapter 6 then treats Descartes' Fourth Meditation resolution of the problem of error. That resolution might appear to require that Descartes hold that finite minds possess libertarian freedom – a two-way ability to affirm or deny that puts the responsibility for error on us and not on the incompetence of our creator. I argue instead that Descartes holds that God preordains all of our volitions, but He also preordains the union of our mind to a body, and our ideas become confused as a result of that union. At any given moment, we affirm the clear and distinct idea that God wills that we affirm, but as a result of mind-body union, we also in many cases affirm confused material that attaches to the idea like a tail, and our affirmation is false. There are numerous benefits to embodiment, Descartes thinks, and a finite mind attached to a body has more perfection than it would have if it were not embodied and its ideas were not confused.

In Chapter 7, I consider Descartes' multiple arguments for the view that finite minds are immaterial substances. I argue that at least one of these is still a contender in contemporary debates about the nature of mind and that it might even get the upper hand. Descartes is arguing more generally that finite minds are immaterial and are made in the image of supreme perfection. A finite mind is a substance already, but it has room to move further in the direction of a level of substantiality (and independence) that is more advanced.

Chapter 8 is a discussion of Descartes' arguments for the existence of material things. Descartes holds that we know with the highest level of confidence that there exist bodies with features like size, shape, and motion, and he holds that we know with the highest level of confidence that these bodies are the cause of our perceptions of sensible particulars. But he concludes that we do not know nearly as well the *details* of sensible particulars – for example, tables, chairs, mountains, and rivers, or pieces of wax, or the microscopic bodies that compose any of these. Still, sensory perception provides us with guidance that is "sufficient… for application to ordinary life."[8]

---

8 *Principles* IV. 205, AT 8A:327, CSM 1: 289–290.

Chapter 9 is a discussion of Descartes on how to live. For Descartes, the exemplar of perfection is God – a being that is (among other things) independent, immutable, and omniscient. Finite beings live well to the degree that they increase their perfection, which is to say that they live well to the degree that they be become more independent, more unflappable, and more informed. Descartes is a Stoic, and his particular variant of Stoicism is informed by his understanding of a perfection that we will never reach but to which we would be wise to aspire.

Chapter 10 is then a brief conclusion.

Now we turn to an initial presentation of the view of reality that Descartes defends and the principles that he mobilizes to defend it.

The pre-eminence of intellectual perception

A *methodological* tenet to which Descartes subscribes is that clear and distinct perceptions are the province of the intellect and not the senses. He writes,

> if there is any certainty to be had, the only remaining alternative [after we rule out sensory perception] is that it occurs in the clear perceptions of the intellect and nowhere else.[9]
>
> certainty does not lie in the senses but solely in the understanding, when it possesses evident perceptions.[10]
>
> intuition is the indubitable conception of a clear and attentive mind which proceeds solely from the light of reason.[11]

He reveals the same in a number of other texts – for example, in "To Princess Elizabeth, 28 June 1643," AT 3:692, CSMK 227; the Second Mediation (AT 7:30–31, CSM 2:20–21); Fifth Replies (AT 7:385, CSM 2:264); "To Mersenne, 27 May 1638," (AT 2:138, CSMK 102–103); and "To Mersenne, 16 November 1639," (AT 2:622, CSMK 141).[12]

---

9 *Second Replies*, AT 7:145, CSM 2:104.

10 Preface to the French edition of *Principles of Philosophy*, AT 8A:7, CSM 1:182.

11 *Rules for the Direction of the Mind*, AT 10:368, CSM 1:14.

12 A good deal of philosophers in the twenty-first century would argue that philosophy is a partly empirical discipline, but Descartes is working in a tradition that takes philosophical truth to be a matter of a priori conceptual analysis and

Descartes articulates the view that clear and distinct perceptions are the province of the intellect alone, and he also applies the view – for example, in the case of our perception of sensory particulars. After concluding in the Sixth Meditation that material bodies exist insofar as they possess the properties "which, viewed in general terms, are comprised within the subject-matter of pure mathematics" (AT 7:80, CSM 2:55), he proceeds to inquire into our grasp of the sensory aspects of a body. He raises the question,

> What of the other aspects of corporeal things which are either particular (for example that the sun is of such and such a size or shape), or less clearly understood, such as light or sound or pain, and so on?
>
> (AT 7:80, 55)

He then immediately answers the question: he says that there is a "high degree of doubt and uncertainty involved here." He adds later in the Meditation that

> the proper purpose of the sensory perceptions given me by nature is simply to inform the mind of what is beneficial or harmful for the composite of which the mind is a part, and to this extent they are sufficiently clear and distinct. But I misuse them as reliable touchstones for immediate judgments about the essential nature of the bodies located outside us; yet this is an area where they provide only obscure information.
>
> (AT 7:83, CSM 2:57–58)

He adds that "knowledge of the truth about such things seems to belong to the mind alone, not to the combination of mind and body" (AT 7:82–83, CSM 2:57). For Descartes, sensory perceptions are not entirely clear and distinct. They do help us "to distinguish the sky, the earth, the seas, and all other bodies, one from another"

---

purely mental scrutiny. For a recent collection of work that takes the opposite approach – "experimental philosophy" – see Knobe and Nichols (2008). For Descartes, philosophical truth is intuitive, unrevisable, and irrevocable.

(AT 7:75, CSM 2:52), but that is just to say that they provide us with pragmatic information that is critical to our survival.[13] What we perceive with the highest level of clarity and distinctness about bodies (or anything else) is grasped by the intellect alone.

The view that clear and distinct perceptions are the province of the intellect is especially prominent in Descartes' famous discussion of wax at the end of the Second Meditation. Earlier in the Second Meditation Descartes had argued that the first result that survives the skeptical onslaught of Meditation One is "I am, I exist" – a result that we do not grasp via our senses. We arrive at that result by doubting the existence of any sensory features that might pertain to our thinking (and doubting) mind, and we are still left thinking of something: "thought; this alone is inseparable from me" (AT 7:27, CSM 2:18). We think of our insensible thinking, but shortly thereafter, we become puzzled, or at least Descartes anticipates that we will become puzzled. If we are in the grip of the view that the kinds of things that we know best are things that we know via the senses, we will wonder how it can be that the first result that we secure in the *Meditations* is *not* known via the senses. Descartes writes,

> From all this I am beginning to have a rather better understanding of what I am. But it still appears – and I cannot stop thinking this – that the corporeal things of which images are formed in my thought, and which the senses investigate – are known with much more distinctness than this puzzling 'I' which cannot be pictured in the imagination. And yet it is surely surprising that I should have a more distinct grasp of things which I realize are doubtful, unknown, and foreign to me, than I have of that which is true and known – my own self.
>
> (AT 7:29, CSM 2:20)

Lest we become confused and dismiss the reasoning of the first half of the Meditation as smoke and mirrors, Descartes proceeds to reinforce that the existence of our thinking mind is just as evident as

---

13 The pragmatic utility of sensory perceptions will be one of the main topics of Chapter 8.

we thought it was – even though it is not sensible. He does this by pointing to another example of something that we know and that we will admit that we know, but that we do not know through the senses. First he has us consider a piece of wax "that has just been taken from the honeycomb" (AT 7:30, CSM 2:20) – an entity that manifests color, scent, taste, and (if we bang on it) sound. Then he asks us to reflect on what would happen to the piece of wax if we manipulated it and all of its sensible features were to change (AT 7:30–32, CSM 2:20–21). For example, we melt the piece of wax, and it exhibits a different color, and it loses its smell. We do this over the course of a short period of time, and before us is "a body which presented itself to me in these various forms a little while ago, but which now exhibits different ones" (AT 7:30, CSM 2:20). We recognize that "the same wax remain[s]… It must be admitted that it does; no one denies it, no one thinks otherwise" (ibid.). We then ask how we know this. We do not know it through sense perception: by hypothesis, none of the features that we sensed to be present in the wax at the start of the thought experiment is present at the end. We recognize something to be present across all of the permutations of the piece of wax – its extension, flexibility, and changeability (AT 7:31, CSM 2:20). We also recognize that these admit of "countless changes" (AT 7:31, CSM 2:21) – more than the finite number that we have sensed. What we understand best about the piece of wax is not its color, taste, sound, or smell – these continue to change before our eyes, and in some permutations, the wax is (for example) odorless and transparent. What we understand best about the wax is its extension, and we understand that by an act of "purely mental scrutiny" (ibid.).

By the end of the wax experiment, we are no longer thinking the sensible piece of wax that we had in mind at the start.[14] We are grasping its general extension, flexibility, and changeability; we are grasping "the nature of this piece of wax" (AT 7:21, CSM 2:31), which in the final analysis Descartes takes to be the nature

---

14 See also the discussion in Patterson (2013), 249–253. I take it that the same analysis applies in the case of the Second Replies claim about the level of clarity of distinctness that we can achieve with respect to our perception of a region of the sea (AT 7:113, CSM 2:81).

of *any* corporeal thing.[15] He adds a few sentences later in the Second Meditation that our perception of the wax "can be imperfect and confused, as it was before, or clear and distinct, as it is now."[16] For Descartes, what it is to have a clear and distinct perception is to have a non-sensory perception.

The features that do (and do not) apply to body

A methodological tenet to which Descartes subscribes is that clear and distinct perceptions are the province of the intellect and not the senses. A tenet at which he *arrives* via non-sensory perception is that the material universe has extensive modifications like size, shape, and motion, but not intensive modifications like color, smell, taste, and sound. In the Second Meditation, Descartes had argued that the sensory features of a body are not particularly well known. It turns out that one of the *reasons* that the sensory features of a body are not well known is that bodies do not possess such features at all. Instead, color, taste, sound, and the like are subjective and mind-dependent: they exist only as sensations in our thought. He writes,

> In order to distinguish what is clear in connection from what is obscure, we must be very careful to note that pain and colour and so on are clearly and distinctly perceived when they are regarded merely as sensations or thoughts. But when they are judged to be real things existing outside of our mind, there is no way of understanding what sort of things they are.[17]

---

15 For example in *Principles* I.53, AT 8A:25, CSM 1:210–211.

16 Note that I am disagreeing with Schmaltz, who argues that in the Second Meditation "this piece of wax" is perceived clearly and distinctly. See Schmaltz (2018), 8–10.

17 *Principles* I.68, AT 8A:33, CSM 1:217. See also *Comments on a Certain Broadsheet*, AT 8B: 358–359, CSM 1: 304, and Nelson (1997). It is now the standard view in modern science that color is not literally in bodies, but instead there are entities like wavelengths that give rise to our perceptions of color. (See for example Malacara (2011), Chapter 1.) Descartes was extremely influential in getting the view off the ground, and by the end of the seventeenth century, it was already

Here Descartes is positing that colors and other sensory qualities are unintelligible as mind-independent entities. To be sure, there is something in bodies that plays a role in the production of sensations in our thought.[18] Descartes is even happy to use the language of sensations to label that (mind-independent) something, so long as we keep straight the distinction between what is mind-dependent and what is not. For example, he is happy to use the word "color" to pick out the mind-independent sizes and shapes that give rise to our sensations of color,[19] but strictly speaking color is a sensation or thought. So long as we get the ontology right, the language does not matter. There is a debate about whether or not features like color exist mind-independently in Descartes' ontology, or whether they are merely sensations.[20] That debate would appear to be merely verbal. Descartes is happy to say that sensory qualities like color exist only as mind-dependent sensations *and* that they exist mind-independently insofar as they are the cause of those sensations. Sensations and the causes of sensations are actual existents, but they are very different things.

Descartes subscribes to the view that strictly speaking sensory qualities like color are not modifications of body. The first step of his argument for the view is that the features of a substance are

---

accepted by many. One of the very vivid statements of the view is in the work of his near-contemporary Ralph Cudworth:

> it was not the intention of God or nature to abuse us herein, but a most wise contrivance thus to beautify and adorn the visible and material world, to add lustre or embellishment to it, that it might have charms, relishes, and allurements to it, to gratify our appetites. Whereas otherwise reality in itself, the whole corporeal world in its naked hue, is nothing else but a heap of dust or atoms, of several figures and magnitudes, variously agitated up and down. So that these things, which we look upon as such real things without us, are not properly modifications of bodies themselves, but several modifications, passions, and affections of our own souls.
>
> (Cudworth 1678, 148–149)

18 In Chapter 8, there is a detailed discussion of Descartes of the role of bodies in sensory perception.

19 *Principles* IV.198, AT 8A:322–323, CSM 1:285.

20 See for example Jolley (1990), 83, Wilson (1992), and Wolf-Devine (1993), 46. For a treatment of all the different interpretive options, see MacKenzie (1994), and also Nolan (2011).

either its basic essential features or features that can be understood and explained in terms of its basic essential features. He says in *Principles* I.53,

> each substance has one principal attribute which constitutes its nature or essence, and to which all of its other properties are referred. Thus extension in length, breadth and depth constitutes the nature of corporeal substance; and thought constitutes the nature of thinking substance. Everything else which can be attributed to body presupposes extension, and is merely a mode of an extended thing; and similarly, whatever we find in the mind is simply one of the various modes of thinking. For example, shape is unintelligible except in an extended thing; and motion is unintelligible except as motion in an extended space; while imagination, sensation and will are intelligible only in a thinking thing.
>
> (AT 8A:25, CSM 1:210–211)

The conclusion that sensory qualities like color are not modifications of body is now supposed to follow very quickly, though with a good amount of background that Descartes is assuming to be obvious. In the Second Meditation (and elsewhere), he takes himself to establish that the nature of body is to be extended in length, breadth, and depth. The argumentational addition of *Principles* I.53 is to posit that any features that a substance has aside from its essential features are features that can be understood and explained in terms of its essential features. In the Second Meditation Descartes speaks of the wax as losing its taste and smell, and he clearly has in mind (though he does not explicitly say) that it could lose its color as well – for example, if it were to become transparent.[21] A body could lose any of its sensory qualities, Descartes is supposing, and it would still be a body. The one thing that it cannot lose is its three-dimensional extension. What that means (for Descartes) is that if a body is ever going to have any

---

21 For example, in the case of things like air, glass, and water, which for Descartes are not unusual anomalies. He will defend the view that there is no empty space and that well over 99% of the bodies that surround us (like air) are transparent. A discussion of that view is just below.

additional features, they will be features that are explicable in terms of extension or in terms of features that are themselves explicable in terms of extension. He supposes that it is obvious that extended bodies allow for features like size, shape, and motion:

> I have observed as a result that nothing whatever belongs to the concept of body except the fact that it is something which has length, breadth, and depth and is capable of various shapes and motions....[22]

However, there is no way to explain how a body with only such features could all of a sudden come to have sensory qualities like color or taste or sound.[23] A body without color, taste or sound could be molded or manipulated into a larger body that has no color or taste or sound. However, if color or taste or sound ever appeared, Descartes is supposing, it would be magic. Sensory qualities therefore are not modifications of bodies. We are aware of them as modifications of mind, and mind is indeed where Descartes houses them.

Corporeal substance

Another tenet of the Cartesian system is that the created material universe is a continuous plenum of bodies. Descartes arrives at this view by applying the a priori metaphysical axiom that nothingness has no properties. If nothingness has no properties, then there is never any empty space between two bodies, but the extent of the distance between them must be the property of some reality. He writes,

> As I have often said, nothingness cannot possess any extension. Hence, if someone asks what would happen if God were to take away every single body contained in a vessel, without allowing any other body to take the place of what had been removed, the answer must be that the sides of the vessel would, in that case

---

22 Sixth Replies, AT 7:440, CSM 2:297.
23 See *Principles* IV.198; AT 8A:322, CSM 1:285. See also Downing (2011), and Chamberlain (2019), 304–305.

have to be in contact. ...And it is a manifest contradiction for
them to be apart, or to have a distance between them, when the
distance in question is nothing; for every distance is a mode
of extension, and therefore cannot exist without an extended
substance.[24]

If two bodies have nothing in between them, Descartes is supposing,
then they have nothing in between them, and hence, they are
touching. If two bodies are separated by some distance – for example
by a distance that can be measured as the length of a line – that
length is the length of something, and it is the length of the sort of
thing that can have length as a property, namely an extended thing.
We might say that "empty space" separates two distant bodies, or
that there is an extended distance between the two bodies without
that distance being the property of anything, but Descartes has to
conclude that in such cases we are using language that is confused
or not referential.[25] He appreciates that his plenum metaphysics is
counter-intuitive to those "whose reason extends no farther than
their fingertips,"[26] but he would remind us that there are things like
wind and air that are invisible and that are far from nothing.[27] In
the "empty space" between bodies, there is just as much being as
anywhere else, even if our attention is not directed at it. We might
find unintuitive the view that there is the same amount of matter in
a region that appears to be empty and a region that exhibits color
and sound, but Descartes again holds that strictly speaking bodies
do not have color or sound. The extended substance that appears to
be colored is a lot more like the "empty" region than we tend to
imagine. In the Second Meditation, he argues that "I am, I exist" is
far more evident than any result that we uncover through the senses.
He thereby clears a path to a non-sensory representation of the

---

24 *Principles of Philosophy* II.18, CSM 1:231. See also *Principles* II:22, AT 8A:52, CSM
   1:232.
25 Descartes says that when people use expressions like *empty space* "[t]here is thus
   no correspondence between their verbal expressions and what they grasp in
   their minds" (*Principles* II.9, AT 8A:45, CSM 1:227).
26 *The World*, AT 11:21, CSM 1:87.
27 Ibid., AT 11:23, CSM 1:88.

corporeal world that is similarly evident and that is to be accepted over its sensory analogue.

Nothingness has no properties, according to Descartes, and there is no empty space between distant physical bodies. We might wonder then how he will locate a distinction between different corporeal substances when he would seem to be committed to the view the entire physical universe is a single continuous stretch of body. He might try to do it by positing the existence of a single (gigantic) corporeal substance and then inquiring into changes that it might undergo: returning to the Second Meditation discussion of wax, it might be changed "from [having] a round shape to a square shape, or from a square shape to triangular shape" (AT 7:31, CSM 2:20). Alternately, it might be molded to have multiple (but smaller) shapes, like a square that abuts a triangle. But it would still be the same substance that remains after "countless changes of this kind" (AT 7:31, CSM 2:21).[28]

Or instead Descartes might point to modifications that are inserted throughout the stretch of body (that is the universe) and that would appear to mark boundaries – like the line that is the border of both the square and the triangle that it abuts. However, any such modifications would just be modifications of the single body. The line would be like a fence that protrudes across a single plot of land. Nor is the situation any different if we drop the language of inserting modifications and we instead reference the modifications that the single stretch of body has already. Descartes thus owns that there is an important sense in which it is the entire physical universe that is a substance, and not its particular regions:

> We need to know that all substances, or things which must be created by God in order to exist, are by their nature incorruptible and cannot ever cease to exist unless they are reduced to nothingness by God's denying his concurrence to them. Second, we need to recognize that body, taken in the general sense, is a substance, so that it too never perishes. But the human body, insofar

28 See also the discussion in Curley (1988), 17–18.

as it differs from other bodies, is simply made up of a certain configuration of limbs and other accidents of this sort...[29]

Here Descartes is sounding very much like Spinoza, at least with respect to his understanding of body.[30] Descartes says that individual bodies are not substances but are accidents – or what he often calls *modes*[31] – of substance. By way of contrast, he does not subscribe to the Spinozistic view that all modes of thought are modes of a single continuous mind.[32] Finite mental substances exist, for Descartes, and in many cases, they are united to bodies, but there are large and continuous stretches of body that exhibit no mentality at all. Thinking is not ubiquitous, but instead there are isolated pockets of thinking that exist within the single extended substance that is the material universe – in something like (but very much unlike) the way in which freestanding heat-signatures might be observed on a screen that is tracking suspects who are in a building and under surveillance. Descartes does not subscribe to the Spinozistic tenet that finite thought is always bound or limited by additional finite thought,[33] and so he does not conclude from that tenet that the thinking that is united to any individual human body is bound and limited by thinking that ranges across the entire universe.[34] But he

---

29 "Synopsis of these following six Meditations," AT 7:14, CSM 2:10.

30 See for example Spinoza (1677), Part I, Proposition 5, 218–219. Here I am disagreeing with commentators who hold that for Descartes individual bodies are substances – for example Schmaltz (2018), 3–10; Kaufman (2014) and Reid (2014). Below I say a little bit about a deflationary sense in which Descartes allows that individual bodies are substances. But whatever that deflationary sense is, it squares with the datum that the contiguous material universe is a single substance and individual bodies are modifications of it.

31 For example in the Third Meditation, AT 7:45, CSM 2:31; *Principles* I.53, AT 8A:25, CSM 1:210–211.

32 See for example Spinoza (1677), Part II, Corollary to Proposition 1, 250.

33 Spinoza (1677), Part I, Definition 2, 217. But Descartes does come close in "To Clerselier, 23 April 1649," AT 5:356, CSMK 377, and "To [Silhon], May 1637," AT 1:353, CSMK 55. See the discussion at the end of Chapter 5, pp. 187–192.

34 See for example Spinoza (1677), Part II, Proposition 7, 247.

does subscribe to the view (that Spinoza later picked up from him) that modes of extension are modes of a single extended substance.[35] In Principles I.51 Descartes says that one of the criteria that a thing has to meet to be a substance is to be ontologically independent. He writes,

> By substance we can understand nothing other than a thing which exists in such a way as to depend on no other thing for its existence.
>
> (AT 8A:24, CSM 1:210)

Strictly speaking only God is a substance, and

> as for corporeal substance and mind (or created thinking substance), these can be understood to fall under the common concept: things that need only the concurrence of God in order to exist.[36]

The material universe is a substance in a secondary sense, according to Descartes, insofar as it depends for its existence on God but nothing else. It "cannot ever cease to exist unless [it is] reduced to nothingness by God's denying his concurrence to them," and so it is a mostly independent entity (AT 7:14, CSM 2:10). There is then a tertiary sense in which we might identify individual bodies as

---

35 See also Gueroult (1968), 541; Gueroult (1953), 107–108; Keeling (1968), 129–130; Williams (1978), 126–129; Cottingham (1986), 84–88; Dicker (1993), 212–217; Lennon (1993, 191–210); Sowaal (2004); and Gombay (2007), 105–106. Note that in Principles I.60, Descartes says that we can "be certain that... each and every part of it [matter], as delimited by us in our thought, is really distinct from the other parts of the same substance" (AT 8A:28–29, CSM 1:213). But Descartes does not say here that we have clear and distinct perceptions of individual corporeal substances. He says that to the degree that we clearly and distinctly perceive individual bodies as substances, they are really distinct, but individual bodies are never perceived with full clarity and distinctness (for example, AT 7:31, CSM 1:21), and in addition the colors and sounds by which we delineate individual bodies (AT 7:75, CSM 2:52) are not really in them. See also the discussion in Paul (2020).

36 Principles I.52, AT 8A:25, CSM 1:210.

substances,[37] though it is not clear exactly what we are buying when we secure that designation for them. An individual body depends for its existence on God – like all creatures – but it also depends for its structural integrity and its existence *qua* individual on the bodies that surround it and the bodies that surround those. We cannot say of it that it cannot ever cease to exist unless it is denied the concurrence of God: individual bodies decompose and disintegrate all the time. Still, a body might become more independent, and hence more substantial, to the extent that it is able to fend off the influence of bodies that attempt to overtake it.[38] But individual bodies never come close to being as independent as the single substance that is the material universe, and they merit the title of "substance" in the most derivative sense only. I do appreciate that it sounds nutty to say that for Descartes what exists is basically a Siamese n-teplet, or a single material substance to which are united a large number of minds. But he will allow that there are buffers by which individual bodies (and also minds) might increase their independence.

Descartes does not hold that finite minds are so ubiquitous that they are united to all regions of the extended universe, but he does expect that a supreme being would be a bountiful creator and that more minds would sprinkle the plenum of bodies than just the ones in our immediate vicinity. He writes,

> The prerogatives which religion attributes to human beings need some explanation, since they seem difficult to believe in, if the extension of the entire universe is supposed indefinite. ...I do not see that the mystery of the Incarnation, and all the other favours God has done to man, rule out his having done countless other great favours to an infinity of other creatures. ... [I]f the indefinite extension of the universe gives ground for inferring that there must be inhabitants of places other than the earth, so does the extension which all the astronomers attribute to it; for every one of them judges that the earth is smaller in

---

37 See Sowaal (2004).

38 I am assuming that for Descartes the extent to which a creature depends for its existence on God never fluctuates, but that a creature might become more (or less) causally independent.

comparison with the entire heavens than a grain of sand in comparison with a mountain.[39]

Here Descartes is saying that a supreme being would create in ways that reflect Its perfection, and so presumably, there exist other planets that host life, and perhaps even minds that are more noble and exalted than we are. He adds that "we do not know that we are obliged to believe that we are the end of creation" (AT 5:53, CSMK 321) and that "[God] has created so many things of which we are only a tiny part."[40] Pockets of created reality abound, Descartes supposes, and it would be a surprise if the single substance that composes the material universe is not united to thinking far and wide. In Chapter 9 – "How Best to Live" – there will be a discussion of what Descartes takes to be the ethical implications of the interdependence of creatures. In short, he thinks that

> none of us could subsist alone and that each one of us is really one of the many parts of the universe.... And the interests of the whole, of which each of us is a part, must always be preferred to those of our own particular person....[41]

Commentators have not made much of this passage, perhaps because Descartes focuses so heavily on the activity of the isolated thinking ego in his metaphysical work.[42] But we are embodied minds also, and the activity that is appropriate to an embodied mind is not the same as the activity that is appropriate to an ego that is more solitary. An embodied mind is united to a body that is contiguous with bodies that are contiguous with bodies, and among these are bodies that are united to other minds. Descartes will accordingly speak of the benefit that accrues to human beings who optimize their contiguity with the rest of creation – a contiguity from which we could never extricate ourselves anyway.

---

39 "To Chanut, 6 June 1647;" AT 5:56, CSMK 322.
40 "To Chanut, 1 February 1647," AT 4:608, CSMK 309.
41 "To Princess Elizabeth, 15 September 1645," AT 4:293, CSMK 266.
42 An important exception is Wee (2002).

Descartes argues that the material universe is a continuous plenum of bodies, but noteworthy is that he refrains from saying that it extends infinitely. Instead, he says that it is indefinitely extended in the sense that "we are unable to discover a limit" to it.[43] He does not want to attribute an infinitude of being to any entity apart from God,[44] and so he concludes that the material universe is not infinitely extended. He says that "we fail to recognize any limits [in God and]... that our understanding positively tells us that there are none" (AT 8A:15, CSM 2:202), but "in the case of other things our understanding does not in the same way positively tell us that they lack limits in some respect" (ibid.). What is puzzling (at least to me) is why Descartes does not conclude positively that the material universe has a limit in the sense that it is finite in its extension. He holds that God creates the material universe and then conserves it in existence,[45] and so he would appear to hold that the amount of corporeal substance that exists is a constant. He also insists that something cannot come from nothing,[46] and so it is not clear how additional material substance would arise from the material substance that already exists. Nor is there any empty space that bounds the material universe – empty space into which the universe could expand. Descartes would appear to be committed to the view that the material universe is finite in its extent and that there is nothing beyond it – no ontological grid of any kind. But he does not say that anywhere. And in a very late (1649) letter, he goes in the opposite direction and suggests that the material universe might in fact be infinite. He says of "things like the extension of the world and the number of parts into which matter is divisible" that "I confess that I do not know whether they are absolutely infinite; I merely know that I know no end to them."[47] The question of extent of the material

---

43 Principles I.26, AT 8A:15, CSM 1:202. See also "To Chanut, 6 June 1647," AT 5:56, CSMK 322.

44 Principles I.27, AT 8A:15, CSM 1:202; "To More, 5 February 1649," AT 5:274–275, CSMK 364.

45 For example in the Third Meditation, AT 7:48–49, CSM 2:33. See Chapter 3, pp. 83–88.

46 For example in Second Replies, AT 7:135, CSM 2:97.

47 "To More, 5 February 1649," AT 5:274, CSMK 364.

universe – of how there could be a boundary that is surrounded by nothing, or alternately how matter could extend infinitely if something cannot come from nothing – is a mind-bender. As we will see, it is one of many metaphysical questions on which Descartes is silent.

The material universe is a continuous plenum of bodies that is very different from what we experience it to be through our senses, or so Descartes is arguing. It does not have the colors or tastes or sounds that we sense it to have. It does not contain any empty space.[48] It also contains immaterial finite minds that as best we can tell are sprinkled far and wide across the single corporeal substance to which they are united.

An initial discussion of the immateriality of mind

One of Descartes' arguments for the immateriality of finite minds is isomorphic with his argument for the view that bodies do not possess sensory qualities. The argument in effect is that there is no way to explain how bodies could ever come to have modifications like ideas and volitions if they just had features like size, shape, and motion to start. Such bodies could come to have larger sizes, and different shapes, and faster motions, but no trace of thinking could arise from ingredients that exhibit no trace of thinking themselves. As Descartes puts it in the *Principles* IV.198 passage, "there is no way of understanding how these same attributes (size, shape, and motion) can produce something else whose nature is quite different from their own." He supposes (in *Principles* I.53) that "each substance has one principal attribute which constitutes its nature or essence" – an attribute which is "presuppose[d]" by all of its other properties and "to which all of its other properties are referred." But "shape is unintelligible except in an extended thing; ... while imagination, sensation and will are intelligible only in a thinking thing" (AT 8A:25, CSM 1:210–211). We have seen this argument elsewhere:

---

48 This also is not an uncommon view in modern science. Many physicists argue that what we call "empty space" is filled with radiation and other forms of material energy. See for example Riek et al. (2015).

Can a thing extended in length, width, and depth reason, desire, sense? Undoubtedly not, for all the ways of being of such an extended thing consist only in relations of distance; and it is evident that these relations are not perceptions, reasonings, pleasures, desires, sensations – in a word, thoughts. Therefore this I that thinks, my own substance, is not a body, since my perceptions, which surely belong to me, are something entirely different from relations of distance.[49]

It must be confessed, moreover, that perception and what depends on it are inexplicable by mechanical reasons, that is, by figures and motions. If we pretend that there is a machine whose structure enables it to think, feel and have perception, one could think of it as enlarged yet preserving its same proportions, so that one could enter it as one does a mill. If we did this, we should find nothing within but parts which push upon each other; we should never see anything which would explain a perception.[50]

Descartes, Malebranche, and Leibniz are clearly on to something. It seems obvious (to me at least) that the reflective activity that Descartes takes to be part and parcel of thinking is not and cannot be the product of the behavior of smaller scale bodies that exhibit no trace of thinking.[51] Or at the very least: if thinking is the product of the behavior of such bodies, there is no satisfying account that will explain how and why and when bodies with zero mentality all of a sudden come to be (even a little bit) minded. If Descartes and Malebranche and Leibniz are right, bodies would be able to think so long as thinking is super-added to bodies as a result of an inexplicable miracle, but not as a result of resources that are native to bodies on their own.[52] To say that mentality arises from the behavior of entities that are wholly non-mental is to provide no explanation at all.

---

49 Malebranche (1688), 6.
50 Leibniz (1714), section XVII, 215.
51 See also Cavendish (1666), 27, Strawson (2008), 60–74, and Cunning (2023).
52 See also Locke (1689), III.iv.6, 540.

An initial discussion of supreme perfection or God

Another tenet of Descartes' system is that there exists a supremely perfect being. An argument that he offers for this tenet is from the objective reality (or roughly speaking the content) of ideas. At the start of the Third Meditation, he is still in the mode of a skeptic, and he has not yet posited the existence of anything other than his thinking. He notices that the items at his evidentiary disposal include introspectable ideas, and he notices further that his ideas differ insofar as they represent different things:

> in so far as different ideas represent different things, it is clear that they differ widely. Undoubtedly, the ideas which represent substances to me amount to something more and, so to speak, contain more objective reality than the ideas which merely represent modes or accidents. Again, the idea that gives me my understanding of a supreme God, eternal, infinite, omniscient, omnipotent, and the creator of all things that exist apart from him, certainly has in it more objective reality than the ideas that represent finite substances.
>
> (AT 7:40, CSM 2:28)

Here Descartes is supposing that there is something that is in an idea that allows us to tell when the idea is of one entity as opposed to another.[53] If so, he goes on to contend, the existence of an idea of God is evidence that God exists in fact. An idea is not of God unless it mirrors the amount of being that God would have if God

---

53 I state that Descartes is "supposing...," but in the case of many of the claims that he advances, he thinks that he is identifying truths that are obvious and non-negotiable. I will sometimes use expressions like "Descartes supposes" and "Descartes posits," but only because it would be highly repetitive in every case to state that he is advancing what he takes to be an unrevisable and foundational starting point. I also use the more humble language of "supposing" and "positing" in order to acknowledge that there are numerous claims that Descartes sees as obvious but that – because he seems them as obvious – he does not defend in any way. He is in good company, however, if a philosopher has to assume at least some basic principles and axioms to be intuitive and not defensible *ad infinitum*.

existed, and so an idea of God would have an infinite amount of what Descartes calls *objective reality*. But no finite being has enough efficacy to produce an entity with an infinite amount of reality – even if that entity is only an idea – and so there exists a being with infinite power (AT 7:45, CSM 2:31). That *has* to be right, Descartes is thinking. It is an axiom that something cannot come from nothing, and so our idea of God must have a cause.[54] A finite being (like a mind) might have within itself the power to produce a *finite stretch* of the infinitude in the idea of God, but the remaining (and still infinite) stretch of reality in that idea would also require a cause, and since it is infinite it would require a cause with infinite power. Descartes draws the conclusion that there exists a being with infinite power; he then proceeds to argue that that being does not *just* have infinite power. There is an inseparable connection between infinite power and features like omniscience and eternality, he argues, and so an infinitely powerful being would carry those features along with it (AT 7:50, CSM 2:34). It would be the supreme being itself.

We might object here that Descartes is wildly mistaken and that his reasoning does *not* have to be right. Part of what is compelling about the argument, however – at least in terms of its validity – is that Descartes is positing as a premise that we have an idea that is so grand and unprecedented that it could only be produced by God. Then he draws the conclusion that God exists. If we consider Descartes' argumentation from that level of generality – from 30,000 feet so to speak – it is in much better shape. He is certainly right that if we have an idea that has an amount of content that could only be produced by God, then God exists. So long as Descartes is right that we have the idea of God that he says we do, the conclusion follows straightaway. Much of the rest of the Third Meditation is thus an effort by him to get us to see that our idea of God is as he describes it (AT 7:45–50, CSM 2:31–34). There are efforts outside of the *Meditations* as well:

> if someone says of himself that he does not have any idea of God, in the sense in which I take the term 'idea', he is making

---

54 Unless it is in some way self-caused, or unless we (the minds that have the idea) are self-caused, but Descartes will argue that we and it are not.

the most impious confession he could make. He is saying that he does not know God by natural reason, but also that neither faith nor any other means could give him any knowledge of God. For if one has no idea, i.e. no perception which corresponds to the meaning of the word 'God', it is no use saying that one believes that God exists.[55]

Here Descartes is referencing individuals who hold that although there is no proof of the existence of God, we can still stand toward God via faith. Descartes says to them: we cannot have faith in the existence of God unless we have an idea that represents God – just the sort of idea that is posited in the Third Meditation. If an individual is able to read from her idea of God that the idea picks out the infinite being (and not something less), she can have faith, but she can also apply the premise that something cannot come from nothing and demonstrate the existence of God via argument. If there is nothing in the individual's idea that picks out God in particular, she cannot even say that she has faith. Or so Descartes is arguing. He clearly supposes that we have an idea of God and that it has a lot more being than many would be prepared to admit.

Descartes concludes that God exists and then appeals to the idea of God to deliver more information about what that entity is. For example, God is eternal and immutable.[56] He is also a necessary and wholly independent existent.[57] He does not have a cause: His "essence is so immense that he does not need an efficient cause in order to exist,"[58] but instead "he has existed for eternity and will

---

55 *Appendix to Fifth Objections and Replies*; AT 9A:209–210, CSM 2:273.

56 AT 7:45, CSM 2:31. See also *Principles* II.36, AT 8A:61–62, CSM 1:240; and *The World*, AT 11:37–38, CSM 1:93.

57 Descartes says that God has "necessary existence" throughout *First Replies*, AT 7:109–119, CSM 2:78–85. He also elaborates: God "exist[s] by [his] own power" (AT 7:119, CSM 2:85); "this power is so great that it is plainly the cause of his continuing in existence" (AT 7:110, CSM 2:79); and that God "possesses such great and inexhaustible power that [He] never required the existence of anything else in order to exist in the first place" (AT 7:109, CSM 2:78).

58 *Fourth Replies*, AT 7:241, CSM 2:168.

abide for eternity."[59] Nor does He (or anything else) produce His attributes: "His essence is such that He possesses from eternity" all the divine attributes, and "it is impossible for such a being to have the power and will to give itself something new."[60] But God is the cause of all *creaturely* reality, and insofar as creatures are concerned "every basis of truth and goodness depends on His omnipotence."[61] An opponent of Descartes might subscribe to a weaker conception of omnipotence according to which there exist independent standards of good and bad that God has to consult if He is going to create good things. God is in charge of creating *things*, the opponent might say, but He is not in charge of the criteria in the light of which they are properly identified as good or bad. Descartes disagrees. He holds that God decrees those criteria, and not on the basis of standards that are independent of Him. There are no such standards.

But that does not mean that God is totally in the dark and that the criteria that He authors are random.[62] There are no criteria of good or bad that are independent of God and that constrain Him to will as He does, Descartes argues, but there is such a thing as supreme perfection. The *Meditations* alone includes more than ten passages that refer to supreme perfection, for example, when Descartes writes that God is "supremely perfect" (AT 7:62, CSM 2:43) and is "a supremely perfect being" (AT 7:66, CSM 2:46). Then there are additional references to God as supremely perfect in Descartes' replies

---

59 The Fifth Meditation, AT 7:68, CSM 2:47. Descartes says that in some contexts it is fine (and it can even be useful) to speak of God as His own cause, so long as we recognize that we are speaking loosely and in a way that borders on incoherent – just like Archimedes would go to lengths to explain sphericality in terms of rectilinear figures, even though the notion of a rectilinear sphere is a contradiction (Fourth Replies, AT 7:241–245, CSM 2:168–171).

60 *Fourth Replies*, AT 7:241, CSM 2:168.

61 "For [Arnauld], 29 July 1648," 5:224, CSMK 358. See also *Sixth Replies;* AT 7:435, CSM 2:293–294.

62 A common view in the literature – tracing back to Frankfurt (1977) and Wilson (1978), 120–130 – is that (according to Descartes) God's omnipotent will is wholly arbitrary: it can even make two and three add to something other than five, or make God's essence something other than it is. At the end of Chapter 5, pp. 192–211, I argue that that view is mistaken and that according to Descartes the divine will is not so unhinged.

to the seven sets of objections, and in other texts as well.[63] God is supremely perfect, and hence, what it is to be supremely perfect is among other things to be omniscient, independent, immutable, eternal, and omnipotent.[64] God does not look to an independent standard of supreme perfection in order to tell that He is supremely perfect. That would make no sense.

Descartes holds that there exists perfection and that it is identical to God. He also holds that God creates with an eye to perfection. He writes for example that

> the way to reach the love of God is to consider that he is a mind, or a thing that thinks, and that our soul's nature resembles his sufficiently for us to believe that it is an emanation of his supreme intelligence, a 'breath of divine spirit'. Our knowledge seems to be able to grow by degrees to infinity, and since God's knowledge is infinite, it is at the point towards which ours strives.[65]
>
> [T]he mere fact that God created me is a very strong basis for believing that I am somehow made in his image and likeness.[66]

Finite minds fall far short of God, but they exist on a scale of perfection, and on a scale that leaves us room to progress. Descartes says for example in his discussion of the passions that to become more independent and free "renders us in a certain way like God

---

63 For example, Second Replies, AT 7:138, CSM 2:99; and Appendix to Fifth Objections and Replies, AT 9A:209, CSM 2:273. In the Sixth Meditation Descartes also appeals the "the goodness of God" (AT 7:83, CSM 2:58; AT 7:85, CSM 2:59; AT 7:88, CSM 2:60) and to "the immense goodness of God" (AT 7:88, CSM 2:61).

64 According to Descartes these conceptual interconnections fall out of the idea of God. See Principles I.14, AT 8A:10, CSM 1:197; Principles II.36, AT 8A:61–62, CSM 1:240; the Third Meditation, AT 7:45, CSM 2:31.

65 "To Chanut, 1 February 1647," AT 4:608, CSMK 309.

66 The Third Meditation, AT 7:51, CSM 2:35. See also the Fourth Meditation, AT 7:56–57, CSM 2:39–40, and De Peretti (2015), 220–223.

by making us masters of ourselves."[67] He also speaks elsewhere of creatures as being more and less perfect. He writes,

> [E]ven though we are *less perfect* than an angel, there is no need for the idea [of an angel] to be produced in us by an angel....[68]
> [A] second thing we must know [in addition to the nature of God] is the nature of our soul. We must know that it subsists apart from the body, and is much nobler than the body....[69]

In these passages, Descartes is referencing a scale of perfection with the supremely perfect being at the top, finite minds farther below, and other creatures farther below still. He also speaks of bodies as exhibiting perfections:

> The true function of reason... in the conduct of life is to examine and consider without passion the value of all the perfections, both *of the body and of the soul*, which can be acquired by our conduct.[70]

There are no completely perfect bodies, just as there is no completely perfect finite mind, but we do have ideas of body which are ideas of things that are "as perfect as a body can be."[71] For example, Descartes references the immutable order that is exhibited in the behavior of bodies – an order that is that product of (the perfection of) the divine will.[72]

---

67 *Passions* III.152, AT 11:445, CSM 1:384.

68 *Second Replies*, AT 7:138–139, CSM 2:99, emphasis added.

69 "To Princess Elizabeth, 15 September 1645," AT 4:292, CSMK 265. See also *Second Replies*, AT 7:139, CSM 2:100.

70 "To Princess Elizabeth, 1 September 1645," AT 4:286–287, CSMK 265, emphasis added.

71 *Second Replies*, AT 7:138, CSM 2:99. He adds in *Principles* III.45 that "the world was created right from the start with all the perfection that it now has" (AT 8A:99, CSM 1:256), and then says a few sentences later that "if we consider the infinite power of God, we cannot think that he ever created anything that was not wholly perfect of its kind" (AT 8A:100, CSM 1:256). See also *Second Replies* – AT 7:118, CSM 2:84, and AT 7:134, CSM 2:96 – and Shapiro (2011), 18–20.

72 *Principles* II.36, AT 8A:61, CSM 1:240.

A datum is that Descartes holds that God is the author of the criteria in virtue of which creatures are properly identified as good or bad. Another datum is that he holds that there exists a standard of perfection that is the divine being Itself. In the Fourth Meditation, he speaks of a scale of perfection that ranges from God (at the top) to non-being at the bottom. He writes,

I possess not only a real and positive idea of God, or a being who is supremely perfect, but also what may be described as a negative idea of nothingness, or of that which is farthest removed from perfection. I realize that I am, as it were, something intermediate between God and nothingness, or between supreme being and non-being....[73]

Here he identifies being and perfection. In a later text he identifies being and goodness: he speaks interchangeably of "non-being, non-good, or non-true" and says that "these three things are the same."[74] Being at the highest level is perfection, but as we have seen Descartes says that creatures exhibit perfections and that some creatures are more (or less) perfect than others. God is not the author of what counts as perfection, but he is the author of the criteria in virtue of which creatures are properly identified as good or bad. For example, He decides how far up the scale a thing needs to be in order to be identified as good. Something that is very close to non-being does not automatically merit identification as good, and on an infinite scale it is not obvious how and where to draw lines. There are lines, however, and it is axiomatic (Descartes supposes) that God decides them.[75]

---

73 AT 7:54, CSM 2:38. See also *Conversation with Burman*, AT 5:147–148, CSMK 334.
74 "To Clerselier, 23 April 1649," AT 5:357, CSMK 378. For a discussion of the historical background to the view that being and goodness are to be equated, see Stump and Kretzmann (1991).
75 A (very rough) analogy is the continuity on the political spectrum of liberal to conservative. In the United States, there was a time when politicians like Dwight Eisenhower and Richard Nixon were regarded as conservative. They are both on the spectrum from liberal to conservative, but the spectrum itself does not indicate when to identify a politician as conservative. That is up to convention.

Descartes subscribes to the view that God exists and is the standard of supreme perfection. The implications for his larger system are enormous. He does not suppose that God just randomly wills a model of goodness that we are then supposed to instantiate. It is not clear how a model of that sort would have anything to speak in its favor, and one of the reasons that Descartes' ethics has not been broadcast as an especially useful aspect of his philosophy, I suspect, is that it is easily interpreted as appealing to such a model exactly.[76] But Descartes does not offer an ethics that is random. He offers an ethics that is pegged to (what he takes to be) the standard of supreme perfection. Finite minds are higher on the scale of perfection than bodies, Descartes supposes, and finite minds increase their perfection by closer approximating supreme perfection – for example by becoming more knowledgeable, more independent, more immutable, and proportionally speaking more active. We also experience new and higher levels of pleasure.[77] We focus more of our time on things that are higher on the scale of perfection, and less of our time on things that do not matter. The former include finite minds and the unions and connections that we form with them. We work in concert with each other to become more active and independent, and to appreciate the material world and its wonders.

Further reading

There are a number of outstanding points of entry into Descartes' philosophical system. These include:

Janet Broughton and John Carriero (eds.), *A Companion to Descartes*, Oxford: Blackwell (2008).
John Cottingham, *Descartes*, London: Blackwell (1986).

---

76 Many commentators have argued that Descartes holds that the definition of goodness is arbitrarily decreed – for example for example Frankfurt (1977), 41–44; Webb (1989), 464–465, 470; Ragland (2006), 382; Brown (2006); Christofidou (2009); and Shapiro (2011). I am arguing that he takes goodness to be tied to supreme perfection.
77 *The Passions of the Soul* III.153–154, AT 11:446–447, CSM 1:384; *The Passions of the Soul* III.212, AT 11:488, CSM 1:404; and "To Princess Elizabeth, 4 August 1645," AT 4:265–266, CSMK 257–258.

Karen Detlefsen (ed.), *Descartes' Meditations: A Critical Guide*, Cambridge and New York: Cambridge UP (2012).

Georges Dicker, *Descartes: An Analytical and Historical Introduction*, Oxford: Oxford UP (1993).

Willis Doney (ed.), *Descartes: A Collection of Critical Essays*, New York: Doubleday (1968).

Stephen Gaukroger (ed.), *The Blackwell Guide to Descartes' Meditations*, Malden, MA: Blackwell (2006).

André Gombay, *Descartes*, Hoboken, NJ: Wiley -Blackwell (2007).

Marjorie Grene, *Descartes*, Indianapolis, IN: Hackett (1985).

Martial Gueroult, *Descartes' Philosophy Interpreted According to the Order of Reasons*, trans. Roger Ariew, Minneapolis, MN: Minnesota UP (1984).

Gary Hatfield, *Descartes and the Meditations*, New York: Routledge (2003).

Paul Hoffman, *Essays on Descartes*, New York and Oxford: Oxford UP (2009).

Norman Kemp Smith, *Studies in the Cartesian Philosophy*, New York: Russell and Russell (1962).

Anthony Kenny, *Descartes: A Study of His Philosophy*, Bristol: Thoemmes Press (1968).

Jean-Luc Marion, *On Descartes' Metaphysical Prism*, trans. Jeffrey L. Kosky, Chicago and London: Chicago UP (1999).

Georges J.D. Moyal (ed.), *René Descartes: Critical Assessments*, New York: Routledge (1991).

Steven Nadler, Tad M. Schmaltz, and Delphine Antoine-Mahut (eds.), *The Oxford Handbook of Descartes and Cartesianism*, Oxford: Oxford UP (2019).

Amélie Oksenberg Rorty (ed.), *Essays on Descartes' Meditations*, Berkeley and Los Angeles: California UP (1986).

Jorge Secada, *Cartesian Metaphysics: The Scholastic Origins of Modern Philosophy*, Cambridge and New York: Cambridge UP (2000).

Bernard Williams, *Descartes: The Project of Pure Enquiry*, London: Routledge (1978).

Catherine Wilson, *Descartes's Meditations: An Introduction*, Cambridge and New York: Cambridge UP (2012).

Margaret Wilson, *Descartes*, in the series *The Arguments of the Philosophers*, New York: Routledge and Kegan Paul (1978).

There is an important literature on Descartes and the question of whether or not individual bodies are substances. A cross-section of this literature includes:

Dan Kaufman, "Cartesian Substances, Individual Bodies, and Corruptibility," *Res Philosophica* 91 (2014), 71–102.

Thomas M. Lennon, "The Eleatic Descartes," *Journal of the History of Philosophy* 45 (2007), 29–45.

Calvin G. Normore, "Descartes and the Metaphysics of Extension," in *A Companion to Descartes*, ed. Janet Broughton and John Carriero, Hoboken, NJ: Blackwell (2007), 271–287.

Jasper Reid, "Descartes and the Individuation of Bodies," *Archiv für Geschichte der Philosophie* 96 (2014), 38–70.

Marleen Rozemond, "Real Distinction, Separability, and Corporeal Substance in Descartes," *Midwest Studies in Philosophy* 35 (2011), 240–258.

Tad M. Schmaltz, "Descartes on the Metaphysics of the Material World," *The Philosophical Review* 127 (2018), 1–40.

Edward Slowik, "Descartes and Individual Corporeal Substance," *British Journal for the History of Philosophy* 9 (2001), 1–15.

Alice Sowaal, "Cartesian Bodies," *Canadian Journal of Philosophy* 34 (2004), 217–240.

There is also an important literature that discusses Descartes' views on sensory qualities like color and taste. This literature includes:

Keith Allen, "Mechanism, Resemblance and Secondary Qualities: From Descartes to Locke," *British Journal for the History of Philosophy* 16 (2008), 273–291.

Lisa Downing, "Sensible Qualities and Material Bodies in Descartes and Boyle," in *Primary and Secondary Qualities: The Historical and Ongoing Debate*, ed. Lawrence Nolan, Oxford UP (2011), 109–135.

Anna Ortín Nadal, "Descartes on the Distinction between Primary and Secondary Qualities," *British Journal for the History of Philosophy* 27 (2019), 1113–1134.

Lawrence Nolan, "Descartes on 'What We Call Color'," in *Primary and Secondary Qualities: The Historical and Ongoing Debate*, ed. Lawrence Nolan, Oxford UP (2011), 83–108.

Kurt Smith, "Descartes's Ontology of Sensation," *Canadian Journal of Philosophy* 35 (2005), 563–584.

At the end of Chapter 5 is a list of readings that address Descartes' arguments for the existence of God, including work on the distinction between the infinite and the indefinite. At the end of Chapter 7 is a list of readings that discuss Descartes' arguments for the immateriality of mind.

Two

Life and works

René Descartes was born on March 31, 1596 in La Haye (now Descartes), France. He was baptized and raised Catholic, and in a time of regular conversions between Catholicism and Protestantism (and sometimes back), he himself remained a Catholic throughout his entire life. One thing that is curious (to me at least) is the connection between the philosophical conception of God that he eventually develops and the conventional understanding of God that would have been presented to him in his youth and promulgated at mass. As we will see, in the final analysis Descartes subscribes to the view that God is the author of all reality past, future, and present, with one of His perfections being a will that is eternal and entirely immutable.[1] Descartes appreciates the immediate consequences of the view. For example, he says in correspondence with Princess Elisabeth,

> When Your Highness speaks of the particular providence of God as being the foundation of theology, I do not think that you have in mind some change in God's decrees occasioned by actions that depend on our free will. No such change is theologically tenable; and when we are told to pray to God, that is not so that we should inform him of our needs, or that we should try to get him to change anything in the order established from all eternity by his providence[,]... but simply to obtain whatever he has, from all eternity, willed to be obtained by our prayers.[2]

---

1 See for example the following sections of Principles of Philosophy – I.23, AT 8A:14, CSM 1:201; II.36, AT 8A:61–62, CSM 1:240; I.56, AT 8A:26, CSM 1:211.

2 "To Princess Elizabeth, 6 October 1645," AT 4:315–316, CSMK 273.

DOI: 10.4324/9781351210522-2

In other texts, he exhibits a corresponding affinity for interpreting the language of scripture metaphorically and in ways that leave open its final meaning. We might read that the earth was created in six days, for example, or that it is the unmoving center of the universe and (by nonlogical implication) that human beings are its central inhabitants. Descartes supposes that the passages in question are certainly getting at something, if they appear in the infallible text of scripture, but they might have been crafted with an eye to a particular audience and not with an eye to literal truth. He writes in a letter to Chanut,

> The six days of creation are indeed described in Genesis in such a way as to make man appear its principal object; but it could be said that the story in Genesis was written for man, and so it is chiefly the things which concern him that the Holy Spirit wished particularly to narrate, and that indeed he did not speak of anything except in its relation to man. ...I do not see that the mystery of the Incarnation, and all the other favours God has done to man rule out his having done countless other great favours to an infinity of other creatures.[3]

Descartes was no doubt sincere in his commitment to Catholicism, or at the very least there is no reason to doubt that commitment given that he never explicitly backs away from it while having plenty of opportunity to do so. Nor is there any text in which he gives up his philosophical conception of God in favor of the conception of God on which he was raised. There *are* some passages in which he says that divine revelation always trumps philosophy.[4] He also makes clear however that truth is always consistent with truth and hence that a given divine revelation will never conflict with a truth of metaphysics.[5] If a feeling or intuition *does* run counter to a truth of metaphysics, that is a definite sign that it is not an instance of revelation after all. Descartes spent much of his adult life in regions in

---

3 "To Chanut, 6 June 1647," AT 5:54–55; CSMK 321. See also the similar language throughout Galileo (1615).

4 For example, *Principles of Philosophy* I.76, AT 8A:39, CSM 1:221–222.

5 *Letter to Father Dinet*, AT 7:581, CSM 2:392 and AT 7:598, CSM 2:394; *Appendix to Fifth Replies*, AT 9A:208, CSM 2:272–273.

which religious tolerance was encouraged – in the United Provinces (which is roughly the current-day Netherlands). We might wonder then why he did not abandon his Catholicism.

One reason, perhaps, is tactical. As we will see, Descartes wanted to be an influential voice in terms of overthrowing the entrenched natural science of Aristotle, and he had no incentive to amplify his outsider status by picking fights with Catholic theologians (who had embraced much of the thinking of Aristotle as orthodoxy). He could have easily limited himself to an austere philosophical conception of God if he had not been trying to convince anyone of anything, especially in the more-or-less tolerant United Provinces, but he wanted to have a voice that would be heard.

Reasons of strategy aside, Descartes also appears to have held that there are multiple routes to the worship of God and that God even prescribed these:

> we believe that God employs various means of drawing souls to him. ...As for those of a different faith, if they speak badly of such a person, we may challenge their judgement; for in all affairs where there are different sides, it is impossible to please one without displeasing the other. If they recall that they would not belong to the church to which they belong if they, or their fathers, or their grandfathers had not left the Church of Rome, then they will have no reason to ridicule those who leave their church, or to accuse them of inconstancy.[6]

Descartes writes elsewhere that he "do[es] not wish to appear to be assuming the right to question someone else's religion."[7] He is thereby echoing the language of *Discourse on the Method*, where he pledged to

> obey the laws and customs of my country, holding constantly to the religion which by God's grace I had been instructed from my childhood.
>
> (AT 6:23, CSM 1:122)

---

6 "To Princess Elizabeth, January 1646," AT 4:351–352, CSMK 281.

7 *Comments on a Certain Broadsheet*, AT 8B:353, CSM 1:300. See also *Letter to Father Dinet*, AT 7:598, CSM 2:394.

He adds that "some things are believed through faith alone" and that "it diminishes the authority of Scripture to undertake to demonstrate questions of [faith] by means of arguments derived solely from philosophy" (AT 8B:353, CSM 1:300).[8] Descartes indeed appears to hold that there are many behavioral routes to interfacing with God and that since reasons do not undergird our initial theological commitments, they are never a ground to backtrack and select a new route instead. A speculation is that he saw his Catholicism as a historically contingent attachment that was familiar and orienting and in no need of expurgation. He was raised in Catholicism from his infancy, and he was educated at the Catholic Jesuit school La Flèche from 1606 to 1614, where he would have continued to practice many of the religious traditions of his family and his youth. He would encounter sympathy for religious diversity and tolerance at La Flèche, which was founded by Henry IV in 1604, a Protestant who converted to Catholicism for pragmatic reasons (at least in part).[9] Descartes then inhabited a climate of religious tolerance later in the United Provinces. His comfort with religious tolerance might have inclined him to retain his Catholicism, among other factors that inclined him as well. He clearly found it appropriate in some contexts to subscribe to positions that, in his view, have no epistemic ground.

Early education

Descartes enrolled at La Flèche in 1606, and although there are no extant records of his own coursework, we do know much about the curriculum around which his education and the education of his fellow students would have been structured. The first years of study involved training in Latin and Greek grammar, discussions of classical texts by Cicero, Ovid, Catullus, and others, and also a treatment of rhetoric in such authors as Quintilian. Of particular interest with regard to the latter, it might be noted that Quintilian

---

8 See also the discussion in Cottingham (2019), 64–67.

9 King Henry was assassinated in 1610 – by a figure who thought he was not quite Catholic enough – but La Flèche would still host a celebration of his life on the anniversary of his assassination for years to come.

wrote much about the phenomenon of compelling assent in the course of reaching different audiences.[10] Later in the 1641 *Meditations on First Philosophy* Descartes invites readers from a range of intellectual backgrounds to take their own first-person perspective in locating cracks in the foundations of existing knowledge and rebuilding from ground that is more stable. To say that Descartes is inviting us to take the first-person point-of-view in evaluating the argumentation of the *Meditations* is not controversial; he supposes that if we do not assess the plausibility and coherence of a view on the basis of our own faculty of judgment, we are "behaving more like automatons or beasts than men."[11] However, it has not been sufficiently appreciated how Descartes is self-consciously writing to a *variety* of intellects in the *Meditations*,[12] or how he is aware that the transcript of the first-person reasoning of one meditator will not always be the same as the transcript of the first-person reasoning of another.[13] For example, in the First Meditation he argues that even if we can never be certain whether or not we are dreaming, we can be certain that there is something external to us that is a precondition of our having any sensory perceptions at all – what he identifies as the simple elements that are a presupposition of waking and dream perception both (AT 7:20–21, CSM 2:13–14). An Aristotelian scholastic reader would suppose that those simples include entities like color and heat, and a mechanist reader (like Hobbes or Gassendi) would suppose that they only include extensive features like size, shape, and motion. Descartes accordingly leaves the list of simples open-ended in the

---

10 See also Gaukroger (1995), 119–123; and Quintilian (1920–1922), 27–35.

11 *Appendix to Fifth Objections and Replies*; AT 9A:208, CSM 2:273. See also Vilmer (2008), 478–481.

12 For example, *Seventh Replies*, AT 7:482, CSM 2:324–325; *First Replies*, AT 7:120, CSM 2:85; *Second Replies*, AT 7:163–164, CSM 2:115.

13 See Cunning (2010), 56–59. Commentators like John Carriero are certainly correct that followers of Aquinas are represented by the "I" of the *Meditations*, but the "I" also carefully reflects the first-person reasoning of atomists, geometers, theists, atheists, mechanists, and others – a "variety of different minds" (*First Replies*, AT 7:120, CSM 2:85) that are in need of emendation. See also Nelson (2011).

First Meditation (AT 7:20, CSM 2:14)[14] – as he should if he expects
that a variety of minds are to reason from their own first-person
perspective and continue into the Second Meditation, where a result
of real epistemic stature is finally advanced. The First Meditation also
offers alternating versions of an argument for the conclusion that it
is possible that our minds are deceived about matters that are utterly
evident to us.[15] One (for theists) is an argument from the possibility
of radical divine deception (AT 7:21, CSM 2:14); one (for atheists
and atheistic mechanists) is an argument from the possibility that
human beings (and our cognitive faculties) evolved to their current
state by a process of random chance (AT 7:21–22, CSM 2:14–15);
and a third (for theists who are not prepared to allow that God might
be a radical deceiver) is an argument from the possibility that an evil
demon is tricking us every time we settle on a result that we find to
be obvious (AT 7:22–23, CSM 2:15). The attention-getting imagery
of an evil demon further echoes the rhetorical themes in the work of
Quintilian, as does the luscious piece of wax that Descartes presents
in the Second Meditation to recover our attention and navigate us
back to the insight that non-sensory perceptions (of truths like I am,

---

14 He concludes that the simple elements that have to exist (if we are to have any
sense perceptions at all) are "corporeal nature in general, and its extension; the
shape of extended things; the quantity, or size and number of these things; the
place in which they may exist, the time through which they may endure, and
so on." Some commentators have argued that because Descartes only includes
features like size, shape, and motion in his description of the simple elements,
he does not take the simples to include sensory qualities like color or sound
(Bermudez 1998, 238). Other commentators have noted that because Descartes
has not yet provided any reason to doubt the existence of features like color and
sound (in the First Meditation), he would be reckless to conclude that color and
sound are not among the simples (Rozemond 1996, 38–39), and so he doesn't.
For example, an Aristotelian reader who is working through the Meditation
would hold that the simple elements that have to exist (if we are to have any
sense perceptions at all) would possess size, motion, and color. What Descartes
concludes in the First Meditation is that the simples include size, shape, "and so
on" (AT 7:20, CSM 2:14); he leaves open the ontology of the simple elements
in a way that reflects that he has written the *Meditations* with an eye to a variety
of minds.

15 See also Cunning (2010), 59–64, and Bouchilloux (2015), 6–8.

I *exist*) are far more perspicuous and vivid than their sensory analog (AT 7:30–31, CSM 2:20–21). As the *Meditations* unfolds, Descartes puts forward axioms and arguments that he takes to be true and obvious, but prior to that he is not putting forward axioms and arguments that he takes to be true and obvious.[16] Instead, he is attempting to reach us.

Descartes also would have studied natural philosophy and metaphysics at La Flèche. The main catalog of readings would have included works of Aristotle – the *De Anima*, the *De Caelo*, the *De Generatione*, the *De Mundo*, the *Metaphysics*, and the *Physics* – along with parts of the *Summa Theologica* by St. Thomas Aquinas and also medieval commentaries on the work of Aristotle.[17] Later in life, Descartes will propose a scientific worldview that is largely opposed to the system of Aristotle, and indeed he makes explicit that one of the aims of the *Meditations* is to overthrow that system.[18] A central innovation that we encounter in scientific methodology in the seventeenth century (although not all would identify it as an innovation) is the use of mathematical quantification in explanations of natural phenomena. Such explanations not only provide an extremely high level of certainty and evidence, but they also promise to be more explanatory.[19] Kepler and Galileo had already made great strides in their efforts to measure particular phenomena – for example in laws of planetary motion, and in equations that track the motion of falling bodies – but Descartes was taking on the project of isolating quantitative laws that govern the behavior of *all* bodies. These laws would be in

16 The first half of Chapter 4 is a further defense of this contention.

17 See Gaukroger (1995), 55–61. Note however that Clemenson argues that most likely students at La Flèche would have only read summaries of these texts. See Clemenson (2018), 13–14.

18 "To Mersenne, 28 January 1641," AT 3:297–298, CSMK 172–173. But note that Descartes says in *Principles of Philosophy* IV.200 that his system is largely consistent with the system of Aristotle (AT 8A:323, CSM 1:286), so perhaps the language in the letter to Mersenne is a bit exaggerated. A question for example is whether or not Descartes ends up excluding force as a feature of body or if his turn against Aristotle is less radical. A discussion of this question is in Chapter 3 below, pp. 83–88.

19 See Gaukroger (1995), 114–116, 185–186.

terms of the size, shape, and motion of bodies, and they (the laws) would also incorporate as a datum the immutable order that is to be expected in a universe that is the product of a supremely perfect being. Aristotle of course posited size, shape, and motion as features to be found in natural bodies, but Aristotelian explanations also make reference to qualitative features like color and heat and to teleological properties that (allegedly) are present in bodies and explain their regular behavior. Descartes will spend much of the 1620s and 1630s attempting to arrive at mathematicized understandings of music, parahelia, vision, acoustics, light, lenses, color, heat, anatomy, barometric pressure, tides, and rainbows, among other objects of study.[20] In both published and unpublished writings, he will offer explanations of all of these phenomena in terms of size, shape, and motion alone. In the 1630s – for example in The World and Treatise on Man – he will argue that although bodies might possess (Aristotelian) features in addition to these, his own explanations are simpler and also more explanatory.[21] In the 1640s – in Meditations on First Philosophy and Principles of Philosophy – he will go further and argue that many of the features that an Aristotelian attributes to body are not features of body at all. Explanations of bodily behavior should be in terms of size, shape and motion, Descartes will insist, and not just because they are simpler. Bodies do not have features like color, heat, and telos, and so explanations in terms of such features are a non-starter.[22]

Travel and trajectory

Descartes completed his program of study at La Flèche in 1614 or 1615. Shortly thereafter he enrolled at the University of Poitiers, receiving his baccalaureate degree and license in law in 1616. As was customary, he defended a set of theses just prior to graduation – in this case theses (around forty in total) that centered on legal

---

20 See Gaukroger (1995), 217–222, 227, 255, 270–274, 334, 393, 405, 414.
21 For example, in Treatise on Man, AT 11:201–202, CSM 1:108.
22 See Chapter 1 above, pp. 10–13.

problems that arise in the validation of wills and bequests.[23] As a philosopher, I am just so grateful that Descartes did not proceed in the direction of a career in legal contracts. We are talking here about an almost unprecedented philosophical, mathematical, and scientific genius. If Descartes had chosen to go into law, perhaps he would have used his talents to have an impact on the full spectrum of legal practice – to be a leader in the foundations of legal theory, and to effectively promulgate insights that improve legal contracts and other day-to-day legal matters. Lucky for us he pursued larger questions still. His family though had an entirely different trajectory in mind for him. Descartes' father Joachim was a counselor in the parliament of Brittany, and other members of the family were medical doctors, lawyers, tax collectors, or were otherwise members of the French civil service.[24] In many cases, a person of Descartes' social background would purchase a civil position as a kind of investment and then receive a salary in the course of performing the work that the position entailed. It was expected (or at least hoped) that Descartes would have pursued a traditional professional trajectory as well. He did not. His family, and more specifically his father, did not approve, and it appears that he saw his son as something of a failure.[25]

As might not be surprising, Descartes was not particularly close with his father; nor was he close (at least later in life) with his brother, Pierre, or his sister, Jeanne. He also had four half-siblings – the children of Joachim and his second wife Anne Morin, who married Joachim in 1600 when Descartes was four years old. Descartes' mother Jeanne (Brochard) died just a year after he was born, and he was raised mostly by his maternal grandmother Jeanne Sain, with his father often away at Brittany or else managing family properties and other affairs. Jeanne Sain died in 1610, when Descartes was fourteen and had already been in residence at La Flèche. Descartes had little contact with his family from that point. There are a couple of exchanges of letters between Descartes and his brother Pierre in

23 See also Rodis-Lewis (1998), 20–23, and Clarke (2006), 32–33.
24 See Clarke (2006), 9–12.
25 See also Watson (2002), 46–48, 117, 124.

the 1620s, largely about matters of business, and there are letters that Pierre sent to Descartes in 1640 pertaining to the death of their father and to the management of the family estate. But Descartes did not know of his father's death at the time that it occurred. He did return (from the United Provinces) to France in 1644 and visit briefly with Pierre, and also with his half-sister, Anne, and half-brother, Joachim, but most of the four-month trip he spent away from them, in Paris, and the time that he did spend with his siblings was in large part devoted to the execution of his father's will.

The thought that René Descartes might have been a disappointment in the eyes of his family is amusing to entertain. However, we might try to see things just a little bit from their point-of-view. Descartes graduated from La Flèche, and then from the University of Poitiers a year later, but he spent much of the next ten years or so traveling throughout Europe and surviving (quite comfortably) on what was basically a trust fund. He was gifted a number of family properties, some of which he sold, and some of which provided regular income. He worked in a military capacity for a time, serving under Prince Maurice of Nassau in the United Provinces in 1618–1619 and under Maximilian I in and around Ulm and Bavaria (in modern-day Germany) in 1619–1620. He also appears to have been present at the Battle of White Mountain in 1620, at which the father of Princess Elisabeth of Bohemia – with whom Descartes would have a significant correspondence in the 1640s – was removed from an extremely short stint as King of Bohemia. We do not know if Descartes actually fought in the battle that led to the dethroning of Frederick V, and indeed we know very little about the nature of his short military career.[26] Ulm had a military engineering college, where Descartes appears to have spent much of his time interacting with the mathematician Johannes Faulhaber.[27] It is no surprise that the Descartes that we know from history would opt to study the mathematizable motions of military projectiles (with Faulhaber), rather than focus on training for combat. He proceeded similarly during his time in Breda under the command of Maurice of Nassau.

---

26 But see Cook (2018), 117–150, and Barret-Kriegel (1990), 381–384.
27 See also Rodis-Lewis (1998), 50–52.

Descartes met Isaac Beeckman in Breda in November 1618, when both had stumbled upon a public placard that displayed a mathematical challenge – a not uncommon sight at the time. Beeckman was a mathematician and natural scientist who took Descartes as an apprentice in Breda and had an enormous influence on his eventual thinking.[28]

Descartes was not going to pursue a life in the military, or the law, or in civil service or medicine. His family was frustrated by his choice of career (or lack thereof), and we can sort of understand why. I try to imagine living back in the first half of the seventeenth century with my daughter, where she insists that her paramount career ambition is to overthrow the natural science and metaphysics of Aristotle in a climate in which one of the most powerful and far-reaching institutions in Europe (the Catholic Church) is heavily aligned with the teachings of Aristotle and in which a university position flouting the views of Aristotle is a virtual impossibility. Massive obstacles of gender discrimination aside, I would like to think that I would encourage her, but that is easier said than done. In the current day, parents and loved ones get nervous enough when a young person aspires to be a movie star or music idol, but those trajectories are arguably much more in the cards than were Descartes' ambitions in the 1620s and beyond. He does appear to have at least entertained the idea of pursuing a career that was more modest; in 1625, he wrote to his father about the possibility of accepting a civil service position, for example, but nothing ever came of it.[29] Fortunately for us, Descartes did attempt to follow through on the goal of overthrowing the natural science and metaphysics of Aristotle. To be sure, he did not come close to achieving the goal in his own lifetime, and from his own point-of-view his progress toward that goal had to appear precarious at best, all the way through to his final days. Descartes did not become *Descartes* until well after his death – when his mechanistic picture of human and animal physiology became standard (even if he got many of the details wrong); when his picture of nature as governed by immutable laws set the

---

28 See also Gaukroger (1995), Chapter 3, and Watson (2002), 84–92. There is some additional discussion of Beeckman and Descartes later in the is chapter.

29 See Gaukroger (1995), 64.

stage for contemporary physics (even if Newton and others who built on that picture also corrected for its errors); and when his interventions in epistemology and metaphysics shaped those sub-areas of philosophy into what they are today. Descartes had the enormous benefit of a trust fund to do much of the work that he did, but unlike other individuals in a similar camp (and many individuals since) he dedicated all of his resources to the slow and cumbersome acquisition of information and knowledge.

Attachment to finitude

After ten years or so of travels – the initial year in Breda, then in Ulm and Bavaria, then Paris from 1622 to 1623, then Italy for two years, then Paris again – Descartes returned to the United Provinces, which he would make his home for the next two decades. He did change his address quite often – living in or near Amsterdam, Leiden, Utrecht, and other cites, and also in small country villages like Egmond-binnen and Egmond aan den Hoef. He moved more than twenty times during his years in the United Provinces, in part to maintain his cherished privacy and isolation, and perhaps in some cases for reasons of health (given the spread of the Plague). Especially note-worthy is that in 1635, Descartes had a daughter. He was living in Amsterdam at the time, and he had a brief relationship with a maid, Hélène, who worked at the residence where he was living. Descartes and Hélène did not marry, and we know very little about her. Descartes did acknowledge paternity of Francine in the record of her baptism (as a Protestant), and it appears that she stayed with him for significant periods of time in 1637–1639.[30] Descartes also made plans for her eventual education in Paris. Very sadly, Francine died of scarlet fever in September 1640. Descartes was devastated, writing a few months later in a separate condolence letter to a friend:

> Not long ago I suffered the loss of two people who were very close to me, and I found that those who wanted to shield me from sadness only increased it, whereas I was consoled by the kindness of those whom I saw to be touched by my grief.

---

30 See also Gaukroger (1995), 332–333.

So I am sure that you will listen to me better if I do not try to check your tears than if I tried to steer you away from a feeling which I consider quite justified.[31]

Here, Descartes is referring most likely to the death of Francine and also to the death of his sister, Jeanne, with whom he was close as a child.[32] As best we can tell the period that Descartes spent with Francine was the happiest of his life, and he missed her terribly.

Descartes was a very embodied individual – immersed in the affairs of the earthly realm – and not just in the sense that he had a body like the rest of us. He was interested not only in abstract subjects like mathematics, but he also wanted to apply mathematics to the sensory objects that surrounded him. He did this from very early on. In 1619, he wrote *Compendium Musicae*, in which he attempted to locate the mathematical ratios and patterns that would seem to underlie harmonies. In the 1620s, he was interested not only in the geometry of lenses but also in the practice of grinding real-life lenses and optimizing their production in the light of the insights of mathematics.[33] He was fascinated with parahelia, barometric pressure, rainbows, and with the physiology of human and non-human animal bodies. He did a significant amount of work dissecting animal corpses, in some cases appropriating them from his local butcher.[34] There is also the episode in which he got so excited upon learning of the existence of (solar) parahelia that he dropped everything in order to study them further.[35] He speaks in addition of the benefits of

> observing the greenness of a wood, the colours of a flower, the flight of a bird, or something else requiring no attention. This is not a waste of time but a good use of it....[36]

---

31 "To [Pollot], mid-January 1641," AT 3:278–279, CSMK 167.
32 Descartes' father died in October 1640, but again it seems unlikely that Descartes is referring to him in the letter to Pollot. See also Gaukroger (1995), 22–23.
33 See also Clarke (2006), 98–100, and Gaukroger (1995), 191.
34 See also Clarke (2006), 304.
35 "To Mersenne, 8 October 1629," AT 1:23, CSMK 6. Also Gaukroger (1995), 219.
36 "To Princess Elizabeth, May or June 1645," AT 4:220, CSMK 250.

He tended a garden at many of the homes where he resided. He enjoyed taking long walks with his dog, Monsieur Grat. He reflects in his correspondence that he wanted to live to be a hundred years old.[37] There is also the wonderful passage in which he says that his hair is greying and that the most pressing order of business on his agenda is to conjure a remedy:

> White hairs are rapidly appearing on my head, which brings it home to me that the only thing I should be devoting myself to is ways of slowing down their growth.[38]

Descartes famously argues for the result that minds are immaterial and that "the decay of the body does not imply the destruction of the mind,"[39] and he thinks that minds are high on the scale of perfection. But rather than cast his glance toward a future disembodiment, he has a steady lock on the here and now.

Descartes indeed has a great admiration for the bodily realm and for embodiment. His writings on natural science are basically an ode to body – for example in The World, Treatise on Man, Optics, Meteorology, Description of the Human Body, Principles of Philosophy (Parts II, III, and IV), and The Passions of the Soul. In all of these texts, he treats the material world as almost a wonderland.

We might begin with The World. One of Descartes' aims in The World is to argue that the order and organization that we encounter in material bodies need not be the result of Aristotelian mind-like entities that guide the behavior of bodies and keep them on the rails (AT 11:39–40, CSM 1:93–94). Bodies instead have the resources on their own to engage in all of the most sophisticated behaviors that we observe in them – without the assistance of a mind. Descartes is careful not to assert definitively that The World describes the behavior of the bodies of our own local solar system; that would be to invite controversy and backlash. Instead, he describes an alternate world that is very much (if not exactly) like our own and in

---

37 "To Hyugens, 4 December 1637," AT 1:649, CSMK 75. See also Clarke (2006), 178, and Gaukroger (1995), 274.
38 "To Hyugens, 5 October 1637," AT 1:434, CSMK 66.
39 "Synopsis of the following six Meditations," AT 7:13, CSM 2:10.

which explanations of natural phenomena are in terms of extensive qualities like size, shape, and motion only. He is describing our actual world, of course, even if he feels the need to put the description into the form of a fable. What he says about this wholly material world is that its bodies exhibit an "immutable" order (AT 11:38, CSM 1:93). Immutability is a divine perfection, and God acts in the light of that perfection to create accordingly (AT 8A:61, CSM 1:240). Descartes says that bodies exhibit an immutable and law-like order no matter how God might have configured them initially:

> For God has established these laws in such a marvellous way that even if we suppose he creates nothing beyond what I have mentioned, and sets up no order or proportion within it but composes it from a chaos as confused and muddled as any of the poets could describe, the laws of nature are sufficient to cause the parts of this chaos to disentangle themselves and arrange themselves in such good order that they will have the form of a quite perfect world.
>
> (AT 11:34–35, CSM 1:91)

It bears repeating: what Descartes is describing is the form of a "quite perfect world" – a world that he takes himself (and us) to inhabit.

For Descartes, material bodies exhibit perfection.[40] Some of his biographers describe the delight that he must have felt in witnessing the marvelous grottoes of the Royal Gardens when he lived in St. Germain.[41] The grottoes were statues of animals that through a process of hydraulics could move, dance, and even sing. Descartes references these himself in *Treatise on Man*:

> you may have observed in the grottos and fountains in the royal gardens that the mere force with which the water is driven as it emerges from its source is sufficient to move various

---

40 See the discussion in Chapter 1 above, p. 28.

41 For example, Gaukroger (1995), 105–112, who suggests that Descartes' encounters with the grottoes were likely a source of inspiration for his mechanistic understanding of bodies.

machines, and even to make them play certain instruments or utter certain words depending on the various arrangements of the pipes through which the water is conducted. Indeed, one may compare the nerves of the machine [the human body] I am describing with the pipes in the works of these fountains, its muscles and tendons with the various devices and springs which serve to set them in motion, its animal spirits [or nerves][42] with the water which drives them, the heart with the source of the water, and the cavities of the brain with the storage tanks. Moreover, breathing and other such activities which are normal and natural to this machine, and which depend on the flow of the spirits, are like the movements of a clock or mill, which the normal flow of water can render continuous.

(AT 11:130–131, CSM 1:100)

Descartes takes material bodies to be capable of highly sophisticated activity. He is granting that there is all of the same wonder and marvel in nature that its admirers had found in it before – absent the immaterial entities that were thought to pervade it – and he is showing it a proportional amount of respect.[43] There is much that bodies cannot do – for example they cannot think – but for Descartes a world that is wholly material still exhibits a degree of perfection.

The language that he uses to describe the material plenum is also quite applaudatory in Optics. We do not need Descartes to tell us about the wonder of the human eye and the larger nervous system that makes possible its operation. But tell us he does. Indeed, there could be an entire book titled *Descartes: An Ode to Body* with "An Ode to the Eye" as one of its fifty chapters. The intricacy of the eye, and its pupil and retina, and the sophistication of the processes by which it forms images of external objects – these are extraordinary, and Descartes reports as much in picture and in word. He provides multiple drawings to illustrate the elegant geometry of the refraction of light and its effect on the optic nerves.[44] He describes the effective

---

42 See Sepper (2015).

43 In Chapter 3 (pp. 83–88), I argue that Descartes holds that bodies also possess (a degree of) force by which they impact other creatures.

44 For example, at AT 6:93, 98–105. See also the discussion in Hatfield (2015), 123–129.

and efficient work of those nerves to produce images of external objects that allow us to make the discriminations that are central to daily life:

> we cannot discriminate the parts of the bodies we are looking at except in so far as they differ somehow in colour; and distinct vision of these colours depends not only on the fact that all the rays coming from each point of the object converge in almost as many different points at the back of the eye, and on the fact that no rays reach the same points from elsewhere[,] ... but also on the great number of optic nerve-fibres in the area which the image occupies at the back of the eye.[45]

The human eye is *extremely* sophisticated.[46] Without all of the optic nerves making their numerous and varied contributions, vision would not be a thing; nor would we be able to (visually) encounter the immutable order that surrounds us. The eye and the optic nerves exhibit extraordinary organization and order, as do all the bodies that are involved in visual perception. Descartes describes the bodies that compose the light that affects the eye on analogy with balls that carom off a surface: he says that in vision the behavior of those bodies is "uniform throughout" and that the bodies "obey the same laws as motion itself" (AT 6:89, CSM 1:155). The bodies that compose the eye and the optic nerves exhibit an immutable order even if "the position of these nerves is changed by [an] unusual cause" (AT 6:141, CSM 1:173) and the orderly behavior of the nerves results in a misperception for us.

Descartes continues along the same lines in *Treatise on Man*. The text begins with an almost fawning description of the human body and its workings:

> We see clocks, artificial fountains, mills, and other such machines which, although only man-made, have the power to move of their own accord in many different ways. But I am

---

45 AT 6:132–133, CSM 1:168. See also the Sixth Meditation, AT 7:75.
46 See also *Optics*, AT 6:109–114, CSM 1:164–166, and *Treatise on Man*, AT 11:175–176, CSM 1:105–106.

supposing this machine to be made by the hands of God, and I think you may reasonably think it capable of a greater variety of movements than I could possibly imagine in it, and of exhibiting more artistry than I could possibly ascribe to it.[47]

Man-made machines are sophisticated, and a human body is a composite of the same kind of matter, but it is not assembled through human artifice. It is the product of a process that is far more grand. The human body is material through and through, but Descartes is suggesting that it exhibits a level of organization and artistry that is unprecedented. He writes for example of

the arteries which carry blood to the brain from the heart, after dividing into countless tiny branches which make up the minute tissues that are stretched like tapestries at the bottom of the cavities of the brain....

(AT 11:129, CSM 1:100)

He ends *Treatise on Man* with more general acclaim for all of the organs that work to keep a human body whole – "the diverse composition and marvellous artistry which is evident in the structure of the visible organs" and in the bodies that undergird these and that "cannot be perceived by any sense."[48]

The attention to the details of the behavior of bodies is also striking in *Metereology*. Descartes does not employ quite as much complimentary language as in other texts, but he does engage an extended and almost relentless discussion of meteorological phenomena – a discussion that a more conceptually driven philosopher might dismiss as an assortment of minutiae, but that Descartes takes to be of great significance. In *Meteorology* he devotes over 130 pages (in the Adam and Tannery numbering) to the particulars of wind, air, rain, moisture, clouds, tempests, thunder, lightning, and similar topics. He also includes twenty-nine detailed illustrations. One of

---

47 AT 11:120, CSM 1:99. See also *Discourse on the Method*, Part 5, AT 6:56, CSM 1:139.
48 AT 11:201, CSM 1:108. See also the similar language in *Discourse on the Method*, Part 5, AT 6:46–55, CSM 1:134–138.

the observations that he attempts to explain is why the countries in and around Europe see an increase in winds in March and the subsequent months of spring. He argues that in the prior months, there is more snow and moisture in the air: the weight of that snow and moisture weighs down the (invisible) air molecules of the surrounding plenum and keeps wind formations from being as active.[49] We may not see these molecules with the naked eye, but they are there, and they encumber. Descartes also provides a drawing to illustrate the effect that the (invisible) light of the sun has on different parts of the planet at different times of year (ibid., 291). He also attempts to explain why the winds that appear above the Pacific Ocean are calmer than the winds of the Atlantic and other oceans. He argues that there is always more wind along a coastline – especially a coastline that features mountains and other instances of uneven terrain – because the air in such an environment collides into more bodies and is more stirred up, but air that is farther from a coastline would be more peaceful (ibid., 296). *Meteorology* also contains laudatory language, with Descartes making reference to the harmony and beauty that are ubiquitous throughout the material world. He speaks for example of snowflakes that exhibit geometrical organization and precision:

> at approximately eight o'clock I again observed another kind of hail, or rather snow, of which I have never heard anyone speak. It was composed of small blades which were completely flat, highly polished, and very transparent; they were… so perfectly cut in hexagons with six sides that were so straight, and six angles so equal, that it is impossible for men to make anything so exact.
>
> (313–314)

He speaks in similarly glowing terms about the rainbow and offers an explanation of its occurrence – appealing to laws of refraction and other principles of his mechanistic science (332). Rainbows are remarkable, and the material plenum exhibits a law-like order and

---

49 *Meteorology*, 292–293. Note that for *Meteorology* I am using the translation in Olscamp (2001).

organization through which they and other impressive entities arise as a matter of course.

We might also consider the treatise, *Description of the Human Body*. The treatise was not published in Descartes' lifetime, and a scholar who is not careful might conclude that the primary reason is that it was woefully unfinished. But that is not so. The excerpted text in the CSM volume that contains it runs just eleven pages (or around seventeen pages in Adam and Tannery numbering), but the full text runs seventy-three pages. It contains four substantive sections – on the movement of the heart and the blood, on nutrition, on the development of organisms from seminal material, and on the formation of veins and arteries. The text offers mechanistic explanations of all of these in full anticipation that readers might not think that bodies are up to the task:

> It is true that we may find it hard to believe that the mere disposition of the bodily organs is sufficient to produce in us all the movements which are in no way determined by... thought.
> (AT 11:226, CSM 1:315)

But Descartes supposes that bodies have been underestimated, and in his own lifetime he clearly prioritized the examination and study of material things.

Descartes also celebrates the level of perfection of a mind-body union. In the Sixth Meditation – after offering a demonstration of the existence of material things – he abandons his focus on (what he takes to be) the thinking and immaterial half of a human being and turns his attention to embodiment. He grants that we do not sense everything in our environment that might be relevant to our preservation, but "this is not surprising, since man is a limited thing, and so it is only fitting that his perfection should be limited" (AT 7:84, CSM 2:58). He then points out just how high on the scale of perfection we land. A human body is of the same sort that he described in *Treatise on Man* – an intricate machine that admits of a remarkable degree of organization and artistry – but he gets into further detail still. A human body is highly sophisticated, and a mind is interfaced with its body in a way that is sophisticated as well. He writes,

I am not merely present in my body as a sailor is present in a ship, but... I am very closely joined and, as it were, intermingled with it, so that I and the body form a unit. If this were not so, I, who am nothing but a thinking thing, would not feel pain when the body was hurt, but would perceive the damage purely by the intellect, just as a sailor perceives by sight if anything in his ship is broken.

(AT 7:81, CSM 2:56)

We feel pain when an external body crashes into us, for example, and we then have an immediate (and very strong) inclination to avoid that body (AT 7:88, CSM 2:60–61). We do not need to construct a discursive argument that informs us that that body is to be avoided; we just immediately register the need to move away. We are constructed similarly in the case of our need for food and water. If we do not eat, we experience a sensation of hunger, and if we wait so long to eat that our body runs a risk to its health, we have a sensation of hunger that takes first billing over other interests that we might have.[50] Features like pain and thirst, and color and taste, are not literally in material objects, according to Descartes, but our sensations of such features help us to make discriminations that are relevant to our survival. Perhaps we might have been created differently, with our minds not as intimately connected to our bodies. Descartes speaks for example of angels who might have bodies but whose minds and bodies do not compose an intermingled unit. He says that

if an angel were in a human body, he would not have sensations as we do, but would simply perceive the motions which are caused by external objects, and in this way would differ from a real man.[51]

---

50 See also the discussions in Simmons (2001) and Laporte (1928).
51 "To Regius, January 1642," AT 3:493, CSMK 206. See also Simmons (2011), 57–61.

Here Descartes is describing an immaterial mind that has some affiliation with a body but does not have sensations by which to learn of benefits and harms to that body. Instead, it gets a kind of intellectual readout of those benefits and harms and is motivated to act accordingly. In the case of a human being, there is an intimate connection between its mind and its body – a connection through which we do not "simply perceive the motions which are caused by external objects." Such a connection allows us to experience harmonic music and the hexagonal shapes of a snowflake, and to experience passions that are some of the "sweetest pleasures of this life."[52] Perhaps we might have been created in such a way that we have sensations and passions *and* we receive the non-sensory readout, and it is vivid enough to get our attention. Perhaps God did make creatures of that kind, and they have more perfection than we do. As we have seen, Descartes emphasizes in his correspondence with Chanut that human beings are not the end of creation and that for all we know God has authored a bounty of creatures that exhibit all ranges of feature (AT 5:53–56 CSMK 320–322). We are not perfect, but we are pretty great.

We also make errors in our capacity as a mind-body composite, but Descartes would remind us again that although we are high on the scale of perfection, we are not at the top. For example, he points to instances in which a human being has a strong inclination to pursue or avoid something that we take to be of benefit or harm to the body, but we are in error. One reason that we err is that as finite beings we fail to take in all the information about our environment: we do not notice the toxic elements that might be present in the air that we breathe; we do not have a sensation of pain when cancer cells are forming in a region of our body; we fail to detect the poison that might be in the water that we are about to drink. Descartes discusses the latter example in the Sixth Meditation and says quite correctly that

> in this case, what the man's nature urges him to go for is simply what is responsible for the pleasant taste, and not the poison, which his nature knows nothing about. The only inference that

---

52 *The Passions of the Soul*, III.202, AT 11:488, CSM 1:404.

can be drawn from this is that his nature is not omniscient. And this is not surprising....

(AT 7:84, CSM 2:58)

Descartes also discusses cases of dropsy – in which we are thirsty but our body would be harmed from drinking water – and phantom limb cases in which we feel pain in a limb that we no longer have.[53] Descartes writes in the last sentence of the Sixth Meditation (and the last sentence of the *Meditations*) that "we must acknowledge the weakness of our nature" (AT 7:90, CSM 2:62). As he had put it, our perfection is very limited, but that is still to say that perfection is something in which we participate. One of the reasons that we err in matters that concern our physical well-being is that we are not omniscient. Another is that we are attached to remarkable bodies that are subject to (and never divert from) the same immutable laws of nature that apply ubiquitously.[54] If an angel were associated (but not intermingled) with a body just like ours, it would employ its non-sensory readout to take in the immutable order of the bodies that surround it and admire the intricacy and sophistication of its human (or in this case angel-body) machine. Our experience is different. We have sensations, and a byproduct of our union with a body is that occasionally we have sensations that incline us to pursue items that harm us and to avoid items that would do us good. The bodies inside of a human body interact with each other, and surrounding bodies have an impact as well, but part of what it is for these bodies to behave in accord with a perfect and immutable order is to not take into account the structural integrity of the larger composites that they comprise. Immutable order is preserved downstream, so to speak – and throughout the entire plenum – but in a way that results in error. Still, we are more than compensated by our attachment to perfection:

If the body did not induce this misleading state, it would not be behaving uniformly and in accordance with its own laws; and

---

53 For the discussion of dropsy, see AT 7:84, CSM 2:58. For the phantom limb case, see AT 7:86–87, CSM 2:60, and "To Plempius for Fromondus, 3 October 1637," AT 1:420, CSMK 64.

54 Again see *Principles* II.36; AT 8A:61, CSM 1:240, and *The World*, AT 11:37–38, CSM 1:93.

then there would be a defect in God's constancy, since he would not be permitting the body to behave uniformly, despite the existence of uniform laws and modes of behavior.[55]

The fact that the behavior of bodies does so often work in our favor is then remarkable.[56]

Descartes expresses nothing but admiration for the plenum of bodies to which he found himself interfaced and united. That should come as no surprise. He spent much of the 1620s and 1630s gazing with wonder at the intricacy and elegance of bodies, and he then spent much of the 1640s laying out the metaphysical foundations that help to expose the immutable order that is manifested in their behavior. He coupled that with yet additional work in natural science, recording descriptions of the complicated machinery of the human body in *The Passions of the Soul* at the end of the decade, and offering accounts of a wide range of natural phenomena in *Principles of Philosophy* Parts III and IV. He intended for *Principles of Philosophy* (1644) to include Parts V and VI on "living beings, i.e. animals and plants, and… on man" (AT 8A: 315, CSM 1:279), with a heavy emphasis on physiology.[57] However, the many experiments that he would need to perform in order to complete all of his research on these would require significant assistance from others and a significant expenditure of time – neither of which he saw on the horizon.[58] We can only imagine all that he might have done in the 1650s and beyond if he had not died at the age of fifty-three. We might also imagine how his reputation as a philosopher might have been passed down to us differently if his trajectory from the 1620s through the 1680s had been a contiguous string of work in the natural sciences and

---

55 *Conversation with Burman*, AT 5:164, CSMK 346.

56 There is a further discussion of error in Chapters 6 and 8 below, but note for the moment that Descartes is clear that a supremely perfect being creates beings that inevitably err. We err as a result of our embodiment, but we are also compensated (by embodiment) in spades.

57 See also Gaukroger (1995), 364.

58 "To Hyugens, July 1645," AT 4:260–261. See also Clarke (2006), 305. But in the end Descartes did do a significant amount of research on natural bodies. See Baldassarri (2019) for a terrific discussion of his studies of plants in particular.

mathematics and a couple of small metaphysical interludes to make that work better grounded.

It should also be noted that Descartes had a number of intimate friendships throughout his life.[59] Henri Reneri was appointed to a chair in philosophy at the University of Deventer in 1631 and then in 1634 to a similar position at the University of Utrecht. He and Descartes were extremely close, and Descartes followed Reneri to both cities, just as he followed him to Leiden when he (Reneri) accepted a tutorial position in early 1630. Descartes maintained his friendship with Reneri until the death of the latter in 1639. Descartes was also a close friend and regular correspondent of Jean Gillot. Descartes tutored Gillot in mathematics, who eventually became the director of the school of engineering at the University of Leiden. Descartes also had a tight friendship with Cornelius Van Hogelande, a Catholic medical doctor. The two worked together in Van Hogelande's medical office in Leiden, and Descartes stayed at his residence for a time. Descartes also entrusted all of his papers to Van Hogelande when he moved to Sweden in 1649. Another good friend of Descartes was Constantijn Hyugens, the father of the famous chemist Christian Hyugens and an extremely accomplished figure in his own right.[60] Descartes was also very close with Hector-Pierre Chanut and Claude Clerselier (who were brothers-in-law). Chanut corresponded extensively with Descartes in the second-half of the 1640s and successfully convinced him to move to Sweden to be tutor to Queen Christina (and to be near Chanut as well). Clerselier helped Descartes in an editorial capacity and later saw to the posthumous publication of *Treatise on Man* (1664) and *The World* (1677). There was also Descartes' friendship with Henri Regius, even if it did not end particularly well.[61] All of this is just to highlight once again that although Descartes valued his privacy and was sometimes reclusive, he remained squarely in the world of embodied feeling

59 See also Rodis-Lewis (1998), 25–30, 74, 91–94, 145, 150–151, 157.
60 See the helpful discussion in Clarke (2006), 105–108, 124–25, 179, 212, and in Gaukroger (1995), 293–295, 333, 414.
61 The blow-up with Regius is discussed below on pp. 63–67.

creatures and engaged in the kinds of earthly activities that are not unusual for them.

Vulnerability and conflict

Descartes devoted much of the 1630s to work in natural science. By 1633, he completed drafts of *The World* or *Treatise on Light* and *Treatise on Man* – though neither was published in his lifetime. Then in 1637, he published *Discourse on the Method*, *Optics*, *Meteorology*, and *Geometry*. The latter were not as explicit in their opposition to Aristotelian principles, and they did not go as far in their defense of the (anti-Aristotelian) view that explanations of the behavior of bodies need only make reference to terms of size, shape, and motion.[62] The four (published) texts are so restrained, in fact, that many of Descartes' contemporaries had raised questions and objections to the views presented in them, and Descartes had to offer promissory notes in response – adding that his fuller account was to be found in work that he could not yet make available, namely, *The World* and *Treatise on Man*.[63] He had every intention of publishing both of these, but he did an about-face when he learned of the condemnation of Galileo in 1633. *Dialogue Concerning the Two Chief World Systems* had defended the doctrine that the sun is at the center of the solar system and the earth rotates around the sun and on its own axis. But the argumentation of *The World* entailed that same doctrine. Descartes delayed the publication of *The World* and *Treatise on Man* immediately upon learning of the condemnation of Galileo, and he was also aware of other instances in which criticism of orthodoxy was severely sanctioned. In 1616, the Roman Inquisition condemned a treatise by Foscarini in which heliocentrism was defended as wholly consistent with Christian doctrine. In 1624, there was held a public meeting in Paris to critique the views of Aristotle specifically, and the three organizers – Jean Bituald, Étienne de Claves, and Antoine Villon – were exiled

---

62 See also Petrescu (2015), 38–43. He argues that although *Meteorology* is merely offering an alternative to Aristotelian explanations, Descartes already lays out his full-blown rejection of such explanations much earlier in (the unpublished) *Rules for the Direction of the Mind*.

63 Also Clarke (2006), 174.

from the city on pain of death.[64] Then there was 1633, along with later incidents as well – including a ban on all teaching of anti-Aristotelian views in the city of Utrecht in 1642. And we are not talking about isolated pockets of suppression. Unless the political and ideological momentum was somehow going to stop on a dime, there would be a thread (or a rope or thick vapor) of continued surveillance running through the 1640s as well. Descartes was not just concerned for his physical welfare. He hoped to provide his fellow human beings with a natural science and metaphysics that was nothing short of revolutionary, but the immensity of the task was even more pronounced in the face of the many efforts that would bring it down. Even if he mustered a proof that he was entirely correct, he would still need the right kind of mouthpiece and an audience that was willing to listen and hear.

Toward the end of the decade, Descartes took a different approach toward the overthrow of Aristotle. In the (published) texts of the 1630s, he still left open that Aristotelian explanations of natural phenomena were a contender and that the not-mathematizable entities posited by Aristotelians were real existents. In *Meditations on First Philosophy* and *Principles of Philosophy*, he takes a different tack. Neither begins with natural science. Instead, they both get underway with a metaphysical discussion of the kinds of entities that exist and the kinds of features that it is intelligible to suppose those entities to have. He does not accept the picture of reality that would appear to be presented to the naked eye – with empty spaces, colored and scented objects, and thinking brains. He analyzes his concepts to consider what kinds of entities are intelligible and what kinds are not, and he posits only the former. In both texts, he draws the conclusion that bodies do not have many of the features that are posited by Aristotle, or at the very least he provides us the unmistakable resources for drawing that conclusion ourselves. As such, he is not standing his own explanation up against the tradition and saying that it is another option, but he is rejecting the tradition outright. For example, in the Second Meditation he proposes that we consider our idea of an observable body – like a sensible piece of wax – and then strip it down to the point that it includes only its essential

---

64 Also Gaukroger (1995), 136.

and inextricable constituents. The latter include three-dimensional extension, flexibility, and changeability (AT 7:30–31, CSM 2:20–21), he argues, but they do not include most of the features that pop up in Aristotelian explanations.[65] It is then a somewhat short step for us to ask how the occurrence of such features could be understood or explained in terms of what definitely *are* the features of a body.[66] Descartes walks us through that step explicitly in *Principles of Philosophy*, arguing that every substance has an essence or principal attribute through which its other modifications can be understood and that if a modification cannot be understood through a given principal attribute, it is a modification of a different substance (with a different principal attribute).[67] Features that are intelligible in terms of the principal attribute of body include size, shape, and motion, but not features like heat, color, or goal-directedness. The metaphysical and epistemological focus of the *Meditations* and Part I of *Principles of Philosophy* is no doubt motivated by an interest in questions about self, the immateriality of mind, and the existence and nature of God, but it also provides a subtle and not very prickly route to the rejection of Aristotle.

But combat still of course ensued. One of the reasons that it ensued is that Descartes was not especially diplomatic in the face of criticism of his views and methods. Indeed, a theme throughout his life is that his passions often got the best of him. In 1629, Beeckman wrote in a letter to Mersenne that he [Beeckman] had shared some of his views on the nature of music with Descartes back in 1619. Beeckman reported that to Mersenne, and things went south very quickly. But first, some background. Beeckman and Descartes were in Breda in 1619, and shortly thereafter Descartes started writing his *Compendium Musicae*. Beeckman had been a mentor and something of a father figure to Descartes, influencing his views on music and other subjects, and Descartes acknowledged as much. In a letter to Beeckman in 1619, he speaks with almost giddy excitement about work that he says Beeckman had inspired – for example the use

---

65 See also Chapter 1 above, pp. 8–10.
66 See also Garber (1992), 77–80.
67 See for example *Principles* I.53, AT 8A:25, CSM 1:210, and the discussion in Chapter 1, pp. 10–13.

of quadratic equations to untangle problems that had long gone unsolved, and the use of geometry to improve the art of navigation.[68] In another early letter, he says to Beeckman,

> it was you alone who roused me from my state of indolence, and reawakened the learning which by then had almost disappeared from my memory; and when my mind strayed from serious pursuits, it was you who led it back to worthier things. Thus, if perhaps I should produce something not wholly to be despised, you can rightly claim it as all your own.[69]

Descartes and Beeckman were on extremely good terms when Descartes left Breda in 1619, but things went south with the 1629 letter from Beeckman to Mersenne – the contents of which Mersenne communicated to Descartes in summary. In reaction, Descartes kind of lost it. He wrote to Beeckman to demand the return of his copy of *Compendium Musicae*, and then in a letter approximately one year later he really unloaded:

> I retrieved my Music from you last year, not because I needed it, but because I was told that you talked about it as if I had learned it from you. ...[S]ince many other things have confirmed that you prefer stupid boasting to friendship and truth, I shall warn you in a few words. If you claim to have taught something to someone, it is repulsive to do so even if you speak the truth; when it is false, however, it is much more repulsive; finally, if you yourself learned it from this person, it is most repulsive. ...I could not have imagined that you are so stupid and ignorant about yourself that you really believe that I ever learned, or ever could learn, anything more from you than I usually do from all natural things – than I usually learn, I say, even from insects and flies – or that you could teach me anything.[70]

---

68 "To Beeckman, 26 March 1619," AT 1:157–160.
69 "To Beeckman, 23 April 1619," AT 10:163, CSMK 4.
70 "To Beeckman, 17 October 1630," AT 1:155–58. Here I am using the translation in Clarke (2006), 49–50.

Whoa. Descartes had some time – almost a year – to put things in perspective after hearing that Beeckman might be claiming some influence on Descartes' mathematical approach to music. The 1629 letter from Beeckman to Mersenne is no longer extant, but as we are talking about a third-person report, Descartes might have bracketed any initial response of frustration and done a bit more investigating. Instead, he lashed out. To be sure, he was concerned about his reputation as an original thinker, and he was no doubt feeling vulnerable about how he might be viewed by the larger intellectual audience of his time. He would want to defend himself. If he was going to make a mark, he would have to confront the headwinds that he was already facing and also minimize the occurrence of additional headwinds still. But instead of looking into the content of the Beeckman letter more closely, and diplomatically amassing a body of allies who might improve his chances at forward progress, he went on the attack.[71]

Descartes did this on a number of occasions actually, and it did not serve his interests. In July 1640, the Jesuit theologian Pierre Bourdin hosted a critical discussion of Descartes' *Dioptrics* at Clermont College in Paris. Descartes learned of the event through Mersenne and then quickly wrote to the Jesuit rector of the College, Father Julien Heyneuve, to take issue. Descartes was apparently concerned that, because Jesuits usually spoke with one voice, the forum at Clermont College might come across as a collective Jesuit critique of Cartesian natural science. Descartes then communicated via Mersenne – who had exceedingly wide contacts – that he would like any Jesuit criticisms of his work to be presented in print and on the record. Soon thereafter, in January 1642, Bourdin sent Descartes a set of (written) objections to the *Meditations*. Descartes was quite dismissive of these, saying to Mersenne that "I have never seen a paper so full of faults."[72] Descartes then included the objections, along with his oft-mocking responses, as part of the second edition of the *Meditations* published later in 1642.[73] He also attached to the

---

71 See also the discussion in Clarke (2006), 46–52, and Rodis-Lewis (1998), 85–89.
72 "To Mersenne, March 1642," AT 3:543, CSMK 211.
73 The first edition of *Meditations on First Philosophy* was published in 1641 and included six sets of objections and replies.

set of objections and replies a letter that he had written to the Jesuit Jacques Dinet to register multiple complaints against Bourdin. Father Dinet had taught at La Flèche when Descartes was a student, and he was a fairly senior member of the Jesuit hierarchy in Paris. He might exercise some of his influence to offset Bourdin's criticisms, Descartes perhaps was thinking, or even promote Descartes' work for use in instruction at Jesuit schools. But the bulk of the letter to Dinet is extremely charged and extremely negative. Descartes says of Bourdin's objections,

> I would have expected to find learning, sound reasoning and intelligence; but instead I found no learning at all..., no reasoning (except what was either invalid or false), and a sharpness of intellect more suited to a bricklayer than to a Jesuit priest.[74]

Descartes goes on to speak of many slanders that Bourdin had levied against him, but in all fairness these were just criticisms to which Descartes had been given every opportunity to reply. In addition, Bourdin was a relatively minor figure and did not have any special influence over his fellow Jesuits. Descartes' management of the situation with Bourdin was extremely reactive and was out of proportion to the circumstances and events to which it was a response.

Descartes also used the letter to Dinet to register concerns about another figure with whom he was having some trouble – the Protestant Calvinist rector of the University of Utrecht, Gisbert Voetius – and here he over-reacted yet again.[75]

In 1640, Henri Regius was teaching at the University of Utrecht and was more or less a convert to Cartesian natural science. He organized a public debate on a number of theses in June of that year, focusing on issues surrounding the circulation of blood. Regius was tightly connected to Descartes, having provided edits on early drafts of *Meditations on First Philosophy* and meeting with Descartes on a regular basis to discuss Cartesian methods. The public debate

---

74 *Letter to Father Dinet*, AT 7:565, CSM 2:385.
75 See also the helpful discussion in Watson (2002), 87–89, 158, 187, 216, 225–231.

sparked a significant amount of controversy in the United Provinces, as Regius knew it would, spreading as far as the intellectual circles of England. He (Regius) then continued to be a provocateur, writing a set of disputations in 1641 in which he defended the Cartesian view that minds and bodies are individual substances, but in which he also entertained the view that the composite of a mind and a body does not constitute a substance itself. That view might not seem particularly unorthodox, but Regius was calling into question the Aristotelian tenet that united minds and bodies combine to form a hylomorphic unity that is even more of a substance than individual minds and bodies themselves. That tenet was non-negotiable for (many of) the theology faculty at the University of Utrecht, and Voetius quickly inserted himself into the back-and-forth. Descartes became involved in part because Regius had included his name on the title page of the disputations that he had authored. At first he was tactical and diplomatic, telling Regius to retreat from the view that a mind-body composite is less substantive than individual minds and bodies, and also encouraging him to use deferential language in communications with Voetius. But soon thereafter, and in the same letter (to Dinet) in which he complained about Bourdin, Descartes initiated a series of attacks against Voetius. Not mentioning him by name, but calling him "Reverend Rector," Descartes suggests that Voetius should not serve as a commentator on new ways of thinking if his mind is too feeble to so much as cognize them:

> I shall merely ask if someone can have a correct understanding of the philosophy which he wants to condemn if he is so stupid (or, if he prefers, malicious) as to try to get that philosophy suspected of being magical merely because it concentrates on figures and shapes.[76]

Here Descartes is clearly expressing frustration, as he takes his own explanations in terms of size, shape, and motion to be fully explanatory and to leave no remainder. They do not appeal to magic, he thinks, even if they appeal to variables that someone like Voetius is

---

76 *Letter to Father Dinet*, AT 7:596, CSM 2:393.

unable or unwilling to understand. Descartes ends the letter with a reference to the "quarrelsome and foolish Rector."[77] And things become testier still.

In late 1642, Descartes learned of a book that was being written – presumptively by Voetius – entitled *The Admirable Method of the New Philosophy of René Descartes*. Descartes was able to see advance pages of the book, which in its totality was a vicious attack against his person and against all things Cartesian. In 1643, he published an open letter to Voetius, running some 200 pages, in which he pulls very few punches himself. Things were starting to spiral out of control.[78] In March 1642, the academic senate of the University of Utrecht had issued a formal condemnation of the teaching of Cartesian views, directed in large part at Regius, but applying across the board. *The Admirable Method* was then published in 1643, and shortly thereafter appeared Descartes' public letter to Voetius. *The Admirable Method* turned out to have been the work of Martinus Schoock, a professor at the University of Groningen, but a supporter and subordinate of Voetius who wrote the book under his guidance. *The Admirable Method* did not lay out Descartes' most admirable qualities; it called him a liar, a heretic, a skeptic, and an atheist. It suggested that he was a homosexual and that he deserved the same fate as Giulio Vanini – who had been burned at the stake (for being a heretic and a homosexual) in 1619.

Descartes was clearly in a position of vulnerability. He was working to overthrow a metaphysics and natural science that had long been interwoven into the most powerful institutions of his time. It is not clear if there existed a path for him to present his alternative view so that it would encounter less resistance. We just don't know. He did alienate a number of influential leaders along the way, and perhaps if he had acted differently his anti-Aristotelian project would have been differently received. Perhaps Regius and others would have been allowed to continue teaching Cartesian views and methods. Perhaps Descartes might have forged a stronger alliance with the Jesuits in France had he communicated

77 Ibid., AT 7:603, CSM 2:397.

78 See also the discussions in Rodis-Lewis (1998), 165–172, and Clarke (2006), Chapter 8.

very differently with Father Dinet and other influence-brokers. Perhaps. In any case, it is worth noting the respects in which Descartes struggled to be calm-headed. At critical moments of his life, he simply lost his composure. He was attempting an intellectual revolution in the face of a tremendous amount of resistance, but there are other ways that he (or someone different) might have proceeded. His irritability is important to register in the context of his historical biography, and in the context of the delivery and reception of his ideas while he was still alive, but it is hard to think that it did not have at least some connection to his work on the regulation of emotions. Descartes offers a systematic treatment of the regulation of emotions in *The Passions of the Soul* (in 1649), with important elements of that work appearing in print as early as 1637.[79] The topic was of great interest to him. He also treats it extensively in the 1640s in his correspondences with Princess Elisabeth and Chanut. Descartes clearly recognized the import of understanding the passions – just as he would seek to understand any other part of reality – and he recognized the import of developing the skills to navigate if not master them. He also had to notice that his emotions often got the best of him, and in ways that were counter-productive. He even lost his very close friendship with Regius, who in some cases disagreed with Descartes on the implications of basic Cartesian principles. After Regius utilized some of those same principles to arrive at his own philosophical views – arguing for example that human minds and bodies are so organically connected that for all we know ideas are modifications of body[80] – Descartes ended their friendship immediately.[81] He did not take well to criticism, and he did not take well to the suggestion that his views might be developed in ways that he did not sanction. We might add that Descartes had a falling out as well with Pierre Fermat, the brilliant mathematician. Fermat was not yet in his prime, but it is believed that he was on track to write one of the official sets of objections that would be

---

79 For example, in *Discourse on Method*, AT 6:24–27, CSM 1:123–124.
80 See for example "Regius to Descartes, 23 July 1645," AT 4:254.
81 See also Rodis-Lewis (1998), 174–175, and Clarke (2006), 312–317.

attached to the *Meditations* – in addition to those written by Hobbes, Gassendi, Arnauld, Mersenne, Bourdin, and others. In the end he opted out.[82] That is a loss for history and a loss for us.

The impact of a genius

Descartes faced a significant number of headwinds in the 1640s, but as in the 1630s, he had an extraordinarily fruitful and productive decade. He published the *Meditations*, along with the attached sets of objections and replies, and in 1644 he published *Principles of Philosophy*, which contains a metaphysical discussion of the kinds of things that exist in Part I, a discussion of the basic principles and laws of physics in Part II, and explanations of a sweeping range of natural phenomena in Parts III and IV. Descartes had hoped that *Principles of Philosophy* might be adopted as a textbook at Jesuit and other colleges, as a way of countering instruction in Aristotelian natural science or at the very least helping to level the playing field. *Principles* was not widely adopted as a textbook, but it did help to expand the influence of Cartesian thinking up to the time of Newton and beyond. Descartes also published *The Passions of the Soul* in 1649, his systematic catalog of the causality behind emotion and a guidebook for redirecting neural pathways toward the production of emotions that are healthy and generative. With proper adjustments to our habits and ways of cognition, Descartes argues, we become more independent, more immutable, and in a word – more perfect.[83] In the 1640s, he published *Meditations on First Philosophy*, *Principles of Philosophy*, and *The Passions of the Soul*, and he also had a number of extremely productive correspondences. To reference just a few, he engaged with Denis Mesland on the relation between will and intellect; with Hector-Pierre Chanut on the relation between God and the creation; with William Cavendish on the question of animal thinking; and with Princess Elisabeth of Bohemia on almost everything.

The exchanges with Princess Elisabeth run largely uninterrupted from 1643 to 1649 and constitute a window on much of Descartes' system. Elisabeth presents clear and incisive objections

---

82 Watson (2002), 201, and Gaukroger (1995), 323.
83 This again is the topic of Chapter 9, "How Best to Live."

to Descartes – for example about how minds and bodies can be united even though a mind has no surface and minds and bodies have nothing in common.[84] Some of his responses are quite elucidating, though there are other instances in which Elisabeth corners Descartes into revealing (but not quite admitting) that his best defense of a particular position is not very compelling at all. With respect to the latter, we might reference his explanation of mind-body interaction in terms of Aristotelian qualities that he himself takes to be unintelligible.[85] With respect to the former, we might reference his discussion of the small number of primitive notions on the basis of which we form all of our conceptions and his contention that human beings are not built for abstract metaphysical thinking.[86] We must also reference his view that we become less malleable and more independent to the extent that our behavior is informed by firm and determinate judgments.[87] Indeed, Descartes' correspondence with Elisabeth appears to have inspired much of his thinking on the emotions, and it is difficult to read that correspondence and not affirm that it led directly to much of the argumentation in *The Passions of the Soul*.[88]

---

84 See Princess Elisabeth (1643), 9–10. And Elisabeth is not just interested in the metaphysical issue of mind-body union. She also calls attention to the bodily grounds of human emotions and mental health – in ways that run counter to much of the tradition. See the discussion in Jeffery (2017), 551–555.

85 "To Princess Elizabeth, 21 May 1643," AT 3:667–668, CSMK 219.

86 "To Princess Elizabeth, 21 May 1643," AT 3:665–667, CSMK 218–19; "To Princess Elizabeth, 28 June 1643," AT 3:691–695, CSMK 226–228.

87 "To Princess Elizabeth, 18 August 1645," AT 4:277, CSMK 262.

88 Descartes admired Elisabeth to such an extent that he dedicated *Principles of Philosophy* to her. Some commentators (myself included) have found it odd that, however much he respected Elisabeth, he did not dedicate *Principles of Philosophy* to a prominent Jesuit or similar figure who would have had more influence on whether it would be incorporated as a textbook. This is so especially in the light of the struggles that Descartes had in the early 1640s with Bourdin, Voetius, and others. Princess Elisabeth did not have much in the way of political or other resources – even though she had a distinguished title and bloodline – and it does not appear that she would have been particularly well-positioned to help. Descartes ends up dedicating *The Passions of the Soul* to Queen Christina – very clearly for reasons of influence and support – but in terms of content, the

The 1640s were an extraordinarily productive decade for Descartes. Given the conflicts and struggles that he faced, however, and given that his metaphysics and natural science were a repudiation of a program that was widely entrenched, he was on very shaky ground in terms of the influence that he hoped to secure.[89] His work was also condemned en masse by the University of Leiden in 1647. We now know how the story turns out – in terms of Descartes' actual impact on the worlds of natural science and philosophy – but he could not have had any real confidence that things would go that way himself. He sensed as much when he wrote in a letter to Chanut that what he needed was a patron and protector:

> Because I have not taken the same care to abstain from writing, I do not have as much leisure or peace as I would if I had the wit to keep quiet. But since the error has already been committed and I am known by countless Schoolmen, who look askance at my writings and try from every angle to find in them the means of harming me, I have good reason to wish to be known by persons of greater distinction, whose power and virtue might protect me.[90]

Perhaps with that thought in mind he relocated to Paris in 1648, after the King of France offered him a pension to sponsor his continued thinking and research. Initially Descartes moved into the heart of Paris, where he would have a lot less privacy than he preferred, and

---

book would have made the most sense to dedicate to Elisabeth. One speculation (which is totally ungrounded but I think highly plausible) is that Descartes dedicated *Principles of Philosophy* to Elisabeth not only because he respected her greatly but also because he thought that her connection to her uncle, King Charles I of England, might have furthered his intellectual and scientific cause. Charles I was executed in 1649, but prior to that (and during the English Civil War) there was an open question about whether or not he would return to power. Descartes also makes reference to (what he thought were) the Catholic sympathies of the King, even though officially he was a Protestant. See "To Mersenne, 1 April 1640," AT 3:50, CSMK 146.

89 Also Gaukroger (1995), 386.

90 "To Chanut, 1 November 1646," AT 4:535, CSMK 299.

much more visibility.[91] He might have been thinking that in order to extend the reach of his work, it would need to be positioned via more and more nodes of influence – and that proximity to the royal court and its environs was the best option toward that end.[92] He left Paris after just a couple of months, however, as widespread political turmoil upended his plans and his pension never materialized. He returned to the United Provinces, where he had to decide if a life of relative privacy and isolation was in the end the best vehicle to advance his work, or if another patron and protector might be a better alternative still.

In 1649, Descartes was corresponding with Chanut – by then the French Ambassador to Sweden – when Chanut encouraged him to relocate to Stockholm at the request of Queen Christina. Descartes and Chanut had been exchanging letters since 1646, and Descartes corresponded with Queen Christina about the regulation of passions in 1647 and 1649.[93] The invitation to Stockholm was very attractive: Descartes would be part of an international institute of scholars and scientists, and he would be personal tutor to the Queen herself. Still, he had serious reservations.[94] Stockholm was cold, and it was cold for many months of the year. Descartes also did not know the exact details or even the rough outline of his expected daily routine, though he knew that he would have to adjust to the royal schedule. In the end, he decided to leave the United Provinces for Stockholm. Perhaps he was thinking that any toxicity that had retreated in places like Utrecht and Leiden was still latent and would continue to show its face. Perhaps he was thinking that an extremely powerful patron could help to clear the way for his metaphysics and natural philosophy to obtain a fair hearing. He arrived in Stockholm in October 1649, but his tutorial sessions with Queen Christina did not start until mid-January. He was then required to wake up early (in the cold winter morning) and be ready to begin each lesson

---

91 Also Gaukroger (1995), 410–411.
92 See also the discussion in Watson (2002), 263–264.
93 There is also a single (and very brief) letter from Queen Christina to Descartes dated December 12, 1648, AT 5:251–252.
94 Also Gaukroger (1995), 288–295.

at 5:00 am.[95] Descartes' close friend Chanut became ill later that month, and Descartes appears to have caught the same. He died on February 11, 1650, at the age of 53.

Descartes had a number of extraordinary intellectual achievements in his lifetime, even if many of them were not fully appreciated until well after his death. But it is also important to recognize that he was very much an embodied person, interested in embodied affairs. He was a mathematician, but he wanted to do mathematics in large part to understand and explain earthly (and celestial) phenomena. He wanted to apply his mathematical and mechanistic methods to understand the physiology of organisms – and to create medicines that would improve the health and extend the life of embodied human beings. He was fascinated by parahelia, barometric pressure, lenses, and plants. He wanted to live to be a hundred years old, to walk his dog, and to treat his increasingly grey hair as he aged. Abstract metaphysical inquiry supplies us with an important ground for the rest of what we do, he allows, but it is the rest of what we do that merits the bulk of our attention.

Further reading

There are a number of biographical works on Descartes. These include:

Roger Ariew, "What Descartes Read: His Intellectual Background," in *The Oxford Handbook of Descartes and Cartesianism*, ed. Steven Nadler, Tad M. Schmaltz, and Delphine Antoine-Mahut, Oxford: Oxford UP (2019), 25–39.

Desmond M. Clarke, *Descartes: A Biography*, Cambridge and New York: Cambridge UP (2006).

Harold John Cook, *The Young Descartes: Nobility, Rumor, and War*, Chicago and London: Chicago UP (2018).

Stephen Gaukroger, *Descartes: An Intellectual Biography*, New York and Oxford: Oxford UP (1995).

---

95 Perhaps noteworthy is that early in life Descartes had been subject to bouts of ill-health, and (for example) at La Flèche he was excused from the standard 5:00 am wakeup. In a 1631 letter, he reports that as often as possible he would sleep for ten hours each night ("To Balzac, 15 April 1631," AT 1:198, CSMK 30). See also Rodis-Lewis (1998), 12.

A.C Grayling, *Descartes: The Life and Times of a Genius*, New York: Walker and Company (2006).

Steven Nadler, *The Philosopher, the Priest, and the Painter: A Portrait of Descartes*, Princeton, NJ: Princeton UP (2015).

Geneviève Rodis-Lewis, *Descartes: His Life and Thought*, trans. Jane Marie Todd, Ithaca, NY: Cornell UP (1998).

Richard Watson, *Cogito Ergo Sum: The Life of Descartes*, Jaffrey, NH: David R Godine Publishing (2002).

In addition, there is a very early two-volume biography of Descartes, written by Adrien Baillet (1691) – *La Vie de M. Descartes*, Paris. This biography is extremely engaging, and it was written much closer to the time in which Descartes was alive, but Baillet also speculates quite a bit, and later biographers have walked back a good number of his claims. Note that an English translation of *La Vie de Descartes* is available online through the Early English Books site at the University of Michigan, though not much is known about the edition or about the translator.

There is also a lot of outstanding scholarship that addresses Descartes' work in natural science and his focus on material bodies. These include:

Delphine Antoine-Mahut and Stephen Gaukroger (eds.), *Descartes' Treatise on Man and Its Reception* (2016). This is volume 43 of *Studies in History and Philosophy of Science*, Dordrecht: Springer.

Dennis Des Chene, *Physiologia: Natural Philosophy in Late Aristotelian and Cartesian Thought*, Ithaca, NY: Cornell UP (1996).

Desmond Clarke, *Descartes' Philosophy of Science*, University Park, PA: Penn State UP (1990).

Karen Detlefsen, "Descartes on the Theory of Life and Methodology in the Life Sciences," in *Early Modern Medicine and Natural Philosophy*, ed. P. Distelzweig, Dordrecht: Springer (2016), 141–171.

Daniel Garber, *Descartes' Metaphysical Physics*, Chicago and London: Chicago UP (1992).

Daniel Garber, *Descartes Embodied: Reading Cartesian Philosophy through Cartesian Science*, Cambridge and New York: Cambridge UP (2000).

Stephen Gaukroger, *Descartes' System of Natural Philosophy*, Cambridge and New York: Cambridge UP (2002).

Melissa Lo, *Skepticism's Pictures: Figuring Descartes's Natural Philosophy*, University Park, PA: Penn State UP (2023).

Margaret Osler, "Descartes, Natural Philosopher," *Studies in History and Philosophy of Science Part A* 23 (1991), 508–518.

Three

The limits of our metaphysical tether

Descartes arrives at a number of metaphysical views – for example, that God exists, that minds are immaterial substances, that bodies exist with extensive features like size, shape, and motion but not intensive features like color and taste, and that the universe is a continuous plenum. But the number of metaphysical views at which he arrives is in fact quite small, as is the number of pages of his corpus that are dedicated to metaphysical inquiry. In a letter to Princess Elisabeth, Descartes says famously and, a bit jarringly, that in his own life, he has spent a very small amount of time on metaphysical matters and the remainder on matters of imagination and the senses. He writes,

> I am almost afraid that your Highness may think that I am not now speaking seriously; but that would go against the respect which I owe her and which I will never cease to show her. I can say with truth that the chief rule I have always observed in my studies, which I think has been the most useful in acquiring what knowledge I have, has been never to spend more than a few hours a day in the thoughts which occupy the imagination and a few hours a year on those which occupy the intellect alone. I have given all the rest of my time to the relaxation of the senses and the repose of the mind.[1]

---

1 "To Princess Elizabeth, 28 June 1643," AT 3:692–693, CSMK 227.

DOI: 10.4324/9781351210522-3

We might suppose that Descartes is just doing some autobiography here, and that he is merely reporting on his own individual pro-clivities. In that case, we might still be surprised that the figure who is sometimes introduced as the Father of Modern Philosophy would have dedicated so little time to metaphysical reflection.[2] But Descartes is not just making an autobiographical statement in the letter to Elisabeth. Later in the same, he makes a more general statement that he takes to apply to all:

> I think that it is very necessary to have properly understood, once in a lifetime, the principles of metaphysics, since they are what gives us the knowledge of God and our soul. But I think also that it would be very harmful to occupy one's intellect fre-quently in meditating upon them, since this would impede it from devoting oneself to all of the functions of the imagination and the senses. I think that the best thing is to content oneself with keeping in one's memory and one's belief the conclusions which one has drawn from them, and then employ the rest of

---

2 Descartes does not provide an explicit definition of the activity that is meta-physical inquiry, though he clearly has in mind a sense of what we are to avoid when he says that "one should not devote so much effort... to metaphysical questions" (*Conversation with Burman*, AT 5:165, CSMK 346). In the preface to the French edition of *Principles of Philosophy*, he provides a list of metaphysical topics, along with a reference to the (non-sensory) tools by which such topics are approached:

> the first part of philosophy is metaphysics, which contains the principles of knowledge, including the explanation of the principal attributes of God, the non-material nature of our souls and all the clear and distinct notions which are in us.
>
> (AT 9B:14, CSM 1:186)

For Descartes, metaphysics is a matter of arriving at results that are grasped through the "clear and distinct notions that are within us" – notions that as we have seen are accessed via "one's intellect" (AT 4:695, CSMK 228), in which we "draw the mind... away from physical and observable things" (AT 5:165, CSMK 346) and focus on that "which occup[ies] the intellect alone" (AT 3:693, CSMK 227) and is uncovered via "purely mental scrutiny" (AT 7:31, CSM 2:21). See also *Letter to Father Dinet*, AT 7:580, CSM 2:391.

one's study time to thoughts in which the intellect co-operates with the imagination and the senses. (AT 4:695, CSMK 228)

Descartes expresses the same sentiment in his October 1645 letter to Elisabeth as well.[3] He is also reported to have said in his 1647 interview with Franz Burman that the pursuit of metaphysical questions is not the most appropriate activity for us. He writes,

A point to note is that one should not devote so much effort to the *Meditations* and to metaphysical questions.... [T]hey draw the mind too far away from physical and observable things, and make it unfit to study them. Yet it is just these physical studies that it is most desirable for people to pursue, since they would yield abundant benefits for life.[4]

Descartes struggles to engage *some* metaphysical questions, but as we will see, in many cases, he points out that a given question is beyond us, and he moves on to matters that are of greater consequence.[5]

Descartes is famous for isolating the existence of his insensible thinking self after the skeptical deluge of the First Meditation – what he identifies as an Archimedean point for all knowledge (AT 7:24). He states in another text that "there is no more fruitful exercise than attempting to know ourselves," but with a very different self in mind:

There is no more fruitful exercise than attempting to know ourselves. The benefits we may expect from such knowledge not only relate to ethics, as many would initially suppose, but also have a special importance for medicine. I believe that we would have been able to find many reliable rules, both for curing illness and for preventing it, and even for slowing down the ageing

---

3 "To Princess Elizabeth, 6 October 1645," AT 4:307, CSMK 268–269.

4 *Conversation with Burman*, AT 5:165, CSMK 346–347.

5 Here I am arguing in the spirit of Marion (1999) and Garber (2012), 62–63. Marion argues that Descartes is not so much presenting metaphysics as a "first philosophy" (10, 27–31). See also Marignac (1980), 302–308, 312, and Watson (1984).

process, if only we had spent enough effort on getting to know the nature of our body....[6]

Here in the first paragraph of *Description of the Human Body and of All Its Functions* Descartes is touting the importance of self-knowledge, but the self in question is the mind-body composite. In the remaining pages – of which just a small fraction are excerpted in CSM – he proceeds to describe a wide range of bodily processes in great detail, suggesting implications for the improvement of both physical and mental health. He adds in yet another text that "[t]he preservation of health has always been the principal end of my studies...."[7] In *Principles of Philosophy*, he says famously that

> the whole of philosophy is like a tree. The roots are metaphysics, the trunk is physics, and the branches emerging from the trunk are all the other sciences, which may be reduced to three principal ones, namely medicine, mechanics and morals. ...Now just as it is not the roots or the trunk of the tree from which one gathers the fruit, but only the ends of the branches, so the principal benefit of philosophy depends on those parts of it which can only be learnt last of all.[8]

In this passage, Descartes is saying about as clearly as one could that the most fruitful kinds of inquiry are not of the metaphysical variety but instead are practical and applied. Metaphysics is not the fruit of the tree of philosophy. It is the roots, and once the roots of a tree are firmly in place, they do not need a lot of tending. For the most part, they lie hidden beneath the ground, but they do infuse the trunk, the branches, and the harvest that is borne from them. In the development of new metaphysical foundations, we do not swap out the old roots with the new and then affix the original trunk and branches. We grow a new tree, and the fruits that arose before are a shadow of the

---

6 *Description of the Human Body and of All Its Functions*, AT 11:223–24, CSM 1:314.
7 "To [The Marquess of Newcastle], October 1645," AT 4:329, CSMK 275. See also Nyden and Dobre (2013) for an extensive treatment of the empirical and applied work of seventeenth-century followers of Descartes.
8 *Principles of Philosophy*, "Preface to the French edition," AT 9B:14–15, CSM 1:186.

fruits that take their place. Descartes engages in abstract metaphysical enquiry — no one is denying that — but he does so in the service of natural science and the betterment of (embodied) human life.

Embodiment and metaphysical inquiry

One of the reasons why Descartes thinks that metaphysics is not an especially appropriate activity for us is that (he thinks that) embodied finite minds are not built for it. He says in one passage that a finite mind would have clear and distinct ideas quite easily if it had no body, or if "in thinking it received not just no assistance from the body but also that it received no interference from it."[9] But we *are* embodied:

> The senses often impede the mind in many of its operations, and in no case do they help in the perception of ideas. The only thing that prevents all of us noticing equally well that we have these ideas is that we are too occupied with perceiving the images of corporeal things.
>
> (ibid.)

And we are impacted by corporeal things almost constantly.[10] There are the macroscopic bodies that we notice and that are overtly relevant to our well-being, and there are the less-observable bodies that span the plenum and exert an influence as well. If the influences of the body were short-circuited, a mind "would have exactly the same ideas of God and itself that it now has, with the sole difference that they would have been much purer and much clearer."[11] Descartes accordingly says that embodiment is "The only thing that

---

9 *Fifth Replies*, AT 7:375, CSM 2:258.

10 I take this to be obvious, but see *Fourth Replies*, where Descartes references "the fact that the mind is closely conjoined with the body, which we experience constantly through our senses" (AT 7:228–29, CSM 2:160). See also "For [Arnauld], 29 July 1648," AT 5:219, CSMK 356.

11 This is a continuation of the passage in *Fifth Replies*, AT 7:375, CSM 2:258.

prevents all of us noticing" our clear and distinct ideas.[12] He adds
in a letter to Princess Elizabeth that there are a small number of
"simple notions" that a (not-embodied) finite mind "possesses…
by nature" and from which "we derive all our other conceptions."[13]
He says that "It is in our own soul that we must look for these simple
notions" (AT 3:666, CSMK 219), but he writes in another text that
"there can be no falsity save in composite natures which are put
together by the intellect" and that we "we term 'simple' only those
things which we know so clearly and distinctly that they cannot be
divided by the mind into others which are more distinctly known."[14]
Descartes holds that without the interference of mind-body union
all of our ideas would be clear and distinct.[15] But as things stand, we
are embodied, and clear and distinct ideas are few and far between.

According to Descartes, there are numerous obstacles that interfere
with the ability of a finite mind to engage in abstract metaphysical
inquiry. Sections 71–74 of Part I of *Principles of Philosophy* is a dedicated
discussion of such obstacles. One is a habit of affirming that anything that is not sensible has no reality at all. In early childhood, we
focus attention exclusively on the sensible bodies that might benefit
or harm us, and we assume that if we do not sense something it is
not there:

> since the mind judged everything in terms of its utility to the
> body in which it was immersed, it assessed the amount of
> reality in each object by the extent to which it was affected by

---

12 He writes in another passage that "the first and most important reason for our
   inability to understand with sufficient clarity the customary assertions about
   the soul and God" – for example that finite minds are immaterial or that God
   exists – is that "[o]ur ideas… have up till now been very confused and mixed
   up with the ideas of things that can be perceived by the senses" (*Second Replies*, AT
   7:130–31, CSM 2:94).

13 "To Princess Elizabeth, 21 May 1643," AT 3:665–666, CSMK 218–219.

14 *Rules for the Direction of the Mind*, AT 10:399, CSM 1:32, and AT 10:418, CSM 1:44.

15 Also, Descartes says in *Principles* III.45 that "if we consider the infinite power of
   God, we cannot think that he ever created anything that was not wholly perfect
   of its kind" (AT 8A:100, CSM 1:256). It is difficult to see how a finite intellect would be wholly perfect of its kind if it had ideas that were intrinsically
   confused. See also the second half of Chapter 6 – on the Fourth Meditation.

it. As a result, it supposed that there was more substance or corporeality in rocks and metals than in water or air, since it felt
more hardness and heaviness in them. Indeed, it regarded air as
a mere nothing, so long as it felt no wind or cold or heat in it.[16]

The habit is useful in terms of registering what is and what is not
relevant to our survival, but it is not useful in terms of gauging the
reality of things that are insensible or abstract.[17] Instead, it sets us
back. Descartes supposes that we also develop a habit of thinking by
way of imagistic ideas. We focus on embodied needs from birth –
deliberating and fretting over the sensible objects that are relevant to
our survival – and the idea of a sensible entity becomes the model
or template by which we think *anything*. Metaphysical inquiry then
becomes difficult to impossible:

> our mind is unable to keep its attention on things without some
> degree of difficulty and fatigue; and it is hardest of all for it to attend
> to what is not present to the senses or even to the imagination. This
> may be due to the very nature that the mind has as a result of being
> joined to the body; or it may be because it was exclusively occupied
> with the objects of sense and imagination in its earliest years, and
> has thus acquired greater practice and aptitude for thinking about
> them than it has for thinking about other things.[18]

If we attempt to think of an insensible entity by picturing it – for
example as having a shape and a color – we will struggle. We will
either fail to think of the insensible entity – because an idea of a
sensible entity does not represent an insensible entity – or else we
will conceive of the insensible entity as having (sensible) features
that do not pertain to it. For example, we might have an idea of
God that has become mixed up and combined with an idea of

---

16 *Principles* I.71, AT 8A:36, CSM 1:219. See also *The World*, where Descartes says that
   there are many "who suppose that there is nothing in the world except what
   they touch" (AT 11:21, CSM 1:87).
17 For example, when we step back to assess the reality and existence of our
   thinking in the Second Meditation (AT 7:29-30, CSM 2:20).
18 *Principles* I.73, AT 8A:37, CSM 1:220.

a bearded man on a cloud, in such a way that the idea is of God, but it misrepresents God.[19]

In yet another passage Descartes says that

> Our nature is so constituted that our mind needs much relaxation if it is to be able to spend usefully a few moments in the search for truth. Too great application to study does not refine the mind, but wears it down.[20]

In the Second Meditation, we saw Descartes' meditator become exhausted after the difficult work of arriving at a non-sensory and clear and distinct idea of his own thinking. In the Third Meditation, the meditator concludes that God exists, but his "mental vision is blinded by the images of things perceived by the senses, and it is not so easy for me to remember why the idea of a being more perfect than myself must necessarily proceed from some being which is in realty more perfect" (AT 7:47–48, CSM 2:32–33). At the end of the Second and Fourth Meditations, the meditator stops to take a break from the strenuous effort that he has exerted in each (AT 7:34, CSM 2:22–23; AT 7:62, CSM 2:43), and at the end of the Third, he pauses to rehearse a clear and distinct perception to the degree that his "darkened [and embodied] intellect can bear it" (AT 7:52, CSM 2:36). One of the views that Descartes puts forward about the nature of things is a view about the nature of embodied minds: they are not particularly suited to metaphysical inquiry.

It is not surprising then that just a small percentage of his 8,000-page corpus is dedicated to the pursuit of metaphysical questions, and to a small number of them. In the very brief part IV of Discourse on the Method (1637), he argues that God exists, that minds are immaterial substances, and that material things exist. The Discourse is basically a preview of Meditations on First Philosophy (1641), in which Descartes indicates that his principal aim is to demonstrate the existence of

---

19 In Chapter 4 (pp. 109–116), there is a further discussion of this kind of case, along with a further discussion of the cognitive obstacles treated in Principles I.71–74.

20 "To Princess Elizabeth, 6 October 1645," AT 4:307, CSMK 268–269.

God and the real distinction between mind and body (AT 7:17).[21]
He also writes a long set of replies to objections to the *Meditations*,
but there he is discussing (and elaborating on) the same material yet
again. He addresses a small number of metaphysical topics in *Principles
of Philosophy* Part I (and in a few sections of Part II), but as we will
see his aims there are modest as well. A small fraction of Descartes'
correspondence treats metaphysical issues – around 550 pages (in
the Adam and Tannery numbering) out of the total 4,000.[22] The
Meditations, Part IV of the *Discourse*, and the first one and one-half parts
of *Principles of Philosophy* total around 150 pages. Including the metaphysical material of the correspondence, we have a total of around
700 pages, but Descartes' corpus totals around 8,000 pages.[23] We
can also include his replies to the seven sets of objections to the
Meditations, which add up to a few hundred pages, but again these are
focused on the small number of views and arguments that appear
in the *Meditations* itself. Only a small amount of Descartes' corpus is
dedicated to abstract metaphysical inquiry, as we would expect if
Descartes held that finite embodied minds are not built for it and
that we are wise to keep it to a minimum.

Metaphysical matters that are beyond our reach

There is a large number of metaphysical issues that Descartes takes to
be beyond us. We are built to focus our attention on other things. In
addition, when we do succeed at bracketing our embodiment for "a
few moments," our ideas do not deliver a whole lot of information.

For example, and as we have seen, one issue on which Descartes
thinks we are able to make very little ground is the question of
whether or not the extent of the universe is infinite or finite. Descartes
says that the material universe is indefinitely extended in a way that

---

21 He also argues that material things exist, in the Sixth Meditation.
22 But note that the 550 (or so) pages of metaphysical material in the correspond-
    ence include a lot of discussion of natural science and a lot of passing references
    to everyday personal matters.
23 And to the 700 pages, we should also add the 33 pages of the dialogue, *The Search
    for Truth*, and the 30 pages of *Comments on a Certain Broadsheet*. In these Descartes is
    clarifying material that he covered in the *Meditations*.

we do not fully understand – and that for all he knows it might be infinite. In addition, he holds that individual bodies are indefinitely divided in a way that we do not fully understand. He writes in *Principles* II.34–35 that there is

> is an infinite, or indefinite, division of the various particles of matter; and the resulting subdivisions are so numerous that however small we make a particle in our thought, we always understand that it is in fact divided into still smaller particles. ...We cannot grasp in our thought how this indefinite division comes about, but we should not doubt that it occurs. For we clearly perceive that it necessarily follows from what we <already> know most evidently of the nature of matter, and we perceive that it belongs to the class of things which are beyond the grasp of our finite minds.
>
> (AT 8A:59–60, CSM 1:239)

Descartes supposes that we recognize not just that a body is always divisible but that it is always in fact divided. We do not recognize that bodies are infinitely divided, but instead their level of division is somewhere between finite and infinite, and is in some way closer to the latter. Descartes does not tell us how far the division of a body falls short of infinite – not even approximately – but we recognize that it is more than finite. To his credit, Descartes does not take a stand on a metaphysical issue that is a mind-bender.

Nor does Descartes take a stand on the ontology of mind-body union or on how minds and bodies are united even though they are substances with nothing in common. A mind is not spatially intermixed with a body if minds are not spatially extended. And minds do not come into contact with bodies if contact is always a matter of the meeting of two surfaces and if minds do not *have* surfaces. When Gassendi and Princess Elisabeth object to Descartes that he has no explanation of how mind-body union is achieved, he does not contradict them. He replies to Gassendi that "it is not necessary for the mind itself to be a body, although it has the power of moving the body."[24] He replies to Elisabeth that we do not understand mind-body union

---

24 *Fifth Replies*, AT 7:389, CSM 2:266.

by way of an idea, but through the "the ordinary course of life and conversation."[25] Descartes is famous for his silence on the question of how exactly minds and bodies form a union if bodies are extended and minds are not. But that silence is not an outlier. There is a wide range of metaphysical matters on which he does not take a stand. Our tether reaches only so far. But that is no loss for us; we have other matters to which to attend that are more pressing.

Nor does Descartes take a stand on the ontology of the force by which bodies interact. In the Third Meditation, he defends (or at least articulates) the doctrine that the power by which a creature is preserved in existence is the same as the power by which it is created:

> it is quite clear to anyone who attentively considers the nature of time that the same power and action are needed to preserve anything at each individual moment of its existence as would be required to create that thing anew if it were not yet in existence. Hence the distinction between preservation and creation is only a conceptual one, and this is one of the things that are evident by the natural light.[26]

He presents the doctrine as obvious, which is to say that he does not go to any lengths to motivate it.[27] The plausibility of the doctrine aside, it would appear to have direct implications for Descartes' view on force. Descartes holds that the power to preserve a creature in existence is identical to the power to re-create it. If so, and if he is right, we might conclude that a body does not move other bodies by means of a force that modifies it. Instead, God just re-creates bodies from moment to moment in their new position. Or even

---

25 "To Princess Elizabeth, 28 June 1643," AT 3:692, CSMK 227.

26 AT 7:49, CSM 2:33. See also *The World*, AT 11:43–44, CSM 1:96.

27 But there is some counterfactual reasoning that makes it at least somewhat intuitive: if God is in the course of willing that a creature remain in existence, and He decides to no longer do that, then He would cease to will that it exist, and it would cease existing; but if God changed His mind and decided to continue preserving it in existence, then God's volition that it exist would keep it from going out of existence, which is to say that God would exert the same power as if He created it anew.

if we suppose that Descartes does not hold that bodies are literally re-created at each and every moment, we might conclude that he holds that God plays such an all-encompassing role in the behavior of bodies that force is not a modification of bodies but is reducible to divine activity.[28]

But Descartes does hold that force is a modification bodies. He holds that force is a modification of bodies and that God preserves creatures in existence from moment to moment, even if we do not understand the line at which creaturely activity starts and divine activity ends. That is one of the many things that is beyond us.

There is a large number of passages in which Descartes speaks of force as a modification of bodies. For example, he says that

> From the time they began to move, they also began to change and diversify their motions by colliding with one another.... [F]rom this first instant the various parts of matter, in which these motions are found unequally dispersed, began to retain them or transfer them from one to another, according as they had the force to do so.[29]

Here Descartes could not be much more explicit that bodies have force. In another passage, he says that "the mechanism of the body... is so constructed by nature that it has the ability to move in various ways by its own power."[30] Descartes clearly holds that force is a

---

28 See for example Garber (1992), 298. For similar interpretations, see Hatfield (1979), Des Chene (1996), and Manchak (2009).

29 *The World*, AT 11:37–43, CSM 1:93–96. See also *Principles* II.25, AT 8A:54, CSM 1:233, Platt (2011), and Platt (2011b).

30 *Principles* I.71, AT 8A:35, CSM 1:219. See also *Description of the Human Body and all its Functions*, AT 11:224, CSM 1:314; *Optics*, AT 6:94, CSM 1:157; and *Principles* II.43, AT 8A:66, CSM 1:243. In a generous email correspondence, Garber has confirmed that, on his view, Descartes is describing reality at a merely phenomenal level in the texts in which he attributes force to body; he is not describing reality at its deepest (metaphysical) level. For example, Leibniz is doing this in passages in which he attributes force to body – Garber (1994, 283–284) – and Garber holds that Descartes is doing the same. A worry is that there is not the same kind of textual evidence that Descartes is making the distinction (between two levels of reality) as there is in the case of Leibniz.

modification of bodies. He does not hold that bodies are completely inert.[31] Bodies move each other via force, and indeed it is inexplicable how they would be able to move each other in any other way:

> it does not seem possible to conceive how one body could move another except through its own movement.[32]

For Descartes, force is a modification of body. He nowhere goes out of his way to make explicit how it is to be explained in terms of the principal attribute of extension, but he would appear to have the resources to offer such an explanation on the basis of his view that motion is a modification of extension. He is very clear that motion is a modification of extension, for example, in Principles I.53 (AT 8A:25, CSM 1:210) and "To More, August 1649" (AT 5:403–404 CSMK 381). He then adds in the AT 11:8 passage that there is no way to understand "how one body could move another except through its own movement."That is to say, motion is a modification of extension, and force is explicable in terms of motion. To be sure, our idea of the principal attribute of extension does not entail that bodies possess motion (or force). Some bodies are at rest.[33] Indeed, Descartes does not hold that the conceptual relation between the principal attribute of a substance and its modes goes from left to right, but from right to left. We do not predict the modes of a substance from its principal attribute. Instead, we specify a mode first, and then we ask if it can be explained in terms of the principal attribute. Motion can be

---

31 To borrow the language from Gaukroger (1995, 350, 376–377), who holds (with Garber and others) that for Descartes force is not a modification of body. I disagree. See also the Sixth Meditation, in which Descartes argues that there is an "active faculty" in bodies that produces our sensory perceptions (AT 7:79, CSM 2:55). In Principles II.1, he argues similarly that bodies "give rise" to our sensory perceptions (AT 8A:40, CSM 1:223).

32 The World, AT 11:8, CSM 1:83.

33 For example, Principles II.43, AT 8A:66, CSM 1:243. Descartes also says in Principles I.53 that "it is possible to understand extension without... movement" (AT 8A:25, CSM 1:211).

explained in terms of the principal attribute of extension, Descartes is arguing, and force is explicable in terms of motion.[34]

Descartes holds that force is a modification of bodies, but he nowhere attempts to mark the line at which the constant creation of a body stops and the activity of the body begins. He says that the power by which God preserves a body from moment to moment is the "same" as the power by which He creates a body anew, but he does not thereby conclude that bodies are newly created in their entirety at each and every moment. He writes for example that

> it follows of necessity, from the mere fact that he [God] continues thus to preserve it, that there must be many changes in its parts which cannot, it seems to me, properly be attributed to the action of God…[35]

For Descartes, there is some aspect or proportion of a body that remains in existence from moment to moment. That is to say, he holds that there is such a thing as divine preservation and that there is sense in which something persists of a creature from moment to moment. That is why it is the same creature that exists from moment

---

34 One of Garber's reasons for thinking that force is not a modification of body (for Descartes) is that force is not explicable in terms of the principal attribute of extension. See Garber (1992), 77–80. A different piece of evidence that Garber offers is that Descartes says in Principles II.36 that the "universal and primary cause… of all the motions in the world… is nothing other than God Himself" (AT 8A:61, CSM 1:240; Garber (2000), 182). Descartes adds in Principles II.37 that there exist "particular and secondary causes" (AT 8A:62), but Garber argues that those are to be identified with divine activity also (ibid., 183–184, 206–208). In the CSM translation of Principles II.37, Descartes says that "from God's immutability we can also know certain rules or laws of nature, which are the secondary and particular causes of the various motions that we see in individual bodies" (AT 8A:62, CSM 1:240). But the CSM translation adds an article before "causae secundariae ac particulares," and in Latin, there is no such article. The Latin does not specify that the secondary and particular causes of the behavior of bodies reduce to divine activity, but just that divine activity (in the form of laws of nature) is among those causes.

35 The World, AT 11:37, CSM 1:92–93; emphasis added.

to moment to moment, and not just a stream of look-alikes.[36] He does not suppose that preservation is *nothing more than* constant creation or that what God *really* does is to constantly create. Instead, he holds that "the same power and action are needed to preserve anything at each individual moment... as would be required to create that thing anew." The self-same power is involved in both cases, and that power is no more the one – the power to create – than it is the other – the power to preserve. Descartes does not proceed to flesh out what exactly this power is – not in the Third Meditation and not anywhere else – and indeed it does not appear that there is anything that he could say to flesh it out. If he tells us that it is preservation, and we ask what that is, he can say that it is constant creation. If we ask what that is, he can say that it is preservation. If we ask again what preservation is, he might say that it is a unitary thing that is at the same time constant creation and preservation both. At that point, we might get frustrated – or worry that he is failing to offer an account – but we might also notice that he himself does not attempt to provide an account. And that is to his credit. He does not report that he has an account of the activity that is both creation and preservation – and ask for a drumroll – and then announce with great (but anti-climactic) fanfare that they are identical. He nowhere provides an exact account of the sense in which creatures depend for their existence on God and the sense in which they are independent substances, but to his credit that is *extremely* hard to do. I do not have such an account myself – and neither does anyone else[37] – and I would not want to critique Descartes for failing to provide an account himself if he never pretends to put one on offer. He does say in *Principles* I.51 that a substance is something "which can be said

---

36 Even *Malebranche* subscribes to this view, although he is known for taking the doctrine of constant creation to the most radical extreme possible. He says for example that "I believe and feel I must believe that after the soul's action there remain in its substance certain changes that really dispose it to this same action." See Elucidation Seven of *Elucidations of the Search After Truth*, in Malebranche (1674), 578; and Cunning (2008).

37 For a discussion that does attempt to make sense of Descartes' view on the relation between divine preservation and constant creation, see Schmaltz (2007), 71–83.

to depend on no other thing whatsoever" (AT 8A:24, CSM 1:210), and hence that there is a sense in which creatures are independent substances and a sense in which they are not. But he nowhere draws the line, and for good reason. A lot of metaphysical issues are simply beyond our reach.

Nor does Descartes go to any lengths to offer an account of the ontology of number. In *Principles* I.58–59, he says that, like many other things, number has two manners of existence – one in thought, and one in reality. He writes that

> number, when it is considered simply in the abstract or in general, and not in any created things, is merely a mode of thinking....
>
> (AT 8A:27, CSM 1:212)

Number "in the abstract or in general" is not a mind-independent substance of any kind,[38] as Plato and Aristotle took it to be.[39] Instead, it is a modification of mind. Descartes then offers an account of the *formation* of our idea of number. He says for example that

> [w]hen we see two stones, ... and direct our attention not to their nature but merely to the fact that there are two of them, we form the idea of the number which we call 'two'; and when we later see two birds or two trees, and consider not their nature but merely the fact that there are two of them, we go back to the same idea as before.
>
> (ibid.)

Here Descartes is telling us about number "when it is considered simply in the abstract or in general," and not when it is considered in created things. But he takes number to exist in created things also.[40]

38　Descartes writes in *Principles* I.55 that "we have a very distinct understanding of... number, provided we do not mistakenly tack onto [it] any concept of substance" (AT 8A:26, CSM 1:211).

39　See Fine (1983).

40　Just like he takes duration to exist in things. In *Principles* I.55–57, he discusses the difference between duration as it exists in thought (as an abstract universal)

He indicates as much when he says that we form our idea of two-ness by noticing the twoness in objects. He does not give an account of that twoness, except to say that "we should not regard order or number as anything separate from the things which are ordered or numbered."[41] But that is again to say that number is in the things that are ordered or numbered. Descartes' account of the formation of the idea of twoness is quick and minimal, but his account of the ontology of number as it exists outside of thought is non-existent. In the short one and one-half (Adam and Tannery) pages in which he engages the discussion, he does not come across as having even the slightest interest in the ontology of number.[42] He is virtually silent. Contemporary mathematicians would note that numbers are in *re* all around us – for example, the Fibonacci sequence as it manifests in plants, music, and human anatomy, and the number pi as it shows up in probability calculations, waves, music, and rivers.[43] But no one pretends to understand the exact sense in which the numbers them-selves are in the world. Descartes would appear to agree.

Nor does Descartes offer an account of the ontology of geometrical properties. In the Fifth Meditation, he focuses on truths that fall out of his idea of a triangle – for example, that "its three angles add to

---

and duration as it exists in things (AT 8A:26–27, CSM 1:211–212). In the same discussion, he is treating the distinction between number as it exists in thought and number as it exists in *re*. See also the discussion of the notion of a concep-tual distinction at the end of the current chapter.

41 *Principles* I.55, AT 8A:26, CSM 1:211.

42 Here I am disagreeing with Nolan (1998), who argues that Descartes does offer an account of the ontology of number – a conceptualist account according to which number is nothing more than a modification of mind. I agree with Nolan's explanation of how it is that (Descartes thinks) we form an idea of number, but Descartes is clear that there is such a thing as number in *re* – something that we notice and then give the name *number*. Nolan is correct when it comes to Descartes' view on how we form an idea of number, but (I think) he is mistaken to argue that number is a modification of mind only. A realist about number might even accept (the rough parameters) of Descartes' view on how we form an idea of number, but the realist would add that to accept that view is not to accept a conceptualist account of number.

43 For a brief but wonderful discussion, see https://iowa.pbslearningmedia.org/resource/nvmm-math-pifibonacci/pi-the-fibonacci-sequence/.

two right angles, that its greatest side subtends its greatest angle, and the like" (AT 7:64, CSM 2:45). There he concludes that "since I am clearly aware of the[se properties], ...and everything of which I am clearly aware is true, ...therefore they are something" (AT 7:65, CSM 2:45). He is applying his notion of truth as "the conformity of thought with its object, ...a notion so transcendentally clear that nobody can be ignorant of it."[44] He concludes that his ideas of geo-metrical properties conform to something – a "true and immutable nature" which "cannot be called nothing" (AT 7:64, CSM 2:44) – but he does not yet know exactly what that something is. Perhaps it is a third-realm Platonic entity; perhaps it is an aspect of the divine nature; perhaps it is an aspect of finite minds.[45] We do not know yet, and so we cannot say. We might suppose that the most obvious candidate for the conformable of an idea of a geometrical property is that property itself insofar as it exists in material things. But in the Fifth Meditation Descartes has not yet established that material things exist, and he does not think that we are entitled to infer from the existence of a true idea of body (or its geometrical properties) that material things exist. He writes in a letter to Mersenne,

> you quote as an axiom of mine: 'Whatever we clearly conceive is or exists.' That is not at all what I think. ...For although the objective being of an idea must have a real cause, it is not always

---

44 "To Mersenne, 16 October 1639," AT 2:597, CSMK 139. See also the similar view in Spinoza (1677), Part I, axiom 6: "A true idea must agree with that of which it is the idea" (218).

45 See Kenny (1968), 150–156, and Kenny (1970) for the view that true and immutable natures are third-realm Platonic entities. See Schmaltz (1991) for the view that true and immutable natures are (divine decrees) in the mind of God. See Nolan (1997) for the view that true and immutable natures are finite ideas considered with respect to their objective reality. I think that it is a mistake to say that Descartes definitively identifies true and immutable natures with any of these entities. In the Fifth Meditation, he says that they are "something," and he leaves open their ontological status. I return to a discussion of true and immutable natures – and the views of Kenny, Schmaltz, and Nolan – in Chapter 5, pp. 151–161.

necessary that this cause should contain it *formally*, but only eminently.[46]

Descartes holds that "it does not admit of any doubt" that "everything of which I am clearly and distinctly aware is a true entity."[47] However, he does not think that we can always tell just from inspecting our clear and distinct idea of an entity what that true entity is.[48] He writes for example that we do not know that material things exist just from having a clear and distinct idea of body:

> I proved the existence of material things not from the fact that we have ideas of them but from the fact that these ideas come to us in such a way as to make us aware that they are not produced by ourselves but come from elsewhere.[49]

The epistemic issue that arises when we attempt to identify the conformable or truthmaker of a true idea of X is that in many cases, a true idea does not expose its truthmaker straightaway.[50] We might sympathize with Descartes here. Inquiry is in part about identifying truths – for example, that the square of the hypotenuse of a right triangle is equal to the sum of the squares of its two shorter sides; or

---

46 "To Mersenne, March 1642"; AT 3:544–545, CSMK 211. See also *Discourse on the Method* Part 4, where Descartes speaks of clear and distinct demonstrations concerning geometrical properties but says that "there was nothing at all in these demonstrations which assured me of the existence of" (AT 6:36, CSM 1:129) the properties themselves.

47 The first quoted piece of text is from *Second Replies*, AT 7:112, CSM 2:81. The second is the principle that Caterus advances in *First Replies* (AT 7:95, CSM 2:69) and that Descartes says does not admit of any doubt.

48 Here I am disagreeing with Arbib (2013), 504–505.

49 "To Hyperaspistes, August 1641," AT 3:428–429, CSMK 193.

50 See also Cunning (2003). Descartes says in *Second Replies* that

> Whatever exists in the objects of our ideas in a way which exactly corresponds to our perception of it is said to exist *formally* in those objects. Something is said to exist *eminently* in an object when, although it does not correspond exactly to our perception of it, its greatness is such that it can fill the role of that which does correspond.
>
> (AT 7:161, CSM 2:114)

that time passes – but the philosophical component of inquiry often begins when we seek out the truthmaker of a truth.[51] The philosopher of math (or time) will confirm that the particular truth itself does not tell us all that we want to know.

Later in the Sixth Meditation, Descartes marshals some additional machinery to argue that material things exist and "possess all the properties which I clearly and distinctly understand, that is, all those which, viewed in general terms, are comprised within the subject-matter of pure mathematics" (AT 7:80, CSM 2:55). That is to say, the "something" whose existence we secure in the Fifth Meditation – the being to which our true idea of a triangle conforms – is an actually existing property of extended substance, even if we were not in a position to identify it at the time. He adds elsewhere that in the case of a geometrical property that exists, the essence or nature of the property is nothing other than the existing property itself. He says that

> when I think of the essence of a triangle, and of the existence of the same triangle, these two thoughts, as thoughts, even taken objectively differ modally in the strict sense of the term 'mode'; but the case is not the same with the triangle existing outside thought, in which it seems to me manifest that essence and existence are in no way distinct.[52]

I engage a further discussion of what Descartes calls a merely *conceptual* distinction at the end of the chapter, but for the moment note that he holds that in the case of an existing triangular figure, the essence or nature of the figure is to be identified with the existing figure itself.

Now we return to the topic of Descartes on the limits of our metaphysical tether. In the Sixth Meditation, he concludes that our ideas of geometrical properties conform to body insofar as it is the

---

51 Thomasson (2021) discusses the historical tendency of philosophers to seize on truths and then seek out the truthmakers whose existence is thereby guaranteed, going back to Plato. It is not surprising that Descartes would be among them.

52 "To ***, 1645 or 1646," AT 4:350, CSMK 280.

subject-matter of pure mathematics. But there is an important sense in which he still does not specify their ontology. For example, he does not say if they are perfect geometrical figures that exist in bodies, or if they are approximate shapes that exist in bodies, or if they are something else. In Fifth Objections, the question is put to Descartes directly (AT 7:321–322, CSM 2:223–224). In reply he reiterates that ideas of perfect geometrical objects are underdetermined by the inputs of the senses: "I do not, incidentally, concede that the ideas of these figures ever came into our mind via the senses, as everyone commonly believes."[53] Then he considers the question of whether or not true ideas of geometrical properties conform to perfect geometrical figures that exist in bodies. He punts:

> For although the world could undoubtedly contain figures such as those the geometers study, I nonetheless maintain that there are no such figures in our environment except perhaps ones so small that they cannot impinge in any way upon our senses. Geometrical figures are composed for the most part of straight lines; yet no part of a line that was really straight could ever affect our senses.... Hence, when in our childhood we first happened to see a triangular figure drawn on paper, it cannot have been this figure that showed us how we should conceive of the true triangle studied by geometers, since the true triangle is contained in the figure only in the way in which a statue of Mercury is contained in a rough block of wood.
>
> (AT 7:381–382, CSM 2:262)

Descartes does not say in any text what is the exact sense in which material things possess the properties that are the subject-matter of pure mathematics. He says that "the true triangle is contained in the figure" that is drawn on paper in something like the way that a statue of Mercury is contained in a block of marble, but that is not to say much. He nowhere identifies the exact sense in which material things possess the properties that are the subject-matter of pure mathematics, and arguably that is too his credit. True ideas of

---

53 *Fifth Replies*, AT 7:381, CSM 2:262.

geometrical properties conform to extended being, but the exact details of their conformity are unclear. If Descartes had promised to give an account of the ontology of geometrical properties, we might be upset when he comes up short. But he does not promise to give an account of the ontology of geometrical properties or the ontology of much else. Instead of a drumroll in anticipation of a final reveal, he tells us up front that finite embodied minds are not built for metaphysical inquiry and that any results at which we arrive will be few and far between.[54]

Definition and its limits

Descartes does arrive at *some* metaphysical conclusions – for example, that God exists and is a supremely perfect being; that bodies have extensive features like size, shape, and motion, but not intensive features like color or taste; and that finite minds are immaterial substances. He also attempts to provide us with additional resources by which we might understand those conclusions as well as possible.

For example, he provides definitions of the notions of substance, attribute, and modification. In *Fourth Replies*, he defines substances as

> things that subsist on their own, …possessing the power to subsist on their own.
>
> (AT 7:222, CSM 2:157)

He uses similar language elsewhere:

> In the case of those items which we regard as things or modes of things, it is worthwhile examining each of them separately.

---

54 Note that Descartes also does not provide any account (or attempt to provide any account) of the truthmaker for metaphysical axioms like that something cannot come from nothing. See Phillips (2014), 127–136. Descartes also makes little to no headway unpacking the nature of the eternality of God – whether it is temporal or atemporal – and he makes no headway on the question of how the infinitude of the mind of God leaves room for the existence of any mentality that is finite. On the former, see Gorham (2008). On the latter, see Chapter 5, pp. 87–192.

> By *substance* we can understand nothing other than a thing which exists in such a way as to depend on no other thing for its existence.[55]

He also says that substances are things that have modifications and that are in some sense different from those modifications:

> *Substance.* This term applies to every thing in which whatever we perceive immediately resides, as in a subject...[56]

To be a substance, for Descartes, is to be a kind of ground-floor existent. A substance is not a property or feature of a yet further existent, but it is the sort of thing that has properties and features itself. It does not depend for its existence on its properties, and as Descartes is attempting to illustrate in the Second Meditation discussion of wax, it can undergo changes in those properties and still be the same underlying substance that it was before.[57]

In articulating the notion of a substance, Descartes highlights that there are not only the things that have features but also the changing properties and features that are had by them. Some of the features of a substance vary in the sense that the substance might have them at one point of its existence but not others. Descartes calls such features *modifications* or *affections*:

> [A] modal distinction can be recognized from the fact that we can clearly perceive a substance apart from the mode which we say differs from it, whereas we cannot, conversely understand the mode apart from the substance. Thus there is a modal distinction between shape or motion and the corporeal substance in which they inhere; and similarly there is a modal distinction between affirmation or recollection and the mind.[58]

---

55 *Principles of Philosophy* I.52, AT 8A:24, CSM 1:210.

56 *Second Replies*, AT 7:161, CSM 2:114.

57 For a further discussion of how to combine Descartes' two definitions of substance-as a subject of inherence and as an ontologically independent entity - see Schechtman (2016), 187–199.

58 *Principles of Philosophy* I.61, AT 8A:29, CSM 1:214.

An affirmation, for example, has some reality; it is something that is enacted in a mind. A size or shape is similarly the size or shape of a body. Descartes will accordingly use the language of "complete things" to mark that *substances* have enough being to be posited without positing the existence of any other creature – but a modification is different. If we posit the existence of a modification like a size, shape, or affirmation, we are thereby positing the existence of a substance that has that modification – and as we have seen, we are positing the existence of a substance that has a principal attribute or essence in terms of which the modification can be understood. A modification is thus an incomplete being in the sense that it does not exist until and unless there is also an existing substance that it modifies. By contrast, a substance is "sufficient… for it to be considered a complete thing."[59] Descartes does not say much by way of explication of the notions of substance and modification, but he appears to hold that they are so fundamental and primitive that we need to understand them in order to be able to understand other things. He is in good company on this front. Part of the trouble in cognizing his system is in the details of the particular primitive concepts that it asks us to employ, but another part of the trouble is that at some point those concepts – like the basic concepts of any philosophical system – will admit of no further motivation or defense.[60] It is not clear that there are any simpler notions to which Descartes could appeal to explain the notions of a substance or modifications, and if there were such notions, he would have to leave *those* unexplained. He opts to stop at the notions of substance and modification instead.[61]

---

59 *Fourth Replies*, AT 7:223, CSM 2:157.
60 See also Leibniz (1714), 217, which is *Monadology* Section XXXV. He says (almost with excitement and pride) that there are notions that are so simple and obvious that they admit of no possible support. That leads to trouble of course if we are not in agreement on which those notions are.
61 Descartes also says that in the end abstract definitions are not all that helpful. He writes for example that

> it is much easier for us to have an understanding of extended substance or thinking substance than it is for us to understand thinking on its own, leaving out the fact that it thinks or is extended. For we have some difficulty

The notion of a conceptual distinction

The category of attribute is also very important in Descartes' ontology. Some of the features of a substance are features that change in the substance over time; these again are its modifications.[62] An attribute is not a modification but instead is a feature that a substance has permanently and that is inextricable from it. As we have seen, a principal attribute is an attribute through which the modifications of a substance are explicable.[63] Examples of principal attributes include thought and extension, as these are a constant that a (thinking or extended) substance would need to have for the duration of its existence if it is also to have a varying array of modifications – for example, thoughts and volitions in a mind, or sizes and shapes in a body. In addition, if varying modifications are going to be able to appear throughout a substance, the substance must exhibit its principal attribute ubiquitously. Descartes thus writes that there is no sense that can be made of a separation or distinction between a substance and its principal attribute:

> Thought and extension can be regarded as constituting the natures of intelligent substance and corporeal substance; they

---

in abstracting the notion of substance from the notions of thought and extension.

(Principles I.63, AT 8A:31, CSM 1:215)

(See also Fourth Replies, AT 7:222, CSM 2:156; De Peretti (2016), 213–215; and the famous discussion in Locke (1689), II.xxiii.2.) We sometimes have a clear idea of thinking substance, Descartes says, but when we do it is not by first considering an extremely abstract idea of substance in general. That would lessen our handle on the idea of thinking substance, just like it would lessen our handle on a sound argument to turn our attention away from the tight connection between its premises and conclusion and think instead about the abstract laws of logic that tell us that the argument has the appropriate form. See Rules for the Direction of the Mind, AT 10:405–406, CSM 1:36. See also Owen (2002), Chapter 2, and Gaukroger (2002), 11–25.

62 Descartes accordingly says that God does not have modifications because God is wholly unchanging and immutable. See Principles of Philosophy I.56, AT 8A:26, CSM 1:211.

63 See the discussion in Chapter 1, pp. 10–13 and 21–22.

must then be considered as nothing else but thinking substance itself and corporeal substance itself – that is, as mind and body.[64]

He adds that there is merely a conceptual distinction between the principal attribute or essence of a substance and the substance itself.[65] There is no distinction between the two in reality, Descartes supposes, but only in our thought.

Part of what it means to say that a substance and its principal attribute or essence are conceptually distinct is that an idea of the substance is a different mental item than an idea of its principal attribute. Descartes had said in "To ***, 1645 or 1646" that in the case of two things that are conceptually distinct, our ideas of them, "as thoughts, even taken objectively differ modally in the strict sense of the term 'mode'" (AT 4:350, CSMK 280). If so, the idea of the principal attribute of a substance is different from the idea of the substance itself. Fair enough. But Descartes is also arguing that outside of thought an existing substance and its principal attribute are in no way distinct. He says in "To ***, 1645 or 1646" that "essence and existence are in no way distinct" in the case of things existing outside of thought (ibid.) and he adds in the same letter:

> when I say Peter is a man, the thought by which I think of Peter differs modally from the thought by which I think of man, but in Peter himself being a man is nothing other than being Peter.
> (AT 4:350, CSMK 280–281)

Part of what it means to say that a substance and its principal attribute or essence are *merely* conceptually distinct is that outside of our thought, a substance and its principal attribute are not different. Still, a question remains as to what it means to say *that*.

In some passages, Descartes suggests that what it means to say that a substance and an attribute are not different is that they are inseparable. For example, he is clear that in the case of the substance

---

64 *Principles of Philosophy* I.63, CSM 1:215.
65 See also *Principles* I.62, AT 8A:30, CSM 1:214.

God, will and intellect are "the same thing,"[66] but he also says that the divine attributes are inseparable in reality: "the inseparability of all of the attributes of God is one of the most important of the perfections which I understand him to have" (AT 7:50, CSM 2:34).[67] If Descartes subscribes to the view that what it means to say that an attribute of a substance is "nothing other than" the substance is that outside of thought the two are inseparable, we still need to be careful in how we understand that view. We might consider the makeshift analogy of a series of blocks that are attached to each other by a kind of metaphysical glue that is unbreakable. Descartes does not have anything like that in mind, and not just because the analogy involves blocks and glue. If a series of blocks are stacked together, there is still a sense in which each is a discrete existent that is identifiable as such, and the first is not "nothing other than" the second. Descartes clearly has something else in mind in the case of the relation between a substance and its principal attribute. A substance does not consist of two blocks that are stacked together – for example, the substance component and the principal-attribute component. Instead, the principal attribute of a substance exists ubiquitously across the substance in such a way that any part of the substance might have a modification that is explicable in terms of that principal attribute. A substance and its attributes are not on a par with blocks that are inseparable, but they are so interwoven that there is no point at which the one stops and the other begins.

Descartes holds that a substance and its principal attribute are conceptually distinct but not distinct in reality. He holds in addition that there is merely a conceptual distinction between a substance

---

66 "To [Mersenne], 27 May 1630," AT 1:153, CSMK 25–26. See also "To [Mesland], 2 May 1644," AT 4:119, CSMK 235, and *Principles* I.23, AT 8A:14, CSM 1:201.

67 A number of commentators have defended a version of the view that Descartes holds that what it means for a substance and its attributes to be conceptually distinct is for them to be inseparable in reality. See for example Kenny (1968), 66; Wilson (1978), 77 and 83; Curley (1986), 166; Christofidou (2001), 229–230; and Hoffman (2002), 61. Note that Descartes cashes out the notion of a *real distinction* in terms of the separability of substances, for example in *Second Replies*, AT 7:162, CSM 2:114, and so it would certainly make sense if he held that entities are conceptually distinct when they are in-separable.

and any "attribute of that substance without which the substance is unintelligible."[68] An example that he provides is the attribute of duration: he says that "since a substance cannot endure without also ceasing to be, the distinction between the substance and its duration is merely a conceptual one" (ibid.). I think that this is an extremely helpful example. In the case of an existing mind, it is not as though there is one part of that mind that is its substance and another part that is its duration. Instead, whatever part of the mind that is its substance *also endures*. Returning to the block analogy, the duration of an existing substance does not sit atop the substance – inseparable from it – but is one with it in the sense that every bit of the substance-block endures. If so, then perhaps what Descartes has in mind when he speaks of a substance as inseparable from one of its attributes is that the substance and the attribute are metaphysically and permanently intermingled. But he seems to mean more than that. He says in *Principles* I.63 that thought and extension must "be considered as nothing else but thinking substance itself and corporeal substance itself," and he says in "To ***, 1645 or 1646" that outside of thought the essence of Peter is "nothing other than Peter himself." And again he says that in the case of God – the one entity that is a substance in the strict sense – will and intellect are the "same thing." That is presumably to say that in God the attribute of omnipotence just is the attribute of omniscience.

Descartes holds that in the case of a conceptual distinction between a substance and its attributes, our idea of the substance and our idea of its attributes are different mental items. What is not as clear is what he takes to be the relationship between a substance and its attributes outside of thought. As we have seen, one interpretive option is to defend the view that Descartes holds that outside of thought a substance and its attributes are utterly inseparable to the point that they practically coincide – for example, in the case of a substance and its duration. A problem with this view is that Descartes also says that in the case of a conceptual distinction the attributes of a substance are

---

68 *Principles* I.62, AT 8A:30, CSM 1:214. See also "To ***, 1645 or 1646," AT 4:349, CSMK 280, where Descartes says that (for example) a "thing cannot be outside our thought without its existence, or without its duration."

nothing other than the substance. Another interpretive option is to defend the view that Descartes holds that outside of thought a substance and its attributes are identical.[69] A problem with this view is that it is in tension with his claim that a substance and its attributes are inseparable, and it conflicts with his definition of substance in *Second Replies* (AT 7:161, CSM 2:114).[70] It also conflicts with a claim that Descartes makes in "To ***, 1645 or 1646." He writes,

> I do not recognize any distinction made by reason *ratiocinantis* – that is, one which has no foundation in reality – because we cannot have any thought without a foundation....
>
> (AT 4:349, CSMK 280)

If Descartes holds that outside of thought a substance and its attributes are identical, he cannot say that there is a foundation in reality that grounds the conceptual distinction between them.[71]

---

69 A number of commentators have defended a version of the view that Descartes holds that what it means for a substance and its attributes to be conceptually distinct is for them to be identical in reality. See for example Lennon (1995); Nolan (1997b), 129–140; Sowaal (2011); and Nelson (2013).

70 It also conflicts with his claim in *Second Replies* that "It is a greater thing to create or preserve a substance than to create or preserve the attributes or properties of that substance" (AT 7:166, CSM 2:117).

71 Here Descartes is sounding a lot like his near contemporary Francisco Suarez:

> Mental distinctions are usually considered to be of two kinds. One, which has no foundation in reality, is called a distinction of the reasoning reason (distinctio rationis ratiocinantis), because it arises exclusively from the reflection and activity of the intellect. The other, which has a foundation in reality, is called by many a distinction of the reasoned reason (distinctio rationis ratiocinatae).... [T]his [the latter] kind of distinction can be understood as pre-existing in reality, prior to the discriminating operation of the mind...
>
> (Suarez 1597, 18)

Descartes says in "To ***, 1645 or 1646" that he is employing the notion of a "distinction made by reason *ratiocinatae*" (AT 4:349, CSMK 280). We do not know for certain if he read Suarez, but he was clearly familiar with the language that was used to describe different kinds of conceptual distinction, and he says that in his own work, he has in mind the kind that has a foundation in reality. Note

One interpretive option is to argue that Descartes holds that a substance and its attributes are conceptually distinct in the sense that they are wholly inseparable. There are texts for and against. A second interpretive option is to argue that Descartes holds that a substance and its attributes are conceptually distinct in the sense that they are identical. There are texts for and against. A third interpretive option arises in the light of Descartes' view on the limits of our metaphysical tether: a substance and attributes are utterly inseparable and interwoven, to the degree the attributes of a substance are "nothing other than" the substance, but our clear and distinct ideas leave us short of grasping any more than that. This third interpretative option would embrace the texts that speak in favor of the other two; it would add that in those texts, Descartes is simply struggling to make headway on a metaphysical issue that is extremely difficult. He is trying to make sense of the difference between (for example)

---

that Sowaal (2011) has argued that for Descartes a substance and its attributes are conceptually distinct in the sense that they are identical outside of thought – and that what Descartes means when he says that a conceptual distinction has a "foundation in reality" is that it has a foundation in the cognitive operations of finite minds (which of course are part of reality). I find it hard to see how such a distinction would not just be a distinctio rationis ratiocinantis, but there is a larger worry for Sowaal's view. She focuses on the divine substance and argues that in God there do not exist different attributes like omniscience, omnipotence, and supreme independence; instead, God is a single unitary being: "Strictly speaking there is one Attribute of God (it is God himself), and loosely speaking there are many attributes of God (e.g. necessary existence, actual infinity, simplicity, independence, substantiality, omnipotence, omniscience)" (420). Sowaal argues that what it is to think omniscience as opposed omnipotence is not to think of any differences in the attributes of the divine being itself, but to arrive at an idea of God by way of different "cognitive routes" (442). For example, if we arrive at a clear and distinct idea of God as a result of reflecting on our own finite knowledge, the terminus of our thought process is an idea of the unitary being that is God, and we call that idea an idea of "omniscience." Sowaal's view is ingenious, but an insurmountable problem for it (I think) is that it entails that the attribute of omnibenevolence applies to God only "loosely," but as we will see Descartes appeals to that attribute to do a lot of real work. For example, he appeals to the "the goodness of God" for argumentative purposes in the Sixth Meditation (AT 7:83, CSM 2:58; AT 7:85, CSM 2:59; AT 7:88, CSM 2:60), and to "the immense goodness of God" (AT 7:88, CSM 2:61).

the duration of a mental substance and its thinking, even though any bit of thinking – no matter how we break it down – thereby endures. The relation between a substance and its duration is a mind-bender if there ever was one.

Descartes and Hume

Descartes is not Hume, but he is more like Hume than is usually thought. He allows (contra Hume) that some metaphysical efforts are generative and an appropriate use of our time, but not many. He supposes that those that *are* generative are almost entirely in the service of science, medicine, and morals. Hume takes metaphysical inquiry to be beyond the scope of human cognition altogether.[72] He also holds that our attempts to do it are unnatural and forced:

> Man is a sociable, no less than a reasonable being: But neither can he always enjoy company agreeable and amusing, or preserve the proper relish for them. Man is also an active being; and from that disposition, as well as from the various necessities of human life, must submit to business and occupation. But the mind requires some relaxation, and cannot always support its bent to care and industry. It seems, then, that nature has pointed out a mixed kind of life a most suitable to [the] human race, and secretly admonished them to allow none of these biasses to *draw* too much, so as to incapacitate them for other occupations and entertainments. Indulge your passion for science, says she, but let your science be human, and such as may have a direct reference to action and society. Abstruse thought and profound researches I prohibit.... Be a philosopher; but, amidst all your philosophy, be still a man.[73]

For the most part, Descartes would agree, even if not for all the same reasons. He would say that nature prohibits abstruse and

---

72 That is, unless metaphysics were to become naturalized in such a way that neither Hume nor Descartes would any longer recognize it as such.
73 Hume (1748), Section 1, 89–90.

profound researches in the sense that embodied human beings find it near-impossible to sustain abstract clear and distinct perceptions and very difficult to have them in the first place.

Descartes and Hume would also agree that on their own the roots of the tree of philosophy have less to offer than we might hope or expect. Hume supposes that we cannot reason (or even think) about such things as God, abstract non-sensory geometrical figures, the necessary connections that link objects and events, or the eternity of time.[74] Descartes allows that we can have ideas of these, but he supposes that our understanding of them is still quite limited. The anti-metaphysical current of the early modern period stretches from Montaigne and Charron to Locke, Hume, and Kant, but it includes Descartes as well.[75] Where Montaigne famously insists that "we have no communication with being," [76] Descartes allows that being communicates with us, but that it does so only a little. As we have seen, he offers no account of the ontology of number insofar as it exists in re, and he offers no account of the extent of the division of matter. He offers no account of the ontology of geometrical properties. He provides no account of the ontology of force, and he

---

74 See for example Hume (1739), I.iii.14, 160; I.ii.4, 50–52; I.iii.14, 166–170; I.ii.3, 36–37.

75 Montaigne (1575–1576/1578–1580) was famously skeptical of our ability to arrive at confident results about pretty much any matter. Pierre Charron, a disciple of Montaigne, was similarly skeptical, but he argued in addition that if we recognize that metaphysical truth is beyond us, we more easily settle into faith (Charron 1601, 52–67). Hume (1748) writes that "if we take in our hand any volume… of divinity or metaphysics," and its language is not traceable to empirical or other observations, "Commit it then to the flames: For it can contain nothing but sophistry and illusion" (211). Kant (1781) offers a slightly more sanguine conclusion about our ability to do metaphysics. He argues that in some instances, we are able to secure a priori knowledge of the features of objects – but only of features that "we ourselves put into them" (23). He uses the analogy of the Copernican Revolution and argues that in something like the way that our experience of the motion of the sun is due to our own viewing position, our experience of any object is framed by cognitive factors on our own end (21–23). He famously argues that we can know a priori the features that we "put into" objects, but those are not features of objects in themselves.

76 Montaigne (1575–1576/1578–1580), 455.

does not tell us where the dependence of a creature stops and its independence and substantiality begin. He does not offer much of an account of almost anything, even if there are instances in which he makes one or two comments that are somewhat suggestive. There have been numerous attempts to extrapolate Descartes' view on a given metaphysical issue, and these attempts have of course sparked an enormous literature. However, it would appear that in many such cases, Descartes does not have a final view himself. A literature is still sparked – perhaps because we are interested in a given issue, and because Descartes offers just enough metaphysical tools to start approaching the issue, but not nearly enough to circumscribe and contain it. One possibility is that Descartes did have a final view on a large number of metaphysical topics, and he thought them to be of great importance, but for some reason he did not take the time to articulate his own thinking. Another possibility is that he was hardly interested in metaphysical matters at all. A third possibility is that he was interested in metaphysical matters to some degree, with an eye to their implications for everyday embodiment, but he thought that for the most part, the subject-matter of metaphysics is beyond us. If the latter, something very interesting is happening when we (as commentators) appeal to Cartesian principles to reconstruct Descartes' own position. In many cases that is not what we are doing at all. We are not reconstructing a position that Descartes actually had or developed, but instead we are identifying Cartesian principles – and bits of texts that are the equivalent of crumbs – and we are working in concert with him to see where (if anywhere) they might lead. He might even cheer us on. But in that case, we are using Cartesian axioms and tenets to do metaphysics, and Descartes does not know where things will end up any more than we do. As a philosopher, I tend to gravitate toward the metaphysical and epistemological aspects of Descartes' thinking, and from the pages of literature that have been produced, it is easy to conclude that those are of paramount concern to him as well. But they are not.

Further reading

There is a large archive of outstanding scholarly work on the topics that have been addressed in this chapter. Below is a cross-section.

Descartes on the limits of metaphysical inquiry

Daniel Garber, "Descartes against the Materialists," in *Descartes'* Meditations: *A Critical Guide*, ed. Karen Detlefsen, Cambridge and New York: Cambridge UP (2012), 45–63.

Pascal Marignac, "Descartes et ses concepts de la substance," *Revue Métaphysique et de Morale* 85 (1980), 298–314.

Jean-Luc Marion, *On Descartes' Metaphysical Prism*, trans. Jeffrey L. Kosky, Chicago and London: Chicago UP (1999), chapter one.

Richard Watson, "Descartes Knows Nothing," *History of Philosophy Quarterly* 1 (1984), 399–411.

Descartes on mind-body union

Lilli Alanen, "Reconsidering Descartes's Notion of the Mind-Body Union," *Synthese* 106 (1996), 3–20.

Janet Broughton and Ruth Mattern, "Reinterpreting Descartes on the Notion of the Union of Mind and Body," *Journal of the History of Philosophy* 16 (1978), 23–32.

Andrea Christofidou, "Descartes: A Metaphysical Solution to the Mind–Body Relation and the Intellect's Clear and Distinct Conception of the Union," *Philosophy* 94 (2019), 87–114.

Daisie Radner, "Descartes' Notion of the Union of Mind and Body," *Journal of the History of Philosophy* 9 (1971), 159–170.

Alison Simmons, "Mind-Body Union and the Limits of Cartesian Metaphysics," *Philosophers' Imprint* 17 (2017), 1–36.

Descartes on preservation versus constant creation

Geoffrey Gorham, "Cartesian Causation: Continuous, Instantaneous, Overdetermined," *Journal of the History of Philosophy* 42 (2004), 389–423.

Richard Hassing, "Descartes on God, Creation, and Conservation," *Review of Metaphysics* 64 (2011), 603–620.

Andrew Pessin, "Does Continuous Creation Entail Occasionalism? Malebranche (and Descartes)," *Canadian Journal of Philosophy* 30 (2000), 413–439.

Tad M. Schmaltz, *Descartes on Causation*, New York and Oxford UP (2007), chapter two.

Descartes on number and other universals

Vere Chapelle, "The Theory of Ideas," in *Essays on Descartes'* Meditations, ed. Amelie Oksenberg Rorty, Berkeley and Los Angeles: California UP (1986), 177–198.

Helen Hattab, "Descartes on the Eternal Truths and Essences of Mathematics: An Alternative Reading," *Vivarium* 54 (2016), 204–249.

Lawrence Nolan, "Descartes' Theory of Universals," *Philosophical Studies* 89 (1998), 161–180.

Marleen Rozemond, "Descartes's Ontology of the Eternal Truths," in *Contemporary Perspectives on Early Modern Philosophy*, eds. Paul Hoffman, David Owen, and Gideon Yaffe, Peterborough, Ontario: Broadview Press (2008), 41–63.

Descartes on substance

Vere Chappell, "Descartes on Substance," in *A Companion to Descartes*, ed. Janet Broughton and John Carriero, Oxford: Blackwell (2008), 251–270.

Peter Markie, "Descartes's Concepts of Substance," in *Reason, Will and Sensation: Studies in Descartes's Metaphysics*, ed. John Cottingham, Oxford: Clarendon Press (1994), 63–87.

Anat Schechtman, "Substance and Independence in Descartes," *Philosophical Review* 125 (2016), 155–202.

Descartes on the conceptual distinction between a substance and its attributes

Paul Hoffman, "Descartes's Theory of Distinction," *Philosophy and Phenomenological Research* 64 (2002), 57–78.

Alan Nelson, "Conceptual Distinctions and the Concept of Substance in Descartes," *ProtoSociology* 30 (2013), 192–205.

Lawrence Nolan, "Descartes' Theory of Universals," *Philosophical Studies* 89 (1998), 161–180.

Justin Skirry, "Descartes's Conceptual Distinction and Its Ontological Import," *Journal of the History of Philosophy* 42 (2004), 121–144.

Alice Sowaal, "Descartes's Reply to Gassendi: How We Can Know All of God, All at Once, but Still Have More to Learn about Him," *British Journal for the History of Philosophy*, 19 (2011), 419–449.

Four

Skepticism

It would be natural to begin a discussion of Descartes' metaphysical views about God, mind, and body with a discussion of the skeptical arguments that he offers as a precursor to them. For example, early in *Meditations on First Philosophy*, he offers a skeptical argument that highlights the difficulty of distinguishing dream experience from waking experience: if we cannot distinguish the two, we can never tell when a given sensory perception is veridical (AT 7:19, CSM 2:13). He then adds a series of hyperbolic skeptical arguments to the effect that it is possible that we are deceived about matters that are utterly evident to us.[1] If so, any result at which we arrive is up for grabs, even if we find the result to be utterly transparent and obvious (AT 7:21–23, CSM 2:14–15).[2] Descartes more or less repeats the First Meditation skeptical arguments at the start of *Principles of Philosophy*, in Part I, Sections 4 and 5 (AT 8A:5–6, CSM 1:193–194). In addition, the metaphysical chapter of *Discourse on the Method* begins with a presentation of skeptical arguments (AT 6:31–32, CSM 1:126–127), though Descartes omits the hyperbolic worry

---

1 Descartes identifies these arguments as "very slight" and exaggerated in the Third Meditation (AT 7:36, CSM 2:25).

2 Descartes says in *Seventh Replies* that until we have dislodged hyperbolic doubt "there will be *nothing* which we may not justly doubt" (AT 7:460, CSM 2:309, emphasis added). He adds that "so long as we attend to a truth which we perceive very clearly, we cannot doubt it" (ibid.), but we can doubt it if we are presented with hyperbolic doubt and we are not in a position to neutralize it. See also the Fifth Meditation, AT 7:69–70, CSM 2:48; Newman and Nelson (1999); and Cunning (2007).

DOI: 10.4324/9781351210522-4

that it is possible that we are mistaken about matters that we find utterly evident.[3] Descartes also writes a dialogue, *The Search for Truth*, in which skeptical arguments are presented as an antecedent to the grasp of metaphysical truth (AT 10:495–515, CSM 2:400–409). We might suppose that if Descartes begins each of his metaphysical writings with a presentation of skeptical arguments, any monograph that attempts to lay out his system ought to begin with a treatment of those arguments as well. But here I am going to take a different approach and argue that there is an important sense in which Descartes takes skepticism to be little more than an afterthought.

Confused ideas and the method of synthesis

Many philosophers of the seventeenth century get right down to business and present the views that they take to be true, along with the reasoning that undergirds them. Leibniz begins *Monadology* with a series of statements in defense of the view that immaterial monads are the fundamental building blocks of created reality.[4] He then proceeds to offer arguments that flesh out the nature of monads and the nature of the (divine) entity that has to exist if monads are what we take them to be.[5] Spinoza proceeds in a more explicitly syllogistic order still. He begins *Ethics* Part I with definitions and axioms that he assumes we will be able to intuit as obvious; then he points to the conclusions (or propositions) that they entail. Descartes takes a very different approach. He does not begin his philosophical treatises with a statement of his views or the argumentation that he takes to entail them. He first does a significant amount of legwork to increase the chances that we will understand his argumentation once it is finally introduced.

At the end of the second set of objections to the *Meditations*, Mersenne asks Descartes if he might put the arguments of the

---

3 Later in this chapter, there will be a discussion of why the *Discourse* is different in this regard.

4 This is in Leibniz (1714), Sections I–III, 213.

5 For example, Leibniz (1714), Sections IV–XLII, 213–218. See in particular Section XXXV on axioms and primary principles that are to be used in the demonstration of other claims and that cannot be demonstrated themselves.

Meditations into syllogistic form, starting with definitions, postulates, and axioms.[6] That way, it would be clearer exactly what the conclusions are that Descartes is defending and what the reasons are that he takes to support them. Descartes obliges at the end of his reply to Mersenne's objections – in an addendum known as the *more geometrico* (AT 7:160–170) – but before he does that he provides an explanation as to why he did not take the more syllogistic (or "synthetic") route in the first place.[7] He says that if he had, most of his readers would have failed to fully grasp the definitions, postulates and axioms in question, and the effort of the *Meditations* would have been largely for naught. Syllogistic arguments are appropriate for subjects like geometry, where the premises tend to cohere with our sensory experience and are easily understood, but the metaphysician is largely in the business of arguing that reality is very different from how it appears. Descartes writes,

> The difference is that the primary notions which are presupposed for the demonstration of geometrical truths are readily accepted by anyone, since they accord with the use of our senses. Hence there is no difficulty there, except in the proper deduction of the consequences, which can be done even by the less attentive, provided they remember what has gone before. ...In metaphysics by contrast there is nothing which causes so much effort as making our perception of the primary notions clear and distinct. Admittedly, they are by their nature as evident as, or more evident than, the primary notions which the geometers study; but they conflict with many preconceived opinions derived from the senses which we have got into the habit of holding from our earliest years, and so only those who really concentrate and meditate and withdraw their minds from corporeal things, so far as is possible, will achieve perfect knowledge of them.[8]

To consider a geometrical example, we might register that two parallel lines never intersect and then draw the conclusion that the

---

6 *Second Objections*, AT 7:128, CSM 2:92.

7 *Second Replies*, AT 7:155–157, CSM 2:110–111.

8 Ibid., AT 7:156–157, CSM 2:111. See also the very influential discussions in Curley (1986), Garber (1986), and Hatfield (1986).

opposite angles that are formed by a third intersecting line are equal. The conclusion can be demonstrated as obvious – from the fact that a line has exactly 180 degrees, among other considerations – and it also squares with the verdict of the naked eye. But Descartes supposes that the premises and conclusions of a metaphysical argument show up very differently.

Consider for example the axiom that nothingness has no properties. Descartes appeals to that axiom to argue that there is no empty space and that in between the bodies that we sense there is just as much matter as there is in the bodies themselves.[9]

Or consider the axiom that every substance has a principal attribute through which all of its modifications can be explained and understood.[10] Descartes leverages the axiom to defend the view that the world of material bodies is devoid of sensory features like color and sound, but on its face that view is ridiculous.

Or consider the axiom to which Descartes appeals in his Third Meditation argumentation for the existence of God – that nothing comes from nothing.[11] This is an axiom that Descartes expects that some will take to be false. For example, there are minds that might suppose that there is such a thing as chance and that things (or aspects of things) just poof into existence out of nowhere. But that would just be an indication of ignorance:

> For when a thing we considered to depend on Fortune does not happen, this indicates that one of the causes necessary for its production was absent, and consequently that it was absolutely impossible and that no similar thing has ever happened, i.e. nothing for the production of which a similar cause was also absent.[12]

We are sometimes in a circumstance in which we witness all of the same causes that we noticed in a previous situation, but in which a different effect ensues. We might then conclude that it is possible for the same set of causes to lead to a different effect and that there

---

9 Principles of Philosophy II.18, AT 8A:50, CSM 1:231.
10 Principles of Philosophy, I.53, AT 8A:25, CSM 1:210–211.
11 AT 7:40–41, CSM 2:28–29. See also Second Replies, AT 7:135, CSM 2:97.
12 The Passions of the Soul II.145, CSM 1:380, AT 11:438.

is nothing that accounts for the difference. Descartes indeed would find it surprising if many of us did not believe in chance. He holds that the material universe is a plenum and that in-between the sensible bodies that surround us are bodies that make a difference but that we tend not to notice.[13] If he is right, we will often fail to appreciate many of the causes that contribute to the production of an effect. If we assume that the only operative causes are the causes of which we are aware, we will be reinforced in the view that there are things and aspects of things that arise due to no cause at all. We will have little hope of registering the force of the axiom that something cannot come from nothing, and any arguments that rely on that axiom − for example Descartes' Third Meditation argument for the existence of God − will seem unmotivated as well.

And things get even worse. Descartes, Spinoza, and Leibniz all aim to argue that there are things that are real that are not sensible, but as we have seen Descartes holds that most embodied minds are saddled with the view that what is not sensible has no reality.[14] We regard entities as real to the extent that we notice and sense them, and we come to believe as "utterly true and evident" that the idea of a thing that is not sensible is an idea of nothing at all:

> Right from infancy our mind was swamped with a thousand such preconceived opinions; and in later childhood, forgetting that they were adopted without sufficient examination, it regarded them as known by the senses or implanted by nature, and accepted them as utterly true and evident.
>
> (ibid.)

If (at a later point in life) we attempt to grasp that finite minds are insensible and real, or that there exists an insensible entity that is infinitely real, we will be wholly befuddled.

Descartes supposes quite rightly that the sensible bodies that surround us are relevant to our continued existence. We manipulate

---

13 *Principles* II.17−18, AT 8A:49−50, CSM 1:230−231; and *Principles* I.71, AT 8A: 35−36, CSM 1:218−219.
14 *Principles* I.71, AT 8A:36, CSM 1:219.

these, and anticipate them, and deliberate about them – to the point that ideas of sensible objects become the primary kind of idea by which we think.[15] If Descartes is right, they become the template and anchor for our every thought. A heavy toll is then exacted on our ability to think and reason about entities like God and finite mind:

> All of our ideas of what belongs to the mind have up till now been very confused and mixed up with the ideas of things that can be perceived by the senses. This is the first and most important reason for our inability to understand with sufficient clarity the customary assertions about the soul and God.[16]

Here Descartes speaks of ideas of mind and God that are "mixed up with" ideas of sensible bodies.[17] A compound idea that includes an idea of mind (or God) as one of its components is still of mind (or God), Descartes is allowing. However, it will misrepresent mind or God to the extent that the other ideas that it includes – for example ideas of sensible bodies – do not apply to mind or God. A compound idea that does not have an idea of mind (or God) as one of its components is not an idea of mind (or God) at all. It does not represent mind (or God), and it does not misrepresent mind (or God). It is an idea of something else entirely.

Our epistemic position leaves something to be desired if we have ideas of mind and God that misrepresent mind and God.[18] But if

---

15 See the initial discussion in Chapter 3, pp. 78–80.

16 *Second Replies*, AT 7:130–131, CSM 2:94.

17 See also the analysis in Nelson (1996, 1997), to which I am heavily indebted.

18 And our idea of body suffers the same fate as well. It gets mixed up with ideas of sensations to the point that an idea of body yields the result that bodies have features like color and sound – as though it were (what we now call) an analytic truth. But it is not a truth at all. In youth, our

> body...twisted around aimlessly in all directions in its random attempts to pursue the beneficial and avoid the harmful; at this point the mind that was attached to the body began to notice that the objects of this pursuit had an existence outside itself. And it attributed to them not only sizes, shapes, motions, and the like, ...but also tastes, smells, and so on.
>
> (*Principles* I.71, AT 8A:35–36, CSM 1:219)

Descartes is right, that is exactly the position in which an embodied mind finds itself at the start of inquiry – and for the entirety of its existence, if its ideas are not emended. If we think of an insensible entity by way of an idea that includes a sensory image or picture, our idea will misrepresent the entity. Our idea will attribute to the entity – for example mind or God – features that do not pertain to it. However, if we come to conceive of the entity by way of an idea that includes no sensory image or picture, and we are saddled with the view that an entity is real to the extent that it can be sensed, we will be skeptical that our idea is of anything at all. Descartes writes in *Principles* I.73 that "most people have nothing but confused perceptions throughout their entire lives" (AT 8A:37, CSM 1:220), and he is not kidding.

Our epistemic position leaves something to be desired if we have ideas of mind and God that misrepresent mind and God, but there is a remedy. We can analyze such ideas into their component parts, which is one of the core activities of *Meditations on First Philosophy*. For example, in the Second Meditation Descartes grasps the existence of his thinking, and then he applies the skeptical arguments of the First Meditation to call into doubt the existence of any sensible features that a pre-*Meditations* idea of mind might recklessly attribute to that thinking.[19] He strips down his composite idea of mind and "subtract[s] anything" that is not inextricable from it (AT 7:25, CSM 2:17); he rids it of the ideas with which it has been mixed up and confused. He is left with an idea of something which is not sensible, but "which is real and which truly exists" (AT 7:27, CSM 2:18). To highlight the being of such a thing – just in case we are suspicious that it has no reality – Descartes provides a "considerable list" of its features (AT 7:28, CSM 2:19). Still, an embodied mind that is breaking down its ideas for the first time occupies an epistemic position that is extremely precarious. After the difficult efforts of the first

---

In this early and frenetic state, our ideas of size, shape, and motion become mixed together with ideas of sensible qualities to the point that an idea of a body is fused with ideas of features that body does not have. See also Chapter 1, pp. 10–13.

19 See also Broughton (2002), Chapter 7; Cunning (2010), Chapter 3; Moyal (2016), 99–103; Paul (2018); and Griffioen (2022).

half of the Second Meditation – efforts that go against the grain – it will likely become exhausted and then lose hold of its cognition of its non-sensory thinking. It might come up for air, so to speak – and start to wonder if it had been thinking anything at all. The argument for the existence of God that appears just a few pages later will have almost no hope of being understood if Descartes does not make an intervention. In the Third Meditation, he will argue that there exists an entity that is not sensible and that has an *infinite* amount of reality. He will do so by positing the existence of a mere idea – one that is without sensory content and that (he supposes) has an infinite amount of reality as well. He will also rely on the abstract metaphysical axiom that something cannot come from nothing. Good luck.

Descartes of course does make an intervention. The wax discussion works to establish and reinforce that there are things that we grasp through "purely mental scrutiny" (AT 7:31, CSM 2:21) – for example, the existence of our thinking, the insensible components of body, and (eventually) the axioms and primary notions of metaphysics. It also displays in full view that there are things that are insensible but have a significant amount of being. We are now ready to enter Meditation Three.[20] But imagine if Descartes had proceeded more along the lines of Spinoza and Leibniz and offered his argumentation for the existence of God in Meditation One. In its first few sentences, we would consider the premise that something cannot come from nothing, and we might counter – very sincerely and honestly – that the premise is false. In our experience, there are things that occur by chance and do not have a sufficient cause, and there are aspects of things that do not have a cause at all. But perhaps we continue to reason (in our alternate First Meditation*), and we grant for the moment, and for the sake of argument, the axiom that something cannot come from nothing. Perhaps we think the axiom by way of linguistic (and imagistic) squiggles. We then apply it to our pre-*Meditations* idea of God, which mischaracterizes God as a sensible body. The pre-*Meditations* idea is still *of* God so long as it is a composite of an actual idea of God and some ideas of sensible bodies. But against the background of our sensory proclivities, we

---

20 See also Cunning (2010), 102, and Secada (2012), 208.

only notice the latter elements of the idea, and we conclude honestly and sincerely that an idea of God does not require a divine being for its cause.[21]

Descartes does not skip the First Meditation, and for good reason. He makes clear that the skeptical arguments therein are an indispensable precursor to achieving clarity on the argumentation for the existence of God. He writes,

> The certainty and evidence of my kind of argument for the existence of God cannot really be known without distinctly recalling the arguments which display the uncertainty of all of our knowledge of material things...[22]

That is to say, we do not appreciate the certainty and evidence of the argumentation for the existence of God unless we work through the skeptical arguments of the First Meditation and unleash them on our "mixed up" ideas of mind and body in the Second – breaking them down into ideas that are a model for thinking that is far clearer.[23] In the absence of that exercise, we do not appreciate the force of the premises that are advanced in the Third Meditation, and we do not grasp the conclusion that they entail. The skeptical arguments expose the ungroundedness of our beliefs about sensible bodies, but more importantly they motivate the need to look for knowledge elsewhere. Instead of looking outward, so to speak, we look inward.[24] But we do not just report on the deliverances of ideas

---

21 Or even worse, perhaps we have the same idea of "God" that Descartes attributes to Gassendi – an idea that is not of God but of an extremely wise and powerful bearded man on a cloud (*Fifth Replies*, AT 7:365, CSM 2:252). This idea might still have a tremendous (but finite) amount of content, in which case we might conclude that "God" is its cause. That is to say, we might conclude that somewhere there exists an extremely powerful finite entity and that it is the supreme being. For a very amusing discussion of this kind of example, see Malebranche (1674), VI.ii.7, 492.

22 "To [Vatier], 22 February 1638," AT 1:560, CSMK 86.

23 Again see Broughton (2002), Chapter 7.

24 In Mercer (2014, 2017), there is a discussion of the way in which Descartes is working in the introspective and meditative tradition of Teresa of Ávila.

that are confused. We labor to break down such ideas – to uncover an idea of insensible thinking (at AT 7:26–27), and an idea of the insensible aspects of body (at AT 7:30–31). We grasp these ideas with a newfound (and unprecedented) level of clarity and evidence, and we register that our pre-*Meditations* standard of clarity and evidence falls far short of that. Then with a bit of prompting (in the Third Meditation), we register non-sensory axioms like that something cannot come from nothing. Such axioms are waiting to be discovered by an act of purely mental scrutiny:

> when we recognize that it is impossible for anything to come from nothing, the proposition *Nothing comes from nothing* is… an eternal truth which resides within our mind. Such truths are termed common notions or axioms. …It would not be easy to draw up a list of all of them; but nonetheless we cannot fail to know them when the occasion for thinking about them arises…[25]

We cannot fail to grasp the self-evident axioms of metaphysics when the occasion for thinking about them arises, and in the case of the axiom that something cannot come from nothing, that occasion is Meditation Three. So long as we have followed the skeptical arguments of the First Meditation and engaged in the appropriate acts of mental scrutiny in the Second, we will grasp that something cannot come from nothing and that something *would come* from nothing if our idea of God has the amount of content that it does and God does not exist.

Descartes accordingly says about the skeptical arguments that

---

Her *Interior Castle* (1588) was well known in Descartes' time, and it is very hard to read it and believe that it did not inform the approach of the *Meditations*.

25 *Principles* I.49, AT 8A:23–24, CSM 1:209. See also *Principles* I.13, AT 8A:9, CSM 1:197. In *Principles* I.48, Descartes adds that eternal truths "have no existence outside our thought" (AT 8A:22, CSM 1:208). As truths, eternal truths are ideas – and more specifically they are ideas that conform to reality ("To Mersenne, 16 October 1639," AT 2:597, CSMK 139). See also the Fourth Meditation, where Descartes makes clear that what it is for a mind to make a judgment is for its will to affirm an idea that is presented by its intellect (AT 7:56, CSM 2:39).

although the usefulness of such extensive doubt is not apparent at first sight, its greatest benefit lies in freeing us from all our preconceived opinions, and providing the easiest route by which the mind may be led away from the senses.[26]

The skeptical arguments lead us away from the senses by forcing us to turn our attention toward non-sensory cognitions that will survive the skeptical arguments. The arguments do not free us from preconceived opinions right away, if preconceived opinions (and like cognitive proclivities) sometimes come back against our will.[27] But they do free us eventually, after we have employed acts of purely mental scrutiny to arrive at results that contradict those opinions and that make them appear amateurish by comparison.[28] Descartes begins many of his philosophical treatises with skeptical arguments, but they are simply a tool that helps us to grasp axioms and premises that would otherwise go over our head. A very different philosopher would lay down axioms and premises straight out of the gate and be indifferent to our inability to understand them. Descartes seeks to be more inclusive.

Confused ideas and the method of analysis

Descartes puts forward skeptical arguments to expose the force of arguments that he takes to be far more perspicuous. Indeed, the skeptical arguments that precede his metaphysical discussions involve

---

26 "Synopsis of these following six Meditations," AT 7:12, CSM 2:9.

27 For example in the First Meditation, AT 7:22, CSM 2:15; *Principles* I.72, AT 8A: 36–37, CSM 1:219–220; The Second Meditation, AT 7:29, CSM 2:20; and the Third Meditation, AT 7:47, CSM 2:32.

28 Descartes adds in *Second Replies*,

> I ask my readers to ponder on all the examples that I went through in my *Meditations*, both of clear and distinct perception, and of obscure and confused perception, and thereby accustom themselves to distinguishing what is clearly known from what is obscure. This is something that it is easier to learn by examples than by rules, and I think that in the *Meditations* I explained, or at least touched on, all the relevant examples.
>
> (AT 7:164, CSM 2:116)

claims that by his own lights range from false to inane.[29] Consider for example the First Meditation claim that it is possible that God has created us in such a way that we are mistaken about matters that are utterly evident to us:

> two and three added together are five, and a square has no more than four sides. It seems impossible to me that such transparent truths should incur any suspicion of being false. ...And yet firmly rooted in my mind is the long-standing opinion that there is an omnipotent God who made me the kind of creature that I am. ...[S]ince I sometimes believe that others go astray in cases where they think they have the most perfect knowledge, may I not similarly go wrong every time I add two and three or count the sides of a square, or in some even simpler matter, if that is imaginable?
>
> (AT 7:20–21, CSM 2:14)

Here Descartes is advancing the premise that it is possible that God has created us in such a way that we are mistaken about the most basic matters of cognition. If the premise is true, we are in big trouble. We will accept claims and arguments as we proceed through the *Meditations* – and long after we are done – but if it is true that it is possible that we are mistaken about matters that are utterly evident to us, then any such claims and arguments will be suspect. Fortunately, however, it is not true that it is possible that our minds are mistaken about matters that are utterly evident to us. Or at least Descartes does not think that it is. In subsequent Meditations, he arrives at premises that he takes to be much more obvious and intuitive and that leave the contentions of the First Meditation in the dust. In the Third Meditation, he recognizes the truth of the axiom that something cannot come from nothing. Then appeals to the non-sensory content of his idea of God – an idea that he thinks we are

---

29 Spinoza, Leibniz, and other contemporaries would offer a similar assessment of skeptical arguments, but it is important to note that Descartes would offer that assessment as well. For more on Spinoza on skeptical arguments, see Spinoza (1660), 22, and Della Rocca (2007). For more on Leibniz on skeptical arguments, see Pelletier (2013).

only able to recognize after the Second Meditation – and argues that something would have to come from nothing if God did not exist as the cause of that idea. He then notes that it is an a priori conceptual truth that God is "subject to no defects whatsoever" and that "it is manifest by the natural light that all fraud and deception depend on some defect" (AT 7:52, CSM 2:35). Later in the Fifth Meditation, he draws the same conclusion on similarly evident grounds (AT 7:70–71, CSM 2:48–49). In the light of so much epistemic progress, we might ask what stance we are to take toward the First Meditation contention that it is possible that God has created us in such a way that our minds are defective, when that contention is in direct contradiction to truths that are far more obvious. Descartes is advancing the uncontroversial thesis that we are to reject the former. In effect, we are deciding to put a **T** in front of one of the two claims, and he is suggesting that we remove it from its tentative location in front of the First Meditation contention and instead put it in front of evident truths and the results that they entail.[30]

The same applies in the case of the First Meditation claim that it is possible that God does not exist and that "I have arrived at my present state by fate or chance or a continuous chain of events" (AT 7:21, CSM 2:14). It follows from evident truths that God is a necessary existent that created "myself and everything else... that exists" (AT 7:45, CSM 2:31), and so the claim is false. Nor is it true that it is possible that "some malicious demon of the utmost power and cunning has employed all of his energies in order to deceive me" (AT 7:22, CSM 2:15). It follows from evident truths that God would not create such a demon, and so it does not exist. Similar considerations apply in the case of the other skeptical arguments that Descartes advances in the First Meditation and to the assumptions that motivate them. He offers a dream argument that posits that "there are never any sure signs by means of which being awake can be distinguished from being asleep" (AT 7:19, CSM 2:13). But that is not true, he would insist, or least it is not true upon reflection. In the Sixth Meditation, he notices that there is an obvious

---

30 See also Cunning (2010), 145–147; Cunning (2019); and Stuchlik (2017), 77–79.

distinction between waking perception and dream perception and that God would be a radical deceiver if the distinction were that obvious and we still could not trust it (AT 7:90, CSM 2:62).[31] Also false is the First Meditation contention that "Whatever I have up till now accepted as most true I have acquired either from the senses or through the senses" (AT 7:18, CSM 2:12). Upon further reflection (in the Second Meditation), we notice that our perception of the extension, flexibility, and changeability of a body "is a case not of vision or touch or imagination – nor has it ever been, despite previous appearances – but of purely mental scrutiny" (AT 7:31, CSM 2:21, emphasis added). Also false is the First Meditation meta-contention that the skeptical argumentation of the First Meditation "is based on powerful and well thought-out reasons" (AT 7: 21–22, CSM 2:15). That argumentation is based on terrible reasons, even if they appear to be good reasons from the first-person point-of-view of a mind that is at the early stages of inquiry and is deeply confused.

We might worry that Descartes would not be in the business of advancing false claims in the First Meditation. He is a philosopher, and he would be interested in advancing truth only. But that is not so. In an exchange with Gassendi, he says that sometimes it is very appropriate to put forward false claims in the course of pointing out truth:

> A philosopher would be no more surprised at such suppositions of falsity than he would be if, in order to straighten out a curved stick, we bent it round in the opposite direction. The philosopher knows that it is often useful to assume falsehoods instead of truths in this way in order to shed light on the truth, e.g. when astronomers imagine the equator, the zodiac, or other circles in the sky, or when geometers add new lines to given figures. Philosophers frequently do the same.[32]

---

31 A full discussion of the Sixth Meditation rebuttal of the dream argument is in Chapter 8.

32 Fifth Replies; AT 7:349–350, CSM 2:242. See also Cunning (2010), Chapter 1, and Arbib (2013), 495–497.

Descartes had said in his letter to Vatier that the clarity and evidence of his arguments for the existence of God cannot be appreciated without first working through skeptical arguments that call into question our long-standing commitments. It is clear how the skeptical arguments are of such assistance – they enable us to arrive at a clear grasp of the axioms and other non-sensory factors on which the arguments for the existence of God rely. If we were presented with those arguments in the First Meditation straightaway, we would fail to understand them, or we would reject them as absurd. Spinoza and Leibniz might accept that outcome, but Descartes seeks to reach as many minds as possible. In the *Meditations*, he does not begin with true premises and then derive the conclusions that they entail. That would be to employ the method of synthesis. Instead, he employs the method of analysis – a method of "discover[y]" by which premises might be seen to be true in the first place.[33]

It is tempting to begin a discussion of Descartes' system with an extended and comprehensive treatment of the skeptical arguments that he proposes, but that would be a mistake.[34] He does offer

33 Descartes describes the "analytic" method as a method of discovery in *Second Replies* (AT 7:155–156, CSM 2:110–112). Note that if I am arguing that Descartes takes some of the claims of the *Meditations* to be false, and that he puts them forward for heuristic purposes only, I will need to be careful when I attribute a view to Descartes on the basis of a claim that is made in the *Meditations*. I will need to make sure that in any such case there are texts outside of the *Meditations* that corroborate the attribution of the view to Descartes.

34 Descartes says more about the epistemic pedigree of the claims of the First Meditation in *Seventh Replies*. Bourdin had argued (in *Seventh Objections*) that the entire project of the *Meditations* is a non-starter: Descartes is attempting to arrive at results that are wholly unimpeachable, but he does not (even try to) establish that any of the premises of the First Meditation are unimpeachable, and if so, any results that depend on its argumentation – for example, the results of the Second Meditation and beyond – are on shaky ground as well. Bourdin writes,

> The method is faulty in its principles.... It chops off renounces and forswears all former beliefs without exception... The method is faulty in the implements it uses, for as long as it destroys the old without providing any replacements, it has no implements at all. ...Hence everything is doubtful and shaky, and your very inferences are uncertain... [W]e have nothing left which will be the slightest use for investigating the truth.
>
> (AT 7:527–529, CSM 2:358–360)

skeptical arguments, but only as an instrument for achieving clarity about axioms and claims that those arguments do not touch.[35] He does not begin with a presentation of rigorous axioms and claims; he does not throw us into the deep end with an onslaught of material that he expects we will not understand. He aims to establish results that are "stable and likely to last" (AT 7:17, CSM 2:12) – and that give metaphysics a firm foothold – but he must tread carefully if he is right about the epistemic proclivities of the vast majority who partake. The First Meditation skeptical arguments are indispensable, but at the same time, they are merely heuristic. We might take the skeptical arguments to be more than that. For example, we might

---

Bourdin is worried in part that the skeptical argumentation of the First Meditation is being used to vet preconceived and other opinions, but is never vetted itself. In effect, it has no epistemic credential. Descartes responds to Bourdin that he is correct that the skeptical argumentation of the First Meditation has no epistemic credential, but he adds that it does not need an epistemic credential to perform its task. He says that "[t]here is nothing at all that I asserted 'with confidence' in the First Meditation; it is full of doubt throughout" (AT 7:474, CSM 2:319). He then explains that there is no need for the skeptical arguments to have premises that are of the same caliber as results that come later – just as there is no need to use the highest quality bulldozer in the clearing away of rubble before the construction of the foundations of an edifice, or in the creation of scaffolding that will be removed once the edifice is in place (AT 7:537–538, CSM 2:366–367). Indeed, it would be a terrible idea to use our best material toward those efforts: we might never be able to kick away the scaffolding if it is too sturdy, and we would want to save the best material for the edifice itself.

35 See also *The Search for Truth*, AT 10:515, CSM 2:409. At one moment in the dialogue Polyander asks,

Is there anyone that can doubt that things that are perceivable by the senses – by which I mean those which can be seen and touched – are much more certain than all the others? I for one would be quite astonished if you were able to make me see just as clearly any of the things which are said about God and the soul.

(AT 10:510, CSM 2:407)

But Eudoxus gets Polyander to do just that – by way of a consideration of skeptical arguments. If Descartes is right, the things that are said about God and the soul are seen with more clarity. For a different (but similarly deflationary) treatment of skeptical arguments and their role in Descartes' thinking, see Fine (2000), Lennon and Hickson (2012), and Larmore (2014).

put a **T** in front of the claim that it is possible that God does not exist or that He is a radical deceiver. If so, we would conclude that any of the reasoning that comes after the First Meditation is entirely precarious, including the argument for the conclusion that God is a necessary existent and that radical deception is inconsistent with His nature. We would assess that that conclusion is up for grabs for the same reason that *any* conclusion is up for grabs – if it is true that it is possible that our minds are radically deceived. We might wonder how Descartes could have missed the obvious blunder of continuing to reason after the First Meditation if any such reasoning has to be hopeless. But Descartes supposes that it is the claims of the First Meditation that are hopeless instead. He does not put a **T** in front of any of them.

One final note needs to be made. In Part 4 of *Discourse on the Method* Descartes does not include the hyperbolic argumentation that posits that we might be mistaken about matters that are utterly evident to us. In a 1637 letter to Mersenne, he reveals why he did not include that argumentation: he excludes it out of a worry that some might take it too seriously. Descartes does not take the hyperbolic skeptical arguments of the First Meditation to have any legitimate epistemic weight. Their role is to expose the clarity of the axioms and premises that come later. He says to Mersenne that in order to make his proof of the existence of God as airtight as possible (in *Discourse* Part 4), he would have needed to "show... which judgements depend only on the pure understanding," but to do that there are particular "doubts and scruples I would have had to propound."[36] He indicates that he has included those doubts and scruples in the "sequel" to *Discourse on the Method* that he is drafting – "the beginnings of a treatise on metaphysics in which" the doubts are "conducted at some length" (ibid.). That sequel of course is the *Meditations*.[37]

---

36 "To Mersenne, 27 February 1637," AT 1:350, CSMK 53.

37 Descartes also refers to the treatise as far back as "To Mersenne, 25 November 1630." He writes, "perhaps I may some day complete a little treatise of Metaphysics, which I began when in Friesland, in which I set out principally to prove the existence of God and of our souls when they are separate from the body, from which their immortality follows" (AT 1:182, CSMK 29). See also "To Gibieuf, 18 July 1629," AT 1:17, CSMK 5.

The doubts that Descartes includes in the *Meditations* but not in the *Discourse* – the doubts that show which judgments depend only on the pure understanding – are the 2-plus AT pages of hyperbolic argumentation to the effect that it is possible that we are mistaken about matters that are utterly evident to us. He does not include these doubts in the *Discourse*, and he tells us why:

> I left this out on purpose and after deliberation, mainly because I had written in the vernacular. I was afraid that weak minds might avidly embrace the doubts and scruples which I would have had to propound, and afterwards be unable to follow as fully the arguments by which I would have endeavoured to remove them. Thus I would have set them on a false path and been unable to bring them back.
>
> (ibid.)

That is to say, Descartes omits the First Meditation hyperbolic doubts from the *Discourse* because he is afraid that "weak minds" would have taken them seriously and ended up on a road from which there is no return. For example, they would have concluded that it is true that it is possible that our minds are mistaken about matters that are utterly evident to us, and they would have concluded that there is no point in moving forward with any subsequent argumentation. Descartes expects that the same concern will not apply in the case of very educated readers – those who would read "a Latin version" (ibid.) – but the *Discourse* was "written in the [French] vernacular."[38] Perhaps he is assuming that his educated readers would recognize the method of analysis and the sort of exercise in which "astronomers imagine the equator, the zodiac, or other circles in the sky, or

---

38 Descartes later approved the French translation of the *Meditations*, which did (of course) contain the First Meditation hyperbolic doubts. So his worry about "weak minds" must have dissipated – perhaps because *Second Replies* contains such an explicit discussion of the teaching method of analysis (AT 7:155–159). The 1637 *Discourse* contained no such discussion. Descartes seems to have expected that readers of the 1641 Latin version of the *Meditations* would have understood that "it is often useful to assume falsehoods instead of truths in this way in order to shed light on the truth" and that "Philosophers frequently do the same."

when geometers add new lines to given figures."[39] He was mistaken, of course. In many instances, readers of the *Meditations* took Descartes to be putting a **T** in front of the First Meditation contention that it is possible that we are mistaken about matters that are utterly evident to us.[40] Perhaps these are not weak minds, as Descartes says they are. Perhaps it is true that it is possible that we are mistaken about matters that are utterly evident to us, and there are readers of the First Meditation who correctly intuit that. But Descartes disagrees.[41] He thinks that a careful consideration of the claim that it is possible that we are mistaken about matters that are utterly evident prompts us to recognize the truth of claims that are far more obvious and that entail that it is false.[42] Descartes is in a real pickle, programmatically speaking. He supposes that we will not register the evidence of the argumentation that comes after the First Meditation unless we engage the hyperbolic skeptical arguments, but as a matter of

---

39 Or the sort of exercise in which Archimedes explains the nature of a sphere in terms of the nature of a rectilinear figure, when strictly speaking a sphere does not have sides (*Fourth Replies*, AT 7:241–242, CSM 2:168).

40 For example, Mersenne in *Second Objections*, AT 7:124–125, CSM 2:89, and Arnauld in *Fourth Objections*, AT 7:214, CSM 2:150.

41 Here I might highlight opponents of Descartes like Hartz and Lewtas (2017).

42 Similarly an ethicist might begin a lesson with a discussion of the views of Nazi soldiers and suggest that if Germany had won World War II and then subsequently colonized the planet, it would be morally acceptable in 2022 to initiate a holocaust. Presumably the ethicist would then take the discussion in a different direction – one that exposes that there are obvious a priori intuitions that entail that Nazi values are absurd. But a student might come up after class and argue that because the sentiments of WWII German soldiers were in favor of Nazi values, it was permissible at the time to initiate a holocaust. Or perhaps the student becomes a Nazi. The ethicist would argue that the student has misconstrued the thought experiment and has a "weak mind;" the student would be on a "false path," and there might no way to "bring them back." The ethicist example is just one of many; the instructor might instead be a logician who attempts to help students to see the truth of the rule *modus ponens* by putting on the board examples that violate the rule egregiously. What Descartes is doing in the First Meditation is not at all uncommon for a philosopher. He is supposing that majority opinion and focus groups and longstanding judgments do not stand a chance against a priori and other non-sensory intuitions, so long as we recognize the latter (and the former) for what they are.

historical fact, it turns out that if we engage those arguments we are likely to conclude that nothing that comes after the First Meditation is credible.

Like Spinoza, Leibniz, and other philosophers who unfold their arguments in a more synthetic manner, Descartes might have begun the *Meditations* with a defense of his views straightaway. I am not suggesting though that Descartes should have employed synthesis rather than analysis. He employs the method of analysis as a precursor to synthesis (AT 7:156, CSM 2:111) – to help to ensure that his readers will understand the basic concepts and axioms that his synthetic demonstrations employ. He employs analysis *and then* synthesis. What I am suggesting is that he would have been better off to proceed in three stages – preliminary synthesis, then analysis, and then synthesis again. If we knew up front which views and arguments he was actually going to defend, and which views and arguments he was going to introduce as a mere heuristic, we would know what (and what not) to take seriously. He might have first laid out the views and arguments that comprise his philosophical system – asking us not yet to make any assessment – and then he might have moved to a second stage of analysis to assist us in grasping those views and arguments. And then he might have employed synthesis again to bring it all home. But perhaps he is damned if he does and damned if he doesn't. If he had done an initial laying out of his views and arguments, asking us not yet to assess them, we might not have been able to resist: we might have rejected them one by one, and with spiraling frustration and contempt.[43]

Dislodging hyperbolic doubt

The First Meditation skeptical arguments are merely heuristic. The hyperbolic argument that it is possible that we are deceived about matters that are utterly evident to us – that argument is epistemic garbage. That is why Descartes takes it to be so easy to neutralize.

Descartes is quite clear that until we defeat the skeptical possibility that we are mistaken about matters that are utterly evident to us, and

---

43 And Descartes predicts exactly that in *Second Replies*, AT 7:157, CSM 2:111.

until we see that possibility for the confusion that it is, knowledge is outside of our reach. He says in the Third Meditation that

> in order to remove even this slight reason for doubt, as soon as the opportunity arises I must examine whether there is a God, and if there is, whether he can be a deceiver. For if I do not know this, it seems that I can never be quite certain about anything else.
>
> (AT 7:36, CSM 2:25)

He adds in *Second Replies* that we do not have *scientia* of a result if it is wholly evident to us but we are not able to rule out the possibility that what is evident to us is nonetheless false. He writes,

> The fact that an atheist can be 'clearly aware that the three angles of a triangle are equal to two right angles' is something I do not dispute. But I maintain that this awareness of his is not true knowledge, since no act of awareness that can be rendered doubtful seems fit to be called knowledge [*scientia*]. Now since we are supposing that this individual is an atheist, he cannot be certain that he is not being deceived on matters which seem to him to be very evident. ...And although this doubt may not occur to him, it can still crop up if someone else raises the point or if he looks into the matter himself.[44]

Here (in a famous passage) Descartes is referencing a scenario in which an individual has a clear and distinct perception and recognizes it to be wholly evident, but for all they know there exists the hyperbolic possibility that what they perceive to be evident is false. To have the highest level of knowledge – or *scientia* – the individual must "be certain that he is not being deceived on matters which seem to him to be very evident." One way to achieve the requisite level of certainty is to have an immediate clear and distinct perception that God exists and is not a deceiver. But Descartes holds that another way is through a mere recollection that God exists and is

---

44 *Second Replies*, AT 7:141, CSM 2:101.

not a deceiver – a kind of cognition that is inextricably bound to our embodiment. An occurrent clear and distinct perception of divine veracity is of course sufficient to neutralize hyperbolic doubt, but as we will see he thinks that a memory of divine veracity does just as well, and he takes memory to be a corporeal faculty. Embodiment does not interfere with the acquisition of metaphysical truth in that instance. It comes to the rescue and saves the day. Corporeal memory is a potent force no matter what. In the service of an individual who has not careened through the gantlet that is the *Meditations*, it might work an entire lifetime to *dismiss* truth – never letting in so much as a morsel.[45] But it might also be retooled in service of the good. A germ or illness can be blocked with (corporeal) medicine, and the incoherent and imagistic prospect that we might be deceived about matters that are utterly evident can be blocked with corporeal instruments as well.

Descartes holds that a mere recollection of divine veracity is enough to neutralize hyperbolic doubt. He could not be more clear about this, and indeed his comments on the dismissal of hyperbolic doubt are almost cavalier:

> a man who has once clearly understood the reasons which convince us that God exists and is not a deceiver, provided he remembers the conclusion 'God is no deceiver' whether or not he continues to remember the reasons for it, will continue to possess not only the conviction, but real knowledge of this and all other conclusions the reasons for which he remembers he once clearly and distinctly perceived.[46]
>
> I have perceived that God exists, and at the same time I have understood that everything else depends on him, and that he is no deceiver; and I have drawn the conclusion that everything which I clearly and distinctly perceive is of necessity true. Accordingly, even if I am no longer attending to the arguments

---

45 See for example *Principles* I.72, where Descartes speaks of the kind of case in which we recognize to be true a result that runs counter to all of our existing opinions, but then our memory of those opinions kicks in and leads us to reject the result as absurd (AT 8A:36–37, CSM 1:219–220).

46 "To Regius, 24 May 1640," AT 3:65, CSMK 147.

which led me to judge that this is true, as long as I remember that I clearly and distinctly perceived it, there are no counter-arguments that can be adduced to make me doubt it, but on the contrary I have true and certain knowledge of it.[47]

There is no question about whether Descartes holds that an occurrent clear and distinct perception of divine veracity is required to rebut the hyperbolic doubts of the First Meditation. He does not.[48] Of course he does not. He said in the February 27, 1637 letter to Mersenne (AT 1:350, CSMK 53) that it is weak minds that fail to recognize that those doubts are confused, temporary, and heuristic, and he is right to suppose that epistemic garbage does not need to be purged with epistemic gold. It is enough that we remember the conclusion that God exists and is not a deceiver.

And for Descartes memory is a corporeal faculty. In *Treatise on Man*, he writes that nerves in the brain

> trace figures… which correspond to those of the objects. At first they do this less easily and less perfectly than they do on [the pineal] gland H, but gradually they do it better and better, as their action becomes better and lasts longer, or is repeated more often. That is why these figures are no longer so easily erased, and why they are preserved in such a way that the ideas which were previously on the gland can be formed again without requiring the presence of the objects to which they correspond. And this is what memory consists in…
>
> (AT 11:178, CSM 1:107)

Descartes says in another text that "memory is no different from imagination," at least in outline.[49] In the case of both, there are tracings of figures on the pineal gland – "forms or images which the

---

47 The Fifth Meditation, AT 7:70, CSM 2:48.
48 Here I am disagreeing with commentators who argue that Descartes holds that a clear and distinct perception of divine veracity is always required to neutralize hyperbolic doubt. See for example Loeb (1992), 206–208; Newman and Nelson (1999), 388–390; and Nolan (2005), 527–530.
49 *Rules for the Direction of the Mind*, AT 10:416, CSM 1:43.

rational soul united to this machine will consider directly when it imagines some object or perceives it by the senses."[50] He adds that "the impressions that are preserved in the memory... are not unlike the folds which remain in [a piece of] paper after it has once been folded."[51] Memory records an image more or less as it was formed in sense perception – and the action of the nerves "becomes better and lasts longer" – and then imagination considers such images and also recombines them into configurations that are more novel.[52] Memory is a corporeal faculty, for Descartes.[53] He does speak of intellectual memory in a few texts,[54] but he says almost nothing about what that is, and more importantly he makes clear that "where purely intellectual things are concerned, memory in the strict sense is not involved."[55] And in the AT 11:178 passage, he was telling us "what memory *consists in*." Memory and imagination are corporeal faculties, for Descartes, and like ideas of "vision or touch or imagination," ideas of memory are "imperfect and confused" and are not a matter of "purely mental scrutiny" (AT 7:31, CSM 2:21). A corporeal memory of divine veracity is not a (wholly intellectual) clear and distinct perception; it is confused.[56] Still, it is sufficient to neutralize the possibility that we are mistaken about matters that are utterly evident to us. Hyperbolic doubt is epistemic garbage. It is debris from the First Meditation, and it is easily swept away.[57]

---

50 *Treatise on Man*, AT 11:177, CSM 1:106.

51 "To Meyssonnier, 29 January 1640," AT 3:20, CSMK 143.

52 See also Sepper (2016), 35–36.

53 See also *Fifth Replies*, AT 7:357, CSM 2:247; "For [Arnauld], 29 July 1648," AT 5:220, CSMK 356; The Sixth Meditation, AT 7:74, CSM 2:51; and "To Hyperaspistes, August 1641," AT 3:425, CSMK 190). For a further discussion of Descartes on (corporeal) memory, see Joyce (1997) and Klein (2002).

54 "To Huygens, 10 October 1642," AT 3:580, CSMK 216; "To [Mesland], 2 May 1644, AT 4:114, CSMK 233; *Rules for the Direction of the Mind*, AT 10:416–417, CSM 1:43.

55 "To Hyperaspistes, August 1641," AT 3:425, CSMK 190. For a further discussion, see Joyce (1997), Clarke (2006), 100–105, and Schmal (2018).

56 See the discussion in Chapter 1, pp. 6–10.

57 Descartes exhibits his trust in (and reliance on) corporeal memory in other contexts as well. At the end of the Second Meditation, he writes,

It is no surprise that Descartes supposes that a thinker who has carefully worked through the *Meditations* (or an exercise like it) will dismiss the hyperbolic doubt of the First Meditation as ridiculous – and without the need of an occurrent clear and distinct perception of divine veracity. The possibility that God has created us in such a way that we are mistaken about matters that are utterly evident to us, the possibility that we are deceived by an evil demon (which God would have had to create), the possibility that God does not exist – by Cartesian lights all of these are silly. They are on a par with the First Meditation claim that what we know best we know through the senses (AT 7:18, CSM 2:12) and the Second Meditation claim that "general perceptions are apt to be somewhat more confused" than perceptions of particulars (AT 7:30, CSM 2:20) – both of which are false upon reflection. The hyperbolic possibilities of the First Mediation appear to be real to a thinker who does not know any better, but there comes a point at which we *do* know better, and the First Meditation possibilities are dismissed just as they should be, with little fanfare on the part of Descartes or his meditator.

Suppose that Einstein had been raised in an extremely isolated region and was taught from an early age that the sum of the squares of the shortest sides of a right triangle sometimes do not add up to the square of the hypotenuse. In this alternate reality, he had an authority-flouting father who drew triangles that were not composed of straight lines, and the empirical measurements would present the impression that the Pythagorean Theorem is false. Then Einstein becomes a mathematician and comes to see

---

> But since the habit of holding onto old opinions cannot be set aside so quickly, I should like to stop here and meditate for some time on this new knowledge I have gained, so as to fix it more deeply in my memory.
>
> (AT 7:34, CSM 2:23)

At the end of the Fourth Meditation, he writes

> I am aware of a certain weakness in me, in that I am unable to keep my attention focused on one and the same item of knowledge at all times; but by attentive and repeated meditation I am nevertheless able to make myself remember it as often as the need arises, and thus get into the habit of avoiding error.
>
> (AT 7:62, CSM 2:43)

that the Pythagorean Theorem is true. He recognizes that what he had learned earlier was just confused. He becomes a professor and teaches advanced mathematics and physics at Princeton, and one day he is doing a lecture that presupposes results from Euclidean geometry. A visitor comes to class that day and suggests that it is possible that there are instances in which the Pythagorean Theorem is false and insists that Einstein cannot continue until he rules out that possibility. The visitor turns out to be Einstein's uncle, who reminds Einstein that when he was an adolescent he put a **T** in front of the claim that it is possible for the sum of the squares of the two shortest sides of a right triangle not to add up to the square of the hypotenuse. Einstein rejects the suggestion of the uncle as inane. For a very short time, and before (the young) Einstein had thought things through, he thought that there existed the possibility that the sum of the squares of the two shortest sides of a right triangle not to add up to the square of the hypotenuse, but then he grew up. He was using his mind to assess that possibility as a child, just as he is using his mind when he assesses the possibility later and upon reflection. The question is which deliverance he should accept. He decides to continue his lecture and to send the visitor on his way. He defeats the confused objection that has been presented to him, but not by harnessing an immediate and opposing clear and distinct perception. That is not always in the cards for a human being, and also it is not necessary.

Descartes holds that for a mind that has undertaken the paradigm-shifting work of *Meditations on First Philosophy*, an embodied memory is enough to defeat confusions like that there exists the possibility that the sum of the squares of the sides of a right triangle not equal the square of the hypotenuse. An embodied memory is also sufficient to neutralize the confused possibility that we are mistaken about matters that are utterly evident to us. Descartes appears to allow however that some minds are sufficiently sharp that they will often defeat a confused objection with a clear and distinct perception that is ready-at-hand and as immediate as the *cogito*. For example, after he demonstrates the existence of God in the Fifth Meditation, he writes:

> as regards God, if I were not overwhelmed by preconceived opinions, and if the images of things perceived by the senses

did not besiege my thought on every side, I would certainly acknowledge him sooner and more easily than anything else. For what is more self-evident than the fact that the supreme being exists, or that God, to whose essence alone existence belongs, exists?

(AT 7:69, CSM 2:47)

Here Descartes is referencing a mind that recognizes the truth that God exists and is not a deceiver immediately upon thinking about whether God exists and is not a deceiver – for example, in the context of entertaining the possibility that our minds are mistaken about matters that are utterly evident to us. Such a mind would dismiss the possibility as soon as it comes up, in the same way that it would dismiss the possibility of the non-existence of its thinking in the Second Meditation.[58] Descartes appears to hold that some minds get to the point where they have clear and distinct perceptions quite easily. He says at the beginning of the Fourth Meditation,

During these past few days I have accustomed myself to leading my mind away from the senses, and I have taken careful note of the fact that there is very little about corporeal things that is truly perceived, whereas much more is known about the human

---

58 See also Newman and Nelson (1999), 386. But I am disagreeing with Newman and Nelson (1999) and also Nolan (2005) on whether or not a self-evident intuition of divine veracity is required to overcome hyperbolic doubt. Both papers argue that in the *Meditations* hyperbolic doubt is not overcome until the meditator achieves a self-evident intuition of divine veracity at the end of the Fifth Meditation (Newman and Nelson (1999), 386–387; Nolan (2005), 527–530). But Descartes is clear that he is writing to a variety of minds in the *Meditations*, and he says very specifically that he offers both the Third Meditation arguments for the existence of God and the Fifth Meditation argument "so as to appeal to a variety of different minds" (*First Replies*, AT 7:120, CSM 2:85). See also *Second Replies*, where he references his arguments for the existence of God and says that "there are certain truths which some people find self-evident, while others come to understand them only by means of a formal argument" (AT 7:164, CSM 2:115). Descartes thus says at the end of the Fifth Meditation that "now" we are able to acquire "full and certain knowledge" (AT 7:71, CSM 2:49) because by that point we have either the one route or the other at our disposal.

mind, and still more about God. The result is that I now have no difficulty in turning my mind away from imaginable things and towards things which are the object of the intellect alone and are totally separate from matter.

(AT 7:52–53, CSM 2:37)

Not all minds have such facility at clear and distinct perception, and indeed the Fourth Meditation is an artificial context that is in place after we have "arranged for [our]sel[ves] a clear stretch of time" (AT 7:18, CSM 2:12) to turn away from things that are sensible and imaginable. In our default state, we have sensory perception after sensory perception – independently of our will and whether we want to have sensory perceptions or not.[59] Descartes adds,

It seems to me very true that, as long as the mind is united to the body, it cannot withdraw itself from the senses whenever it is stimulated with great force by external or internal objects.[60]

There are also the texts in which he says that it is extremely difficult for a human being to secure clear and distinct perceptions and that we become exhausted after securing a clear and distinct perception for even a few moments.[61] There is also the language of *Principles* I.73: "it is hardest of all for it [the mind] to attend to what is not present to the senses or... imagination" (AT 8A:37, CSM 1:220).[62] Descartes

---

59 This is obvious, but see for example the Third Meditation, AT 7:38, CSM 2:26.

60 "For [Arnauld], 29 July 1648," AT 5:219, CSMK 356.

61 For example in "To Princess Elizabeth, 6 October 1645," AT 4:307, CSMK 269.

62 See also the verdict in Russell (1956):

In very abstract studies such as philosophical logic, ...the subject-matter that you are supposed to be thinking is so exceedingly difficult and elusive that any person who has ever tried to think about it knows that you do not think about it except perhaps once in six months for half a minute. The rest of the time you think about the symbols, because they are tangible, for the thing you are supposed to be thinking about is fearfully difficult and one does not manage to think about it. The really good philosopher is the one who does once in six months think about it for a minute. Bad philosophers never do.

(185)

supposes that generally speaking clear and distinct perceptions do not come easily and that for the bulk of us they are few and far between.

But he does allow that some embodied minds are smarter than others. On his own view, any differences in intelligence between minds would appear to be due to differences of embodiment – for example, in the connection of the pineal gland to the mind, or in the relative agility of the animal spirits in the brain and nervous system.[63] As we have seen, he says in *Fifth Replies* that if finite minds were not embodied, or if our bodies did not interfere with our thinking, we would all of us have clear and distinct perceptions straightaway (AT 7:375, CSM 2:258).[64] In other texts, he calls attention to minds that are interfaced with bodies but have clear and distinct perceptions quite easily. In one of the passages in which he speaks with optimism about our ability to overcome longstanding opinions, he writes,

> In order to philosophize seriously and search out the truth about all the things that are capable of being known, we must first of all lay aside all our preconceived opinions, or at least we must take the greatest care not to put our trust in any of the opinions accepted by us in the past until we have first scrutinized their truth and examined them afresh and confirmed their truth. Next, we must give our attention in an orderly way to the notions that we have within us, and we must judge to be true all and only those whose truth we clearly and distinctly recognize when we attend to them in this way. ...*When we contrast all this knowledge with the confused thoughts we had before, we will acquire the habit of forming clear and distinct concepts of all the things that can be*

---

63 Descartes also appears to hold that there is no intrinsic difference between the intellectual capacities of men and women and that differences in intellectual capacity among any human beings are due to differences in pineal gland and the activity of the body. See also Reuter (2010) and Pellegrin (2019). An important early modern Cartesian philosopher who defends the view that men and women are generally speaking equal with respect to cognitive capacities is Mary Astell. See Astell (1694/1697), and Sowaal (2015).

64 See Chapter 3, pp. 77–78.

known. These few instructions seem to me to contain the most important principles of human knowledge.[65]

Here Descartes is featuring a sort of embodied mind that reaches the point where it has clear and distinct perceptions almost at will. It considers its preconceived opinions and arrives at evident truths that show them to be false, and then as those opinions happen to arise again, it dismisses them with an immediate clear and distinct perception. But Descartes does not require that embodied minds always marshal a clear and distinct perception in order to dismiss a confused opinion. A corporeal memory will suffice as well.

Descartes is writing to a variety of minds in the *Meditations*. He is aware that those who are thinking through its argumentation from the first-person point-of-view include Aristotelians, mechanists, skeptics, theists, atheists, and geometers. In the Second Meditation, he thinks through and past multiple hypotheses – for example, that mind is a wind or fire (AT 7:26) and that it involves a nutritive component (AT 7:27). He does the same in the First Meditation – imagining that perhaps God does not exist and that we have reached our current state by chance (AT 7:21–22). In the Third Meditation, he speaks of sensory heat as existing in material bodies (AT 7:41), and he speaks of individual bodies as substances (AT 7:45). He writes more generally that

It was not my intention to make a survey of all the views anyone else had ever held on these matters, nor was there any reason why I should have done so. I confined myself to what I had originally believed quite spontaneously and with nature as my guide, and to the commonly held views of others, irrespective of truth or falsity; for my purpose in making the survey was not to adopt these beliefs, but merely to examine them.[66]

He adds in *First Replies* that the reason why he includes multiple arguments for the existence of God in the *Meditations* is "to appeal

---

65 *Principles* I.75, AT 8A:38–39, CSM 1:221.
66 *Seventh Replies*, AT 7:482, CSM 2:325.

to a variety of different minds" (AT 7:120, CSM 2:85). He is fully aware that Hobbes, Gassendi, Arnauld, Bourdin, Caterus, Mersenne, the atheist geometer of *Second Replies*, and other minds will be working through and processing the argumentation of the *Meditations* from the first-person perspective. The minds that will be engaging his philosophical system have different antecedent commitments, Descartes is right to suppose, but he is also right to suppose that minds differ with respect to their facility at clear and distinct perception. Some have an easier (or harder) time intuiting what is obvious. Some embodied minds glide to a clear and distinct perception of divine veracity that is as immediate as the cogito, even if there might be a second or two in the interim when they are redirecting their attention. We might call such a creature *homo scientia*. At the opposite extreme, there is the mind that will not grasp the results of the *Meditations* even after reading it a thousand times.[67] There are also many cases in-between.

Descartes does not hold that a clear and distinct perception of divine veracity is required to neutralize hyperbolic doubt each and every time that it might attempt to show itself. The thought that our minds might be mistaken about matters that are most evident to us is cognitive garbage – along the lines of a filthy rag that helps us to clear away the gunk on a beautiful floor – but we do not dispense with a filthy rag by calling a Hazmat team. The latter would be effective, but it would also be overkill.

Truth is its own standard

Nor does Descartes suppose that a clear and distinct perception of divine veracity is required to derive the truth of a clear and distinct perception in the first place. He supposes instead that what it is to have a clear and distinct perception of a result is to recognize the result to be true.[68] As we have seen, he says in *Principles* I.75 that "we must give our attention in an orderly way to the notions that we have

---

67 "To Hyperaspistes, August 1641," AT 3:430, CSMK 194.
68 Here I am in agreement with Della Rocca (2005), 7–11, 19, and Cottingham (1986), 69, that what it is to have a clear and distinct perception of *x* is to recognize the truth of *x*. The view that "truth is its own standard" is also in Spinoza (1677), Part II, Proposition XLIII, scholium, 268–269.

within us, and we must judge to be true all and only those whose truth we recognize clearly and distinctly" (AT 8A:38, CSM 1:221).[69] He adds in *Second Replies*,

> I ask them [my readers] to ponder on those self-evident prop-ositions that they will find within themselves, such as 'The same thing cannot both be and not be at the same time', and 'Nothing cannot be the efficient cause of anything', and so on. In this way they will be exercising the intellectual vision which nature gave them, in the pure form which it attains when freed from the senses; for sensory appearances generally interfere with it and darken it to a very great extent. And by this means *the truth of the following axioms will easily become apparent to them.*[70]

---

69 See also The Third Meditation, AT 7: 40–41, CSM 2:28; *Rules for the Direction of the Mind*, Rule 11, AT 10:409, CSM 1:38; *The World*, AT 11:20, CSM 1:87; *Discourse*, Part 4, AT 6:33, CSM 1:127; preface to the French edition of *Principles of Philosophy*, AT 9B:4, CSM 1:181; *Principles* I.30, AT 8A:16, CSM 1:203; *Principles* I.49, AT 8A:23, CSM 1:209; *Principles* I.61, AT 8A:29, CSM 1:214; *Principles* I.63, AT 8A:30, CSM 1:215; *Principles* I.64, AT 8A:31, CSM 1:215; *Principles* II.11, AT 8A:46, CSM 1:227; "To Mersenne, 28 January 1641," AT 3:298, CSMK 173; *Conversation with Burman*, AT 5:177, CSMK 351–352; and "To Mersenne, 1 March 1638," AT 2:24, CSMK 89.

70 AT 7:162–163, CSM 2:115, emphasis added. Della Rocca (2005) makes a distinction between psychological certainty and normative certainty and argues that Descartes holds that to have a clear and distinct perception is to have the latter – not just to be convinced of a result, or to be unable to doubt it, but to recognize it to be true (2–6). I agree with Della Rocca, but I think that the textual evidence that he provides is not as compelling as it might be. For example, he cites the *Principles* I.13 passage in which Descartes says that the mind

> finds within itself ideas of many things; and so long as it merely contemplates these ideas and does not affirm or deny the existence outside itself of any-thing resembling them, it cannot be mistaken. Next, it finds certain common notions from which it constructs various proofs; and, for as long as it attends to them, it is completely convinced of their truth.

(AT 8A:9, CSM 1:197; Della Rocca 2005, 10–11)

This passage is open to an interpretation according to which it is referencing mere psychological certainty, especially in terms of the language at the very end ("it is completely convinced of their truth"). I am focusing on the passages in

Descartes does not hold that we recognize a result as true by having a clear and distinct perception of it and then applying the premise that because God is not a deceiver whatever we clearly and distinctly perceive is true. Instead, we recognize the truth of the result straightaway – by clearly and distinctly perceiving it. We then appeal to divine veracity *afterward* – in case we are prompted to block the incoherent defeater that we might be mistaken about matters that are utterly evident to us. Descartes puts a **T** in front of the claim that God exists and is not a deceiver. But instead of employing that claim as a premise in arguments that derive the truth of a clear and distinct perception, he employs it subsequent to recognizing the truth of the clear and distinct perception. More specifically, he appeals to it to neutralize a defeater that might be introduced as a reason to call into doubt the truth of the clear and distinct perception. As he indicates in *Principles* I.75 and *Second Replies*, there are results whose truth we clearly and distinctly recognize. There is also a subsequent (and wholly incoherent) objection that might be raised against such results after we have clearly and distinctly perceived their truth. The objection is that it is possible that we are mistaken about matters that are utterly evident to us. We have *scientia* so long as we have the resources to dismiss the objection – via a corporeal memory or a clear and distinct perception – but the claim that God is not a deceiver was not a premise in an argument for the truth of the perception to start.

For example, in *Principles of Philosophy* Part I, Descartes derives the rule (that whatever we clearly and distinctly perceive is true) in Section 30 – well after he has already recognized and posited a number of truths. In Sections 14–15, he offers what is in effect the Fifth Meditation argument for the existence and nature of God, and the rule is not an ingredient of his reasoning. In Sections 17–21, he offers what are in effect the Third Meditation arguments for the existence and nature of God; the rule is not an ingredient in

---

Principles I.75 and *Second Replies* because they make explicit that Descartes holds that what it is to have a clear and distinct perception is to recognize a truth. I agree with Della Rocca that in *Principles* I.13 Descartes is referencing normative certainty, but I think that we can only say as much in the light of the language in *Principles* I.75 and *Second Replies*.

his reasoning there either. In Section 13, he recognizes the truth of axioms like that "If you add equals to equals the results will be equal" (AT 8A:9, CSM 1:197), but again the rule is nowhere to be found. Descartes derives the rule later, in Part I Section 30.[71]

And the rule is never a premise in an argument for the truth of a clear and distinct perception.[72] Instead, the rule is harnessed after a truth has been recognized – to neutralize the confused defeater that we might be mistaken about matters that are utterly evident to us. We see this across the board. In *Second Replies*, Descartes refers to the atheist geometer who sees that the three angles of a triangle add to two right angles. The objection then crops up that it is possible that what is utterly evident to us is false, and the geometer needs to defeat that objection or else she does not have *scientia*. But the atheist geometer clearly and distinctly recognized the truth of the result before that. In the Third Meditation, Descartes lists a number of arithmetical and geometrical claims that he had called into question in the First Meditation and asks if he does "not see at least these things clearly enough to affirm their truth" (AT 7:36, CSM 2:25). He reveals that

---

71 And of course, Descartes is not appealing to the rule that clear and distinct perceptions are true (in Section 30) in order to argue (in Sections 14–18) that (1) we have a clear and distinct perception that God exists and hence (2) God exists. He derives the rule from (2), and so he is not using the rule to yield (2). Here I am referencing the notorious problem of the "Cartesian Circle," but I have been arguing that the question of circular reasoning does not even arise for Descartes. He appeals to the rule after arriving at the conclusion that God exists, and he employs it to neutralize the confused defeater that we might be mistaken in matters that are utterly evident to us.

72 There are some arguments – three in total – in which Descartes employs as a premise the claim that God is not a deceiver and has not created us in such a way that we are radically deceived. These appear in the Sixth Meditation: (1) the argument for the existence of material things; (2) the argument for the view that generally speaking sensations track information that is relevant to the preservation of our mind-body union; and (3) the argument that establishes a distinction between waking perception and dream perception. But in these arguments Descartes is not applying the rule that whatever we clearly and distinctly perceive is true; that is because the arguments do not involve clear and distinct perceptions, but strong inclinations to affirm. There is a further discussion of the three arguments in Chapter 8.

he does see their truth that clearly and that "the only reason for my later judgement that they were open to doubt was that it occurred to me that perhaps some God could have given me a nature such that I was deceived even in matters which seemed most evident" (ibid.). He "turn[s] to the things themselves" and recognizes (for example) that nothing could ever "bring it about that two and three added together are more or less than five" (ibid.). He then considers the hyberbolic (and *inane*) objection that it is possible that he has been created with a defective mind and says that until he defeats it on the basis of reasoning that is much clearer, he "can never be quite certain about anything else" (ibid.).

Descartes holds that the divine guarantee of the truth of clear and distinct perceptions is to be employed after we derive the truth of a given clear and distinct perception.[73] We employ the guarantee to block the incoherent objection that it is possible that we are mistaken about matters that are utterly evident to us. Ideally, we reach the point at which we dismiss the objection in the same way that we dismiss the objection that it is possible that seven equals two – where the refutation of that possibility does not require the summoning of an immediate clear and distinct perception either. Or perhaps we reach the point where it is as unintelligible to us as the noises of a person who is combining syllables at random, or who is coughing up phlegm. Hyperbolic doubt is that unintelligible, and if we get to the point where we recognize it as such we give it the attention that it is due and nothing more. We throw at it a corporeal memory of divine veracity, and we are done.

---

73 Note that here I am disagreeing with a number of commentators, including Newman (1999) – who argues that Descartes holds that the Fourth Meditation "truth rule" is a premise in arguments that yield the truth of clear and distinct perceptions (588–589). I am arguing that the Fourth Meditation rule is meant to prevent backsliding after we have already recognized the truth of a clear and distinct perception. In a passage that Newman cites in defense of his interpretation, Descartes says that "These [Fourth Meditation] results need to be known both in order to confirm what has gone before and also to make intelligible what is to come later" (CSM 2:11, AT 7:15). The passage is clear however that the rule is just meant to confirm what has already been established.

Hyperbolic doubt and the analytic method (revisited)

On another telling of the fictional Einstein story, Einstein has a math tutor as child, and the math tutor occasionally makes false claims for the pedagogical purpose of helping Einstein to think them through and confront first-hand just how completely false they are. Perhaps the tutor also supposes that by entertaining incoherencies a student is better able to locate truth and recognize it for what it is. In that case the tutor would be employing a method that Descartes takes to be perfectly appropriate:

> It is exactly the same sort of comparison between a sphere (or other curvilinear figure) and a rectilinear figure that enabled Archimedes to demonstrate various properties of the sphere which could scarcely be understood otherwise.[74]

Descartes adds that "just as no one criticizes these proofs," he is not open to the criticism that he uses analogies and examples that are incoherent. In the case of the hyperbolic arguments of the First Meditation, he writes more specifically,

> take the case of someone who imagines a deceiving God – even the true God, but not yet clearly enough known to himself or to the others for whom he frames the hypothesis. Let us suppose that he does not misuse this fiction for the evil purpose of persuading others to believe something of the Godhead, but uses it only to enlighten the intellect, and bring greater knowledge of God's nature to himself and to others. ...There is no malice at all in his action; he does something which is good in itself, and no one can rebuke him for it except slanderously.[75]

Voetius had rebuked Descartes for inviting us to entertain the thought that it is possible that God is a deceiver in the First Meditation. But Descartes is not being serious in the First Meditation, and Voetius rebukes him slanderously. Descartes is just offering a thought

---

74 Fourth Replies, AT 7:241, CSM 2:168.
75 "To Buitendijck, 1643," AT 4:64, CSMK 230.

experiment that will assist us in moving beyond a confused and imagistic conception of God to a stripped-down idea that attributes to God all and only features that God has in fact:

> [Voetius claims that in my philosophy] 'God is thought of as a deceiver.' This is foolish. Although in my First Meditation I did speak of a supremely powerful deceiver, the conception there was in no way of the true God, since, as he himself says, it is impossible that the true God should be a deceiver.[76]

Descartes supposes that we will not fully register that it is impossible that God is a deceiver – or that bodies are limited to extensive features like size, shape, and motion, or that minds are immaterial, or that God is supremely independent, perfect, and immutable – if we are restricted to the ideas that we have upon entering the *Meditations*. We will not register the truth of the metaphysical axioms from which Descartes' non-sensory picture of reality arises. We will reason from our existing ideas, and we will not get anywhere. So his first order of business is to help to clean up our ideas, and a consideration of hyperbolic doubt is essential to that end. Under the circumstances the pedagogical method that Descartes employs is completely appropriate. As he had said to Gassendi, a philosopher should not be "surprised at such suppositions of falsity" (AT 7:349, CSM 2:242). The Einstein in the second telling of the story arrives at extremely clear and obvious results in mathematics, and he looks back with a proper balance of gratitude and disregard for his adolescent thought that it is possible for the sum of the squares of the two shortest sides to not equal the square of the hypotenuse. He overhears a lesson in which a new batch of adolescent students is learning about mathematics via the method of analysis, and he does not panic that all of his current views are up for grabs. He does not stop everything to isolate clear and distinct perceptions of triangles. He proceeds to give his lecture at the Institute for Advanced Research at Princeton, and without batting an eye.

---

76 "Letter to Voetius, May 1643," AT 8B:60, CSMK 222.

Further reading

There is a large literature on Descartes and skepticism. An important cross-section of this literature includes:

José Luis Bermúdez, "Cartesian Skepticism: Arguments and Antecedents," in *The Oxford Handbook of Skepticism*, ed. John Greco, New York and Oxford: Oxford UP (2008), 57–80.

Janet Broughton, *Descartes's Method of Doubt*, Princeton, NJ: Princeton UP (2002).

Edwin M. Curley, *Descartes Against the Skeptics*, Cambridge, MA: Harvard UP (1978).

Gail Fine, "Descartes and Ancient Skepticism: Reheated Cabbage?," *The Philosophical Review* 109 (2000), 195–234.

Marjorie Grene, "Descartes and Skepticism," *Review of Metaphysics* 52 (1999), 553–571.

Robert Hanna, "Descartes and Dream Skepticism Revisited," *Journal of the History of Philosophy* 30 (1992), 377–398.

Charles Larmore, "The First Meditation: Skeptical Doubt and Certainty," in *The Cambridge Companion to Descartes' Meditations*, ed. David Cunning, Cambridge and New York: Cambridge UP (2014), 48–67.

Thomas M. Lennon and Michael W. Hickson, "The skepticism of the First Meditation," in *Descartes' Meditations: A Critical Guide*, ed. Karen Detlefsen, Cambridge and New York: Cambridge UP (2012), 9–24.

Barry Stroud, *The Significance of Philosophical Skepticism*, New York and Oxford: Oxford UP (1984), chapter one.

Bernard Williams, "Descartes' Use of Skepticism," in *The Skeptical Tradition*, ed. Myles Burnyeat, Berkeley and Los Angeles: California UP (1983), 337–352.

There is also a large literature on the more specific question of how (or whether) Descartes overcomes the hyperbolic doubt that we might be mistaken about matters that are utterly evident to us. A cross-section of this literature includes:

Janet Broughton, "Skepticism and the Cartesian Circle," *Canadian Journal of Philosophy* 14 (1984), 593–615.

Michael Della Rocca, "Descartes, the Cartesian Circle, and Epistemology Without God," *Philosophy and Phenomenological Research* 70 (2005), 1–33.

Willis Doney, "The Cartesian Circle," *Journal of the History of Ideas* 16 (1955), 324–338.

Gary Hatfield, "The Cartesian Circle," in *The Blackwell Guide to Descartes' Meditations*, ed. Stephen Gaukroger, Hoboken, NJ: Wiley-Blackwell (2006), 122–141.

Robert A. Imlay, "Intuition and the Cartesian Circle," *Journal of the History of Philosophy* 11 (1973), 19–27.

Anthony Kenny, "The Cartesian Circle and the Eternal Truths," *Journal of Philosophy* 67 (1970), 685–700.

Louis Loeb, "The Cartesian Circle," in *The Cambridge Companion to Descartes*, ed. John Cottingham, Cambridge and New York: Cambridge UP (1992), 200–235.

Dugald Murdoch, "The Cartesian Circle," *Philosophical Review* 108 (1999), 221–244.

Jennifer Nagel, "Contemporary Skepticism and the Cartesian God," *Canadian Journal of Philosophy* 35 (2005), 465–497.

Lex Newman and Alan Nelson, "Circumventing Cartesian Circles," *Noûs* 33 (1999), 370–404.

D. Blake Roeber, "Does the Theist Have an Epistemic Advantage Over the Atheist?: Plantinga and Descartes on Theism, Atheism, and Skepticism," *Journal of Philosophical Research* 34 (2009), 305–328.

James Van Cleve, "Foundationalism, Epistemic Principles, and the Cartesian Circle," *Philosophical Review* 88 (1979), 55–91.

Five

Arguments for the existence of God

In the bulk of this chapter, I address the arguments for the existence
of God that Descartes lays out in the *Meditations* and other works. At
the end of the chapter, there is a discussion of some of the apparent
implications of these arguments for Descartes' views on the distinction between God and creatures and for his views on possibility and
necessity.

Descartes offers three arguments for the existence of God. Two of
these arguments rely on the assumption that we possess an idea that
has so much being or reality that the positing of that idea entails
that God exists as its cause. At the very least, a being with infinite
power exists as its cause, Descartes argues, but there is an inextricable conceptual tie between infinite power and the other divine
attributes, and so the being with infinite power is God Itself. The
two arguments are very similar and in a way are different versions
of the same: one posits the existence of an idea that requires an
infinitely powerful cause; the other posits the existence of a mind
that possesses that idea and concludes that that mind (together with
its idea) requires an infinitely powerful cause. Descartes also offers
a third argument for the existence of God – an argument from the
assumption that we have a clear and distinct (or true) idea of a being
with the perfection of necessary existence. Like all true ideas, that
idea has a conformable or truthmaker. The being whose existence is
guaranteed by a true idea of God is not eminent being that exists in
some other entity but is the divine being Itself. The Third Meditation
arguments ride on the supposition that the idea of God is so vast that
an entity that falls short of God could not be the cause of its content.
The Fifth Meditation argument rides on the supposition that the idea

DOI: 10.4324/9781351210522-5

of God is so vast that an entity that falls short of God could not be its conformable.

The order of the arguments for the existence of God

We might assume from the order of presentation of the *Meditations* that the Fifth Meditation argument includes as a premise that whatever we clearly and distinctly perceive is true. Descartes argues in the Third Meditation that God exists, and he concludes at the end of the Meditation that "he cannot be a deceiver" (AT 7:52, CSM 2:35). In the Fourth Meditation, he addresses a worry that might bring down the conclusion that God exists and is not a deceiver – namely, that a supremely perfect being would produce creatures that do not err, but finite minds do err, and so perhaps God does not exist at all. He argues in the remainder of the Fourth Meditation that it is a mistake to assume that a perfect being would not produce creatures that err: all of the *clear and distinct* ideas of a creature (of God) would be true, but a perfect being might create finite minds that affirm confused ideas and err as a result.[1] Having restored the Third Meditation conclusion that God exists and is not a deceiver, Descartes proceeds to the Fifth Meditation to derive yet a third time that God exists and is not a deceiver. We might assume that because the Fifth Meditation argument comes after the Fourth Meditation claim that clear and distinct perceptions are true, Descartes is applying that result to a true idea of God in the Fifth Meditation. But that is not what he is doing.

The Fifth Meditation argument for the existence of God is freestanding. In an alternate universe, Descartes might have offered the Fifth Meditation argument immediately after arguments one and two, and the Third Meditation would have contained three arguments for the existence of God. The *second* argument certainly does not depend on the first; Descartes considers it after "his mental vision is blinded by the images of things perceived by the senses" and he finds it "not so easy" to follow the first argument (AT 7:47, CSM 2:32). He then asks whether a mind that "ha[s] this idea [of God]… could exist if

---

1 There is a comprehensive discussion of the Fourth Meditation intervention in the second half of Chapter 6.

no such being [God] existed" (AT 7:48, CSM 2:33). Nor does the third argument (in the Fifth Meditation) depend on the second or first. Descartes says in the Fifth Meditation that his argument for the existence of God still stands "even if it turned out that not everything on which I have meditated in these past days is true" (AT 7:65, CSM 2:45). He also says in multiple texts that the different arguments that he offers for the existence of God are intended for a variety of minds – to increase the chances that those who fail to understand one of the arguments might understand one or both of the others.[2] The arguments do not rely on each other in that case but are independent. The Fifth Meditation argument for the existence of God does not include as a premise that whatever we clearly and distinctly perceive is true. That would be silly: Descartes would in effect be arguing that God exists; clear and distinct perceptions are therefore true; we have a clear and distinct perception that God exists; and so God exists.

In the *Principles of Philosophy* presentation of the Fifth Meditation argument for the existence of God, Descartes reveals even more explicitly that that argument does not depend on either of the arguments that appear in the Third Meditation. In *Principles of Philosophy*, he goes in reverse order and offers the (equivalent of the) Fifth Meditation argument first, in *Principles* I.14–16. He then presents the (equivalent of the) two Third Meditation arguments later, in *Principles* I.17–21.

The *Principles* I.14–16 argument does not employ (or even mention) the claim that clear and distinct perceptions are true. As we have seen, the claim is derived much later, in Part I Section 30. In *Principles* I.14, Descartes proceeds straight to a recognition of the truth of the operative clear and distinct perceptions themselves.[3] He inspects his idea of God and notices that it entails the truth that God has a very particular kind of existence – namely, "necessary and eternal existence" (AT 8A:10, CSM 1:197). That is to say, it is a truth that God has necessary and eternal existence. Descartes also notices other truths that his idea of God entails: the idea is "of a supremely

---

2 First *Replies*, AT 7:120, CSM 2:85; Second *Replies*, AT 7:163–164, CSM 2:115; Seventh *Replies*, AT 7:482, CSM 2:325.

3 See also the discussion in Chapter 4 above, pp. 138–142. Descartes holds that what it is to have a clear and distinct perception is to grasp the truth.

intelligent, supremely powerful, and supremely perfect being"
(ibid.), and so it is true that God is supremely intelligent, supremely
powerful, and supremely perfect. Descartes then takes for granted
the axiom that truth is "the conformity of thought with its object"[4]
to generate the conclusion that God in fact exists. He does not state
the axiom in *Principles* I.14–16 (or in the Fifth Meditation): he thinks
that it is so obvious that no one could possibly be ignorant of it.[5] He
assumes that truth is the conformity of thought with reality, and he
asks what could possibly be the conformable of truths like that God
is omnipotent and has necessary existence. The idea of God "stands
out from all the others" (AT 8A:10, CSM 1:197) in terms of the
truths that it delivers. The conformable of a true idea of God could
only be the divine being Itself.[6]

---

4 "To Mersenne, 16 October 1639," AT 2:597, CSMK 139. See Chapter 3 above,
   pp. 89–94.
5 Ibid. He continues in the letter to Mersenne,
      There are many ways of examining a scale before using it, but there is no way
      to learn what truth is, if one does not know it by nature. What reason would
      we have for accepting anything which could teach us the nature of truth if
      we did not know that it was true, that is to say, if we did not know truth?
6 Note that my reconstruction of the Fifth Meditation argument is controversial, and I defend it below. We might be tempted to read Descartes as instead
   offering the argument that because existence is contained in the idea of God,
   God exists. (See for example Abbruzzese (2007).) But that is a really bad argument, and more importantly, Descartes explicitly distances himself from it
   in *First Replies* (AT 7:115–116, CSM 2:82–83). He adds in "Synopsis of the
   following six Meditations" that he takes himself to be offering a "new" argument for the existence of God in the Fifth Meditation (AT 7:15, CSM 2:11).
   He does say in the Fifth Meditation that "existence is one of the perfections"
   that is contained in the idea of God (AT 7:67, CSM 2:46), but as I will argue,
   what he has in mind is a particular kind of existence – necessary or independent existence – and on his view that the truth that God has *that* kind of
   existence can only have God as its conformable. As he says in *Principles* I:14,
   "necessary existence is included in our idea of God" (AT 8A:10, CSM 1:197).
   Note for the record that Abbruzzese is attempting to read Descartes charitably
   in attributing to him the argument that God exists because the concept of God
   contains existence. Abbruzzese argues that in the Fifth Meditation, Descartes
   is not trying to establish that God exists; he is just trying to point out (to the
   atheist mathematician) that "God exists" follows from the idea of God with
   the same level of certainty that truths about triangles follow from the idea of a

The Fifth Meditation discussion is more fleshed out than the (barely 1-page) discussion in Principles I.14–16, so we might begin there.

True and immutable natures and the third argument for the existence of God

In the Fifth Meditation, Descartes takes for granted the axiom that truth is the conformity of thought with its object and then applies it straightaway. He begins the Meditation with a discussion of geometrical properties and argues that his clear and distinct perceptions of these properties guarantee that they are something. That is to say, he concludes that his clear and distinct ideas of the properties are true and hence conform to some reality. He writes,

> I find within me countless ideas of things which even though they may not exist anywhere outside me still cannot be called nothing; ...but have their own true and immutable natures. ...This is clear from the fact that various properties can be demonstrated of the triangle, for example that its three angles equal two right angles, that its greatest side subtends its greatest angle, and the like...All these properties are certainly true, since I am clearly aware of them, and therefore they are something.
> (AT 7:64–65, CSM 2:44–45)

Here Descartes reports that geometrical properties "cannot be called nothing," and that "they are something." He does not conclude that they exist as properties of actually-existing bodies: he does not yet know if any bodies actually exist, and for all he knows his clear and distinct ideas of geometrical properties conform to reality that is more perfect and whose "greatness is such that it can fill the role" (AT 7:161, CSM 2:114) of actually-existing properties of bodies.[7] As he had said in the March 1642 letter to Mersenne, the entities of which we have clear and distinct ideas might exist, but for all we

---

triangle. But that cannot be right, as Descartes is clear that the Fifth Meditation (and Principles I.14–16) argument is freestanding and establishes the existence of God for minds that did not follow the arguments of Meditation Three.

7 See Chapter 3 above, pp. 90–92.

know our clear and distinct idea of an entity might instead conform to reality that is more noble or exalted.[8] A clear and distinct idea guarantees the existence of an existent to which it conforms – a true and immutable nature (AT 7:64, CSM 2:44) – even if that clear and distinct idea does not tell us the ontology of that existent right away.

The clear and distinct perception of a truth about a geometrical property is a recognition of a truth. It is a recognition of a truth, and like any truth it has a conformable or truthmaker. Descartes takes this to be obvious. He continues,

> All these properties are certainly true, since I am clearly aware of them. And therefore they are something, and not merely nothing; for it is *obvious* that whatever is true is something....
>
> (AT 7:65, CSM 2:45, emphasis added)

There is such a thing as a true idea, Descartes supposes, and there is also such a thing as a true entity – which is the object to which a true idea conforms. As he says to Mersenne, truth is the conformity of thought with its object, but "when it is attributed to things outside of thought, it means only that they can be the objects of true thoughts, either ours or God's."[9] In the Fifth Meditation, Descartes turns to his idea of God and seeks to uncover the true entity that is its truthmaker. One of the truths that the idea delivers is that God is a supremely perfect being that has eternal and necessary existence. Descartes writes,

> Certainly, the idea of God, or a supremely perfect being, is one which I find within me just as surely as the idea of any shape or number. And my understanding that it belongs to his nature that he always exists is no less clear and distinct than is the case when I prove of any shape or number that some property belongs to its nature.
>
> (AT 7:65, CSM 2:45)

---

8 "To Mersenne, March 1642," AT 3:544–545, CSMK 211.
9 "To Mersenne, 16 October 1639," AT 2:597, CSMK 139. See also "To Clerselier, 23 April 1649," in which Descartes identifies truth and being (AT 5:356, CSMK 377).

The true and immutable nature of an entity is the something whose existence is guaranteed by a clear and distinct idea of the entity, even if we do not know the ontology of that something straightaway. Descartes says that it belongs to the nature of God that He always exists. He adds that "it is necessary that he [God] has existed from eternity and will abide for eternity" (AT 7:68, CSM 2:47). He is specifying that there is a particular kind of existence that pertains to God – what he calls *necessary existence*. He is not making the epistemic claim that the concept of God includes existence and therefore that God necessarily exists; he is saying that the concept of God includes necessary existence, or the kind of existence that is had by a being that exists through its own power.[10] He elaborates in *First Replies*:

> when I examine the idea of a body, I perceive that a body has no power to create itself or maintain itself in existence, and I rightly conclude that necessary existence – and it is only necessary existence that is at issue here – [does not] belong to the nature of a body. ...But instead of a body, let us now take a thing – whatever this thing turns out to be – which possesses all the perfections which can exist together. ...[W]hen we think of the immense power of this being, we shall be unable to think of its existence as possible without also recognizing that it can exist by its own power.
>
> (AT 7:118–119, CSM 2: 84–85)

Here Descartes is positing – and in the Fifth Meditation he took himself to be positing – that it is a truth that a supremely perfect being is ontologically independent and exists by its own power. But he also has in hand the axiom that truth is the conformity of thought with reality, and so he infers the existence of a true entity or being – the true and immutable nature of God. He then enquires into the ontology of that entity – an entity to which necessary existence and the other divine perfections[11] are attributable, whatever the entity

---

10 See also Nelson and Cunning (1999), 141–143, Cunning (2010), 164–168, and Wee (2012), 33–34.

11 Again Descartes argues in the Third Meditation that the divine attributes are interconnected and inseparable (AT 7:50, CSM 2:34). See also Nolan (2005) and Vadana (2017).

turns out to be. As we might expect, he supposes that it is obvious that it is God. It is not something that has necessary existence and the other perfections only *eminently*: it is not an entity more exalted than God whose "greatness is such that it can fill the role" of the conformable of our clear and distinct ideas of the divine perfections. Ideas of these conform to God and God alone.

Descartes took himself to be arguing along exactly these lines in the Fifth Meditation, even if the text of the Fifth Meditation might have been clearer. He says in his *First Replies* gloss on the Fifth Meditation discussion that

> .... we shall infer from this that this being really does exist and has existed from eternity, since it is quite evident by the natural light that what can exist by its own power always exists.
>
> (AT 7:119, CSM 2:85)

The conformable of a clear and distinct idea of a being that has the perfection of necessary existence is an existent that exists by its own power. An entity does not have one divine perfection unless it has them all, Descartes supposes, and so the existent has the other divine attributes as well:

> We shall also easily perceive that this supremely powerful being cannot but possess within it all the other perfections that are contained in the idea of God; and hence that these perfections exist in God... by their very nature.
>
> (ibid.)

It may not be obvious to a contemporary reader that a being with necessary existence exists by its own power, or that a being that exists by its own power is omnipotent, or that a being that is omnipotent has every divine attribute, but all three are obvious to Descartes and obvious to the degree that he does not make explicit all of the steps of his reasoning in the text of the Fifth Meditation itself. He does say (in "Synopsis of the following six Meditations") that in the Fifth Meditation, he is offering "a new argument demonstrating the existence of God," and that "several difficulties may arise here, but these are resolved later in the Replies to the Objections"

(AT 7:15, CSM 2:11). Perhaps he should have just re-written the Fifth Meditation to include the additional material that comes later, but he also saw the compilation of the *Meditations* and the objections and replies as a larger philosophical production to be read in its entirety.[12] He makes clear in *First Replies* that in the Fifth Meditation, he is arguing that "That which we clearly and distinctly understand to be belong to the true and immutable nature, or essence, or form of something, can truly be asserted of that thing" (AT 7:115–116, CSM 2:83). But we clearly and distinctly understand necessary existence to belong to the entity whose existence is guaranteed by a clear and distinct idea of God, and the only entity that has necessary existence (and all of the other supreme perfections) is the divine being Itself. That is the only entity that is the conformable of a true idea of God.

Descartes accordingly holds that the true and immutable nature of God and God are one and the same. And that is just what he indicates in *Principles* I.15: "the idea of a supremely perfect being… represents a true and immutable nature which cannot but exist" (AT 8A:10, CSM 1:198).[13] He also reveals that the true and immutable nature (or essence) of God is God in his discussion of the conceptual distinction between a substance and its attributes in the letter "To ***, 1645 or 1646." There he says that in an existing substance, the essence of the substance is "nothing other than" the substance itself (AT 4:350, CSMK 281).[14] He does allow that there is another sense

---

12 He also says that "those who study my arguments for the existence of God will find them more cogent the more they try to fault them" ("To Mersenne, 27 February 1637," AT 1:350, CSMK 53). He appears to hold that the objections and replies are an absolutely critical part of the text of the *Meditations* itself.

13 Descartes does not say in this passage that our idea of God represents a *being* that cannot but exist. He says more specifically that our idea of God represents a *true and immutable nature* that cannot but exist.

14 See also Chapter 3 above, pp. 97–103. I argue there that Descartes does not make entirely clear whether or not the conceptual distinction between a substance and its nature amounts to their inseparability in *re* or their identity in *re*, but in either case he is talking about a substance and its attributes as they exist in *re*.

in which we speak of the essence or nature of an entity – insofar as the entity exists in our thought. He says for example that

> the idea of the sun is the sun itself existing in the intellect by means of an idea – not of course formally existing, as it does in the heavens, but objectively existing, i.e. in the way in which objects are normally in the intellect. Now this mode of being is of course much less perfect than that possessed by things which exist outside the intellect....[15]

God exists in finite thought, for Descartes, but the Fifth Meditation is working to establish the existence of God in reality.[16] It works to establish the existence of the true and immutable nature of God – that is to say, the existence of God in *re* – and not just the "less perfect" version of God that exists as the content of an idea.[17]

---

15 First Replies, AT 7: 102–103, CSM 2:75. For a further discussion of Descartes on objective being (in the intellect) versus formal being, see Clemenson (2007), 47–56.

16 Again, Descartes is writing to a variety of minds in the *Meditations*, and the Fifth Meditation argument is offered in part to establish the existence of God for a mind that has failed to understand fully the argumentation of Meditation Three.

17 A question might still arise about other true and immutable natures – in particular, the natures of entities that do not in fact exist. However, Descartes does not include any such true and immutable natures in his system. He posits the nature of God, the nature of body (and the geometrical modifications that are had by body), and also the nature of mind. He holds that body and mind exist, and he holds that in the case of a thing that exists, the essence of the thing is "nothing other than the thing." In the Fifth Meditation he posits the true and immutable natures of geometrical properties, and later in the Sixth Meditation he concludes that bodies exist and "possess all the properties which... are comprised within the subject-matter of pure mathematics" (AT 7:80, CSM 2:55). It should also be noted that there is just a small number of passages in which Descartes speaks of true and immutable natures at all. Apart from the Fifth Meditation, there are only quick references in *Principles* I.13–16, AT 8A:9–11, CSM 1:197–198), "To [Mersenne], 27 May 1630," AT 1:152, CSMK 25; "To Mersenne, 16 June 1641," AT 3:382–383, CSMK 183–184; First Replies, AT 7:115–116, CSM 2:82–83; Fifth Replies, AT 7:380–381, CSM 2:261–262, and *Conversation with Burman*, AT 5:160, CSMK 343. In these Descartes does not posit any true and immutable natures apart from the nature of God, the nature of body (and its geometrical properties), and the nature of mind. He also says in "To Princess Elizabeth, 21 May

Descartes is not doing anything particularly odd or unusual when he posits that truth is the conformity of thought with reality.[18] We find the same notion of truth in other figures of the period, most explicitly in Spinoza: "A true idea must agree with that of which it is the idea."[19] Indeed, it would be difficult to make sense of much of the period if we did not assume that all of its philosophers embraced at least something like that notion. They are attempting to get at how things are, but if so they at some point would need to supply a bridge between the true claims at which they (take themselves to) arrive and the reality in virtue of which those claims are true. In the case of the Fifth Meditation, Descartes advances the claim that the three angles of a triangle equal two right angles and the claim that the greatest side of a triangle subtends its greatest angle. If these claims are true, he is supposing, there is some reality to which they conform. That is to say, true claims about the properties of a triangle have a truthmaker. He next considers a number of truths about God – truths that he clearly and distinctly recognizes and whose truthmaker he takes to be immediately identifiable. We might disagree with Descartes about whether or not we have a true idea of God in the sense that he has in mind, or we might disagree with him about whether or not that idea must have God for its truthmaker. If so, we have isolated some instances of genuine, and perhaps very deep, philosophical disagreement. But more can be said to motivate Descartes' thinking further. He does not incorporate the substantive elaboration of *First Replies* into the text of the Fifth Meditation itself, but the Fifth Meditation does contain hints of that elaboration. It is still longer than the text of *Principles* I.13–16 – which Descartes seemed to think was sufficient, at least for some – and it helps to make clear why he would hold that the truthmaker for truths about

---

1643" that (apart from our idea of God) there are three "primitive notions… [that] are as it were the patterns on the basis of which we form all our other conceptions." (AT 3:665, CSMK 218–219) – the "the notions we have of the soul, of body, and of the union between the soul and the body" ("To Princess Elizabeth, 28 June 1643," AT 3:691, CSMK 226). We do not have ideas of natures other than these.

18 Again see Thomasson (2021).

19 Spinoza (1677), Part I, axiom 6.

God is not finite thinking, or the material universe, or a dressing gown or fire.

In the Fifth Meditation, Descartes addresses the possibility that our idea of God is invented. If it *were* invented, it could be true that God is a supremely perfect being – just like it is true that a unicorn has a horn, or that a harpy is not a centaur[20] – but we would not be entitled to conclude that God in fact exists. Descartes says very early in the Fifth Meditation that he "find[s] within [him]self countless ideas of things which... are not my invention but have their own true and immutable natures." He repeats the point later in the Fifth Meditation, a reflection of its import:

> There are many ways in which I understand that this idea [of God] is not something fictitious which is dependent on my thought, but is an image of a true and immutable nature.
>
> (AT 7:68, CSM 2:47)

We might construct ideas of things like hippogriffs or unicorns or chimeras, but the truths that we derive from such ideas do not entail the existence of any of those entities. If our ideas of chimeras were tethered to reality in a way that put constraints on our construction of them, things would be very different. But as Descartes puts it in *Principles* I.16, "we are in the habit of making up at will ideas of things that do not exist anywhere and have never done so" (AT 8A:10–11, CSM 1:198). Perhaps some of our invented ideas conform to reality, but if by hypothesis our assembly of them is not sensitive to the order in which things are *arranged* in reality, there is no guarantee. Descartes is then supposing that our idea of God and our ideas of geometrical properties are very different from invented ideas. For example, it is not up to us whether or not to attach to the idea of a three-sided figure that its (three) angles add to something other than two right angles:

> whenever I do wish to consider a rectilinear figure having just three sides, it is necessary that I attribute to it the properties

---

20 To use an example from Locke (1689), IV.iv.1, 563.

which license the inference that its three angles equal no more
than two right angles.

(AT 7:67–68, CSM 2:47)

In the case of triangles, and Descartes is supposing in the case of
God, reality puts constraints on what we can truly assert about it. He
accordingly says that it is not his thought that imposes any necessity on the way that things are, but it is the way that things are that
imposes necessity on his thought. He writes,

> It is not that my thought makes it so, or imposes any necessity on
> any thing; on the contrary, it is the necessity of the thing itself,
> namely the existence of God, which determines my thinking in
> this respect.
>
> (AT 7:67, CSM 2:46)

Descartes holds that we are latching on to an existent when we have
a true idea of God. That existent then puts constraints on the true
beliefs that we can have about it. An invented idea is different, and
we are able to tell that an idea has been invented when we are able to
break it back down into the separate elements that make it up.[21] We
are not able to do that in the case of an idea of a true and immutable
nature:

> I am not free to think of God without [necessary] existence
> (that is, a supremely perfect being without a supreme perfec-
> tion) as I am free to imagine a horse with or without wings.[22]

Truths that are invented carry no guarantee that they conform to an
existent. Truths about geometrical properties and God are different.

A lot of course rides on whether or not Descartes is correct about
what we have in mind when we are thinking of a supremely perfect
being. An opponent might argue that any idea that we report to be

---

21 The discussion in Smith (2002) is very helpful here.
22 AT 7:67, CSM 2:46. See also the corresponding back and forth between
   Gassendi and Descartes – in Gassendi (1641), 225–226, and Fifth Replies, AT
   7:382–84, CSM 2:262–263.

of God would likely fall short of representing a supreme being. For example,

> we have no basis for claiming that we have any authentic idea which represents God; and it is more than enough if, on the analogy of our human attributes, we can derive and construct an idea of some sort for our own use – an idea which does not transcend our human grasp and which contains no reality except what we perceive in other things or as a result of encountering other things.[23]

If Descartes is mistaken about the content of our idea of God – and it does not effectively capture the infinitude and ontological independence of a supremely perfect being – then even if our idea of God has a conformable, it would not be the supremely perfect necessary existent that Descartes assumes that it is. But Descartes of course recognizes that in many cases the idea that is before a person's mind when they report to be thinking of God is not the idea that he is specifying in the Fifth (or the Third) Meditation. Instead, we might just be imagining an enormous bearded man on a cloud, or we might be thinking the linguistic squiggle *Deus*.[24] None of these ideas would be a conception of God, Descartes is supposing, and it would not deliver us any truths from which we could infer the existence of a truthmaker that is a supremely perfect necessary existent. Some of us might have a confused and imagistic idea that is not of God but of "God." Descartes is arguing that in addition to that we have a very different idea – an idea that represents God and nothing less. At a minimum, we all want to say that we have *beliefs* about God – for example that He exists, or that He does not.[25] Descartes is then arguing that it turns out that the only way that we can have beliefs about God is if we have an (un-invented) idea of God that yields the

---

23 Gassendi (1641), 201.

24 See for example *Fifth Replies*, AT 7:365, CSM 2:252 and AT 7:385, CSM 2:264; and "To Mersenne, 6 May 1630;" AT 1:150, CSMK 24–25.

25 *Appendix to Fifth Objections and Replies*, AT 9A:209–210, CSM 2:273.

truth that God is a supremely perfect necessary existent. That truth conforms to an existent, which is God Itself.[26]

The second and third arguments

The Fifth Meditation argument for the existence of God does not include as a premise the Third Meditation conclusion that God

26 Note that here I am disagreeing with Nolan (1997), Vinci (1998), Schmaltz (1991), and Kenny (1968, 1970). Nolan argues that the true and immutable nature of God is the idea of God considered with respect to its objective reality. If Nolan is right, the Fifth Meditation tells us that there exists a modification of mind – the essence of God in thought. However, it is not clear how we are supposed to get from the existence of that sort of essence – whose "mode of being is of course much less perfect than that possessed by things which exist outside the intellect..." (*First Replies*, AT 7:103, CSM 2:75) – to the existence of God in *re*. The same worry arises for the view in Vinci (1998) that Cartesian true and immutable natures reside in finite minds but not as modifications of mind (64–69). Schmaltz (1991) argues that the true and immutable nature of God is to be identified with God, and more specifically with divine decrees. Schmaltz argues that *all* true and immutable natures are to be identified with God, but Descartes makes clear that (for example) the nature of thinking substance is nothing other than thinking substance and that the nature of extended substance is nothing other than extended substance (*Principles* I.63, AT 8A:30–31, CSM 1:215). Kenny argues that the essence of a thing is a third-realm Platonic entity – it is "an eternal creature of God, with its own immutable nature and properties, a real thing lacking only the perfection of actual existence" (697). (See also See Kenny (1968), 150–156, and Kenny (1970), 692–693.) But Descartes holds that the nature of God is nothing other than the divine being Itself. For a further discussion of the views of Nolan, Schmaltz, and Kenny, see Cunning (2003a), 236–239. De Rosa (2011) rehearses the problems with the interpretations of Cartesian true and immutable natures in the work of Kenny, Schmaltz, and Nolan and argues that a fourth alternative needs to be developed. She proposes two possibilities – an adverbial reading according to which true and immutable natures are ways in which God's mind is modified, and a reading according to which they exist in God's mind eminently (620–621). De Rosa does not consider the possibility that true and immutable natures are the non-conceptualist kind of essence that Descartes posits – the kind of essence that in *re* is nothing other than the thing that has it. Descartes posits only two kinds of nature, and if a true and immutable nature is not a nature of the conceptualist variety, then it is the nature of a thing as it exists in *re*.

exists, but it does benefit from the attention to ideas that is the focus of the Third Meditation. The argument from the true and immutable nature of God is a free-standing argument that does not employ the premises of any prior Meditations. However, prior Meditations are still relevant, and for most minds they are critical. For example, one of the aims of the Third Meditation is to unpack the content of a clear and distinct idea of God, and the Fifth Meditation argument (for the existence of God) requires that we have that idea.[27] We turn now to the two arguments for the existence of God in the Third Meditation itself.

Descartes begins his Third Meditation argumentation for the existence of God by noticing (or more accurately by positing) that ideas differ in terms of their content, even if they all have the same status as modifications of mind. He writes that

> In so far as the ideas are simply modes of thought, there is no recognizable inequality among them: they all appear to come from within me in the same fashion. But in so far as different ideas represent things, it is clear that they differ widely.
>
> (AT 7:40, CSM 2:27–28)

Part of what Descartes is saying here seems totally obvious, at least if we find plausible his substance-mode ontology and his view that introspection is a route to the content of ideas. In the Third Meditation, he does not yet have many leads on what in fact exists, but he supposes that the kinds of things that exist (if things do exist) are substances and their modifications. The ideas that we have are modifications – and thus are modifications of substances – and insofar as ideas are of things they are either of substances or modifications. Ideas are modifications one and all, but ideas of substances and ideas of modifications are different in terms of their objects, or as Descartes puts it they are different in terms of their objective reality. We notice this, Descartes assumes, now that we have taken the introspective turn and we view our ideas in a way that we perhaps had never done before. We notice that ideas do not have a different amount of reality in virtue of their status as ideas, but they do have a different amount

---

27 See also Nolan (2005a) and (2014), and Wee (2012), 29–34.

of reality in virtue of their content. That content is something that is mental and introspectable – otherwise there is no way that we could be so confident about it at this point in the *Meditations*[28] – and it is obvious that we are confronting *more* of it in the case of an idea of a substance than in the case of an idea of a mode. Descartes is not expecting that his mere assertion that ideas differ in objective reality will get us to register that they differ with respect to their objective reality; he is once again employing a method of discovery by which we will hopefully see that for ourselves.

We have ideas of substances, Descartes supposes, and in particular we have an idea of an infinite substance. Prior to the Third Meditation, we do not know that any such substance exists, and we do not yet fully register the idea that we have of it, but the discussion of wax at the end of the Second Meditation gets us pretty close. If Descartes is right, that discussion helps us to appreciate that we have an idea whose content far outstrips the pictures of the imagination. In the Second Meditation, we do not yet establish that material things exist and are real. However, as embodied minds in the course of a disciplined meditation we are practically bursting at the seams to affirm that they are real, and the wax discussion helps us to register that if we are right, they include aspects that are insensible and that nonetheless have a considerable amount of being (AT 7:31). We are then ready to take seriously the Third Meditation proposition that we have an idea of an entity that is insensible and has an infinite amount of being. We do not yet know that that entity exists, but we do have an idea of it:

> the idea that gives me my understanding of a supreme God, eternal, infinite, <immutable>, omniscient, omnipotent, and the creator of all things apart from him, certainly has in it more objective reality than the ideas that represent finite substances.
>
> (AT 7:40, CSM 2:28)

---

28 Descartes does not rule out that there is another kind of content that is not introspectable, but in the Third Meditation we have no awareness of any such content, he supposes, and so that is not what he is positing. Objective reality is just the introspectable content of which we are aware, and that is what he is prepared to admit into existence. But see Schmitter (2014) for an exploration of the prospect that Descartes is flirting with an externalist view of content in the Third Meditation.

That is to say, we not only have ideas of finite substances and ideas of modifications of finite substances, but also an idea of an infinite substance. We notice by introspection that these three different kinds of idea have different degrees of objective reality. Descartes is now a short step from the conclusion that God exists in fact.

The next step of the argument for that conclusion is the axiom that something cannot come from nothing. Immediately after pointing out that ideas differ in terms of their objective reality, Descartes writes:

> Now it is manifest by the natural light that there must be at least as much reality in the efficient and total cause as in the effect of that cause.
>
> (AT 7:40, CSM 2:28)

He adds in his *Second Replies* elaboration of the Third Meditation argument that the principle that there must be at least as much reality in a cause as in its effect "is just same as the primary notion 'Nothing comes from nothing'."[29] We might worry straightaway that the two do not appear to be the same and that although the latter might seem to be manifest, the former is not manifest at all. We might worry that even further removed is the Third Meditation claim that "in order for a given idea to contain such and such objective reality, it must surely derive it from some cause which contains at least much formal reality as there is objective reality in the idea" (AT 7:41, CSM 2:28–29). Some commentators have argued that it is a stretch for Descartes to suppose that that claim is obvious and that it is a stretch to think that any of his readers would find it to be obvious.[30] Other commentators have worked to locate versions of the claim in nearby contemporaries, as a way of making sense of why Descartes would think that a reader of the *Meditations* (or at least some readers of the *Meditations*) might take it to be compelling.[31] Even if the latter commentators are correct, the problem still remains that

---

29 AT 7:135, CSM 2:97. See also *First Replies*, AT 7:103–105, CSM 2:75–76. See also Nolan (2014), 132.

30 For example Loeb (1986).

31 For example Schmaltz (2007), Chapter 2; and Nolan (2014), 135–140.

Descartes is guiding us through a process in which we are to see for ourselves the obvious truth of the results that he is advancing, but the Third Meditation causal principle is not obvious at all. He does do an admirable job of exhibiting the distinction between objective reality and formal reality: the first is the kind of reality had by the introspectable content of ideas; the second is the kind of reality had by ideas as modifications of mind and by the things to which those ideas conform (if in fact they exist). He does not give technical definitions of these, for reasons that we have already considered (AT 7:155–159, CSM 2:110–112), but instead he provides vivid illustrations and examples of familiarities like stones and heat, and ideas of stones and heat (AT 7:41–44, CSM 2: 28–30). These are welcome.[32] But he does not go to the same lengths to exhibit the obvious truth of the principle that the objective reality of an idea requires a cause that has at least as much formal reality as the idea has objective reality.

Perhaps. Another interpretive option however is that he did not put things as clearly as he might have. In the Third Mediation, Descartes has yielded very few results about what actually exists, and he is supposing that if *anything* exists, it is either a finite substance, a finite modification, or an infinite substance. He is then supposing that ideas exist and that any idea would be of one of the three categories of being – finite substance, finite modification, and infinite substance. If so, then he is correct to say that, as applied to the objective reality of ideas, the axiom that something cannot come from nothing is the principle that the objective reality of an idea requires a cause that has at least as much formal reality as the idea has objective reality. The objective reality of an idea is something, he supposes, and so it cannot come from nothing. It must be caused by something, and by something that has formal reality:

> just as the objective mode of being belongs to ideas by their very nature, so the formal mode of being belongs to the causes of ideas... by their very nature.
>
> (AT 7:42, CSM 2:29)

---

32 See also *Second Replies*, AT 7:164, CSM 2:116; and Nolan (2014), 138–139.

If so, the objective reality of the idea of a modification requires a cause that has at least the formal reality of a modification. Of course it does. A cause that brings about the content of an idea of a modification is either a modification or a substance, but if it is either of those, it has at least the reality of a modification. The same consideration applies in the case of the cause of the objective reality of an idea of a substance. If the objective reality of the idea of a substance is a modification, the larger cause of that objective reality is never a modification alone but also the substance that it modifies.

With the principle in hand that something cannot come from nothing, Descartes is a short step from the conclusion that God exists. If his idea of God has an amount of content that cannot be produced by a finite substance, then there exists something other than a finite substance. Otherwise there would be some element of that content that would have had to have come from nothing:

> if we suppose that an idea contains something which was not in its cause, it must have got this from nothing: yet the mode of being by which a thing exists objectively <or representatively> in the intellect by way of an idea, imperfect though it may be, is certainly not nothing, and so it cannot come from nothing.[33]

He is now in a position to argue that our idea of God has so much content that it would have an uncaused remainder if it were produced by a finite substance. Finite substances only have the wherewithal and power to produce finite effects, Descartes supposes, but our idea of God has so much content that it could only be produced by a being with infinite power.[34] On the assumption that the divine attributes (including omnipotence) are conceptually interlocked,[35] that being is God Itself.

Descartes takes objective reality to have at least some being. However, ontologically thin it might be, it is being, and it requires a cause that is sufficient to bring about any and all of its manifestations.

---

33 AT 7:41, CSM 2:29. See also *Second Replies*, AT 7:135, CSM 2:97.
34 See also Davidson (2004).
35 AT 7:50, CSM 2:34; also *Second Replies*, AT 7:119, CSM 2:85.

An idea of God manifests an infinite amount of objective reality, Descartes insists, and it would appear to be the best candidate for an entity that forces him to posit the existence of something other than himself. Erring on the side of caution, however, he considers a number of ideas of finite modifications and finite substances and enquires into the cause of their objective reality. After a brief discussion he concludes that, for all he knows, the cause is his thinking mind. For example, his ideas of individual bodies would appear to be ideas of substances, and even if bodies are very different from minds, "they still seem to agree with respect to the classification 'substance'" (AT 7:44, CSM 2:30). If so, a mind might have the wherewithal to generate the objective reality of the idea of a material substance, and it might have the wherewithal to generate the objective reality of the idea of a material mode. Indeed, Descartes highlighted in the First Meditation that in the course of a dream, we often have ideas and perceptions that (as far as we can tell) are not produced by external objects, and so "within me" there may be "a faculty not yet fully known to me, which produces these ideas without any assistance from external things" (AT 7:39, CSM 2:27).[36] The language here is all very tentative, but Descartes is being honest. He does not know for sure the cause of the objective reality of his ideas of finite substances and finite modes, and so he does not say. What he seeks is an idea that has so much objective reality that it requires him to conclude that he is "not alone in the world, but that some other thing which is the cause of this idea also exists" (AT 7:42, CSM 2:29). And what he seeks in particular is an idea whose objective reality is so voluminous that it could only be generated by God Itself.

After running through a cross-section of ideas of finite things, Descartes proceeds to an examination of the idea of God. He supposes that it is an altogether different specimen:

> So there remains only the idea of God; and I must consider whether there is anything in the idea which could not have originated in myself. By the word 'God' I understand a substance

---

36 Or perhaps mind is much more noble than body, and body can be said to exist in mind eminently (AT 7:45, CSM 2:31).

that is infinite, <eternal, immutable,> independent, supremely intelligent.... All these attributes are such that, the more carefully I concentrate on them, the less possible it seems that they could have originated from me alone. So from what has been said it must be concluded that God necessarily exists.

(AT 7:45, CSM 2:31)

That's it. That's the argument. The rest of the Third Meditation is dedicated to responding to objections to the argument, in ways that fill in some of its background assumptions. The argument is that every creature requires a sufficient cause for its existence,[37] that the idea of God is a creature, and that the only entity that has the where-withal to produce the objective reality that is contained in that idea is a being with infinite power – a being that thereby possesses all of the other divine attributes as well.

Descartes moves straightaway to potential objections to the argument and uses them as an occasion to flesh out his reasoning in more detail. The first objection that he considers is that the objective reality of the idea of God does not require the existence of a divine being for its cause because it might have a lot less content than Descartes has said it does. We speak of our idea of God as an idea of an infinite being, but perhaps our idea of infinitude is just

---

37 Note that I am disagreeing with Nolan (2014); he argues that in the argument from objective reality Descartes appeals to the principle that every effect has a cause, and not the principle that every effect has a sufficient cause (132). I do not see how that can be right, as the only reason that Descartes ends up positing the existence of God (in the Third Meditation) is that there is no cause other than God that has enough power to produce the amount of objective reality that is in the idea of God. Nolan does not state his explicit reason for thinking that Descartes subscribes to the weaker principle, but he does suggest that for Descartes the principle of sufficient reason does not apply to God and so is not a truth in Descartes' system (144). I offer a very different reading of Descartes on divine voluntarism at the end of the current chapter. I think that another reason why Nolan is happy to attribute a weaker version of the causal principle to Descartes is that he (Nolan) holds that the Fifth Meditation argumentation for the existence of God is much stronger and that the Third Meditation argumentation is largely preparatory. See also note 58 of Chapter 4.

a composite idea that is within our range to construct. Descartes replies to the objection:

> I must not think that, just as my conceptions of rest and darkness are arrived at by negating movement and light, so my perception of the infinite is arrived at not by means of a true idea but merely by negating the finite.
>
> (AT 7:45, CSM 2:31)

The objection is that perhaps an idea of the infinite is just a composite of an idea of finitude and an idea of negation. Descartes turns the objection on its head and argues that our idea of infinitude "is in some way prior to [the] perception of the finite" (AT 7:45–46, CSM 2:31). He elaborates (a bit) in other texts:

> I say that the notion that I have of the infinite is in me before that of the finite because, by the mere fact that I conceive being, or that which is, without thinking whether it is finite or infinite, what I conceive is infinite being; but in order to conceive a finite being, I have to take away something from this general notion of being, which must accordingly be there first.[38]

In the Third Meditation and elsewhere, Descartes takes it to be obvious that the idea of finitude is a delimitation of the idea of infinitude and thus that the idea of the infinite is prior to the idea of the finite.[39] In the Third Meditation, he also attempts to illustrate the view with an example: he says that the only reason that a finite mind is able to tell that its knowledge is lacking is that it has a sense of the infinite knowledge of which it falls short. That example is not particularly helpful, however, as we can easily develop an awareness of our cognitive shortcomings just from a confrontation with our everyday failures to anticipate and plan. Descartes appears to be resting his case more heavily on the assumption that the idea of the infinitude of God

---

38 "To Clerselier, 23 April 1649," AT 5:356, CSMK 377.
39 See "To [Silhon], May 1637," AT 1:353, CSMK 55. See also Nolan and Nelson (2006), 105–112, and Schechtman (2014).

is "positive in the highest degree" (*First Replies*, AT 7:113, CSM 2:81)
and that "whatever I clearly and distinctly perceive as being real and
true, and implying any perfection, is wholly contained in it" (AT
7:46, CSM 2:32).[40] Or, with an eye to the first-person structure of
the *Meditations*, Descartes appears to be resting his case on our noticing
that the idea of God has the positive content that Descartes describes
it to have. The idea of God is not an idea of finitude and negation, and
it is not an idea that merely tells us the features that its object lacks.
The idea contains an amount of objective reality that mirrors the
amount of formal reality that God would have if God in fact existed.

Descartes expects that we are going to be very reluctant to let
go of the thought that our idea of God is just a negation of an idea
of something finite. Immediately after dismissing the objection that
our idea of infinitude might be a negation of our idea of finitude, he
addresses the almost identical objection that our idea of God might
exhibit "material falsity, which occurs in ideas, when they represent
non-things as things" (AT 7:43, CSM 2:30). He considers for
example the view that an idea of cold is just an idea of the absence
of heat – an idea that reports that cold is a thing when instead it is
the absence of a thing – and he asks whether or not our idea of God
might be the idea of an absence as well. He does not say definitively
that an idea of cold is an idea of the absence of heat. Instead, the
discussion is hypothetical.[41] He writes,

> if it is true that cold is nothing but the absence of heat, the idea
> which represents it to me as something real and positive deserves
> to be called false, and the same goes for other ideas of this kind.
> (AT 7:44, CSM 2:30)

If cold is just the absence of heat, and if it is not uncommon for us to
have ideas that are of absences, we would need to be careful in concluding that the idea of God requires an infinitely powerful being

---

40 See also Vilmer (2009). Descartes might appear to come across as dogmatic
here, but if we think that we have an idea of *infinitude* – and that it would not be
an idea of infinitude if it was just a combination of two ideas that have a very
finite amount of content – then his reasoning is quite intuitive.

41 See also Nelson (1996).

for its cause. Perhaps the idea of God is just an idea of the absence of finitude – in something like the way that an idea of infinitude might be the idea of the negation of the finite – and if so its cause might be quite mundane. Descartes spends very little time on the discussion of material falsity in the Third Meditation – just a few sentences – and he quickly dismisses the objection that the idea of God might be the idea of a lack. He says that the idea

> is utterly clear and distinct, and contains in itself more objective reality than any idea; hence there is no idea which is in itself truer or less liable to be suspected of falsehood.
>
> (AT 7:46, CSM 2:31)

Descartes appears to suppose that if we have meditated properly, we will notice (from the first-person point-of-view) that our idea of God has the positive content that he says it does. We will notice that content through a direct confrontation with the idea. And to Descartes' credit, it is not clear how else he could proceed here. He will not just ask us to take his word for it that the idea of God has an infinite amount of content; in that case, we would be behaving more like automata than women or men. Nor will he cite philosophers of the past or other authorities. He cites what he expects will be our first-person experience.[42]

---

42 There is an enormous literature on what Descartes means to say that an idea is materially false. I agree with Nelson (1996) that a materially false idea of X is a confused composite of an idea of X and an idea of B – a composite idea which predicates B of X even though B does not pertain to X. Descartes says in Fourth *Replies* that a materially false idea of cold as the absence of heat is a composite that includes the idea of the sensation of cold as one of its components. He writes,

> it often happens in the case of obscure and confused ideas - and the ideas of heat and cold fall into this category - that an idea is referred to something other than that of which it is in fact the idea. ...[But] this does have something positive as its underlying subject, namely the actual sensation involved.
>
> (AT 7:233–234, CSM 2:163–164)

That has to be the right, Descartes supposes: an idea would not misrepresent X if it was just an idea of B (or C); it wouldn't be an idea of X at all. A materially false idea of cold is an idea of cold - it is a composite of an idea of the sensation of cold and ideas of features that do not pertain to that sensation. That is why it is

Descartes considers an additional objection before moving onto the second argument for the existence of God in the Third Meditation. He notes that even if we concede that our idea of God has an infinite amount of objective reality, the cause of that objective reality need not be God: perhaps a finite mind participates in divinity in a way that it does not fully appreciate, and it has the ability to produce an infinite effect. Descartes writes,

> But perhaps I am something greater than I myself understand, and all the perfections which I attribute to God are somehow in me potentially, though not yet emerging or actualized.
>
> (AT 7:46–47, CSM 2:32)

The initial reply that Descartes offers to the objection is that the idea of God informs us that in God there is "absolutely nothing that is potential" (AT 7:47, CSM 2:32). This reply does not help much, if the objection is that in a finite mind (like that of Descartes), there is

---

so important to analyze our ideas into their component (and clear and distinct) elements. (See also Chapter 3 above, pp. 77–78, and Chapter 4, pp. 112–115.) For three accounts of Cartesian material falsity that are diametrically opposed to my own – in that they take sensations to be materially false ideas, and ideas that are intrinsically confused – see Wilson (1978), 111–115, Bolton (1986), and De Rosa (2004). I am arguing that Descartes holds that we have ideas of sensations, but that sensations are not ideas themselves. In the Descartes literature there is a long history of speaking of sensations as ideas – and more specifically as "sensory ideas." However there is just one passage in his corpus in which he refers to the "sensation or idea of heat" (the Third Meditation, (AT 7:38, CSM 2:26), and in that passage he is using the blanket term *idea* or *thought* in the course of "classify[ing] my [introspectable] thoughts into definite kinds" (AT 7:36–37, CSM 2:25). In the same discussion he uses the term 'idea' to pick out volitions, but those are not ideas (in the sense of being entities with objective reality) either. In the remaining fifty-plus passages in which he speaks of color and the like, he identifies them as *sensations*. Note finally that Descartes says in *Fourth Replies* that strictly speaking *any* composite idea is materially false if it provides subject-matter for error by attributing to a thing a feature that does not pertain to it (AT 7:233, CSM 2:163). A materially false idea of cold is just one of many examples. But another example is a confused idea of mind that has become so tightly associated with ideas of sensible bodies that a consideration of that larger idea entails that mind are material (like wind or fire).

potential being that might have the wherewithal to serve as the cause of the objective reality of the idea of God. Just because God contains nothing that is potential, that by itself does not mean that a finite mind does not contain a lot of potentiality or that it does not contain a kind of potentiality that might produce an idea of God. Descartes does not say a lot more to dislodge the objection that perhaps he has enough potential being to be the cause of the objective reality of the idea of God. Perhaps, he is thinking that the cause of the objective reality of the idea of God has to have infinite power actually – and not just potentially – and that a being with actual infinite power cannot have any of the other divine attributes just potentially. A being with actual infinite power is also omniscient and eternal for example and is God Itself.

Descartes supplies a second argument for the existence of God at the end of the Third Meditation. The argument from objective reality had built on the datum that there exists an idea of God; the second argument builds on the datum that there exists an idea of God and also a finite mind that possesses that idea. Descartes sees the two arguments as different versions of the same:

> my purpose here was not to produce a different proof from the preceding one, but rather to take the same proof and provide a more thorough explanation of it.[43]

The first argument assumes that there exists an idea with an infinite amount of objective reality and concludes that God must be its cause. The second argument assumes that there exists an idea with an infinite amount of objective reality and then draws the sub-conclusion that there exists a mind that has an idea with an infinite amount of objective reality. The argument concludes that if a mind exists that has that idea, God must be its cause. From 30,000 feet, both arguments are positing that if there exists an idea with an infinite amount of objective reality, then God exists. The objective reality of the idea requires an infinitely powerful cause, as does the mind that has the idea. The cause either owes its existence to itself,

---

43 First Replies, AT 7:106, CSM 2:77.

in which case it "has the power of existing through its own might" (AT 7:50, CSM 2:34), or it owes its existence to something else that has that power. In either case, there exists a being with infinite power, and a being with infinite power would have the other divine attributes as well.

The first argument for the existence of God – the argument from objective reality – operates at an almost stratospheric level of abstraction, and Descartes anticipates that if we have followed it carefully we will become exhausted. As he did in the middle of the Second Meditation, he acknowledges the difficulty that is associated with abstract thinking, and as he did at the end of the Second Meditation he proceeds with a discussion that gives us a bit more on which to chew. He says that

> If one concentrates carefully, all this [the argument from objective reality] is quite evident by the natural light. But when I relax my concentration, and my mental vision is blinded by the images of things perceived by the senses, it is not so easy for me to remember why the idea of a being more perfect than myself must necessarily proceed from some being which is in reality more perfect. I should therefore like to go further and inquire whether I myself, who have this idea, could exist if no such being existed.
>
> (AT 7:47–48, CSM 2:32–33)

In his second argument for the existence of God, Descartes considers a more substantial and perhaps less ephemeral effect than the objective reality of the idea of God; he argues that if a mind exists that has an idea of God, then God exists as well. The argument is very quick. Descartes first says that his mind either derived its existence from itself or from something else. If it derived its existence from itself, it would have infinite power and would have given itself all the other divine attributes:

> if I had derived my existence from myself, which is a greater achievement, I should certainly not have not denied myself the knowledge in question, which is something much easier to acquire, or indeed any of the attributes which I perceive to be

contained in the idea of God; for none of them seem any harder to achieve.

(AT 7:48, CSM 2:33)

A finite mind that derived its existence from itself would have given itself all of the other divine attributes, but clearly it did not. A finite mind is therefore produced by a different being – one that itself has infinite power. Since a being with infinite power would have all the other divine attributes, God in fact exists.

There is no doubt something odd about the prospect of a mind with infinite power giving itself omniscience and other divine attributes. It would be a being that comes to have divine attributes that it did not have essentially and for eternity, and it would not be God as Descartes understands It. Descartes appreciates though that there is an incoherence to the thought experiment that imagines a being that comes to have a subset of divine attributes. He thinks that the divine attributes are entirely inseparable in such a way God does not come to have any of them. Instead, a being with infinite power has the rest of the divine attributes automatically. Descartes says in Fourth Replies,

The words 'he will give himself all the perfections, if indeed he does not yet have them' are merely explanatory. For the same natural light enables us to perceive that it is impossible for such a being to have the power and will to give itself something new; rather, his essence is such that he possesses from eternity everything which we can now suppose he would bestow upon himself if he did not yet possess it.

(AT 7:241, CSM 2:168)

A being with infinite power has all of the divine attributes already – in light of the conceptual interlocked-ness of the divine attributes – and there is never such a thing as an entity that has infinite power and then develops for example omniscience. Descartes recognizes as much, and his Third Meditation discussion of the prospect of a being (himself) coming to have divine attributes makes no sense. But Descartes makes a lot of claims in the Meditations that make no sense and that by his own lights make no sense. As we have seen, he sometimes undertakes exploratory reasoning that is applicable to the argument or objection at hand, even if in the final analysis that reasoning is deeply confused. If we accept that the existence of our mind (with its idea of God) must have a cause, but object that that cause might just be us, Descartes argues that we would be much more exalted than we are. But we are not.

Descartes considers one final objection to the view that a finite mind (with an idea of God) requires a being with infinite power for its cause. The objection is that perhaps a finite mind is eternal and uncreated and that, if so, it would not require any cause at all. Descartes dismisses this objection quickly. He argues that finite beings are dependent creatures whose existence is in no way guaranteed from moment to moment. He writes,

> I do not escape the force of these arguments by supposing that I have always existed as I do now, as if it followed from this that there was no need to look for any author of my existence. For a lifespan can be divided into countless parts, each completely independent of the others, so that it does not follow from the fact that I existed a little while ago that I must exist now, unless there is some cause which as it were creates me afresh at this moment – that is, which preserves me.
>
> (AT 7:48–49, CSM 2:33)

Descartes supposes that it is obvious that creatures are dependent entities that do not have what he has called necessary existence. He writes in *Second Replies* that

> Possible or contingent existence is contained in the concept of a limited thing, whereas necessary and perfect existence is contained in the concept of a supremely perfect being.
>
> (AT 7:166, CSM 2:117)

A being with contingent existence does not exist unless something else creates it, and that something is not a being that has contingent existence. What Descartes is now adding at the end of the Third Meditation – and what he takes to be obvious – is that a being that has contingent existence as part of its essence in no case comes to have independent existence. Instead, it depends for its existence on another entity from moment to moment, which is to say that it is preserved in existence. Descartes then supposes that it is obvious that the power by which a being is preserved in existence is the same as the power by which it would be created anew: he supposes that a creature would go out of existence if the entity (that keeps it in existence) did not keep it in existence, and so the power by which a creature is preserved is the same as the power by which it is created.[44] Descartes assumes that all of this "is quite clear to anyone who attentively considers" the matter (AT 7:49, CSM 2:33), and so he does not provide any further explication. For example, he does not provide a premise that is clearer still and that entails that the power by which a creature is preserved is the same as the power by which it is created. If he did, he would be suggesting that it is not clear on its face that the power by which a creature is preserved is the same as the power by which it is created. He supposes that it is clear that something remains of a creature from moment to moment (AT 11:37, CSM 1:92–93), and he supposes that the power by which a creature is preserved is the same as the power by which it is created. The power by which a being is created is infinite power, and hence God exists.

At the end of the Meditation, Descartes draws the conclusion that God "is subject to no defects whatsoever… [and] that he cannot be a deceiver, since it is manifest by the natural light that all fraud and deception depend on some defect" (AT 7:52, CSM 35). He takes the conclusion to be obvious, though he does elaborate on it, at least a bit. He writes elsewhere that the claim

> That every deception depends on some defect is manifest to me by the natural light; for a being in which there is no imperfection cannot tend to non-being, that is, cannot have non-being, or non-good, or non-true as its end or purpose, since these three things are the same. It is manifest that in every deception

---

44 See also Chapter 3, pp. 83–88.

there is falsehood, and that falsehood is something non-true and therefore non-being and non-good.[45]

He adds in *Conversation with Burman* that

> since we are composed partly of nothingness and partly of being, we incline partly toward nothingness and partly toward being. As for God, on the other hand, he cannot incline to nothingness, since he is pure and supreme being. This consideration is a metaphysical one and is perfectly clear to all those who give their mind to it. Hence, inasmuch as I have my faculty of [clear and distinct] perception from God, ...I cannot be deceived or tricked by it.
>
> (AT 5:147, CSMK 334)

Descartes does not hold that there is a standard of perfection that is independent of God and that God meets. Instead, being and goodness are identical, and God is nothing other than His perfection. Our idea of supreme perfection conforms to God and God alone, and that idea entails that God does not incline toward non-being or falsity. Descartes accordingly draws the conclusion that it is impossible for a creature (of God) to be deceived about a matter that is utterly evident to it. He supposes that the conclusion is "perfectly clear to all those who give their mind to it," and so he does not say any more. If he did say more, he would be indicating that there are considerations that are more clear and that make the conclusion clearer itself. The identification of God and supreme perfection would appear for him to be rock-bottom.

If Descartes has been successful in the Third Meditation, he has undermined the hyperbolic doubts that are a threat to *scientia*. In the Second Meditation, but not in the First, we registered the "falsehood or uncertainty to be found in all the judgements that depend on the senses and the imagination," and we recognized the truth of

---

45 "To Clerselier, 23 April 1649," AT 5:357, CSMK 378.

"judgments [that] depend only on the pure understanding."[46] We also begin to appreciate that any judgments that conflict with these are confused and amateurish – for example our judgments about wax "before" as compared to our judgments about it "now" (AT 7:31, CSM 2:21). At the start of the Third Meditation, we list additional truths that we grasp by an act of purely mental scrutiny (AT 7:36), and we ask if there are any truths of that caliber that might undermine the hyperbolic doubts of the Meditation One. There are. A "weak mind" (AT 1:350, CSMK 53) might suppose that the First Meditation hyperbolic doubts prevent the argumentation of the Third Meditation from having any authority, but the judgments of the Third Meditation leave the judgments of the First Meditation in the dust. Descartes argues in the Third Meditation that God exists and is supremely perfect, and the hyperbolic doubts of the First Meditation fall by the wayside – as if they had never been presented in the first place.

Objections that Descartes does not raise himself

There are a number of objections to the argumentation of the Third Meditation that Descartes does not raise himself. One is that we are not in a position to survey the entirety of the objective reality of the idea of God to confirm that it is infinite, and so for all we know it is not infinite.[47] Descartes admits that we are not in a position to survey the entirety of the objective reality of the idea of God, but he says that nonetheless we "understand" – using the word as a success term – that the idea is infinite. He writes that

> It does not matter that I do not grasp the infinite...; for it is in the nature the infinite not to be grasped by a finite mind like myself. It is enough that I understand the infinite....
>
> (AT 7:46, CSM 2:32)[48]

---

46 "To Mersenne, 27 February 1637," AT 1:350, CSMK 53. See also the discussion in Chapter 4 above, pp. 109–127.

47 See also Vilmer (2009), 508–511.

48 See also the similar language in "To [Mersenne], 27 May 1630," where Descartes says that

Here Descartes appears to be admitting that a finite mind is never in a position to survey the idea of God to check to see that its content is in fact infinite. Still, he does not retreat and concede that the idea of God might only have the finite amount of content that a finite mind is able to traverse. Perhaps he might point to the datum that we are all prepared to admit that mathematicians have ideas of infinite series of objects, even if (by hypothesis) no one is ever able to reach their end. The mathematician *understands* that the number of integers is infinite, Descartes might say, even if we are also prepared to admit that no human mind ever inventories the entire set of them.[49] Descartes supposes that we somehow see or recognize or appreciate that the idea of God has an infinite amount of objective reality, and there is little more that he can do to get us to register that much objective reality other than by putting us in a position to see it for ourselves. For example, he will not offer an additional *reason* that serves as evidence for the claim that we understand the idea of God to be infinite. If he did offer such a reason, and it was going to be taken as definitive support, then *that* would need to be seen or recognized as obvious and evident, but Descartes is supposing that what is more obvious is the amount of objective reality that we confront in the idea itself. He would not want to downplay (what he takes to be) the clarity and evidence of the infinitude of the idea of God by suggesting that it is not evident on its own, and he would not want to turn our attention away from it to considerations that would never help us to see it better than we do already. Descartes will take the same approach in other cases in which he supposes that there is something that we recognize to be obvious. He will try to put us in a position to recognize truth for ourselves, in many cases by way of meditational meandering. We can sympathize with

---

our soul, being finite, cannot grasp or conceive him. In the same way we can touch a mountain with our hands but we cannot put our arms around it as we could put them around a tree or something else not too large for them.

(AT 1:152, CSMK 25)

49 But it is not clear that Descartes would be totally comfortable with the comparison to mathematical infinities, given his view on the distinction between the infinite and the indefinite. See *Principles* II.21, AT 8A:52, CSM 1:232, and the discussion in Chapter 1 above, pp. 20–21.

him if philosophy is a discipline in which the defense of a view is a matter of constructing arguments from axioms or tenets that are supposed to be intuitive and are largely non-empirical. To object to such a tenet, one would need to point to considerations that undermine the tenet but that are more intuitive and obvious than it. We might offer opposing intuitions, along with thought experiments that generate and reinforce those intuitions, and then stand them up against the views of our opponent. If such efforts fail, another thing that we might do is conclude that in the end we are stuck in a kind of yelling match – where we and our opponent have nothing more to say to ground our non-empirical contentions. Some might even draw the snarky conclusion that there is never any further ground for saying that one philosophical view is better than its opposite.[50] Descartes does not do that, of course, and neither do many of the rest of us. He would no doubt encounter some eye-rolling from his insistence on intuitions that many (at least today) would find objectionable. To his credit, however, he would note that with respect to the not-further-groundedness of these intuitions, he is not alone.[51] If we do not recognize the same truths that Descartes does, he would chastise us to think harder.[52] He supposes that there are matters of pure understanding that are obvious upon reflection but that are not obvious at first glance. If we do not recognize the truth of these, we are confused, and there is (almost) nothing that we could say to provide him with a compelling reason to reject his own argumentation.

---

50 Here we might think for example of the approach in Feyerabend (1975) or Rorty (1981). Or we might reference Burton Dreben's famous contention that "Philosophy is garbage, but the history of garbage is scholarship." This is quoted from Dennett (2013), 423.

51 Or as David Lewis (1986) famously puts it, "one man's reason is another man's *reductio*" (207). See also Butchvarov (2021) and Strawson (2008c), 37. Butchvarov worries that because a priori philosophical intuitions are not further grounded, they are on a par with tenets of faith.

52 For example, he quips that in the case of the objective reality of the idea of God in particular, "Some people will perhaps not notice it after reading my *Meditations* a thousand times." This is in "To Hyperaspistes, August 1641," AT 3:430, CSMK 194.

If we are not in a position to survey the entire infinitude of our idea of God, perhaps we should refrain from concluding that we have the idea that Descartes says we do. Perhaps our idea of God is just the imagistic picture that Gassendi (or Hobbes) says it is, and if so, a finite mind might have easily constructed it. But Descartes would insist that what we *do* see in our idea of God is enough for us to recognize that we did not construct it. For example, he writes,

> To provide a solution to your objection about the idea of God, we must observe that the point at issue is not the essence of the idea, in respect of which it is only a mode existing in the human mind and therefore no more perfect than a human being, but its objective perfection.... Suppose someone said that anyone can paint pictures as well as Apelles, because they consist only of patterns of paint and anyone can make all kinds of patterns of paint. To such a suggestion we should have to reply that when we are talking about Apelles' pictures we are not just considering a pattern of colours, but a pattern skillfully made to produce a representation resembling reality, such as can be produced only by those very practiced in this art.[53]

I might present an extremely clunky painting and claim with pride that it is my own work and not that of Apelles, and Descartes would no doubt take my word for it. He might then present a very different (and much higher quality) painting and ask if I had created *that*. I might respond that at the very least it was in my skill set and power to create the painting, but any effort to demonstrate as much would immediately betray me. Descartes would then point out that for any painting that I am able to produce – he is not talking about *that* painting, but a different one. He uses similar language in his description of the idea of an intricate machine.[54] We might think that anyone could muster such an idea, but the idea that Descartes has in mind is far more grand and is only produced by a few. The idea of God is then of a different order still. Any idea that we take ourselves to

---

53 "To Regius, June 1642," AT 3:566–567, CSMK 214.
54 *First Replies*, AT 7:103–104, CSM 2:75–76.

have created is not an idea of God, Descartes is supposing, because it would not have enough content to mirror the being that God would have if God in fact existed. Descartes accordingly expends a significant amount of effort to divert our attention away from ideas that we have assembled and toward ideas that (he argues) we have not.

As we have seen, in many cases, the route to the latter is *via* the former. Descartes allows that our imagistic picture-ideas of body (and mind) are of body (and mind), but only if they are a composite idea that includes a non-imagistic idea of body (or mind) as one of its components.[55] For example, the idea of a sensible piece of wax includes an idea of extension – an idea whose content outstrips the inputs of the senses and imagination. We do not *assemble* an idea of body that is "capable of being extended in many more different ways than I will ever encompass in my imagination" (AT 7:31, CSM 2:21). Instead, we break down our larger idea of a sensible piece of wax and notice that an idea of extension was already a component of it. The same applies in the case of a true idea of God: it is often "mixed up" with ideas of sensible things, but with effort it can be extracted. There is thus a sense in which we arrive at ideas of God and body (and mind) via cognitive operations that we perform, but not because we construct those ideas. Descartes also allows that there is a related sense in which we arrive at ideas of the divine attributes by reflecting on our existing cognitive machinery. We think of our own finite knowledge and arrive at an idea of omniscience, for example, but we do not thereby *assemble* an idea of omniscience.[56] That idea is part of our existing cognitive machinery in the sense that God has implanted it in us. Presumably we are able to arrive at it by thinking of our own finitude and noticing the conceptual connection between that finitude and the infinitude of the being on which it depends. We might still object and say that for all we know we created *that* idea of infinitude, even if we have read the *Meditations* a thousand times, but Descartes would then insist that our attention must have been diverted and that we are thinking a different idea

---

55 See also chapter 4 above, pp. 112–115, and Chapter 3, pp. 77–80.
56 See for example *Third Replies*, AT 7:188, CSM 2:132, and "To Hyperaspistes, August 1641," AT 3:427–428, CSMK 192. See also Nelson (2013) and Miles (2010).

than the one that he is aiming to highlight. We have yet another idea, he would insist – an idea that has so much content that it could only be produced by a being with infinite power. If Descartes is right that we have such an idea, he wins.

Another objection to the argumentation of the Third Meditation is that perhaps there doesn't exist objective reality at all. Perhaps the content of an idea is not even something that exists internal to a mind. A contemporary and very common view is that an idea can be said to be of a thing just by virtue of standing in the right causal relationship to it: a person on earth entertains a mental image of clear bluish liquid, and another person has before their mind the same exact content, but they are on a planet where the bluish water is not H_2O, but XYZ. In that case, both are entertaining the same introspectable content, but one is thinking of water and the other is not.[57] If that is how ideas refer, then what it is to think of God would not be to introspect and notice an idea with an infinite amount of objective reality; it would instead be to notice an idea that has a much smaller amount of objective reality (if we still want to retain that language), but that stands in the right kind of causal relation to (the existent being that is) God. Descartes cannot run his argument from objective reality if "meanings are not in the head" – for two reasons. First, he would not be able to assert that the idea of God has an infinite amount of objective reality, at least as he understands objective reality. Second, he would not be able to say that his idea is of God without confirming first that God in fact exists. He would not thereby retreat from his own view, of course, and he would not be under any obligation to retreat, if he and his opponents were both appealing to ground-floor suppositions that by definition have nothing underneath them.

There are other objections to Descartes' Third Meditation argumentation that we might consider. One is that we might agree that an infinitely powerful cause is required to bring about the objective

---

57 Here I am referencing the famous though-experiment in Putnam (1973). I also like to think of the idea of energy, which in my own case has the slimmest of introspectable content but that is of energy by virtue of its relationship to the thing (energy) in the world. But Descartes would argue (perhaps very plausibly) that I have no idea of energy at all.

reality of the idea of God, but we might question whether infinite power is inseparable from omniscience and the other divine attributes. If so, we might allow that Descartes is correct to conclude that an infinitely powerful being exists (as the cause of the objective reality of the idea of God) but then say that he is mistaken to conclude that that being is God. We know how Descartes will respond here – he will argue that there is a conceptual connection between infinite power and all other divine attributes and hence that the infinitely powerful being is God Itself. We might disagree and say that there is no such conceptual connection, or we might hold (with someone like Hume) that on matters of such stratospheric intellection our tether does not reach far enough to give us confidence either way.[58] I myself do not have a clear enough understanding of infinite power to know what it would or would not entail, in which case I have a deep philosophical disagreement with Descartes, and a disagreement that offers no apparent route to resolution.

Demonstrations vs. self-evident intuitions

A final observation to make about the Third Meditation arguments for the existence of God is that there is something imprecise about identifying them as arguments simpliciter. Indeed, there is something imprecise about speaking of the Third Meditation or the Fifth Meditation as offering arguments. Descartes in some instances refers to the Fifth Meditation claim that God exists as a self-evident intuition, but he also refers to it as a demonstration. He says in the Fifth Meditation that he is locating a "basis for another argument to prove the existence of God" (AT 7:65, CSM 2:45), and that he is "inferring that the first and supreme being exists" (AT 7:67, CSM 2:47). He says at the end of the Fifth Meditation however that the existence of the supreme being is "self-evident" (AT 7:69, CSM 2:47). The Third Meditation certainly *seems* to be offering arguments that have discrete steps, but Descartes also says elsewhere that whether or not we regard something as a proof or an intuition is to some degree relative to the cognizer. He writes,

---

58 Hume (1739), 142.

Now that we possess all the premises, the only thing that remains to be shown is how the conclusion is to be found. This is… a matter of deriving a single fact which depends on many interconnected facts, and of doing this in such a methodical way that no greater intellectual capacity is required than is needed for the simplest inference.[59]

Here Descartes is suggesting that whether or not something is a demonstration or intuition depends in part on the reasoning aptitude of the grasper. If we run through discrete premises in such a way that we see the obvious force of a conclusion that they entail, we have entertained an argument, but we might acquire such a grasp of the argument that we are more accurately described as having a single intuition. Descartes says explicitly in *Second Replies* that "there are certain truths which some people find self-evident, while others come to understand them only by means of a formal argument" (AT 7:164, CSM 2:115). The passage specifically references the truth that God exists – and the different routes that finite minds might take to reach that truth – but it applies generally. Even the result "I am, I exist" would appear to be alternatingly a conclusion that we infer, as in *Discourse* Part 4 (AT 6:32, CSM 1:127) and the Second Meditation (AT 7:25, CSM 2:17), and an immediate intuition (*Second Replies*, AT 7:145-46, CSM 2:104).[60] The reasoning of the Third Meditation is presented as argumentation for the existence of God, but Descartes

---

59 *Rules for the Direction of the Mind*, AT 10:429, CSM 1:51.

60 See also the discussion in Hintikka (1962). A similar account of the distinction between intuition and demonstration appears later in Spinoza. An example that he offers to illustrate the distinction is the demonstration that for any three numbers, there is a fourth number that is the quotient of (1) the product of the second and the third and (2) the first, and that has the same relation to the third as the second has to the first. Either we run through the demonstration and recognize that because d is b*c/a, d/c is therefore b/a; or else we just *see* that d/c = b/a. (See Spinoza (1662), Part II, Chapter 1, 62–63.) Descartes is clearly anticipating (or just initially offering) the view in Spinoza that there are truths whose identification as a conclusion or intuition is a function of the details of the mind that is cognizing them.

suggests in the *Regulae* that some minds would be able to grasp each of its two arguments as a single intuition.[61]

Spinozistic leanings – the boundary between God and creatures

A final theme to address in connection with the Third Meditation arguments for the existence of God is the overlap between the systems of Descartes and Spinoza. We know that Spinoza read Descartes, and in many respects he appears to be adopting basic Cartesian tenets and arguing that they entail conclusions that Descartes himself would rather avoid.[62] Spinoza argues for example that there exists a single substance – God – and that all minds and bodies are just modifications of that substance.[63] God is an immutable and eternal being that constitutes all of reality, according to Spinoza, and all minds and bodies are necessitated to act as they do by immutable laws of nature.[64] Descartes is not Spinoza, but in some passages the daylight between their systems becomes harder and harder to see.

After providing his demonstration for the existence of material things in the Sixth Meditation, Descartes writes that

> if nature is considered in its general aspect, then I understand by the term nothing other than God himself, or the ordered system of created things established by God.
>
> (AT 7:80, CSM 2:56)

Here Descartes is perhaps identifying God and the natural world, but at the very least he would appear to be identifying God and the orderly laws (or Spinozistic infinite modes)[65] that apply to

---

61 See also *Conversation with Burman*, AT 5:149, CSMK 335.
62 See for example the axioms and definitions of Spinoza (1677), Parts I and II. For an introduction to the work of Spinoza, and a discussion of some of the ways in which Spinoza is assuming basic Cartesian tenets to derive conclusions that Descartes did not, see Nadler (2006).
63 See for example Spinoza (1677), Part I, Propositions XIV and XV, 224–226.
64 See for example Spinoza (1677), Part I, Propositions XXVI–XXIX, 232–234.
65 Curley (1969), 67–68.

the changes that bodies undergo.[66] We might think that the Sixth Meditation passage is an outlier, but just a few pages earlier Descartes flirts with Spinozism yet again when he attributes imagination and memory to God. In the Fourth Meditation – almost in passing, and in a way that it is quite easy to overlook – he writes,

> if I examine the faculties of memory or imagination, or any others, I discover that in my case each one of these faculties is weak and limited, while in the case of God it is immeasurable.
>
> (AT 7:57, CSM 2:40)

Descartes makes clear in numerous passages that imagination and memory are corporeal.[67] But if imagination and memory are corporeal, and there are such things as the imagination and memory of God, then God would appear to have a body.[68] And not just any old body. God would have a body that is contiguous with additional bodies that are contiguous with additional bodies – all of these comprising a single body with an array of modifications throughout – and God of course has a mind that would be united to that body. In that case, God would be a mind that is united to a very large body – the single body that composes the entirety of the material universe.[69]

---

66 See Baier (2014), and Spinoza (1677), Part I, Proposition 29, scholium, 234.

67 *Treatise on Man*, AT 11:178, CSM 1:107; *Fifth Replies*, AT 7:357, CSM 2:247; "For [Arnauld], 29 July 1648," AT 5:220, CSMK 356; The Sixth Meditation, AT 7:74, CSM 2:51; "To Hyperaspistes, August 1641," AT 3:425, CSMK 190. See also the discussion in Chapter 4 above, pp. 130–131.

68 See Baier (2014).

69 As we have seen, there is also the passage in *Principles* I.51 in which Descartes writes:

> By *substance* we can understand nothing other than a thing which exists in such a way as to depend on no other thing for its existence. And there is only one substance which can be understood to depend on no other thing whatsoever, namely God.
>
> (AT 8A:24, CSM 1:210)

I do not want to lean too heavily on this passage, however. Schechtman (2018) has argued (convincingly I think) that Descartes' *Principles* I.51 claim that only God is a substance is getting at something different than the view that Spinoza

Descartes also approaches Spinozism from the other direction – from assumptions about finite minds and bodies. He holds that in the case of a human being, a mind is united to its body not just at the pineal gland (in the brain), but instead the human body is the "the whole of the matter which is united with the soul of that man."[70] He does say that the pineal gland is the "part of the body where [the soul] exercises its functions more particularly than in all the others,"[71] but he also says that

> we need to recognize that the soul is really joined to the whole body, and that we cannot properly say that it exists in any one part of the body to the exclusion of the others.[72]

He adds that "the soul… is the true substantial form of man."[73] But he *also* appears to hold that what it is for a thing to be finite is for it to be a delimitation of infinitude.[74] A finite mind is united to

---

had in mind. See also the discussion in Renault (2015), 126–130. I am focusing instead on other texts in which Descartes sounds a lot like Spinoza.

70 "To Mesland, 9 February 1645," AT 5:166, CSMK 243. For the view that the soul of a human being is united to its body at the pineal gland, see for example *Treatise on Man*, AT 11:129, CSM 1:100.

71 *Passions* I.31, AT 11:352 CSM 1:340.

72 *Passions* I.30, AT 11:351, CSM 1:339.

73 "To Regius, January 1642," AT 3:505, CSMK 208.

74 As we have seen, he writes:
> I say that the notion I have of the infinite is in me before that of the finite because, by the mere fact that I conceive being, or that which is, …what I conceive is infinite being; but in order to conceive a finite being, I have to take away something from this general notion of being, which must accordingly be there first.
>
> ("To Clerselier, 23 April 1649," AT 5:356, CSMK 377)

See also "To [Silhon], May 1637," AT 1:353, CSMK 55. A similar view is in Spinoza:
> A thing is said to be finite in its own kind when it can be limited by another thing of the same nature. For example, a body is said to be finite because we can always conceive of another body greater than it. So, too, a thought is limited by another thought. But body is not limited by thought, nor thought by body.
>
> (Spinoza (1677), Part I, Definition 2, 217)

the matter that constitutes the human body – up to and including the modifications that are the boundary between that body and its surroundings. That body is surrounded by additional body, *ad indefinitum*, and its mind would appear to be delimited by additional mentality as well.[75]

Descartes does not arrive at the view that God and creatures coincide.[76] He does however make claims that are suggestive of that view, and in one series of letters – to Henry More in 1649 – he makes claims that are more than just suggestive. For example, he writes that "it is certain that God's essence must be present everywhere for his power to be able to manifest itself everywhere"[77] and that "the only idea I can find in my mind to represent the way in which God or an angel can move matter is the one which shows me the way in which I am conscious I can move my own body by my own thought."[78] That is to say, Descartes appears to be saying that God's mind is united to the material plenum, and that it is united to it ubiquitously. To be sure, he does not allow that extended substance is infinite with respect to its extension; instead, it is indefinite.[79] However, as we have also seen he concedes that he does not know whether the extension of the universe is infinite or indefinite.[80] If he

---

75 See also *Second Replies*, where Descartes addresses the concern that "the infinite in every category of perfection [would] exclude... every other entity whatsoever" (AT 7:141, CSM 2:101). Descartes' reply is not particularly helpful: he says that "the term 'inifinite' is not generally taken to mean something which excludes the existence of finite things" (ibid.). See also Riquier (2020), 32.

76 He is clear for example that "since being divisible is an imperfection, it is certain that God is not a body" (*Principles* 1.23; AT 8A:13, CSM 1:201). He also says that God has absolutely no modes, "since in the case of God any variation is unintelligible" (*Principles* I.56, AT 8A:26, CSM 1:211).

77 "To More, August 1649," AT 5:403, CSMK 381.

78 "To More, 15 April 1649," AT 5:347, CSMK 375.

79 *Principles* II.21, AT 8A:52, CSM 1:232. See the discussion in Chapter 1, pp. 20–21, and also Vilmer (2010).

80 "To More, 5 February 1649," AT 5:274, CSMK 364. Note that Koyré (1958, 124) comes very close to concluding (on the basis of the letters to More) that Descartes holds that the created material universe positively has no limits. In the light of *Prinicples* I.27 (AT 8A:15, CSM 1:202) that would mean that

abides by the view that what it is to be finite is to be a limitation of infinitude, he is dangerously close to the conclusion that a given mind-body union is a single substance that is infinite with respect to its thought and extension and whose modifications constitute regions of the substance, but not internal borders or divisions. Descartes even says to More that

> It is not my custom to argue about words, and so if someone wants to say that God is in a sense extended, since he is everywhere, I have no objection. But I deny that true extension as commonly conceived is to be found in God or in angels or in our mind or in any substance which is not a body. Commonly when people talk of an extended being, they have in mind something imaginable. In this being... they can distinguish by the imagination various parts of determinate size and shape, each non-identical with the others. Some of these parts can be imagined as transferred to the place of others, but no two can be imagined simultaneously in one and the same place. Nothing of this kind can be said about God or about our mind; they cannot be apprehended by the imagination, but only by the intellect....
>
> (AT 5:269–270, CSMK 361, emphasis added)

Descartes may well be correct that we (commonly) picture an image when we think of body, but that is not the only way that we think of body, at least on his own view. Our clearest grasp of body, he thinks, is by an act of purely mental scrutiny (AT 7:31, CSM 2:21). He also says that strictly speaking body is not known through the senses and that there is a sense in which it is not sensible at all (ibid.). He may be correct that God and finite mind are not extended in the sense in which extension is imagined, but God and finite mind might still be extended in the more rigorous sense in which it is conceived or understood. Descartes rules out that God and finite mind answer to

---

Descartes holds that the material universe is infinitely extended, and not indefinitely extended. I do not think that Descartes wants to go that far. See also the discussions Agostini (2017) and Grobet (2010).

the common way of regarding extension. The extension that "is a case not of vision or touch or imagination" (ibid.) is altogether different.

Spinozistic leanings – God and modality

Descartes also leans in the direction of Spinoza in his views on modality. In his 1648 interview with Franz Burman, he says that

> it is quite unintelligible that God should be anything but com-
> pletely unalterable. It is irrelevant that [his] decrees could
> have been separated from God; indeed, this should not really
> be asserted. For although God is completely indifferent with
> respect to all things, he necessarily made the decrees he did....
> We should not make a separation here between the necessity and
> indifference that apply to God's decrees; although his actions
> were completely indifferent, they were also completely neces-
> sary. Then again, although we may conceive that the decrees
> could have been separated from God, this is merely a token pro-
> cedure of our understanding: the distinction thus introduced
> between God himself and his decrees is a mental, not a real
> one. In reality the decrees could not have been separated from
> God; he is not prior to them or distinct from them, nor could
> he have existed without them. So it is clear enough how God
> accomplishes all things in a single act.[81]

Here we have Descartes saying that God is the author of all reality (other than God)[82] and that since God acts by a single eternal and immutable volition, whatever happens has to happen exactly as it does. That is to say, we have Descartes expressing a variant of the view that is a pillar of the system of Spinoza:

> since all that happens is done by God, it must necessarily be
> predetermined by him, otherwise he would be mutable,
> which would be a great imperfection in him. And as this

---

81 *Conversation with Burman*, AT 5:166–167, CSMK 348.
82 See Chapter 1, pp. 25–26, especially notes 57 and 59. See also *Fourth Replies*, AT 7:238–246, CSM 2:166–171.

predetermination by him must be from eternity, in which eternity there is no before or after, it follows irresistibly that God could never have predetermined things in any other way than that in which they are determined now, and have been from eternity, and that God could not have been either before or without these determinations.[83]

We might be concerned that perhaps Burman has mis-transcribed a word or two in his interview with Descartes, but it is difficult to imagine that he got things completely wrong – for two reasons. One is that (as we saw in Chapter 2) Descartes was extremely protective of his intellectual persona and of the way in which his views were both presented and received. It is hard to believe that he would have given the interview with Burman without a significant amount of oversight. We have no record of his approval of the transcript of the interview – unlike the approval that we know he gave to the French translation of the *Meditations*, for example – but it is hard to believe that in real time Descartes would have just looked the other way. The second (and much more verifiable) reason is that the argument laid out in the *Conversation with Burman* passage can be pieced together from other texts in Descartes' corpus.

A tenet that bears on Descartes' understanding of modality is that God is not only omnipotent and supremely independent, but also wholly immutable. He writes,

it is easy to accept that God, who is, as everyone must know, immutable, always acts in the same way.[84]

we understand that God's perfection involves his not only being immutable in himself, but also his operating in a manner that is always utterly constant and immutable.[85]

For Descartes, the immutability of God falls out of the idea of God – it follows a priori from God's perfection.[86] God does not act by one

---

83 Spinoza (1662), I.iv, 51–52.
84 The World, AT 11:38, CSM 1:93.
85 Principles II.36, AT 8A:61, CSM 1:240.
86 See also Garber (2000), 164.

volition, and then switch to another, and then another, but instead
He acts by a single volition that is wholly unchanging:

> even his understanding and willing does not happen, as in our
> case, by means of operations that are in a certain sense dis-
> tinct from one another; we must rather suppose that there is
> always a single identical and perfectly simple act by means of
> which he simultaneously understands, wills and accomplishes
> everything.[87]

But Descartes also holds that God "created both [him]self and
everything else (if anything else there be) that exists" (AT 7:45,
CSM 2:31). That is all to say, Descartes holds that God acts by a single
immutable volition that brings about all reality apart from God:

> the power of God is infinite – the power by which he knew
> from eternity not only whatever is or can be, but also willed it
> and preordained it.[88]

The divine volition is immutable and eternal, but we might ask if
(contra the language of the AT 5:147 *Conversation with Burman* passage)
Descartes allows that God might have willed a different series of
creatures immutably and for eternity. I think that the answer is clearly
no. He says in the Third Meditation that the idea of God reflects that
in God there is no potential being whatsoever: "although I have
many potentialities which are not yet actual, this is all quite irrelevant to the idea of God, which contains absolutely no potential
being" (AT 7:47, CSM 2:32). He then emphasizes a few sentences
later that "potential being... is strictly speaking nothing" (ibid.). In
God, there does not exist the latent potential to will alternative series
of creatures. Instead, God is wholly active, and "the idea which we
have of God teaches us that there is in him only a single *activity*,
entirely simple and entirely pure."[89] Descartes does not say in the

---

87   *Principles* I.23, AT 8A:14, CSM 1:201.
88   *Principles* I.41, AT 8A:20, CSM 1:206.
89   "To [Mesland], 2 May 1644," AT 4:119, CSMK 235, emphasis added. Of
     course, it is important to mark that "the idea which we have of God [that]

Third Meditation that there are *some* respects in which God has no potentiality; he says that in God there is no potentiality whatsoever. He then echoes the same result later in *Conversation with Burman*: "It is irrelevant that the decrees could have been separated from God; indeed, this should not really be asserted." Descartes holds that God wills the entire series of creaturely reality by a single immutable and eternal volition, and there is no potentiality in God by which He might have willed a different series instead. Or as he puts it: "We should not make a separation here between the necessity and indifference that apply to God's decrees; although his actions were completely indifferent, they were also completely necessary."

It is controversial to argue that Descartes subscribes to the view that there is no possibility that things be other than they are in fact.[90] But I think that the view fits quite nicely into his system. It squares particularly well with (1) his view that the truths of math and logic are necessary, (2) his conception of divine freedom, and (3) his understanding of the relationship between God's will and intellect.

Descartes is clear that there are mathematical and other truths that are necessary. For example, in the course of the 1630 letters to Mersenne on the truths of mathematics he says that "the necessity of these truths does not exceed our knowledge."[91] As a matter of interpretive charity, it is a good thing that he says (and thinks) that mathematical truths are necessary, or else he would be saddled with the view that it is possible that (for example) two and three might have added to something other than five. Descartes accordingly says in the Third Meditation that

> when I turn to the things themselves which I think I perceive very clearly, I am so convinced by them that I spontaneously

teaches" us such a result is not the confused and amateurish idea of the First Meditation. See also Bouchilloux (2015), 6.

90 Some version of the opposite view appears in the work of numerous commentators – for example, Wilson (1978), 120–131, Frankfurt (1977), 39–46, Curley (1984), 576–583, Wagner (1983), Alanen (1991), Christofidou (2001), Ragland (2005), and Pessin (2010), among others.

91 "To Mersenne, 6 May 1630," AT 1:150, CSMK 25.

declare: let whoever can do so deceive me, he will... never bring it about that two and three added together are more or less than five, or anything of this kind in which I see a manifest contradiction.

(AT 7:36, CSM 2:25)

Descartes does consider the prospect that (a fully omnipotent) God might alter the truth value of a truth like that that the radii of a circle are equal or that two and three add to five, but he rejects it – because the will of God is wholly immutable. He writes,

It will be said that if God had established these truths he could change them as a king changes his laws. To this the answer is: Yes he can, if His will can change. 'But I understand them to be eternal and unchangeable.' – I make the same judgment about God.[92]

Descartes dismisses the possibility that God might alter the truth value of a necessary truth. Note however that he is not thereby supposing that there are things that God cannot do. It is a necessary truth that two and three add to five, and so it is not possible that two and three not add to five.[93] That is to say, the possibility that two and three add to five does not exist. It isn't anything – it is wholly unintelligible, and it is not something that God's immutable will has authored. It is not anything, and more specifically it is not something that God cannot bring about. Descartes does say in one passage that "the only things that are said to be impossible for God to do are those which involve a conceptual contradiction, that is,

---

92 "To Mersenne, 15 April 1630," AT 1:145–146, CSMK 23.

93 Here I am proceeding in the reverse direction of Frankfurt (1977) – who argues that Descartes holds that God could have made it true that two and three add to something other than five, and hence that it is not a necessary truth that two and three add to five. But Descartes holds that it is a necessary truth that two and three add to five. In Curley (1984) there is an ingenious attempt to argue that for Descartes the truths of math and logic are necessary even though God has the power to falsify them. But I agree with Van Cleve (1994) that that attempt is unsuccessful.

which are not intelligible."[94] But, again, that is not to say (or even to suggest) that there actually are things that it is impossible for God to do. An incoherent and contradictory non-entity is not anything, and Descartes is happy to say that God cannot bring about one of those. We are not imposing a limit on God's power in such cases, but owning that the "it" that we thought we had specified isn't an "it" at all.[95] Descartes also says that

> the nature of God is immense, incomprehensible and infinite, and I also know without more ado that he is capable of countless things whose causes are beyond my knowledge.[96]

As we have seen, he speaks to "the immensity of [God's] works" and suspects that "the indefinite extension of the universe gives ground for inferring that there must be inhabitants of places other than the earth."[97] There is a lot that is done by a supremely perfect being – a being that is purely active – and our finite thought reaches the tip of the iceberg at best. We only cognize so much, but Descartes is not thereby committed to the view that there exists the possibility that God do what is incoherent.[98] Among the things that are the product of

---

94 "To Regius, June 1642," AT 3:567, CSMK 214. An example is that "it is impossible for... [the divine] being to have the power and will to give itself something new" (AT 7:241, CSM 2:168).

95 But if it is an it – that is to say, if it is something of which we have a clear and distinct idea – then we ought not say that God cannot bring it about. See for example "For [Arnauld], 29 July 1648," AT 5:224, CSMK 358. See also the discussion in Bennett (1994), and Nelson and Cunning (1999). Anything of which we have a clear and distinct idea either exists formally or else it exists eminently in an entity that is more perfect. See Chapter 3 above, pp. 90–92.

96 The Fourth Meditation, AT 7:55, CSM 2:39.

97 "To Chanut, 6 June 1647," AT 5:56, CSMK 322.

98 The train of thought in the 15 April 1630 letter to Mersenne then continues as we might expect:

It will be said that if God had established these truths he could change them as a king changes his laws. To this the answer is: Yes he can, if His will can change. 'But I understand them to be eternal and unchangeable.' – I make the same judgment about God. 'But his will is free.' – Yes, but his power is beyond our grasp. In general we can assert that God can do everything that

God's will are truths of mathematics and geometry that are necessary and cannot be otherwise.[99] God produces other things as well, a few of which we can think and many of which we cannot.

Descartes could not be more clear that God is the author of the truths of mathematics. God is not only the creator of anything triangular or circular that exists, but He is also the author of the truths that specify what it is for something to be triangular or circular. Descartes writes,

> You ask me by what kind of causality God established the eternal truths. I reply: by the same kind of causality as he created all things, that is to say their efficient and total cause. For it is certain that he is the author of the essence of created things no less than of their existence; and this essence is nothing other than the eternal truths. ...You ask what God did in order to produce

---

is within our grasp but not that he cannot do what is beyond our grasp. It would be rash to think that our imagination reaches as far as his power.

(AT 1:145, CSMK 23)

99 Descartes even appears to allow that there exist laws of physical nature that are necessary truths − laws that follow from the idea of God as immutable. He writes in Principles II.37 that "[f]rom God's immutability we can also know certain rules or laws of nature, which are the secondary and particular causes of the various motions that we see in particular bodies" (AT 8A:62, CSM 1:240) − for example that "what is in motion always, so far as it can, continues to move" (AT 8A:62, CSM 1:241). Unless laws of physical nature are in some way more necessary than the truths of math, geometry, and logic, Descartes is proposing that all are on a par in terms of their necessity and cannot be otherwise. In Discourse on the Method Part V Descartes writes,

I showed [in TheWorld] what the laws of nature were, and without basing my arguments on any principle other than the infinite perfections of God, I tried to demonstrate all those laws about which we could have any doubt, and to show that they are such that, even if God created many worlds, there could not be any in which they failed to be observed.

(AT 6:43, CSM 1:132)

See also TheWorld, AT 11:47, CSM 1:97, and Curley (1984), 573. Olson (1988) argues that Descartes is committed to the view that the laws of physical nature are necessary truths, but that the eternal truths of mathematics and geometry are not. See also the discussion in Osler (1985).

them. I reply that from all eternity he willed and understood them to be, and by that very fact he created them.[100]

He then offers an example of one of these essences: namely, that "the radii of the circle are equal" (ibid.). God does not confront the independently settled fact that the radii of a circle are equal; rather, it is true that the radii of a circle are equal because God has decreed that the radii of a circle are equal.[101] That is in part to say, God is the author of all reality and truth apart from the being of God Itself.

Descartes subscribes to the view that the truths of mathematics are necessary. We might worry though that Descartes cannot subscribe to that view if he also subscribes to the view that God is free with respect to His creative activity. But that worry does not arise unless we superimpose onto Descartes' system a conception of divine freedom that he himself does not advance. He unpacks divine

---

100 "To [Mersenne], 27 May 1630," AT 1:151–152, CSMK 25. In the next sentence Descartes says, "Or, if you reserve the word *created* for the existence of things, then he established them and made them" (AT 152–153, CSMK 25). Here Descartes is anticipating that Mersenne or others might want to use a different term than 'create' to pick out God's authoring of eternal truths – in case we do not want to say that God created the eternal truths – but one of the alternate terms that Descartes suggests is 'made', which is little different from 'create'. Descartes also makes clear in the larger passage that what God does in all cases is just to will.

101 On the question of the ontology of the eternal truths, Descartes says that "eternal truths... have no existence outside our thought" (*Principles* I.48, AT 8A:22, CSM 1:208) and that each "eternal truth resides within our mind" (*Principles* I.49, AT 8A:23, CSM 1:209). For Descartes, eternal truths are creatures and more specifically they are ideas in finite minds. We might worry that eternal truths cannot be ideas in finite minds if they are eternal, but Descartes actually distances himself from the label 'eternal'. In "To Mersenne, 15 April 1630" he speaks of "[t]he mathematical truths which you call eternal" (AT 1:145, CSMK 23), and in "To Mersenne, 27 May 1638," he mentions "those truths which are called eternal" (AT 2:138, CSMK 103). He allows that things can be identified as 'eternal' so long as they "are always the same" (*Fifth Replies*, AT 7:381, CSM 2:262). An eternal truth is a truth, which is in part to say that it is an idea that conforms to reality. Descartes appears to retain the label 'eternal truth' so that he can communicate about the entity that he and his contemporaries are attempting to analyze.

freedom in terms of God's independence of any influences that might impact His activity. He says in Sixth Replies,

> As for freedom of the will, the way in which it exists in God is quite different from the way in which it exists in us. It is self-contradictory to suppose that the will of God was not indifferent from eternity with respect to everything which has happened or will ever happen; for it is impossible to imagine that anything is thought of in the divine intellect as good or true, or worthy of belief or action or omission, prior to the decision of the divine will to make it so. ...There is no problem in the fact that the merit of the saints may be said to be the cause of their obtaining eternal life; for it is not the cause of this reward in the sense that it determines God to will anything, but is merely the cause of an effect of which God has willed from eternity that it should be the case. Thus the supreme indifference to be found in God is the supreme indication of his omnipotence.
>
> (AT 7:431–432, CSM 2:291–292)

As Descartes says in many other passages, there is nothing that is independent of God that puts any constraints on His creative power.[102] He wills all creaturely reality in a single immutable and eternal act, and not on the basis of any facts or considerations that are separate from Him. He does (in a sense) respond to the unfolding of the series of creatures – for example to the behavior of saints – but only in the sense that His single immutable act already reflects what His will is going to effect. As Descartes had said similarly in a letter to Elizabeth,

> when we are told to pray to God, that is not so that we should inform him of our needs, or that we should try to get him to change anything in the order established from all eternity by his

---

102 See also Bennett (1994), 641–644, Nelson and Cunning (1999), 144–146, and Kaufman (2002). See also Spinoza (1677), Part I, Definition 7, 217, and Part I, Proposition 17, 227–229.

providence[,]... but simply to obtain whatever he has, from all eternity, willed to be obtained by our prayers.[103]

Simply put, God acts by a single immutable volition, and a volition to which He is locked in. He is not locked in due to any authority that is independent of Him; there is no such authority. But He is locked in nonetheless. His activity is free in the sense that there is nothing that is independent of Him that puts constraints on it.[104]

Descartes' view on the relationship between divine will and divine intellect also squares well with the view that there is no possibility that things be other than they are in fact.[105] Descartes holds that in God will and intellect are identical in such a way that there is nothing that God understands that He does not thereby create:

> In God, willing, understanding and creating are all the same thing without one being prior to the other even conceptually.[106]
>
> In God willing and knowing are a single thing in such a way that by the very fact of willing something he knows it and it is only for this reason that such a thing is true.[107]

Descartes does not subscribe to the Leibnizian view that unactualized possibilities exist in the form of ideas in the divine intellect that God thinks but does not instantiate.[108] For Descartes, if God had any such idea of X, God would also will and create X, and it would not be an

---

103 "To Princess Elizabeth, 6 October 1645," AT 4:316, CSMK 273.

104 Commentators have gone to great lengths to interpret Descartes as holding that God has libertarian freedom and that (in some sense) there exists the possibility that God's will be other than it is. See for example Frankfurt (1977), 39–46; Wilson (1978), 120–131; Wagner (1983); Curley (1984), 576–583; Alanen (1991), Christofidou (2001), Ragland (2005), Kaufman (2005), and Pessin (2010), among others.

105 See also Nelson and Cunning (1999).

106 "To [Mersenne], 27 May 1630," AT 1:153, CSMK 25–26.

107 "To Mersenne, 6 May 1630," AT 1:149, CSMK 24. See also "To [Mesland], 2 May 1644," AT 4:119, CSMK 235.

108 See for example Leibniz (1686a), Sections XIII–XIV, 44–48; and Leibniz (1686b), 69–77. See also Frankfurt (1977), 39–41; Nelson and Cunning (1999); and Chukurian (2018), 381–382.

unactualized possibility. Instead, X would be blasted into existence as part of the series that God wills immutably and for eternity. Nor does Descartes hold that the possibility of X is an idea of the *possibility of X* in the divine intellect. If the divine intellect *did* include an idea of what we might call "the unactualized possibility of X," that idea would be instantiated in the form of a creature that is part of the series that God wills in His single immutable and eternal act. The creature would not be the *unactualized possibility of X*, or at the very least there is no reason for a finite mind to identify it as such. It would be a creature that exists as part of the series that God has willed immutably and for eternity, and like everything else in the series, and like the series itself, there does not exist the possibility that it be otherwise.[109]

Descartes does not speak of unactualized possibilities himself, but instead he says things like this:

> we conceive distinctly that it is possible that the world has been made, and therefore it has been made.[110]

In *Second Replies*, he infers that "God created the heavens and the earth and everything in them" from the premise that God has the power to create them and the premise that they are possible (AT 7:169, CSM 2:119). He says in the Third Meditation that "potential being... strictly speaking is nothing" (AT 7:47, CSM 2:32). Descartes does say in some passages that a creature can exist so long as we have a clear and distinct idea of it.[111] But as we have seen, in these passages he is making an epistemic point: he is indicating that so long as our idea of a thing is not confused or incoherent, the thing is at least a candidate for existence, even if we have to do additional work to determine that the thing exists in fact. Descartes also makes a distinction between the necessary existence that is had by God and

---

109 Here I am disagreeing with commentators who argue that Descartes posits the existence or being of *possibilia*. See for example Normore (1986, 1991).

110 "To Mersenne, 30 September 1640," AT 3:191, CSMK 154.

111 For example, at the start of the Sixth Meditation, AT 7:71, CSM 2:50, and in "To Mersenne, March 1642," AT 3:544–545, CSMK 211. See also the discussion in Chapter 3 above, pp. 90–92.

the contingent existence that is had by creatures. God is a necessary existent in the sense that He is an ontologically independent and eternal existent,[112] but creatures "fall under this common concept: things that need only the concurrence of God in order to exist" (AT 8A:25, CSM 1:210). Descartes speaks again to the distinction between necessary and dependent existence in *Second Replies*: he says that "necessary and perfect existence.... is contained in the concept of a supreme being," but creatures have "possible or [*sive*] contingent existence" (AT 7:166, CSM 2:117). Here he is highlighting that creatures do not have necessary existence and that they only exist if God creates them.[113]

Descartes also says in *Second Replies* that we commonly identify something as possible to indicate that our idea of it is coherent (AT 7:150–151, CSM 2:107).[114] There he is responding to Mersenne's worry that if the idea of God turns out to be incoherent, then any argument for the existence of God is hopeless.[115] God is a possible existent, Descartes is happy to allow, but not in the sense that there are two kinds of existence that are had by God – actual necessary existence and also existence of the possible variety. Instead, God is a possible existent in the sense that the idea of God is not self-contradictory. Any creature of which we have a coherent idea is a possible existent in that sense as well.[116] Once we have in hand the result that an entity is a possible existent, we move forward in our effort to demonstrate whether it exists in fact.[117]

Now I would like to consider some potential objections to the view that Descartes holds that there is no other way that things can be other than they in fact. One objection is that in a 1644 letter to

---

112 Again, see *Fourth Replies*, AT 7:235–245, CSM 2:164–171, and *First Replies*, AT 7:116–119, CSM 2:83–85.

113 See also Nelson and Cunning (1999), 141–143.

114 See also the discussion in Bennett (1994).

115 *Second Objections*, AT 7:127, CSM 2:91.

116 I take it that Descartes has the same idea in mind when he says in *Fourth Replies* that "God can bring about everything that I clearly and distinctly recognize as possible" (AT 7:219, CSM 2:154).

117 There are also two more claims about possible existence in the *Regulae* (AT 10:421, CSM 1:46) and *Comments on a Certain Broadsheet* (AT 8B:361, CSM 1:306), but these are overtly epistemic.

Mesland, Descartes speaks of God as having a contra-causal power
to act other than He does. First, he reminds us that on his view "the
power of God cannot have any limits." Then, he adds that

> our mind is finite and so created as to be able to conceive as
> possible the things which God has wished to be in fact pos-
> sible, but not be able to conceive as possible things which God
> could have made possible, but which he has nevertheless wished
> to make impossible. The first consideration shows us that God
> cannot have been determined to make it true that contradict-
> ories cannot be true together, and therefore that he could have
> done the opposite.[118]

Here we have a passage that appears to be very clear evidence for
the view that Descartes holds it is possible for things to be other
than they are in fact. The passage expresses that God is the author of
all reality and truth – even truths about what is possible – and that
God could have willed to be possible the opposite of what He in
fact willed to be possible. If God has so much power with respect to
possibility – and He could have willed (for example) that it is possible that contradictories be true together – then He clearly could
have willed the existence of a different series of creatures than the
one that in fact exists, and He presumably has a two-way libertarian
power with respect to the willing or not willing of anything at all.

The problem of course is that Descartes is not entitled to say what
he says to Mesland, if God acts by a single immutable and eternal volition and if in God there is no potential being whatsoever. Descartes
recognizes as much, and later in the paragraph he takes it all back. In
the first few sentences of the paragraph he was perhaps in the grip
of an effort to not underestimate the extent of divine power, but at
the end of the paragraph he is more restrained:

> if we would know the immensity of his power we should not
> put these thoughts before our minds, nor should we conceive
> any precedence or priority between his intellect and his will; for

---

118 "To [Mesland], 2 May 1644," AT 4:118, CSMK 235.

the idea which we have of God teaches us that there is in him
only a single activity, entirely simple and entirely pure.

(AT 4:119, CSMK 235)

According to Descartes, there is no sense in which God might have
opted to have a different eternal and immutable volition apart from
the single eternal and immutable volition that He has in fact. Nor
is there anything that is independent of God that could make God
have a different immutable and eternal volition. Nor does there exist
independently of God's creative activity the possibility that God
will differently than He does. What exists is God and the series of
creatures that is the product of a single volition that is immutable
and eternal.

Another text that might appear to be evidence that Descartes
holds that it is possible for things to be different than they are in
fact is *Principles* III.45–46. In *Principles* III.45, he reflects on some of
the ways in which his explanations of physical phenomena might
appear to run counter to Christian faith. He says for example that
his explanations tell of the slow and gradual formation of the moon,
stars, plants, human bodies, and the like, but scripture would appear
to suggest that the creation of these occurred over six days. Descartes
owns the discrepancy: "I... take my investigation of their causes
right back to a time before the period when I believe that the causes
actually came into existence" (AT 8A: 99, CSM 1:256). He continues,

For there is no doubt that the world was created right from the
start with all the perfection which it now has. The sun and earth
and moon and stars thus existed in the beginning, and, what is
more, the earth contained not just the seeds of plants but the
plants themselves; and Adam and Eve were not born as babies
but were created as fully grown people. This is the doctrine of the
Christian Faith, and our natural reason convinces us that it was
so. ...Nevertheless, if we want to understand the nature of plants
or of men, it is much better to consider how they can gradually
grow from seeds than to consider how they were created by God
at the very beginning of the world. Thus we may be able to think
up certain very simple and easily known principles which can
serve, as it were, as the seeds from which we can demonstrate

that the stars, the earth and indeed everything we observe in this visible world could have sprung.

(AT 8A:99–100, CSM 1:256)

When I read this passage, I see Descartes referencing principles and explanations that finite minds are able to conjure and that might or might not coincide with how things have actually come to pass. He is making an epistemic point about the different stories that we might "think up" to explain what has unfolded and why, but at most one of those stories will be true, and the rest reside at the level of our imagination. If so, his subsequent comments in Principles III.46 are not evidence that he holds that things could be different than how they are in fact.[119] He writes,

> From what has already been said we have established that all the bodies in the universe are composed of one and the same matter, which is divisible into indefinitely many parts... and have a sort of circular motion.... However, we cannot determine by reason alone how big these pieces of matter are, or how fast they move, or what kinds of circle they describe. Since there are countless different configurations which God might have instituted here, experience must teach us which configurations he actually selected....[120]

As I read the text of Principles III.45–46, Descartes is not saying that God has before His mind a number of ideas of different possible ways that things might unfold; he is saying that we have before our minds a number of ideas of different ways that we might imagine things to unfold, and we need to appeal to experience to uncover which if any God has enacted. The best analogy of which I can think is this. We approach a guarded room and we are told that there is a

---

119 I am grateful to Scott Ragland for highlighting the import of this passage in a generous email correspondence.

120 AT 8A:100–101, CSM 1:256. Note that I have elided five words that appear in the CSM translation, but those words are not from the original Latin. In the CSM the words are – "in preference to the rest." It makes a difference to leave them out.

person inside who has been engaging in an activity for twenty years straight, and each of us is asked to guess what the activity might be. We come up with over a thousand guesses, and then there is a dramatic reveal. We learn that one of us has made the correct guess – the person inside was moving their arms at alternating 30, 45, 60, and 90 degree angles – and most everyone else guessed an activity that had absolutely nothing to do with that. We imagined a wide range of things that the person might have been doing – largely a function of our parochial interests – and we learn that the person had never considered any of them. Instead, they were inside the room the whole time, focused on geometrical movements. Then in a variation of the story we are told that the person (or being) has been engaging in the movements immutably and for eternity. The being wills the movements, and there is no sense in which there exists the possibility that they do otherwise.

Another passage that might appear to be evidence that Descartes holds it is possible for things to be other than they are in fact is the May 27, 1630 letter to Mersenne in which he says that God willed freely that the radii of a circle are equal. I want to break the passage into two parts, just because one of the parts is easy to square with the view that God does not have libertarian freedom, but the second might appear to be more recalcitrant.

In the May 27, 1630 letter, Descartes says that the eternal truth that the radii of a circle are equal is the product of a free act of God. He writes,

> You ask also what necessitated God to create these truths, and I reply that he was free to make it not true that all the radii of a circle are equal – just as free as he was not to create the world.[121]
>
> And it is certain that these truths are no more necessarily attached to his essence than are other created things.[122]

---

121 "To [Mersenne], 27 May 1630," AT 1:152, CSMK 25. This is the first part of the passage (as I am carving it up).

122 Ibid. This is the very next sentence of the letter and the second part of the passage.

Let us focus on the first part of the passage. If we read it on the assumption that Descartes holds that God has libertarian freedom, or if we read it right after reading the initial fragment of the 1644 Mesland letter – but not the part of the letter where Descartes takes it all back – then Descartes would seem to be telling Mersenne that there exists the possibility that God not will that the radii of a circle be equal. That is to say, on Descartes' view, God could have willed that the radii of a circle are not equal, or He could have refrained from willing any truths about radii at all. However, if we read the passage in the light of Descartes' own understanding of divine freedom – in terms of supreme independence – then he is saying something quite different. He is saying that God is supremely indifferent and that there are no antecedent facts about radii that God consults or that constrain His volition that the radii of a circle be equal. But just because there are no antecedent facts about radii that constrain God's activity, that does not mean that there exists the possibility that God will other than He does or that there exists the possibility that the radii of a circle be unequal.

The second part of the passage might appear to be less friendly to my reading – "it is certain that these truths are no more necessarily attached to his essence than are other created things." I agree that this part of the passage does not provide positive evidence that Descartes holds that it is not possible for things to be other than they are in fact. However, I also think that this part of the passage does not provide evidence *against* the view that Descartes holds that it is not possible for things to be other than they are in fact. If Descartes were being cagey in his comments to Mersenne, and if he subscribed to the view that it is not possible for things to be other than they are in fact, he might very well be articulating that all of God's creation is *equally* attached to His essence. And I think that it is extremely plausible that Descartes would have been cagey in communicating with Mersenne. He knew as early as October 1629 that Mersenne had a habit of sharing information that interlocutors communicated to him in private correspondence. We need look no further than the conflict that Mersenne started between Descartes and Beeckman: in early 1629, Mersenne communicated about Descartes with Beeckman, and then in October Mersenne shared information about Beeckman with Descartes, leading to the end of their ten-year friendship.[123] Descartes was extremely protective of his views, and in his May 27, 1630 letter to Mersenne he would have been wise to pull punches in the course of communicating his austere conception of divine freedom. He does come close to articulating that it is not possible for God will other than He does: he says in the same letter that "In God, willing, understanding and creating are all the same thing," and it is hard to see how a divine being so described would be able to think anything that it does not create. But there is reason to believe that he would not have been as forthcoming to Mersenne in 1630 as he was to Burman in 1648.

Another passage in which Descartes might appear to be speaking of unactualized possibilities is *Principles* III.47. There he speaks of configurations of which matter is capable, and he says that over time matter will exhibit all the configurations that are consistent with the laws of nature. He writes,

> by the operation of these laws matter must successively assume all the forms of which it is capable; and if we consider these forms in order, we will eventually be able to arrive at the form which characterizes the universe in its present state.
>
> (AT 8A:103, CSM 1:258)

Here Descartes references states of which bodies are capable, but he is not thereby positing anything in addition to the series of creatures that is the result of God's immutable and eternal act. Even the most strict necessitarian would allow that not everything happens all at once and that there are configurations that bodies exhibit at some moments but not at others. Bodies are capable of all such configurations, but that does not mean that in addition to what actually exists there also exist unactualized possibilities. For Descartes, there is what was, and what is, and what will be, and together these coincide with the states of which bodies are capable.[124] God wills the entire series of creaturely reality by a single immutable and eternal

---

123 See the discussion in Chapter 2 above, pp. 60–62, and "To Mersenne, 8 October 1629," AT 1:24.

124 For example Descartes says in *Principles* I.41 that God "knew from eternity whatever is or can be" (AT 8A:20, CSM 1:206).

act, and that is all. Anything "in addition" that He wills would already be included in His immutable and eternal volition. Anything in addition to that has no reality and is nothing at all.[125]

There is a very strong intuition that it is possible that things could be different than they actually are. David Lewis builds his view of modality on that intuition, at least in part. He writes:

> If an argument is wanted, it is this. It is uncontroversially true that things might be otherwise than they are. I believe, and so do you, that things could have been different in countless ways.[126]

Lewis does not offer an argument in support of the intuition; it is instead an obvious datum to which any account of modality is to be sensitive. Leibniz proceeds in a very similar manner. He supposes that it is a truth that (for example) Julius Caesar could have acted differently than he did, and that it is a truth that reality could have been different in all kinds of ways.[127] He then constructs a view of modality that attempts to do justice to both. But Descartes' corpus is noticeably lacking in references to alternate ways that things might be. He would agree with Lewis and Leibniz that part of the business of the philosopher is to identify intuitions that are as clear and evident as possible and then harness them in the service of a larger understanding of reality. He does not start with common-sensical intuitions about what is possible, however. As we have seen – for example in the case of color, heat, animal minds, empty space, and God's response to prayer – he has little allegiance to common-sense intuitions at all. Descartes does not start with common-sense intuitions so much as he upends them. His views in the case of modality are no different. He begins with data that he takes to admit of the highest level of clarity and evidence – intuitions about God and His omnipotence and immutability – and he follows them to

---

125 I doubt that anyone would take the *Principles* III.47 text as evidence for the view that Descartes holds that there exist possibilia. I mention the text just to be as exhaustive as possible, and also to foreground a point (later in Chapter 7) about what Descartes means to say that mind and body can exist apart.

126 Lewis (1973), 96.

127 Leibniz (1686a), Section XIII, 45–46.

wherever they might lead. He also presents us with texts in which he seems to come right out and say that there is no unactualized possible reality. What we do not find in Descartes are specific texts in which he speaks of specific ways that things could be but are not.[128]

There are two more important objections to the view that Descartes holds that it is not possible for things to be other than they are in fact. One arises in the context of his view on the freedom of finite minds – and whether or not he holds that it is possible for the volitions of a finite mind to be other than what they are in fact. That is the topic of Chapter 6. Another objection is that Descartes holds that there are states of affairs that God can bring about that God has not actualized in fact – for example the separation of minds and bodies that are united. That objection will be addressed in Chapter 7 in the discussion of Descartes' Sixth Meditation argument for mind-body dualism.

Further reading

There is a large literature on Descartes' argumentation for the existence of God. A cross-section includes:

John Edward Abbruzzese, "The Structure of Descartes's Ontological Proof," *British Journal for the History of Philosophy* 15 (2007), 253–282.

Jean-Marie Beyssade, "The Idea of God and the Proofs of His Existence," in *The Cambridge Companion to Descartes*, ed. John Cottingham, Cambridge and New York: Cambridge UP (1992), 174–199.

Georges Dicker, "Meditation III: The Criterion of Truth and the Existence of God," in *Descartes: An Analytic and Historical Introduction*, Second Edition, ed. Georges Dicker, New York and Oxford: Oxford UP (2013), 91–180.

Lawrence Nolan, "The Ontological Argument as an Exercise in Cartesian Therapy," *Canadian Journal of Philosophy* 35 (2005), 521–562.

David M. Stamos, "The Nature and Relation of the Three Proofs of God's Existence in Descartes' Meditations," *Auslegung* 22 (1997), 1–37.

---

128 Note that Kaufman (2005) argues that Descartes has a non-negotiable commitment to the existence of unactualized possible reality, but the only specific basis that Kaufman cites is his view of human freedom. In Chapter 6, I argue that Descartes does not have a view of freedom that commits him to the existence of unactualized possible reality.

Cecilia Wee, "Descartes's Ontological Proof of God's Existence," British Journal for the History of Philosophy 20 (2012), 23–40.

Margaret Wilson, Descartes, New York: Routledge (1978), 100–138.

There is also a large literature that takes up Descartes' concept of infinitude. A cross-section includes:

Igor Agostini, "Descartes and More on the Infinity of the World," British Journal for the History of Philosophy 25 (2017), 878–896.

Roger Ariew, "The Infinite in Descartes' Conversation with Burman," Archiv für Geschichte der Philosophie 69 (1987), 140–163.

Steven Barbone, "Infinity in Descartes," Philosophical Inquiry 17 (1995), 23–38.

Andrew Janiak, "Mathematics and Infinity in Descartes and Newton," in Mathematizing Space, ed. Vincenzo De Risi, Dordrecht: Springer (2015), 209–230.

Louis Loeb, "Is There Radical Dissimulation in Descartes's Meditations?" in Essays on Descartes's Meditations, ed. Amélie Oksenberg Rorty, Berkeley and Los Angeles: California UP (1986), 243–270.

Anat Schechtman, "Descartes's Argument for the Existence of the Idea of an Infinite Being," Journal of the History of Philosophy 52 (2014), 487–517.

Tad M. Schmaltz, "The Indefinite in the Descartes-More correspondence," British Journal for the History of Philosophy 29 (2021), 453–471.

Margaret D. Wilson, "Can I Be the Cause of My Idea of the World? (Descartes on the Infinite and Indefinite)," in Essays on Descartes's Meditations, ed. Amélie Oksenberg Rorty, Berkeley and Los Angeles: California UP (1986), 339–358.

There is also substantial literature on Descartes and modality. A cross-section includes:

Lilli Alanen, "Descartes, Conceivability, and Logical Modality," in Thought Experiments in Science and Philosophy, ed. Tamara Horowitz, Savage, MD: Rowman and Littlefield (1991), 65–84.

Jonathan Bennett, "Descartes's Theory of Modality," The Philosophical Review 103 (1994), 639–667.

E.M. Curley, "Descartes on the Creation of the Eternal Truths," The Philosophical Review 93 (1984), 569–597.

Harry Frankfurt, "Descartes on the Creation of the Eternal Truths," The Philosophical Review 86 (1977), 36–57.

Hide Isheguro, "The Status of Necessity and Impossibility in Descartes," in Essays on Descartes's Meditations, ed. Amélie Oksenberg Rorty. Berkeley and Los Angeles: California UP (1986), 459–472.

Dan Kaufman, "God's Immutability and the Necessity of Descartes's Eternal Truths," Journal of the History of Philosophy 43 (2005), 1–19.

Richard R. La Croix, "Descartes on God's Ability to Do the Logically Impossible," *Canadian Journal of Philosophy* 14 (1984), 455–475.

Steven Nadler, "Scientific Certainty and the Creation of the Eternal Truths: A Problem in Descartes," *The Southern Journal of Philosophy* 25 (1987), 175–192.

Alan Nelson and David Cunning, "Modality and Cognition in Descartes," *Acta Philosophica Fennica* 64 (1999), 137–153.

Calvin Normore, "Descartes's Possibilities," in *Rene Descartes: Critical Assessments*, Volume 1, ed. G.J.D. Moyal, London: Routledge (1991), 68–84.

Andrew Pessin, "Divine Simplicity and the Eternal Truths: Descartes and the Scholastics," *Philosophia* 38 (2010), 69–105.

There is also a literature on connections between Descartes and Spinoza. A cross-section includes:

Annette Baier, "The *Meditations* and Descartes' Considered Conception of God," in *The Cambridge Companion to Descartes' Meditations*, ed. David Cunning, Cambridge and New York: Cambridge UP (2014), 299–305.

John Carriero, "Descartes (and Spinoza) on Intellectual Experience and Skepticism," *Roczniki Filozoficzne* 68 (2020), 21–42.

John Cottingham, "The Intellect, the Will, and the Passions: Spinoza's Critique of Descartes," *Journal of the History of Philosophy* 26 (1988), 239–257.

Denis Kambouchner, "Spinoza and Descartes," in *A Companion to Spinoza*, ed. Yitzhak Melamed, Hoboken, NJ: Wiley & Sons (2021), 56–67.

Derk Pereboom, "Stoic Psychotherapy in Descartes and Spinoza," *Faith and Philosophy* 11 (1994), 592–625.

Anat Schechtman, "The Allegedly Cartesian Roots of Spinoza's Metaphysics," *Philosophers' Imprint* 18 (2018), 1–23.

Six

Human freedom

In this chapter, I explore Descartes' view on human freedom. I argue that Descartes does not subscribe to a libertarian view according to which it is possible for finite wills to will or affirm other than they do in fact. Then I argue that for Descartes the freedom of a finite mind is to be understood in a compatibilist sense – in terms of its independence of influences that would otherwise encumber it. For the latter discussion, I focus on the Fourth Meditation. Descartes holds that God is the cause of our affirmation of clear and distinct ideas. That is to say, God wills and preordains our affirmations of clear and distinct ideas, just as He wills and preordains everything else. Due to our embodiment, however, our otherwise clear-and-distinct ideas become confused, and we end up affirming material that attaches to those ideas like a tail. We do not find out that bodies exist until the Sixth Meditation, but the erring mind of the Fourth Meditation is a mind that is in fact embodied.

Against a libertarian reading

One of the strong pieces of evidence for the view that Descartes does not hold that finite minds possess libertarian freedom is in a 1645 letter to Princess Elisabeth. Descartes is clear that God wills the entire series of creaturely reality by a single immutable and eternal act. The modifications of finite minds are no exception:

> the only way to prove that he exists is to consider him as a
> supremely perfect being; and he would not be supremely perfect

DOI: 10.4324/9781351210522-6

if anything could happen in the world without coming entirely from him. It is true that faith alone tells us about the nature of the grace by which God raises us to a supernatural bliss; but philosophy by itself is able to discover that the slightest thought could not enter into a person's mind without God's willing, and having willed from eternity, that it should so enter. ...God is the universal cause of everything in such a way as to be also the total cause of everything....[1]

It is difficult to imagine how Descartes could be much clearer in expressing the view that nothing can happen in the creaturely realm other than God has decreed it to happen. God is the *total* cause of everything; nothing could ever happen without coming entirely from Him. To make sure that we do not misunderstand, Descartes says later in the same letter that

the greater we deem the works of God to be, the better we observe the infinity of his power; and the better known this infinity is to us, the more certain we are that it extends even to the most particular actions of human beings.

(AT 4:315, CSMK 273)

For Descartes, there is nothing that does not depend for its existence on the creative activity of God – not the eternal truths that two and three add to five or that the radii of a circle are equal, not finite bodies, not the sizes and shapes of finite bodies, not the slightest modification of a mind. Descartes will still allow that finite minds are free, at least in some instances, but whatever sort of freedom they possess, it will square with the datum that God has preordained everything from eternity.

Another piece of evidence for the view that Descartes does not hold that finite minds possess libertarian freedom is in a 1647 letter to Chanut. There Descartes speaks of God and

the extent of his providence, which makes him see with a single thought all that has been, all that is, all that will be and all

---

1   "To Princess Elizabeth, 6 October 1645," AT 4:314, CSMK 272.

that could be, and of the infallibility of his decrees, which are altogether immutable even though they respect our free will.[2]

Descartes does not say here that God's decrees are altogether immutable *apart* from our free will. His decrees are wholly immutable *and* they respect our free will.

Another piece of evidence for the view that Descartes does not hold that finite minds possess libertarian freedom is in the November 3, 1645 letter to Princess Elisabeth. Descartes owns that we have a vivid and undeniable experience of independence and freedom – or "the independence which we experience in ourselves" (AT 4:332–333, CSMK 277) – but he says that whatever that independence is, it is not incompatible with the datum that God has willed all of creaturely reality by a single immutable and eternal act. He writes,

> As for free will, I agree that if we think only of ourselves we cannot help regarding ourselves as independent, but when we think of the infinite power of God, we cannot help believing that all things depend on him, and hence that our free will is not exempt from this dependence. For it involves a contradiction to say that God has created human beings of such a nature that the actions of their will do not depend on his. It is the same thing as saying that his power is both finite and infinite.... The independence which we experience and feel in ourselves... is not incompatible with a dependence of quite another kind, whereby all things are subject to God.[3]

Here Descartes is contending that our experience of independence and freedom is compatible with divine preordination. Of course it is. There is nothing contradictory about the idea of a being that has an experience of independence even though all of that being's decisions and other mental states are preordained from eternity.

---

2 "To Chanut, 1 February 1647," AT 4:608–609, CSMK 309. Descartes says that God sees "*all* that will be." I am reading the "all that could be" language in line with *Principles* III.47, AT 8A:103, CSM 1:258.

3 "To Princess Elizabeth, 3 November 1645," AT 4:332–333, CSMK 277.

There is something puzzling about it, to be sure.[4] What is especially puzzling is that while we are *having* that experience, the prospect that God has preordained everything seems utterly absurd.[5] But Descartes could not be more clear that God is the author of finite minds all the way down to their slightest modification – the experience of independence included.

Still, we might assume that God would not give us that experience if there did not exist the possibility that we affirm otherwise. But that would be hasty.[6] The experience of independence is in fact an echo of our proximity to God, according to Descartes. At the end of the Third Meditation he had said that our idea of God is a kind of birthmark – and one that we should not be surprised to find in ourselves if we are products of God (AT 7:51, CSM 2:35). In the Fourth Meditation, he says more specifically that our experience of independence is an indication that we "bear in some way the image and likeness of God" (AT 7:57, CSM 2:40). We do not register proximity to God in terms of our knowledge, power, or eternality. However, our experience of independence appears to be a kind of announcement to the effect that there are respects in which we come close to approximating the divine nature. Descartes will argue later in his correspondence with Elizabeth and in *The Passions of the Soul* that finite embodied minds achieve more perfection to the extent that they become more independent, more informed, and more immutable.[7] A vivid experience of independence is then an accompaniment to that perfection. We do not *always* have an experience of freedom: for example, the passions of an embodied mind sometimes

---

4   It might be puzzling that we have an experience of independence even though all of our mental modifications are preordained for all eternity, but it is not contradictory. A non-Cartesian evolutionist might say that similarly there is a puzzle about why our nervous system would make us have a vivid experience of freedom when all of our ideas and decisions are due to the way that our neurons were firing just the moment before. But the evolutionist is not thereby exposing a contradiction of any kind.

5   Descartes makes this point in *Principles* I.40–41, a discussion of which is below.

6   Here I am disagreeing with Latzer (2001), 44–45; Shapiro (1999), 254–258; Ragland (2005); Della Rocca (2005), 26–28; Wee (2006); and Gombay (2007), 128.

7   This is the topic of Chapter 9.

pull the will first to one side and then to the other, thus making it battle against itself and so putting the soul in the most deplorable state possible[,]... render[ing] the soul enslaved and miserable.[8]

Descartes adds in a letter to Elizabeth that there is "nothing more distressing than being attached to a body that altogether takes away its freedom."[9] Finite minds do not always have a vivid experience of independence, but that experience is a not unpleasant signal of our participation in the good.

Another (and a very much related) piece of evidence for the view that Descartes does not hold that finite minds possess libertarian freedom is in *Passions* II.145. There he writes that

we should reflect upon the fact that nothing can possibly happen other than as Providence has determined from all eternity.

(AT 11:438, CSM 1:380)

Descartes does not say here that we should reflect upon the fact that some things cannot happen other than Providence has determined from all eternity, or that most things cannot happen other than Providence has determined from all eternity. He says that nothing can happen other than as Providence has determined for all eternity. If something did happen that was not the product of the single immutable and eternal act by which God produces all things, then there would be something that was independent of God, but that (according to Descartes) is absurd. Descartes does of course allow that part of what is included in the Providential act is that finite minds have a vivid and inescapable experience of independence. We (sometimes) have a vivid experience of independence, and when we do, we cannot help but regard ourselves as exempt from divine preordination. Descartes accordingly says in *Passions* II.146 that

we must recognize that everything is guided by divine Providence, whose eternal decree is infallible and immutable to

---

8   *Passions* I.48, AT 11:367, CSM 1:347.
9   "To Princess Elizabeth, 1 September 1645," AT 4:282, CSMK 263.

such an extent that, except for matters it has determined to be dependent on my free will, we must consider everything that affects us to occur of necessity and as it were by fate....

(AT 11:439, CSM 1:380)

The "except" clause here might be read as reflecting that the eternal and immutable decree of God does not apply to the volitions of finite minds, but Descartes had said just a few sentences earlier that "nothing can possibly happen other than as Providence has determined from all eternity." In yet other passages, he says that God decrees *everything* by an eternal and immutable act – an act which reaches all the way down to finite modifications. In the "except" clause of *Passions* II.146, Descartes is referencing what "we must [and must not] *consider*" or regard as taking place by necessity. Finite minds have been constructed in such a way that on some occasions we have a vivid sense of independence. Descartes accordingly does not propose that on those occasions we take a third-person perspective on our behavior and consider it to be the inevitable result of Providence.[10]

Descartes grants that while we are having a vivid experience of freedom, we encounter tremendous difficulty accepting that God wills all of creaturely reality by a single immutable and eternal act. In *Principles* I.40–41, he addresses that difficulty and tension directly. Absent our vivid experience of freedom, we have no trouble recognizing that everything – down to the slightest modification – is the product of His (eternal and immutable) will. In *Principles* I.40, Descartes repeats what he has said in so many other passages:

now that we have come to know God, we perceive in Him a power so immeasurable that we regard it as impious to suppose that we could ever do anything which was not already preordained by him.

(AT 8A:20, CSM 1:206)

He had also just stated a few sections earlier (in *Principles* I.23) that God wills the entire series of creaturely reality by a single immutable

---

10 See also the similar language in Leibniz (1686), Section IV, 37.

and eternal act, and here he asserts that that act reaches to anything "we could ever do." Focusing our attention on one thing at a time, a clear and distinct perception of the divine preordination of all creaturely reality is difficult enough, but a grasp of divine preordination in the face of a vivid experience of independence and freedom is another thing entirely. It is analogous to a recognition of the real distinction between mind and body in the face of a vivid awareness of mind-body union: the latter inclines us to dismiss the prospect of mind-body union as suspicious if not absurd.[11] Descartes accordingly says at the end of *Principles* I.40 that "we can easily get ourselves into difficulties if we attempt to reconcile this divine preordination with the freedom of our will, or attempt to grasp both these things at once" (ibid.). He then begins *Principles* I.41 with the proclamation that

> We shall get out of these difficulties if we remember that our mind is finite, while the power of God is infinite – the power by which he not only knew from eternity whatever is or can be, but also willed it and preordained it.[12]

We have seen this argumentative maneuver before.[13] Descartes identifies a result that we clearly and distinctly perceive, but he also identifies a confused judgment that we are inclined to make and that places the result under suspicion. The result that we clearly

---

11 See for example "To Princess Elizabeth, 28 June 1643," AT 3:693, CSMK 227, and Chapter 7, pp. 287–290.

12 AT 8A:20, CSM 1:206. Note that here, and also in the February 1647 Chanut letter (AT 4:608, CSMK 309), Descartes says that in the single immutable act God preordains all that is and *can* be, and so we might read him as holding that God preordains unactualized possible reality in addition to actual reality. I am instead reading the two passages in line with Descartes' own *Principles* III.47 claim that bodies eventually take on all configurations that are possible for them. See also the discussion in Chapter 5, p. 209–210.

13 In *Principles* II.35, AT 8A:60, CSM 1:239. Descartes says that we understand that bodies are indefinitely divided and that we do not understand how such a division could take place. He argues that instead of affirming that it is impossible for the division to take place – and rejecting a result that we clearly and distinctly perceive – we should just admit that there are things that we do not understand. See also Chapter 3, pp. 81–82.

and distinctly perceive is that God wills all of creaturely reality by a single immutable and eternal act. The confused judgment is that God would not have given us a vivid experience of freedom and independence if He preordained everything from eternity and so He did not preordain everything from eternity. Descartes thus makes sure to remind us that God has enough power to have created a universe in which everything is preordained *and* we have a vivid experience of independence. He says of "the power by which [God] not only knew from eternity whatever is or can be, but also willed it and preordained it" that "We may attain a sufficient knowledge of this power to perceive clearly and distinctly that God possesses it" (AT 8A:20, CSM 1:206). At the time that we are having a vivid experience of independence, however, we do not understand how it could be the case that everything is preordained. We might then affirm that we are mistaken that God wills all of creaturely reality by a single immutable and eternal act.

That would be hasty. Descartes reminds us that it is inappropriate for us to make assertions about what we do not understand, and he adds that it is even more inappropriate to judge on the basis of our inability to understand or grasp one thing that something else that we *do* understand or grasp is false. We cannot make sense of how our vivid experience of independence and freedom squares with the fact that everything is preordained from eternity. Descartes thus suggests that we focus on one thing at a time. We understand that God wills the entire series of creaturely reality by a single immutable and eternal act. In addition,

> we have such a close awareness of the freedom and indifference which is in us that there is nothing we can grasp more evidently or more perfectly. And it would be absurd, simply because we do not grasp one thing, which we know must by its nature to be beyond our comprehension, to doubt something else of which we have an intimate grasp and which we experience within ourselves.
>
> (ibid.)

The result that God has preordained everything from eternity is in severe tension with "the close awareness of the freedom and indifference which is in us." We would be hasty to deny the divine preordination of all events on the basis of the unsubstantiated judgment that it is impossible for God to have preordained everything from eternity *and* to have supplied us with an awareness of independence. We would also be hasty to deny or dismiss our intimate experience of independence and freedom.[14] It is not clear how we would even do that – if the experience is inescapable and will keep coming back. But more importantly, it is a mark of our proximity to God and the perfection that it is within our reach as a model. To dismiss it would be to ignore a signpost that points us in the direction of how to live.

Another passage that is evidence for the view that Descartes does not hold that finite minds possess libertarian freedom is in a 1646 letter to Princess Elisabeth. Descartes writes,

> Before he [God] sent us into the world he knew exactly what all the inclinations of our will would be; it is he who gave us them, it is he who has arranged all the other things outside us so that such and such objects would present themselves to our senses

---

14 Descartes is clear in *Principles* I.40-41 that what is in conflict is (1) the result that God preordains all events from eternity and (2) our experience of independence and freedom. What is in conflict is not (1) and (3) the fact of human freedom. Descartes nowhere speaks of a fact of human freedom that we recognize or grasp, but only of an *experience* of freedom – for example in "To Princess Elizabeth, 3 November 1645," AT 4:332-33, CSMK 277, quoted above, and *Principles* I.41. He instead speaks of a vivid experience of freedom, which he thinks we have at least occasionally. Ragland argues that because libertarian (but not compatibilist) freedom conflicts with divine preordination, Descartes is clearly espousing a libertarian view in *Principles* I.40-41. (See Ragland (2016), 208.) But again Descartes is pointing out in *Principles* I.40-41 that it is our *experience* of freedom that flies in the face of divine preordination freedom – and we have that experience regardless of whether we have libertarian or compatibilist freedom. If Descartes is suggesting a view of freedom in *Principles* I.40-41, he is suggesting a compatibilist view when he says that there is not anything we could ever do which was not already preordained by him. Note that in *Principles* I.41 he adds that we do not grasp as perfectly how divine preordination "leaves the free actions of men undetermined" (Ibid.). I have argued that he holds that the reason why we do not grasp this is that divine preordination does not leave our actions undetermined.

at such and such times, on the occasion of which he knew that our free will would determine us to such and such an action.[15]

Here Descartes says that God knows all the details surrounding our decisions and that he also knows which action our free will opts to pursue. He compares God to a king "who knows with certainty that [two men] will meet, and fight, ...but he does not thereby compel them," and hence their actions are "voluntary... and free" (AT 4:353, CSMK 282). But if God knows that something will happen, it will happen without fail, and in addition Descartes makes clear in numerous passages that (unlike in the case of a king) whatever God understands, He also wills and creates.[16] In the letter, Descartes says that God knows all the details surrounding our volitions and that God knows what we will do, but that is also to say that He preordains what we will do. He adds that "he [God] so willed, but he did not thereby will that our will should be constrained to the choice in question" (AT 4:354, CSMK 282). Here he is gesturing at his compatibilist view of human freedom. We move on to that now.

Freedom and voluntariness

In other texts, Descartes fleshes out the sense in which it is true that finite minds are free and not constrained. In *Third Replies*, he says to Hobbes that

> if we simply consider ourselves, we will all realize in the light of our own experience that voluntariness and freedom are one and the same thing.
>
> (AT 7:191, CSM 2:134)

He says the same in *Principles* I.37: "it is a supreme perfection in man that he acts voluntarily, that is freely" (AT 8A:18, CSM 1:205). He uses very similar language in a 1644 letter to Mesland. He writes that

15 "To Princess Elizabeth, January 1646," AT 4:353–354, CSMK 282.
16 See Chapter 5, pp. 201–202.

"I call free in the general sense whatever is voluntary,"[17] or of the will. He elaborates in the Fourth Meditation and says that an affirmation is free to the extent that it is guided by compelling reasons or similar (mental) dispositions:

> In order to be free, there is no need for me to be inclined both ways; on the contrary, the more I incline in one direction – either because I clearly understand that reasons of truth and goodness point that way, or because of a divinely produced disposition of my inmost thoughts – the freer is my choice.
> (AT 7:57–58, CSM 2:40)

He accordingly speaks of freedom as consisting in the "ease of operation" of the will when reasons compel it to affirm:

> freedom considered in the acts of will at the moment they are elicited… consists simply in ease of operation; and at that point freedom, spontaneity, and voluntariness are the same thing. It was in this sense that I wrote that I moved towards something all the more freely when there were more reasons driving me toward it; for it is certain that in that case our will moves itself with greater facility and force.[18]

He adds that there is a distinctive phenomenological awareness in such cases: "our inclinations are such that we do not feel we are determined by any external force" (AT 7:57, CSM 2:40). We are free in cases in which we do not *feel* that we are compelled by an external force, but more importantly we are free in cases in which we are not in fact compelled to judge by an external force. As Descartes puts it,

> I could not but judge that something which I understood so clearly was true; but this was not because I was compelled so to judge by any external force, but because a great light in the intellect was followed by a great inclination in the will, and thus

---

17 "To [Mesland], 2 May 1644," AT 4:116, CSMK 234.
18 "To [Mesland], 9 February 1645," AT 4:174–175, CSMK 246.

the spontaneity and freedom of my belief was all the greater in proportion to my lack of indifference.

(AT 7:58–59, CSM 2:41)[19]

There are other instances in which finite minds are not free, or at least not as free – for example when corporeal passions "pull the will first to one side and then to the other" (AT 11:367, CSM 1:347), or when a "passion makes us believe certain things."[20]

Descartes holds that affirmations are free to the extent that they are compelled by evident reasons or other wholly mental dispositions. Affirmations are less free to the extent that they are compelled by bodily states and other factors that are external to the mind. That is all to say, affirmations are voluntary or free to the extent that they are due to mind and not body: they are voluntary or free to the extent that they are the product of the mind that makes them.[21] To the extent that an affirmation is due to something else – for example, the states of the body to which that mind is united – the affirmation is due to external and non-volitional causes. It is not of the will. Here we have again a sense in which the supreme independence of God is a model for us.

We are now in a position to consider two passages that might seem to provide evidence that Descartes holds that finite wills do possess libertarian freedom. One is in *Principles* I.37. There Descartes writes (in the CSM translation) that

it is a supreme perfection in man that he acts voluntarily, that is, freely; this makes him in a special way the author of his actions and deserving of praise for what he does. We do not praise automatons for accurately producing all the movements they were designed to perform, because the production of these

---

19 Descartes is not regarding God as an external force in this context, for he supposes that some of our affirmations are free but that all are part of the series of creatures that God immutably wills and decrees.

20 "To Princess Elizabeth, 1 September 1645," AT 4:284, CSSK 263. In the same letter, Descartes also speaks of cases in which a mind is attached to a body that "altogether takes away its freedom" (AT 4:282, CSMK 263).

21 See also Lennon (2013) and Lennon (2014).

movements occurs necessarily. It is the designer who is praised for constructing such carefully-made devices; for in constructing them he acted not out of necessity but freely. By the same principle, when we embrace the truth, our doing so voluntarily is much more to our credit than would be the case if we could not do otherwise.

(AT 8A:18–19, CSM 1:205)

We might suppose that this passage spells doom for the view that Descartes does not hold that finite minds possess libertarian freedom and a two-way contra-causal ability to do otherwise.[22] But we would be making a mistake. The mistake is due in part to a problem of translation and in part to a failure to appreciate (what Descartes takes to be) the distinction between voluntary behavior and the behavior of automata.

The CSM translation of *Principles* I.37 ends with the following – "our doing so voluntarily is much more to our credit than would be the case if we could not do otherwise." But a reference to an ability to do otherwise does not actually appear in the original Latin. The original is "quam si non possemus non amplecti," which does not include a variant of the (loaded) term "otherwise" and is more literally translated – "than if we did not have the ability to not embrace it." The reason why it is so important to highlight the mistake in translation is that Descartes uses almost identical language elsewhere, and he does so in the context of articulating that the ability to affirm and to refrain from affirming truth is not a two-way libertarian power. He says in the Fourth Meditation that "the will *consists* simply in our ability to do or not do something (that is, to affirm or deny, to pursue or avoid)" (AT 7:57, CSM 2:40, emphasis added). But he also holds that in cases of clear and distinct perception of truth, our perception is utterly compelled. He says this in multiple passages, some of which appear in the *Meditations*, and one of which appears in *Principles of Philosophy* just shortly after Section 37 of Part I:

---

22 See for example Ragland (2005), Wee (2006), Wee (2014), and Ragland (2016).

the minds of all of us have been so moulded by nature that whenever we perceive something clearly, we spontaneously give our assent to it and are quite unable to doubt its truth.[23]

That is all to say: the nature of a finite will consists in the ability to affirm or deny; but a thing has the nature that it does in all circumstances in which it exists, and so a will has the nature of a will even when it is unable to refrain from affirming a clear and distinct perception; therefore, the ability to affirm or deny is not a contra-causal two-way ability to do otherwise. Instead, Descartes holds that the will has the two abilities – to affirm and to deny.[24]

---

23 *Principles* I.43, AT 8A:21, CSM 1:207. See also the Fifth Meditation, AT 7:69, CSM 2:48; *Second Replies*, AT 7:166, CSM 2:117; and "To [Mesland], 9 February 1645," AT 4:173, CSMK 245. Descartes holds that while we are having a clear and distinct perception, our will cannot help but affirm it. He does allow however that there are cases in which a different mental modification (other than our will) is able to divert our attention so that we cease to affirm a clear and distinct perception. He says for example in the Mesland letter that "it is always open to us to hold back from pursuing a clearly known good, or from admitting a clearly perceived truth, provided we consider it a good thing to demonstrate the freedom of our will by so doing" (ibid.). If clear and distinct perceptions are utterly will-compelling, there is no way for a will to divert itself from a clear and distinct perception while it is having one, but other mental modifications can (and do) intervene instead. See also Nelson (1997), and Christofidou (2009), 644–648. Note that many libertarian interpreters of Descartes now accept that (for Descartes) clear and distinct perceptions are utterly will-compelling, but the will has libertarian freedom in cases of non-clear-and-distinct perception. See for example Ragland (2016), 160–166. Some commentators (for example Schüssler 2013) argue that Descartes holds that finite will has a two-way power to affirm or not affirm in all cases – including cases of clear and distinct perception. Schüssler appeals to the February 1645 Mesland letter as strong evidence for the view that Descartes holds that it is possible to refrain from affirming a clear and distinct perception (159–160), but in the light of the numerous counter-passages, the letter is most easily read as saying that *while* we are having a clear and distinct perception, it is impossible for the will not to affirm it.

24 See also "To Mesland, 2 May 1644," AT 4:117, CSMK 234, and Lennon (2014), 178–179.

Descartes writes in *Principles* I.37 that we merit praise or blame when we do things voluntarily. He does not hold that when we affirm a clearly and distinctly perceived truth we have an ability to do otherwise, and so he does not hold that praise and blame are only merited in cases in which a being exercises libertarian freedom. He contrasts us with automata, or creatures "which lack reason."[25] These are entities that do not have a will and so do not act voluntarily. They do not act voluntarily, and in addition, there is little sense in which their activity can be properly described as their own. An automaton is a material body in a plenum, and its activity will always be due in part to the behavior of the bodies that surround it and in (large) part to the behavior of the bodies that surround those. The activity of a finite mind is sometimes due to the behavior of things other than itself – for example, bodies that pull it first in one direction and then in another – but there are also instances in which a finite mind is independent of such influences and is the source of its own activity. In such instances, the activity of that mind is attributable to it – and it is that mind that is due any praise. "It is a supreme perfection in us" that like the supremely perfect being we act voluntarily or from volitions, even if our behavior is sometimes due to other causes as well. Descartes nowhere suggests that a mind merits praise or blame for its activity because it has a libertarian two-way ability to do otherwise. Instead, he is operating in a seventeenth-century context in which compatibilist attributions of praise and blame make perfect sense, for example in the work of Leibniz and Hobbes.[26]

An additional reason for thinking that Descartes does not suppose that praise and blame only apply to actions that result from libertarian freedom is that Descartes is clear that God merits praise for the bounty that He has created, but He does not hold that God has libertarian freedom.[27] Descartes writes for example that

---

25 "To Mersenne, 30 July 1640," AT 3:122, CSMK 149. See also Christofidou (2009), 645.

26 Leibniz (1686), Sections viii–xiii, pp. 40–46; Hobbes (1668), chapter xxi, pp. 136–145. Below (on pp. 246–247) there is a discussion of Descartes' Fourth Meditation claim that we use our will correctly when we refrain from affirming perceptions that are confused (AT 7:59–60, CSM 2:41).

27 See the discussion in Chapter 5, pp. 192–202.

the function of the various parts of plants and animals, etc.,
makes it appropriate to admire God as their efficient cause –
to recognize and glorify the craftsman through examining his
works....[28]

Descartes does not hold that God is not worthy of praise or blame.
God has willed all events by a single immutable act for eternity, and
there does not exist the possibility that His eternal and immutable
will be otherwise, but still He deserves praise for the bounteous creation that He has made:

> when we love God and through him unite ourselves willingly
> to all the things he has created, then the more great, noble and
> perfect we reckon them, ...and the more grounds we have for
> praising God on account of the immensity of his works.[29]

God merits praise, on Descartes' view, even though God does not
possess libertarian freedom. The fact that God does not possess libertarian freedom also does not signal that God is an automaton or that
His behavior is caused by the behavior of other beings.

The final piece of textual evidence that would seem to reflect
that Descartes takes finite minds to have libertarian freedom is in
Passions I.41.[30] There Descartes says that "the will is by its nature so
free that it can never be constrained" (AT 11:359, CSM 1:343). On
its face the passage suggests that finite wills are not constrained
under any circumstances. A problem with reading the passage
that way, however, is that as we have seen there are numerous
passages – some in *The Passions of the Soul* itself – in which Descartes
says that finite wills are pulled this way and that by passions and
sensations, and passages in which he speaks of embodied minds
as enslaved. If we are going to apply a principle of charity and
allow Descartes to be consistent, we have to read the *Passions* I.41
passage as stating that on their own and by their very nature finite

---

28 *Fifth Replies*, AT 7:374–375, CSM 2:258.
29 "To Chanut, 6 June 1647," AT 5:56, CSMK 322. See also the Fourth Meditation,
   CSM 2:42, AT 7:60.
30 See also Gilbert (1998) and Shapiro (1999), 252–254.

minds are wholly unconstrained – for example when they are not attached to bodies, or at least when bodily states do not interfere with their activity. The passage is almost a tautology in that case, but not quite. We sometimes speak of a diamond as beautiful by its very nature, even if we are talking about a diamond that is encrusted in centuries of dirt and rock and soil. The diamond is not beautiful at first glance, but there is a sense, and a strong sense, in which it is beautiful by its nature. Or perhaps a better analogy is that of a dancer who is active and exuberant and who exhibits a tremendous amount of spontaneity and energy on stage. We might say of such a dancer that he cannot be contained. Still, the dancer could be contained if someone pinned him down or if an injury hampered his activity. Nor are we saying something trivial or empty when we go out of our way and highlight that the dancer is active and graceful in circumstances in which he is allowed to express himself.

Descartes holds that the nature of a finite will is to be unconstrained in something like the way that a diamond encrusted in dirt is beautiful or the way that a spontaneous and energetic dancer is free and uncontained. For Descartes, a finite mind untethered to a body is extremely active and affirms its clear and distinct ideas. Again, he holds that if a mind were not tethered to a body – or at least if it were not influenced by its body – it would have clear and distinct ideas only.[31] On its own and untethered to a body, a finite mind is a highly active being. It is unconstrained and uncontained in that circumstance, just as its existence is marked by unconstrained activity when it is attached to a body but has achieved a level of independence such that it is (sometimes) the author of its own states. In that circumstance, its affirmations can be attributed to it and it alone.

Creaturely error and the supreme perfection of God

Now we are in a position to turn to the Fourth Meditation resolution of the problem of error.

---

31 See Chapter 3, pp. 77–78.

Descartes begins the Meditation by calling attention to a truth that he had clearly and distinctly recognized at the end of Meditation Three. He writes,

> To begin with, I recognize that it is impossible that God should ever deceive me. For in every case of trickery or deception some imperfection is to be found; and although the ability to deceive appears to be an indication of cleverness or power, the will to deceive is undoubtedly evidence of malice or weakness, and so cannot apply to God.
>
> (AT 7:53, CSM 2:37)

But a worry arises almost immediately. Finite minds make mistakes – a lot of them – and if so, we would not appear to be the product of a supremely perfect being. As Descartes puts it,

> if everything that is within me comes from God, and he did not endow me with a faculty for making mistakes, it appears that I can never go wrong. ...[But] I know by experience that I am prone to countless errors.
>
> (AT 7:54, CSM 2:38)

One approach that Descartes might take to restore the Third Meditation result that a supreme and perfect creator exists would be to argue that appearances aside finite minds do not make false judgments. For good reason, he does not do that. He argues instead that appearances aside it is consistent with the supremacy and perfection of the divine being that Its creatures occasionally err.

We err, and one of the errors that we make is to affirm at the start of the Fourth Meditation that if we are created by a supremely perfect being we "can never go wrong."[32]

Descartes first attempts to disarm that false judgment by pointing out that there is no reason to expect that a supreme and perfect creator would create other beings that are supremely perfect. As the product of a supreme being, we will have perfections, but we will

---

32 See also Ragland (2007), and Ragland and Fulmer (2020).

not be a duplicate of the supreme being Itself. We are "something intermediate between God and nothingness, or between supreme being and non-being" (AT 7:54, CSM 2:38). Descartes continues,

> in so far as I was created by the supreme being, there is nothing in me to enable me to go wrong or to lead me astray; but… in so far as I am not myself the supreme being and am lacking in countless respects, it is no wonder that I make mistakes.
>
> (ibid.)

A supremely perfect divine being would never err, Descartes is supposing, but instead Its judgments would always be true. There is nothing that a supreme being thinks that It does not understand, and there is nothing that It does not think. But "the faculty of judgement which I have from God in my case is not infinite" (ibid.), as there is a lot that we think that we do not understand, and there are many things of which we have no ideas at all. We are "lacking in countless respects," and an entity that is somewhere on the spectrum from non-being to infinite perfection is still infinitely removed from God. Such an entity would be expected to err at least on occasion, or so Descartes reasons initially.

A finite creature would not be a duplicate of God, but Descartes reflects a bit more and wonders why a supremely perfect being would not have created beings that are inferior to God but that still do not err. A finite mind would understand just a small number of things – as a reflection of its position on the scale from non-being to perfection – but if it was the product of a supremely perfect creator, it presumably would affirm what it understands and nothing more:

> The more skilled the craftsman the more perfect the work produced by him; if this is so, how can anything produced by the supreme creator of all things not be complete and perfect in all respects?
>
> (AT 7:55, CSM 2:38)

Descartes therefore identifies error not as a negation of perfection – or a lack of features whose absence constitutes the totally acceptable gap between supreme perfection and finitude – but as a privation.

Finite minds are always going to be less than supremely perfect – as there is only so much that we are going to understand – but if we did not ever mistake the false for the true, we would understand just as much as we do currently and have less imperfection still. Descartes accordingly says that error is "a privation or lack of some knowledge which somehow should be in me" (ibid.), though he does not yet elaborate on what that lack of knowledge is. He supposes that a perfect craftsman would create entities that are "complete and perfect in all respects" of their finitude, and later in the Meditation he adds that

> He could, for example, have endowed my intellect with a clear and distinct perception of everything about which I was ever likely to deliberate…
>
> (AT 7:61, CSM 2:42)

Here Descartes is suggesting that the lack that is error is perhaps due to our possession of ideas that lack full clarity and distinctness. If we had clear and distinct ideas only, we would never err. Indeed, it seems that God might have made us such that our currently confused ideas were fully clear and distinct, or He might have made us without those ideas at all.

There is also a second way that "God could have given me a nature such that I was never mistaken…." (AT 7:55, CSM 2:38). He might have created us in such a way that we think a number of things that we do not understand, but we always refrain from making judgments about them. In the Third Meditation, he had highlighted that there are instances in which we imagine or daydream scenarios without affirming whether or not they obtain. We do not err in such instances if – for reasons of wonder or speculation or pleasure – we are just entertaining ideas that are part of our cognitive toolkit:

> Now as far as ideas are concerned, provided they are considered solely in themselves and I do not refer them to anything else, they cannot strictly speaking be false; for whether it is a goat or a chimera that I am imagining, it is just as true that I imagine the former as the latter. As for the will and the emotions, here too one need not worry about falsity; for even if the things which I

may desire are wicked or even non-existent, that does not make
it any less true that I desire them.

(AT 7:37, CSM 2:26)

A supremely perfect being would not create other supremely perfect
entities; it would create entities that are somewhere on the spectrum
of supreme perfection to non-being. A finite mind might be created
in such a way that it understands whatever it thinks, and so never
makes a false judgment. A finite might also be created in such a way
that it imagines and daydreams, but is one way or another prevented
from affirming what it does not understand. Descartes thus says later
in the Fourth Meditation that a second way that "God could easily
have brought it about that... despite the limitations in my knowledge, I should nonetheless never make a mistake" is "simply [to]
have impressed it unforgettably on my memory that I should never
make a judgment about anything which I did not clearly and distinctly understand" (AT 7:61, CSM 2:42).[33] A supreme being would
create minds that involve a negation of supreme perfection, but still
there are the two ways that It might have made us such that we never
err. God did not make us in either of those two ways – that is pretty
clear – and so the initial explanation of error in terms of creatures
occupying a position on the spectrum of supreme perfection to
non-being "is still not entirely satisfactory" (AT 7:55, CSM 2:38).

In the next few paragraphs of the Meditation, Descartes continues
in the effort to make sense of how an erring mind might be the creative output of a supremely perfect entity. He explores three different
but similarly weighty considerations – each of which chips away at
the assumption that erring minds are too imperfect to have been
made by God.

The first consideration is that we do not always understand why a
supremely perfect being would act as It does. He writes,

---

33 But note that Descartes argues later in the Sixth Meditation that if God had
created us in such a way that "I should never make a judgment about anything
which I did not clearly and distinctly understand" – for example, the sensible
bodies that are relevant to the continued existence of our mind-body union –
we would not survive for very long. See Chapter 8, pp. 318–321.

it occurs to me first of all that it is no cause for surprise if I do not understand the reasons for some of God's actions; and there is no call to doubt his existence if I happen to find that there are other instances where I do not grasp why or how certain things were made by him.

(AT 7:55, CSM 2:38–39)

Descartes might have ended the Fourth Meditation with a discussion of just this first consideration if he did not think that there were other considerations that entail that a supremely perfect being might create minds that err. As we saw in *Second Replies* (AT 7:164, CSM 2:116) and *Principles* I.41 (AT 8A:20, CSM 2:206), he supposes that there are results that we recognize to be true but whose truth seems very unlikely in the face of other factors that show up on our radar. He argues that God has enough power to have created a universe in which all of our clear and distinct perceptions are true – come what may. He makes basically the same point in the next sentence of the Fourth Meditation:

For since I now know that my own nature is very weak and limited, whereas the nature of God is immense, incomprehensible, and infinite, I also know without more ado that he is capable of countless things whose causes are beyond my knowledge.

(AT 7:55, CSM 2:39)

It is true that a supremely perfect being exists, or so Descartes has argued. It is also true that finite minds err and are the product of a supremely perfect being, so God clearly has the power to have made a universe in which there exists a finite being that has a privation or "lacks some perfection that it ought to have." Descartes might have ended the Fourth Meditation with that, but there are two other considerations that he thinks merit presenting, and he presents them.[34]

---

34 One more thing to note about the consideration that "occurs to [Descartes] first of all" is that in explicating it he does not say that whatever it is that God happens to will is good, but that God "always wills what is best" (AT 7:55, CSM 2:38). If whatever it is that God happens to will is good, then we would not have to look at the whole universe to assess "whether the works of God

He also presumably recognizes that an appeal to God's power in a context in which God's existence has been called into question (at the start of the Fourth Meditation) will not be as effective as an appeal to God's power in a context (like *Principles* I.41) in which the existence of God is assumed to be obvious.

The second consideration that Descartes explores is that we are hasty to assert that an erring finite mind "lacks some perfection that it ought to have" or that it is wanting in any way at all. Such a mind certainly *appears* to be wanting – at least when we consider it in isolation. But perhaps we are misled by the hard boundaries that we draw to demarcate creatures, and the apparent imperfection of an entity vanishes when we pay attention to more than just the entity itself. Descartes writes,

> For what would perhaps rightly appear very imperfect if it existed on its own is quite perfect when its function as a part of the universe is considered.
>
> (AT 7:55–56, CSM 2:39)

A familiar example that Descartes does not offer is that of a small section of a masterpiece work of art – a section that would be less impressive in isolation but that does *not* exist in isolation and that contributes to the esthetic of the larger masterpiece whole. The small section is perhaps less intricate, less impactful, and less prominent than other parts of the painting, but the painting is better with than without it. Descartes is then suggesting in the Fourth Meditation that for all we know and contrary to appearances our errant minds are not as imperfect as we take them to be. They "perhaps rightly appear imperfect" on their own, but they are not on their own, and their apparent imperfection does not give us license to conclude that they are imperfect or that there does not exist a supremely perfect being that is their author.

---

are perfect." Instead, we would know that they are good in advance. See also *Conversation with Burman*, where Descartes says that "necessarily willed what was best" (AT 5:166, CSMK 348). See also the discussion in Chapter 1, pp. 25–30.

Finite will and finite intellect

The next (or third) consideration that Descartes presents is that the false judgments of a finite mind are the product of two faculties each of which is quite well-made and of the sort that would be produced by a supremely perfect entity. He writes,

> Next, when I look more closely at myself and inquire into the nature of my errors (for these are the only evidence of some imperfection in me), I notice that they depend on two concurrent causes, namely on the faculty of knowledge which is in me, and on the faculty of choice or freedom of the will; that is, they depend on both the intellect and the will simultaneously.
>
> (AT 7:56, CSM 2:39)

Descartes holds that any judgment – and here he focuses on the erroneous variety of judgment – is the product of both intellect and will. He does not attempt to prove that the judgments of a finite mind are due to both intellect and will. He tries to get us to notice it. Nor does he attempt to prove that a finite mind has faculties of intellect and will. Thus far in the *Meditations*, he has analyzed and broken down the notions of substance and modification, but he has not said much about the ontology of faculties. He is presumably entitled to make the claim that finite minds have ideas, at least if we accept his classification of mental items into different kinds in the Third Meditation (AT 7:37, CSM 2:25). He would also appear to be entitled to assert that there are such modifications as volitions. But he does not demonstrate (or even pretend to try to demonstrate) that there are such things as faculties or that we have a faculty of intellect and a faculty of will. In reconstructing the remainder of the Fourth Meditation, I will make use of Descartes' own language of faculties, but I will try to do so in a way that focuses attention on the ideas and acts of will that (arguably) he seems more entitled to posit.[35]

---

35 Scott Ragland has also pointed out in correspondence that if Descartes is only trying to argue that it is consistent with the divine nature to produce creatures that err, he does not need to demonstrate all of the claims that he advances in the Fourth Meditation. Strictly speaking, he just needs to show that there is

Descartes takes it to be obvious that finite minds have ideas. He also supposes that there are instances in which we have an idea and we affirm that the idea conforms to reality. For example, we might have an idea of a goat, or an idea of supreme perfection attached to an idea of a bearded man on a cloud, or an idea of an entity that is composed of a lion's head, a goat's body, and a serpent's tail. If we affirm that our idea of a goat as a colored material object conforms to reality, and it does conform to reality, then our affirmation is true. If we affirm that our idea conforms to reality but it does not, then our affirmation is false. Descartes thus says in the Third Meditation that to merely entertain an idea is not to err, but that

> the only remaining thoughts where I must be on my guard against making a mistake are judgements. And the chief and most common mistake which is to be found here consists in my judging that the ideas which are in me resemble, or conform to, things located outside me.
>
> (AT 7:37, CSM 2:26)

Descartes is not stating that error occurs only in cases in which we judge that an idea conforms to an object "located outside me" and there is no such object. He says that "the chief and most common mistake" is in that kind of case, but there are other instances of erroneous judgment as well. For example, we might have a confused idea, along with an immature sense of what counts as evident and obvious, and assert falsely that our idea is clear and distinct. We would not be making a judgment about anything located outside of us in that instance, but we would be making a false judgment nonetheless. We also make false judgments about the essences of things: we have an idea of an X and assert that what it is for something to be an X is to be Y, but what it is to be X is not to be Y.[36] We do sometimes make false judgments about the essences or natures of things, even

---

an account of judgment according to which we err and are the product of a supremely perfect being.

36 For Descartes, the essence of a thing exists in two ways – as identical to the in re thing that has the essence, or as an idea in a finite mind. Here I have in mind the latter.

if we do not always employ that precise technical language. Perhaps we have an idea of a body and an idea of a sensation of color, and we affirm that part of what it is to be a body is to be an entity that has color. In that case, we are making a false affirmation about the essence of body. We might worry about how we could ever make false a judgment about an essence if such a judgment would be literally incoherent – for example, the judgment that God is a body or the judgment that two and two add to five. Recall though that Descartes holds that in the case of most judgments, the details of what is before our mind are quite complicated and messy. Often what we line up before our mind is a string of linguistic images that hide the conceptual repugnance of the ideas for which they stand in.[37]

Descartes supposes that it is one thing to arrange a sequence of ideas and affirm it, and that it is something else merely to think or imagine that line-up of ideas. We might affirm that existing bodies have color or that part of what it is to be a body is to have color, but we might also just entertain an idea of body together with an idea of color, where we do not make an affirmation. Or perhaps we entertain an idea of God together with an idea of body and ideas of sensations, but without affirming that God is a sensible body. Or perhaps we think an idea of Descartes together with an idea of the year 2022 and we imagine what Descartes might say about the relationship between science and philosophy if he were alive today.[38] All such composite ideas are the stuff of fiction: we are entertaining

---

37 He writes for example that "because of the use of language, we tie all our concepts to the words used to express them. ...The thoughts of all people are more concerned with words than with things, and as a result people very often give their assent to words they do not understand, thinking they once understood them" (Principles I.74, AT 8A:37, CSM 1:220). See also Chapter 3, pp. 77–80, and Chapter 4, pp. 112–114.

38 An objection of course is that there are no instances in which we are having an idea and not making an affirmation. For example, one might argue that part of what it is to have an idea of a chimera is to affirm that what it is to be a chimera is to be an entity with a lion's head, a goat's body, and a serpent's tail. See for example Spinoza (1677), Part II, proposition 49, pp. 272–273. I am not sure that Spinoza is right about this. Perhaps there are (slight) affirmations at work in the having of each of the component ideas that make up the idea of a chimera, but that is not obvious (at least not to me).

ideas without taking a stand on the nature or existence of Descartes or body or God, but in each case, we are having ideas nonetheless. If we *do* affirm (for example) that God is a sensible body or that God (as a sensible body) exists, that is an additional step – something over and above the thinking of ideas. Descartes accordingly concludes that part of what it is to make a judgment is (first) to "perceive the ideas which are the subjects for possible judgements" (AT 7:56, CSM 2:39). He adds that so long as we are just having an idea and not making an affirmation, we do not err: "when regarded strictly in this light, it [the intellect] turns out to contain no error in the proper sense of that term" (ibid.). Here he is thinking of intellect as a faculty by which we merely consider or entertain ideas. He does define intellect as a "faculta[s] cognoscendi" in the Fourth Meditation (ibid.), but he is not thereby expressing that the role of the intellect is to understand – in the sense of recognizing and affirming truth. CSM translates "faculta[s] cognoscendi" as "faculty of knowledge," but a more contextually sensitive translation is "faculty of cognition." Descartes could not be clearer in his definition of the faculty that on its own intellect does not affirm or judge or *recognize to be true*; it simply presents subjects for possible judgments. He adds that since we are finite, we would expect that there are many such subjects of which we have no idea and about which we will never make a judgment:

> For although countless things may exist without there being any corresponding idea in me, it should not, strictly speaking, be said that I am deprived of these ideas, but merely that I lack them, in a negative sense. This is because I cannot produce any reason to prove that God ought to have given me a greater faculty of knowledge [cognoscendi] than he did; and no matter how skilled I understand a craftsman to be, this does not make me think he ought to have put into every one of his works all the perfections which he is able to put into some of them.
>
> (ibid.)

In this passage, Descartes is saying what we would expect – that a finite mind would not possess ideas of the subjects of all possible judgments, but just a subset of the ideas of those subjects. He is saying that our "faculta[s] cognoscendi" is merely a faculty for considering ideas. If we translate "faculta[s] cognoscendi" as a faculty of knowledge in the sense of a faculty of understanding – or recognizing and affirming truth – Descartes would be contradicting his definition of intellect just as soon as he offers it.

Descartes supposes that the possession of ideas is a pre-condition for making a judgment. We have ideas – which are modifications of mind – but we also have volitions by which we affirm and deny those ideas. God creates finite intellects on the spectrum of non-being to supreme perfection, and finite wills exemplify perfection as well. Through our will we "bear in some way the image and likeness of God" (AT 7:57, CSM 2:40). Like finite intellects, finite wills are still finite, but an increase in the perfection of a finite will is much harder to imagine. A finite intellect could always have one more idea of a thing that is the subject of a possible judgment, or two or three or a thousand, but we encounter difficulty thinking of what might be added to finite will. Descartes writes,

> it is very noteworthy that there is nothing else in me which is so perfect and so great that the possibility of a further increase in its perfection or greatness is beyond my understanding. If, for example, I consider the faculty of understanding, I immediately recognize that in my case it is extremely slight and very finite, and I at once form the idea of an understanding which is much greater – indeed supremely great and infinite…. It is only the will or freedom of choice, which I experience within me to be so great that the idea of any greater faculty is beyond my grasp.
>
> (AT 7: 57–58, CSM 2: 39–40)

Here Descartes is contending that there is nothing that can be added to a finite will that would increase its level of perfection. A finite will is still different from the divine will – "in virtue of the knowledge and power that accompany [the divine will] and make it more firm and efficacious, and also in virtue of its object, in that it ranges over a greater number of items" (AT 7:57, CSM 2:40). Descartes supposes however that if a finite mind came to have more knowledge and power, that new knowledge and power would accompany its will and would not be constitutive of its will strictly speaking. They would not amount to an increase in perfection of the will, but just an increase in the perfection of the mind that has it. By contrast, a finite intellect admits of a large amount of improvement: it presents ideas that are the subjects of judgments that we might make, and there are many ideas that it lacks.

In the Fourth Meditation, Descartes supposes that a finite intellect is the sort of thing that we would expect to be the product of a supremely perfect creator. A finite intellect allows us to consider a large number of ideas that are the subjects of possible judgments, but (as finite) it exists on the spectrum of non-being to perfection, and there are many ideas that it will never have at all. A finite will would appear to be even higher on the spectrum of non-being to perfection. As finite, it is not perfect itself, but it is pretty close, at least in terms of its range and scope. Note however that its scope is not so extensive that it ranges over ideas that the intellect does not possess. Descartes says for example in a letter to Hyperaspistes that "we never will anything of which we have no understanding at all."[39] He adds in Principles I.34 that "In order to make a judgement, the intellect is of course required since, in the case of something which we do not in any way perceive, there is no judgment we can make" (AT 8A:18, CSM 1:204). Descartes is very clear outside of the Meditations that finite will does not outstrip finite intellect in the sense of affirming ideas that are not presented as the subjects for possible judgments, but even the most charitable commentator has to allow that the language of the Fourth Meditation might have been more careful. If the intellect is (by Descartes' own definition) the faculty by which ideas are presented for possible judgments, then the will can never outstrip that, for "we never will something of which we have no understanding at all." He invites confusion, however, when he says in the Fourth Meditation:

> So what then is the source of my mistakes? It must simply be this: the scope of the will is wider than that of the intellect, but

---

39 "To Hyperaspistes, August 1641," AT 3:432, CSMK 195. See also "To Regius, May 1641," AT 3:372, CSMK 182.

> instead of restricting it within the same limits, I extend its use
> to matters which I do not understand.
>
> > (AT 7:58, CSM 2:40)

> Nor do I have any cause for complaint on the grounds that *God*
> *gave me a will which extends more widely than my intellect.*
> > (AT 7:60, CSM 2:42, emphasis added)

Descartes says that will outstrips intellect, but will does not outstrip
intellect insofar as intellect is a faculty for considering ideas – which
is how he defines it. Will outstrips intellect if we are thinking of
intellect as a faculty of understanding – or recognizing to be true –
but that is a totally different issue altogether. I am making what is
perhaps a nitpicky textual point, but I will keep track of it for the
remainder of the discussion as applicable. Descartes says later in the
Fourth Meditation for example that

> I have no cause for complaint on the grounds that the power
> of understanding or the natural light which God gave me is no
> greater than it is; for it is in the nature of a finite intellect to lack
> understanding of many things, and it is in the nature of a created
> intellect to be finite.
>
> > (ibid.)

Fair enough. But here he has explicitly turned the tables: he is identifying intellect as the faculty by which we *understand*. When he initially
introduced intellect in the Fourth Meditation, he defined it quite
differently.

In the Fourth Meditation, Descartes does not undertake to
explain why there are things of which we have ideas but that we
do not understand. That is to say, he does not explain why the intellect does not have clear and distinct ideas only. I will argue that
the reason is that finite minds are embodied, but Descartes is not
in a position to offer that reason in the Fourth Meditation because
he is not in a position to establish the existence of bodies until
Meditation Six.

But first I want to make clear that Descartes does not argue in
the Fourth Meditation that error is due to the mis-use of libertarian

freedom.[40] He is officially neutral on the nature of freedom in the Fourth Meditation, and if anything what he says about freedom is suggestive of a compatibilist view instead.

Compatibilist language in the Fourth Meditation

First, there is the discussion in which he announces that "the more I incline in one direction... the freer is my choice" (AT 7: 57–58, CSM 2:40). He elaborates and says that the case in which "there is no reason pushing me in one direction rather than another is the lowest grade of freedom" (AT 7:58, CSM 2:40) He adds by way of contrast that if he had been created to have clear and distinct perceptions only, his thinking would involve no deliberation and all of his affirmations would be utterly compelled, but he would be entirely free. He writes,

> For if I always saw clearly what was true and good, I should never have to deliberate about the right judgment or choice; in that case, although I should be wholly free, it would be *impossible* for me ever to be in a state of indifference.[41]

Here Descartes is articulating that an affirmation is free to the degree that it is compelled by clear and evident reasons and that to the extent that it is the result of other factors it is not free. He adds elsewhere that what it is for the will to be indifferent is for it not to be impelled by reasons:

> a person... is more indifferent the fewer reasons he knows which impel him to choose one side rather than another; and this, I think, cannot be denied by anybody.[42]

---

40 Here I am disagreeing with Newman (1999), 582–583; Ragland (2006) and (2007); and Wee (2014).

41 Ibid., emphasis added.

42 "To [Mesland], 2 May 1644," AT 4:115, CSMK 233. Descartes then adds a few sentences later that "a great light in the intellect is followed by a great inclination in the will" (AT 4:116, CSMK 233). He says that "if we see very clearly that something is good for us, it is... impossible, as long as one continues in the same thought – to stop the course of our desire" (ibid.). We will not cease to

When a will is free in its affirmation of an idea, it cannot help but affirm that idea.[43] Insofar as a will is unfree, there are factors other than clear and distinct ideas that contribute to its activity. Or better: there are factors other than clear and distinct ideas that contribute to its *behavior*, for the will is active (and is engaging in activity) to the extent that such factors are not operative.

There is also the language two paragraphs further down in the Fourth Meditation in which Descartes speaks of the will as being pushed and pulled when it is affirming in the absence of a clear and distinct perception. He writes that some of the thinking of the *Meditations* is itself the product of the push and pull of reasons:

> although probable conjectures may pull me in one direction, the mere knowledge that they are simply conjectures, and not certain and indubitable reasons, is itself quite enough to push my assent the other way. My experience in the last few days confirms this: the mere fact that I found that all my previous beliefs were in some sense open to doubt was enough to turn my absolutely confident belief in their truth into the supposition that they were wholly false.[44]

Descartes rightly describes the will as sometimes pushed and pulled – as being turned in one direction and then another. He is echoing language that he uses elsewhere to describe the work of reasons in the *Meditations*:

> before we can decide to doubt, we need some reason for doubting; and that is why in my First Meditation I put forward the principal reasons for doubt.[45]

---

affirm a clear and distinct idea if it stays before our mind, but as we have seen, Descartes holds that an embodied mind never sustains a clear and distinct idea for long.

43 See also the Fifth Meditation, AT 7:69, CSM 2:48; *Second Replies*, AT 7:166, CSM 2:117; and *Principles* I.43, AT 8A:21, CSM 1:207. See also Nelson (1997) and Lennon (2014), 178–179.

44 AT 7:59, CSM 2:41.

45 *Appendix to Fifth Objections and Replies*, AT 9A:204, CSM 2:270.

The language that Descartes uses here is quite *anti*-libertarian – we cannot decide to doubt in the absence of a reason for doubting. In the Fourth Meditation, the anti-libertarian stance is not as definitive, but it is strongly suggestive. He says that our affirmations are due to freedom to the extent that they are utterly compelled and that when they are not utterly compelled they are pushed and pulled. At the end of the Meditation, he then repeats that freedom and utter compulsion go hand in hand. He says that

> God could have easily brought it about that without losing my freedom, …I should nevertheless never make a mistake. He could, for example, have endowed my intellect with a clear and distinct perception of everything about which I was ever likely to deliberate.
>
> (AT 7:61, CSM 2:42)

God did not create us in such a way that for everything that we think, we think it clearly and distinctly. Instead, we have ideas that are confused. If all our ideas were clear and distinct, we would never err, but God did not create us in such a way that we have clear and distinct ideas only.[46] Nor did He did create us in a way that we have confused perceptions that we never affirm.

None of the text of the Fourth Meditation entails a libertarian view of human freedom. Descartes does say in one passage that if

> I simply refrain from making a judgement in cases where I do not perceive the truth with sufficient clarity and distinctness, then it is clear that I am behaving correctly and avoiding error.

---

46 That is to say, God did not create the I *of the Fourth Meditation* in such a way that it has clear and distinct ideas only. The I of the Fourth Meditation is embodied, and it has confused ideas, but Descartes cannot fully disclose as much in the Fourth Meditation because he has not yet established that material things exist. He is clear however that a finite mind on its own has clear and distinct ideas only and is perfect of its kind. See Chapter 3, pp. 77–78. Later in the current chapter, there is a discussion of the difference between embodied intellect, which has confused ideas, and intellect, which does not.

But if in such cases I either affirm or deny, then I am not using my free will correctly.

(AT 7:59–60, CSM 41)

But a compatibilist of course can say that. A philosopher like Hobbes might observe an individual who is mis-using a tool and describe them as using it incorrectly – perhaps a calculator that they are employing to pound a nail, or a hammer that they are employing to secure results in math. The individual is using such a tool incorrectly even though they do not possess a two-way ability to use it other- wise. Or perhaps a better example would be that of an individual who is mis-using a tool that is a part of their own person – an indi- vidual who is pressing their ear up against the window of a store in order to see better what is happening inside. The individual is using their ear incorrectly, and Hobbes would point that out even if the individual did not have a two-way ability to do otherwise. Or perhaps a better example still would be that of an individual who is mis-using a faculty of mind. A philosopher like Spinoza or Leibniz might point to an individual who is attempting to use imagination to conceive of immaterial entities. The individual would be mis- using their imagination if they attempted to think of mind by way of ideas that are imagistic pictures, and Spinoza and Leibniz (and Descartes) would be sure to call them out.[47] But neither would posit that an individual mind has a two-way power to act differently than it does. Descartes is also entitled to describe human beings as not using one of their faculties correctly even if they do not possess lib- ertarian freedom.[48]

There is one final passage in the Fourth Meditation in which Descartes might seem to be suggesting that finite wills have liber- tarian freedom. After highlighting the circumstances in which we do and do not employ the will correctly, Descartes speaks of the fault

47 For example, Spinoza (1677), Appendix to Part I, 238–243, and Leibniz (1765), 209.
48 Note that Descartes says two more times in the Fourth Meditation that a finite mind mis-uses its will when it errs – in a passage at AT 7:60 (line 6), and in a passage at AT 7:61 (line 8). He is entitled to do so in all both cases, without being committed to a libertarian view of human freedom.

that is associated with false affirmations. In the CSM translation, we find this:

> If I go for the alternative which is false, then obviously I shall be in error; if I take the other side, then it is by pure chance that I arrive at the truth, and I shall still be at fault since it is clear by the natural light that the perception of the intellect should always precede the determination of the will.
>
> (AT 7:60, CSM 2:41)

Depending on where we stand, the claim that "I shall still be at fault" might ring of libertarian freedom, and very loudly. We might suppose that it only makes sense to say that a being is at fault for committing an act if the being had libertarian freedom and if it possessed a two-way ability to not commit the act. Perhaps we would be right, but in that case, we would want to look more closely at the CSM translation and the original Latin. The latter is "non ideo culpa carebo" which reads – "so I am not without fault." Descartes might be referring here to a level of blame that is attributable to a finite mind in virtue of its possession of libertarian freedom, but he might instead be using the language of not being "without fault" to repeat the Fourth Meditation view that the imperfection of error is "in me" (AT 7:61, CSM 2:42) and "proceeds from me" (AT 7:60, CSM 2:41). Our faculty of will does not have any faults, and our faculty of intellect does not have any faults, but when both of these are present in unison, we do have the fault that we sometimes affirm what we do not understand.

An additional reason for thinking that Descartes does not subscribe to a libertarian view of freedom – in the Fourth Meditation or anywhere else – is both textual and philosophical. In the Third Meditation, Descartes made use of the axiom that something cannot come from nothing as part of his effort to demonstrate that God exists. He argues that if our idea of God was caused by a being with a finite amount of power, there would be a remainder of its objective reality that would have to have come from nothing, but that is absurd. A different but related question arises about the cause of our volitions. Objective reality is a relatively slight kind of reality, even if (Descartes is right that) an infinite amount of it still requires an omnipotent cause, but finite volitions have a not-inconsequential amount of being as well. They are modifications, and so they do not have the same level of reality as a substance, but they are something, and when they appear in a finite mind, we are entitled to ask how they got there. If the answer is that they are uncaused – that they simply blurp into existence in the finite mental substance that has them – they would violate the axiom that something cannot come from nothing. Their occurrence would also leave us with no sense of how the mental substance in question would be in charge of them. Without a cause, there is no reason why they would arise at one moment rather than another, and they would appear to manifest at random. The problem is especially glaring in the context of a substance-mode ontology. If we consider a mental substance that has modifications 1, 2, 3, and 4, and those modifications cause a volition (or modification 5), then the substance does not have libertarian freedom. If modification 5 just arises but is not caused by modifications 1–4, it would appear to blurp into existence at random. If we bracket modifications 1–4 and assume that it is not *modifications* that produce modification 5, but instead the underlying substance is the cause of modification 5, we run into the same issue. Bracketing the modifications, there is no difference in the substance from moment to moment, and so any *new* volition that arises in it would appear to be a random occurrence.[49] If Descartes were explaining error in terms of a libertarian freedom to affirm or not affirm error, it is not obvious how the explanation would explain anything at all.[50] And he veers away from that sort of explanation on his own. He holds that something cannot come from nothing, and he makes very clear outside of the *Meditations* that God has willed all of creaturely reality by a single immutable act – finite modifications included.

---

49 See also Spinoza (1662), Part II, Chapter XVII, 84.

50 Scott Ragland has suggested in correspondence that Descartes might appeal to the notion of agent causation to account for the occurrence of volitions that are free in a libertarian sense. I worry however that that just pushes the problem back a step, as Van Inwagen (1983) has argued. See also Strawson (2008b), 343–345.

Finite will and embodied intellect

Descartes does not argue in the Fourth Meditation that finite minds err because they have libertarian freedom. He argues that we err because the will affirms more than the intellect understands, but in the Fourth Meditation, he does not explain why the will affirms more than it understands. In texts outside of the Fourth Meditation, he does explain why the will affirms more than the intellect understands, or at the very least, he offers the seeds of a more complete account.

In *Fifth Objections*, Gassendi asks Descartes what our ideas would be like if "since being implanted in the body" our "eyes [were] closed" and our "ears stopped" (AT 7:310, CSM 2:216). He wonders –

> with no external senses to enable you to perceive the universe of objects or anything outside you...[,] Would you not have been absorbed in private meditation, eternally turning thoughts over and over?
>
> (ibid.)

As we have seen, Descartes replies that "the mind... would have exactly the same ideas of God and itself that it now has, with the sole difference that they would have been much purer and clearer" (AT 7:375, CSM 2:258). He holds more specifically that the confusion in our ideas is a product of mind-body union and that a mind that is not embodied has clear and distinct ideas only.[51] The will of such a mind still extends to all the ideas that are had by its intellect – for "we never will anything of which we have no understanding at all" – but it does not extend to matters that the intellect does not understand clearly and distinctly, because there aren't any. Descartes subscribes to the view that a finite mind on its own is constructed in such a way that its ideas are clear and distinct – and so never makes a false judgment. We would expect that to be his view, if he holds that God created finite intellect and if "we cannot think that he ever created anything that was not wholly perfect of its kind."[52] He says to Gassendi that "the only thing" (AT 7:375, CSM 2:258) that keeps

---

51 See Chapter 3, pp. 77–78.
52 *Principles* III.45, AT 8A:100, CSM 1:256.

us from a clear and distinct grasp of ideas is our sensory perceptions of bodies. He subscribes to the view that a finite mind by itself has clear and distinct ideas alone.

Descartes does not defend the view in the *Meditations* itself, but he does hint at it – and very strongly. He writes in the Fourth Meditation that an embodied human being that has "accustomed [it]self to leading [its] mind away from the senses... ha[s] no difficulty... in turning... toward things which are objects of the intellect alone" (AT 7: 52–53, CSM 2:37) – at least during the period of its detachment and isolation. Such a mind is able to notice the true ideas that it has possessed all along and that are part of its very fabric:

> the truth of these matters is so open and so much in harmony with my nature, that on first discovering them it seems that I am not so much learning something new as remembering what I knew before; or it seems like noticing for the first time things which were long present within me although I had never turned my mental gaze on them before.[53]

It notices ideas that are part of "the treasure house of my mind" (AT 7:67, CSM 2:46). In the Third Meditation, Descartes says that the argument from objective reality "is quite evident by the natural light, [but when]... my mental vision is blinded by the images of things perceived by the senses" (AT 7:47, CSM 2:32), the argument is not so easy to grasp. In the Fifth Meditation he says that the existence of God would be obvious and self-evident if not for the influence of embodiment.[54] He then argues outside of the *Meditations*

---

53 The Fifth Meditation, AT 7:63–64, CSM 2:44.

54 He says in the Fifth Meditation that "if I were not overwhelmed by preconceived opinions, and if the images of things presented by the senses did not besiege my thought on every side, I would certainly acknowledge [God] sooner and more easily than anything else. For what is more self-evident than the fact that the supreme being exists?" (AT 7:69, CSM 2:47). And as we have seen he holds that it is via the faculty of memory that preconceived opinions capture our thought (*Principles* I.72, AT 8A:36–37, CSM 1:219–220), and memory is corporeal (*Treatise on Man*, AT 11:178, CSM 1:107; *Rules for the Direction of the Mind*, AT 10:416, CSM 1:43; "To Hyperaspistes, 1641," AT 3:425, CSMK 190).

that it is due to embodiment that our true ideas become mixed up together to result in confused composite ideas that do not conform to reality.[55] For example, we have an idea of mind, but until we have worked through an exercise like the *Meditations* this is a composite idea that consists of a true idea of mind and ideas of sensory features that do not pertain to mind.[56] We might break down the (larger) pre-*Meditations* idea into its component elements – as we do in the Second Meditation when we start from an idea of mind as a "wind or fire" (AT 7:26, CSM 2:17) and we arrive at a clear and distinct idea of thinking.[57] We break down a confused idea into its component elements, and we notice that their historical sewing together is due not to conceptual interlinkages but to the pragmatics of embodied survival. For example, in early childhood, we pay exclusive attention to the sensible bodies that are relevant to our preservation – manipulating and deliberating about these – and the template idea by which we come to think about *anything* is the idea of a sensible body.[58] As a result, our true idea of mind (or body or God) becomes fused together with ideas of features that do not pertain to mind (or body or God), which is to say that our idea of mind becomes confused. The survival benefits of our early childhood practice are enormous, but our ideas pay a price.

Descartes emphasizes throughout the *Meditations* that although we grasp that the "I" is a thinking thing, we do not grasp all that it is. Early in the Third Meditation, he reiterates the Second Meditation result that he exists as a thinking mind, but he adds that there might

---

55 See the discussion in Chapter 4, pp. 112–114.

56 *Second Replies*, AT 7:130–131, CSM 2:94.

57 The pre-*Meditations* idea of mind as a wind or fire also includes an idea of a body as a sensible entity, and we break down that idea at the end of the Second Meditation (AT 7:30–31, CSM 2:20–21). We notice that it includes a clear and distinct idea of extension and ideas of features like color and sound. Descartes does not guide us to clear and distinct ideas of the latter in the *Meditations*. He does the analysis in *Principles* I.68 and argues that colors are mind-dependent sensations (AT 8A:33, CSM 1:217).

58 *Principles* I.71–I.74, AT 8A:35–38, CSM 2:218–221. In these sections, Descartes also discusses other ways in which embodiment results in the confusion of ideas.

still be aspects of his self that are "not yet fully known to me" (AT 7:39, CSM 2:27). For example, there might be in him a faculty for producing sense perceptions, in which case his "adventitious" ideas would not be evidence that there exists anything separate from him that produces those ideas (AT 7:39, CSM 2:27). He had also allowed in the Second Meditation that although the self of which he is aware is a thinking being, there might be things "which are unknown to me, [but] which would in the truth of the matter still not differ from that me whom I know" (AT 7:27).[59] In particular, these things might include "that structure of limbs which I call the human body" (AT 7:27, CSM 2:18) – the "very things which I am supposing to be nothing" as a result of the skeptical arguments of the First Meditation. He then repeats at the start of the Fourth Meditation that he is certain of the existence of the "I," but only "in so far as it is a thinking thing" (AT 7:53, CSM 2:37) – leaving open that there might be aspects of it of which he is unaware. Later in the Meditation, he says that he does not yet know if his thinking is material:

> besides the knowledge that I exist, in so far as I am a thinking thing, an idea of corporeal nature comes into my mind; and I happen to be in doubt as to whether the thinking nature which is in me, or rather which I am, is distinct from this corporeal nature or identical with it. I am making the further supposition that my intellect has not yet come upon any persuasive reason in favour of one alternative rather than the other. This obviously implies that I am indifferent as to whether I should assert or deny either alternative, or indeed refrain from making any judgement on the matter.
>
> (AT 7:59, CSM 2:41)

Here Descartes is not just saying that there is a slight chance that there are aspects of what we are that we do not yet appreciate; he is saying that we have no more reason to think that there are than to think that there are not. In the Second, Third, and Fourth Meditations, he is clear that there is much about the "I" that is not yet known.

---

59 Note that here I am using the translation in Heffernan (1992), 34.

One of the things that is not yet known about the "I" in the Fourth Meditation is that it is united to a body in such a way that its ideas become mixed up and fused together. Descartes says in the Fourth Meditation that error is due to "the operation of the will in so far as it is in me" and that error "is undoubtedly an imperfection in me." But error is not "an imperfection in me" insofar as I am just a mind. Error does not take place in a mind that is not attached to a body; such a mind has clear and distinct ideas only. Instead, error is "an imperfection in me" insofar as I am a mind that is part of a mind-body composite. It (error) traces to the way that finite thinking operates as a result of its embodiment. However, in the Fourth Meditation, we have not yet established that bodies exist or that our thinking mind is united to a body. We learn both in the Sixth Meditation, where we also uncover that "the nature of man as a combination of mind and body is such that it is bound to mislead him from time to time" (AT 7:88, CSM 2:61). We learn that the "deception of the senses is natural, because a given motion in the brain must always produce the same sensation in the mind" (ibid.), and the immutable order of the behavior of bodies is not preserved unless we sometimes have sensations that are deceptive.[60] We also find out that the sensory perceptions of a mind-body union are as confused as they are constant (AT 7:82–83, CSM 2:57–58). According to Descartes, embodied selves are constructed in such a way that they are no stranger to error and confusion. The finite mind that is one half of an embodied self is constructed very differently.[61]

Descartes emphasizes in the Fourth Meditation that insofar as our affirmations depend on God they are wholly true and good. He writes,

> I must not complain that the forming of those acts of will or judgments in which I go wrong happens with God's concurrence.

---

60 See *Conversation with Burman*, AT 5:164, CSMK 346, and Chapter 2, pp. 54–56.

61 It is also telling that Descartes would all of a sudden bring up the (epistemic) possibility of his embodiment at AT 7:58–59, in a context in which is he is exploring why the will would affirm more than the intellect understands.

For in so far as these acts depend on God, they are wholly true and good.

(AT 7:60, CSM 2:42)

He also says that error "lies... not in the faculty of will which I received from God, nor even in its operation, in so far as it depends on him" (AT 7:60, CSM 2:41). We might ask what the sense is in which our volitions are wholly true and good even when we affirm a falsehood. They are not wholly true and good in so far as they affirm the false. Instead, an affirmation is wholly true and good in so far as it is the affirmation of a clear and distinct idea, which "must necessarily have God for its author" (AT 7:62, CSM 2:43). Outside of the *Meditations*, Descartes argues that God wills all of creaturely reality in a single immutable act – finite volitions included. What he is indicating in the Fourth Meditation is that God wills our affirmations insofar as they are true – that is, God wills our affirmations of clear and distinct ideas. As a result of our embodiment, however, those same clear and distinct ideas become confused and mixed up. Our affirmations then suffer as a result. We affirm an idea of God, for example, but we are not *only* affirming an idea of God, we are also affirming material that trails that idea. For example, we affirm that God (or finite mind) exists, but as a sensible body. God preordains all of our particular volitions immutably and for eternity – He wills our particular affirmations of clear and distinct ideas – but He also wills that we be attached to a body, and confusion and false judgments follow inevitably.[62] God does not will error, according to Descartes, and presumably that is why he says that "error as such is not something real" (AT 7:54, CSM 2:38) and "is not a thing" (AT 7:61, CSM 2:42). But God is the eternal and immutable author of all that does exist – including finite affirmations of clear and distinct ideas and the union of particular minds and bodies. In the

---

62 Note that Malebranche appears to be making a somewhat similar move in the effort to reconcile the all-encompassing reach of the divine will and the existence of error and sin. See Pessin (2000), and Pessin (2000b), 41–42. The details of the account in Descartes (that I am defending) are very different from the account in Malebranche, but the accounts are similar in that Malebranche appears to hold that error is a by-product of what God wills.

Fourth Meditation, Descartes speaks of "my nature... in so far as I was created by the supreme being" (AT 7:54, CM 2:38). He says that "God could have given me a nature such that I was never mistaken"[63] and that "my own nature is very weak and limited" (AT 7:55, CSM 2:39). There he has in mind, and he is gesturing obliquely at, his nature as an embodied being. He holds that God created his (not embodied) thinking mind with a nature such that on its own it has clear and distinct ideas exclusively and is never mistaken, and so the Fourth Meditation "me" does not have that nature and is something different. It is a larger nature that is not fully known to him. It is the mind that is intermingled with a body.[64] He allowed in the Second, Third, and Fourth Meditations that there might be something else that pertains to him other than just his thinking mind, and that something else is what accounts for error – the body to which his mind is united.

Descartes makes a number of incomplete and imprecise claims in the *Meditations*. He is on the record as employing a pedagogical method in which he will try to reach us where we are and not where we are not. In the Fourth Meditation, he explains the phenomenon of error by appealing to the datum that finite will outstrips finite intellect – in the sense of a faculty of *understanding* – but in the final analysis, he does not take that to be a datum. He does not hold that finite will outstrips finite intellect. He holds that finite will outstrips embodied intellect – *that* is the intellect that he is treating in the Fourth Meditation – but he does not hold that finite will outstrips

---

63 Perhaps we might have been created with no body, for example, or we might have been created like an angel that has a body but is not tightly intermingled with it.

64 See also the discussion in Alanen (1989), 402–403. I am not suggesting that Alanen accepts anything like the interpretation of the Fourth Meditation that I am proposing – according to which the "I" that is responsible for error in the Fourth Meditation is the embodied mind – but Alanen emphasizes the extent to which the first five Meditations are a matter of keeping embodiment at bay before it is unveiled explicitly at AT 7:80–90. Brown (2014) and Chamberlain (2020) argue that there are two notions of self that Descartes unpacks in the *Meditations* – the thinking self of Meditation Two, and the embodied self of Meditation Six. I am arguing that Descartes is already gesturing at the latter in the Fourth Meditation.

unembodied finite intellect. He holds on the contrary that a mind that is not saddled with a body — or that has mitigated the interferences of the body — has clear and distinct ideas only. That is to say, if we are talking about finite will and finite intellect proper, the scope of will and intellect (in the sense of a faculty of understanding) are identical. Finite will outstrips *embodied* finite intellect, and it does so often — it affirms ideas that would otherwise be clear and distinct but that are confused as a result of embodiment. But Descartes cannot yet say in the Fourth Meditation that finite will only outstrips embodied intellect; he does not establish the existence of bodies until Meditation Six.[65]

In the Fourth Meditation, Descartes concludes that "error is a privation or lack of some knowledge which somehow should be in me" (AT 7:55, CSM 2:38). I have argued that it is a lack of clarity in our ideas that results from our attachment to a body. If we were not united to a body, we would have clear and distinct ideas only, but "I have no right to complain that the role God wished me to undertake in the world is not the principal one or the most perfect of all" (AT 7:61, CSM 2:43). Still, we are pretty amazing. Perhaps embodied minds are less perfect in virtue of their tendency to err, but as we have seen Descartes holds that truth is not everything.

---

65 Still, we might ask why he does not provide (in any text) the more complete explanation of human error that is available to him. One possible reason is that he thought that the explanation would be obvious to a reader who has reasoned to the end of the *Meditations* and through the entirety of the objections and replies. He communicates again and again that embodiment is the cause of the confusion in our ideas and that if we were not embodied clear and distinct ideas would come easily. Another possible reason is that he does not think that we need to have that account under our belt in order to dispel the worry that a supremely perfect being would not create beings that err. He just needs to show that it is consistent with the perfection of a supreme being to create beings that err, and He does that. Another possible reason is that in the final analysis he does not think that error is an especially big deal. (See "To Chanut, 1 February 1647," AT 4:609, CSMK 309–310.) A fourth possible reason is that he supposes that the Sixth Meditation makes clear that error is the inevitable offshoot of our embodiment, and so he might not have felt the need to return again to the particular moment of the Fourth Meditation.

Further reading

There is a substantial literature on Descartes on human freedom. A cross-section includes:

Andrea Christofidou, *Self, Reason, and Freedom: A New Light on Descartes' Metaphysics*, New York: Routledge (2013).

Brian Embry, "Descartes on Free Will and Moral Possibility," *Philosophy and Phenomenological Research* 96 (2018), 380–398.

Daniel Fogal, "Descartes and the Possibility of Enlightened Freedom," *Res Philosophica* 94 (2017), 499–534.

Christopher Gilbert, "Freedom and Enslavement: Descartes on Passions and the Will," *History of Philosophy Quarterly* 15 (1998), 177–190.

Robert Anderson Imlay, "Freedom, the Self and Epistemic Voluntarism in Descartes," *Studia Leibnitiana* 28 (1996), 211–224.

Marie Jayasekera, "Descartes on Human Freedom," *Philosophy Compass* 9 (2014), 527–539.

Anthony Kenny, "Descartes on the Will," in *Descartes*, ed. John Cottingham, New York and Oxford: Oxford UP (1998), 132–159.

Thomas M. Lennon, "Descartes's Supposed Libertarianism: Letter to Mesland or Memorandum Concerning Petau?," *Journal of the History of Philosophy* 51 (2013), 223–248.

Andreea Mihali, "The Role of Freedom in Descartes' Ethics of Belief," *Pacific Philosophical Quarterly* 95 (2014), 218–245.

Noa Naaman-Zauderer, *Descartes' Deontological Turn: Reason, Will, and Virtue in the Later Writings*, Cambridge and New York: Cambridge UP (2010).

Lex Newman, "The Fourth Meditation," *Philosophy and Phenomenological Research* 59 (1999), 559–591.

C.P. Ragland, *The Will to Reason: Theodicy and Freedom in Descartes*, New York and Oxford: Oxford UP (2016).

David Rosenthal, "Will and the Theory of Judgment," in Amélie Oksenberg Rorty, *Essays on Descartes's Meditations*, Berkeley and Los Angeles: California UP (1986), 405–434.

Mark C.R. Smith, "The Uses of Thought and Will: Descartes' Practical Philosophy of Freedom," *The European Legacy* 27 (2022), 310–320.

Jemimah Thompson, "Perfection in the Balance of Descartes's Epistemological Project," *History of Philosophy Quarterly* 36 (2019), 139–160.

Cecilia Wee, "Descartes and Leibniz on Human Free-Will and the Ability to Do Otherwise," *Canadian Journal of Philosophy* 36 (2006), 387–414.

Lianghua Zhou, "Descartes on the Source of Error: The Fourth Meditation and the Correspondence with Elisabeth," *British Journal for the History of Philosophy* 30 (2022), 992–1012.

Seven

Immaterial minds

Descartes offers five arguments for the view that minds are immaterial substances. One is an argument from the indivisibility of mind and the divisibility of body. A second is from the inexplicability of modifications like ideas and volitions in terms of three-dimensional extension. A third rests on the contention that there are linguistic and other capacities that are had by substances, but not material substances. A fourth is what we know infamously as the *argument from doubt* – if we can posit the existence of minds while doubting the existence of anything material, then minds are not material. The fifth begins with the assumption that we have a clear and distinct idea of mental substance without [*absque*] any corporeality and concludes that mind and body can exist apart. The five arguments are different but employ the same basic machinery – an understanding of what it is for something to be a substance, an understanding of what it is for something to be a modification, an understanding of what it is for something to be extended, and an understanding of what it is for something to be mental. We would not understand the conclusion that minds are immaterial substances in the absence of that basic machinery, and we would not understand the premises by which to recognize that the conclusion is true. Accordingly, the five arguments overlap to a significant degree. None of the arguments is entirely successful, but they are all consistent and coherent, and some (I think) are quite plausible.

DOI: 10.4324/9781351210522-7

The argument from indivisibility

Descartes offers two arguments for the immateriality of minds in the Sixth Meditation, one of which is from the indivisibility of minds.[1] He makes the latter argument almost in passing: he mentions it in the context of explaining why distal nerves occasionally communicate an erroneous signal to the brain and mislead a mind to think that its body is in harm when it is not. He argues that because bodies are divisible, it will sometimes happen that a nerve in the brain is severed from a more distant nerve or body part, and the nerve in the brain is still impacted just as it was before – communicating the same signal that it would have sent had the severing not occurred. Human bodies (and the larger universe) exhibit a perfect and immutable order, and so the same nerve activity in the brain always produces the same sensation.[2] Occasional error is then a trade-off that results from participation in that order.[3] Descartes proceeds to add that whereas bodies are divisible, minds are not divisible and hence are not extended. He writes,

> The first observation that I make at this point [to account for the erroneous signals that the nerves send to the brain] is that there is a great difference between the mind and the body, inasmuch as the body is by its very nature always divisible, while the mind is utterly indivisible. For when I consider the mind, or myself in so far as I am merely a thinking thing, I am unable to distinguish

---

1 Andrea Christofidou has suggested in correspondence that the Sixth Meditation argument from indivisibility (AT 7:85–86) is not a freestanding argument for the immateriality of mind, but instead is additional support for the (main) argument that Descartes offers at AT 7:78. I do not think that that is right. At the end of the paragraph in which he puts forward the argument from indivisibility, he writes, "This one argument would be enough to show me that the mind is completely different from the body, even if I did not already know as much from other considerations" (AT 7:86, CSM 2:59). I just don't see how Descartes could make more clear that the argument from divisibility is establishing the same result that has already been made clear from earlier considerations, for example from the discussion at AT 7:78.

2 AT 7:87, CSM 2:60. See also Chapter 2, pp. 54–56.

3 AT 7:84–85, CSM 2:58–59. See also *Conversation with Burman*, AT 5:164, CSMK 346.

parts within myself; I understand myself to be something quite single and complete. Although the whole mind seems to be united to the whole body, I recognize that if a foot or arm or any other part of the body is cut off, nothing has thereby been taken away from the mind. As for the faculties of willing, of understanding, of sensory perception and so on, these cannot be termed parts of the mind, since it is one and the same mind that wills, and understands and has sensory perceptions. By contrast, there is no corporeal or extended thing that I can think of which in my thought I cannot easily divide into parts; and this very fact makes me understand that it is divisible. This one argument would be enough to show me that the mind is completely different from the body, even if I did not already know as much from other considerations.

(AT 7:85–86, CSM 2:59)

The reasoning here is fairly quick. Descartes appears to be arguing that bodies are divisible in a way that minds are not and that minds are therefore not extended. They are unextended, and with unextended modifications like volitions, intellections, and sensations, they are unextended substances.[4]

Minds would certainly *appear* to have parts – insofar as they have volitions, intellections, and sensory perceptions. Descartes is quick to specify however that "As for the faculties of willing, of understanding, of sensory perception and so on, these cannot be termed parts of the mind." Here he appears to be articulating that

---

4 In Chapter 1 (pp. 13–18), I argued that Descartes holds that the material universe is a single contiguous substance and that individual bodies are modifications or collections of modifications of that substance. He says for example that a particular "human body... is simply made up of a certain configuration of limbs and other accidents of this sort" ("Synopsis of the following six Meditations," AT 7:14, CSM 2:10). In the Sixth Meditation argument from divisibility, Descartes is not saying that the single corporeal substance that is the entire universe is divisible. Instead, he is saying that it is individual bodies that are divisible. (See also Barry (2015), 69–71.) But we can bracket that controversial issue in the course of addressing his argument from the indivisibility of mind. We just need to consider whether he is correct that there is a sense in which minds are indivisible.

will, intellect, and the ability to have sensory perceptions are not fractional thirds that add up to a whole that is a mind, but that a mind is in some sense prior to these faculties and possesses them. As he says in the larger passage, "it is one and the same mind that wills, and understands and has sensory perceptions." A mind itself is not these faculties – and is not constituted by them. A mind might even lack one of the faculties and still be a mind: Descartes allows for example that angels are minds even though they lack a faculty of sensory perception.[5] There is one feature however that Descartes takes to be wholly inseparable from a mind – its thinking. He says as much in the Second Meditation: "At last I have discovered it – thought; this alone is inseparable from me" (AT 7:27, CSM 2:18). He then elaborates in Fourth Replies:

> As to the fact that there can be nothing in the mind, in so far as it is a thinking thing, of which it is not aware, this seems to me to be self-evident. For there is nothing that we can understand to be in the mind, regarded in this way, that is not a thought or dependent on a thought. If it were not a thought or dependent on a thought it would not belong to the mind qua thinking thing; and we cannot have any thought of which we are not aware at the very moment when it is in us.
>
> (AT 7:246, CSM 2:171)

Descartes holds that a finite mind is to be identified with its thinking, and more specifically with its conscious thinking.[6] And he is contending that conscious thinking has no parts and is indivisible. I have to say that I share Descartes' intuition here (if I am understanding him correctly). So far as I can tell, I do not have a coherent thought before my mind when I attempt to conceive of

---

5 "To Regius, January 1642," AT 3:493, CSMK 206. See also Simmons (2010), 57–61. Descartes also says in "To The Marquess of Newcastle, 23 November 1646" that non-human animals might possess "some thought such as we experience in ourselves, but of a very much less perfect kind" (AT 4:576, CSMK 304). Here he appears to be indicating that something is still thought even if it does not involve all of the faculties that are present in a human mind.
6 See also Principles of Philosophy I.63, AT 8A:30–31, CSM 1:215.

my conscious awareness as carved into two or more regions. I can lose a thought – and become no longer conscious of it – but then I still have conscious awareness of other thoughts, and that conscious awareness would appear to be unitary.[7]

But trouble looms around the corner. Descartes says that "if a foot or arm or any other part of the body is cut off, nothing has thereby been taken away from the mind." That would not appear to be right. There would seem to be cases in which parts of the body are cut off or damaged – namely, regions of the brain – and things *are* taken away from the mind.

Way back in Phaedo, Socrates also appeals to considerations of divisibility to argue that minds and bodies are wholly different kinds of entity. He says to his interlocutor,

> What kind of thing is likely to be scattered? On behalf of what kind of thing should one fear this, and for what kind of thing should one not fear it? We should examine to which class the soul belongs, and as a result either fear for the soul or be of good cheer.[8]

---

7 I certainly do not agree with Descartes that thinking is to be identified with consciousness. For example, there are cognitive states that are clearly unconscious – for example, the thinking that takes place when we fall asleep mulling over a problem, and the solution comes to us shortly after we wake. But if for the moment, we grant Descartes the assumption that thinking is to be identified with consciousness, then I think his argument from divisibility is more plausible than has been thought. Some commentators discuss the argument but quickly dismiss it – for example, Gombay (2007), 104–107 and Wagner (1983), 508–512. Noteworthy perhaps is that the argument from divisibility makes no appearance in (the 1644) Principles of Philosophy. Also, Dutton (2003, 407–414) has argued that although the argument from divisibility is not particularly compelling on its own, Descartes can utilize the assumption that material substance is divisible to make good on his contention that thought and extension are contrary natures. That contention is critical to other arguments that Descartes offers for the view that minds are immaterial substances. See Rozemond (2014) for a discussion of the respects in which Descartes takes the argument from indivisibility to stand on its own.

8 Plato (2002), 116.

Socrates then proceeds to argue that souls are indivisible – and hence cannot decompose or be scattered – and that bodies are divisible.[9] Souls and bodies in fact have a number of opposing qualities, he argues. For example, bodies are visible, tangible, and divisible, whereas souls cannot be seen, or grabbed or touched, or cut into two (116–117). In an effort to be as rigorous as possible, Socrates then considers a potential objection: that even if souls and bodies are different in all of these respects, souls might still be material. He notes that a musical harmony would appear to be invisible, intangible, and indivisible, but still it depends for its moment-to-moment existence on the material instrument that produces it. A musical harmony is an elegant and exalted phenomenon, but a physical phenomenon, and perhaps a soul or mind is similarly a product of the activity of the human nervous system. Socrates writes,

> One might make the same argument about harmony, lyre and strings, that a harmony is something invisible, without body, beautiful and divine in the attuned lyre, whereas the lyre itself and its strings are physical, bodily, composite, earthly, and akin to what is mortal. ... [S]omeone breaks the lyre, cuts or breaks the strings and then insists, using the same argument as you, that the harmony must still exist and is not destroyed....
>
> (124)

The analogy here is very smart. There is a myriad of notes that combine into the stretch of music that is a harmony, but each and every note owes its entire existence – at the exact moment that it occurs – to the particular movement of the harp strings just before. If we hear a C-note, it is because the harp strings moved the way that they did, and it is not possible for the strings to have moved that way and for a D-note to have played instead. Nor is it possible for the C-note to continue playing if the harp strings are cut or destroyed. If we continued to hear the C-note in that instance, we would look around for a different harp that is their source. What

---

9 Starting with Plato, there is a long history of arguments from indivisibility. See for example the papers in Lennon and Stainton (2008).

Socrates is asking is whether or not our thinking and our mental states have a dependence on brain strings that is analogous to the dependence that musical notes have on the strings of the instrument that produces them.

Turning back to the argument from divisibility that Descartes presents in the Sixth Meditation, it might be granted for the sake of argument that bodies are divisible in a way that minds are not, but minds might still be material. Ideas and volitions might be something like what we now identify as emergent properties of bodies – properties that are very different from the more basic material properties from which they result, but which result from those properties nonetheless. A worry in particular is that modern-day procedures like anesthesia would appear to show that the brain is a kind of on-off switch for mentality and that when brain strings are cut, our (material) thinking perishes in the absence of its undergirding support and cause. I am not suggesting that the emergentist is able to offer any kind of *explanation* of how mind emerges from body.[10] The emergentist might just appeal to considerations like mind-body interaction – and to the way in which thinking appears to cease when the brain is modified in the right way – and argue that mental states *somehow* result from brain states, but in a way that we do not understand. The emergentist would then deny that "if a foot or arm or any other part of the body is cut off, nothing has thereby been taken away from the mind." With the right kind of damage to the brain, thinking ceases altogether.

An initial response that Descartes might provide is that the thinking of a mind does *not* cease in the course of anesthesiology and similar interruptions to brain activity. Thinking is always conscious, he supposes, and so a mind exhibits conscious awareness at all times, but a mind does not always *remember* its awareness. In the *Fourth Replies* discussion in which he identifies thinking and conscious thinking, he goes out of his way to add:

---

10 See for example the discussion in Strawson (2008). I suspect that the emergentist has to say (with Hume 1739–1740, I.iii.3, 78–82) that causal relations are not intelligible in some instances and that it is possible for anything to come from anything (or even from nothing).

I do not doubt that the mind begins to think as soon as it is implanted in the body of an infant, and that it is immediately aware of its thoughts, even though it does not remember this afterwards because the impressions of these thoughts do not remain in the memory.

(AT 7:246, CSM 2:171–172)

I have to admit that here I do not share Descartes' intuition. As far as I can tell, there is a lot of thinking that is not conscious, but more importantly Descartes would appear to be in the grip of a theory to say that all of our thinking is conscious and that we simply forget most of it. He could retain the view that the essence of mind is to think, but he might conclude with near contemporaries like Cavendish, More, Cudworth, and Leibniz that mentality often is not conscious at all.[11]

The argument from inexplicability

Descartes has another (and I think much more plausible) way to rebuff the view that mental states are emergent properties of bodies. He offers a second argument for the immateriality of mind – an argument from the inexplicability of modifications like ideas and volitions in terms of three-dimensional extension.

As we have seen, in Principles I.53 Descartes posits that every substance has a principal attribute through which all of its modifications are intelligible.[12] He supposes that there are such things as modifications – which seems fair enough – and he supposes that these do not have the ontological wherewithal to exist in the absence of the substances on which they depend. There are no free-floating sizes and no free-floating ideas, but these are always the sizes and ideas of a substance. But never of the same substance; or so he is

---

11 See Cavendish (1655), unnumbered page between pp. 26 and 27; More (1659), 169; Cudworth (1678), 679; and Leibniz (1714), Section 18, p. 215; Sections 20–24, pp. 215–216; Section 36, p. 217; and Section 56, p. 220. See also Chapter 8, pp. 303–305.

12 AT 8:25, CSM 1:210–211. See also the discussion Chapter 1, pp. 11–13 and 21–22.

arguing. If all that existed were modifications and substances, there would be nothing to block the existence of a substance that had a size and an idea among its modifications. A substance might instead be neutral with the respect to the modifications that it comes to have, and there would be no explanation why it comes to have some modifications rather than others.[13] Descartes supposes however that substances are not neutral with respect to the modifications that they come to have and that in addition to substances and modifications there exist principal attributes.

Descartes holds that substances have a principal attribute in terms of which all of the modifications of the substance are explicable. Bodies have extension as their principal attribute, and bodies accordingly possess modifications like size, shape, and motion. But there is no way to explain how bodies with features like size, shape, and motion would ever come to have a feature like thinking. So they don't. Instead, thinking is a feature of a different substance, and a substance that has a principal attribute through which thinking is explicable. A worry here might be that Descartes is imposing too strong an intelligibility requirement on reality: he is supposing that reality makes sense (or is explicable or intelligible) and that if an account of reality does not make sense then it is to be rejected. Presumably he would be on steady ground if he insisted that an account of reality is to be rejected if it is unintelligible in the sense of being self-contradictory. In that case, we would not be putting constraints on reality so much as we would be putting constraints on ourselves: we would be noticing that what we have offered as a picture of reality is not a picture at all. But Descartes is doing more than rejecting pictures of reality that are self-contradictory. In arguing that ideas and volitions are not modifications of corporeal substance, he is insisting that we would understand how ideas and volitions arise from extension if they did arise from extension, and he is insisting that because we do not understand how ideas and volitions arise from extension they do not. He is arguing – and presumably is right to argue – that it is not intelligible how ideas and volitions would arise from extension, but he is

---

13 See for example the overview in Stubenberg (2018).

presumably mistaken to conclude that ideas and volitions therefore have to be modifications of a different substance (with a different principal attribute). Perhaps there are substances and there is no such thing as a principal attribute, and substances admit of whatever modifications they please.[14] Descartes posits that there are such things as principal attributes, but another philosopher might argue that there does not exist so much as a concept of these.

A related worry is that Descartes does not offer any explicit evidence for the view that extension and thought are so different that there is no explanation of the existence of mental modifications in terms of extension. In the Second Meditation discussion of wax, he exposes thought and extension to be similar in fact – arguing that what we know best about body are features that are wholly insensible and cannot be pictured in the imagination (AT 7:31, CSM 2:21). Perhaps a pre-*Meditations* idea of body has little content in common with a clear and distinct idea of mind, but a considered idea of body tells a different story.[15] Descartes does not offer an *argument* to show that our ideas of extension and thought are so different that there is no way to explain mental modifications in terms of extension, but instead he supposes that the difference between the two is obvious. He does not offer an argument to demonstrate what he finds to be obvious – perhaps because that would be to undermine his case and suggest that it is not obvious at all. He writes for example,

> in the case of body and soul you cannot see any such connection, provided you conceive them as they should be conceived, the one as that which fills space and the other as that which thinks. …I do not know any other pair of ideas in the whole of nature which are as different from each other as these two.[16]

---

14 I am not trying to suggest that other philosophers are somehow on a better footing than Descartes in terms of their most fundamental assumptions and posits. I just want to be honest about the limits to the kind of justification that Descartes is going to be able to provide for his view on principal attributes.

15 See also "To More, 5 February 1649," AT 5:269–270, CSMK 361.

16 "To [De Launay], 22 July 1641," AT 3:421, CSMK 188. See also "To Mersenne, 21 January 1641," AT 3:285, CSMK 169.

The principal attribute of thought and the principal attribute of extension have nothing in common, Descartes insists, and so extended and thinking substances will have nothing in common either. They will be different with respect to their principal attribute, and they will be different with respect to the modifications that are explicable in terms of that attribute.

Another worry for the *Principles* I.53 argument is that it supposes that a substance has only one principal attribute, when for all we know it might have two. Margaret Cavendish, a near-contemporary of Descartes, held that bodies have a rich enough nature to give rise not only to modifications like size, shape, and motion but also to mental modifications. Cavendish was a self-described materialist,[17] but she had a very expansive understanding of body – arguing that the most basic features of body include more than size, shape, and motion. She argues that if the most basic features of body were restricted to size, shape, and motion, and everything was material, then finite thinking would never have come to exist; but exist it does.[18] Cavendish thus agrees with Descartes that bodies with the basic features of size, shape, and motion are not able to generate thought and intelligence. Bodies do think,[19] however, and so matter must already possess thought at the most fundamental level.[20] We might then ask why Descartes does not allow that a substance might have two principal attributes such that some of the features of the substance could be explained in terms of one and some could be

---

17 See for example Cavendish (1664), 69, 195.

18 She writes,

> I shall never be able to conceive, how senseless and irrational Atoms can produce sense and reason, or a sensible and rational body, such as the soul is.... 'Tis true, different effects may proceed from one cause or principle; but there is no principle, which is senseless, can produce sensitive effects; nor no rational effects can flow from an irrational cause....
>
> ("Observations Upon the Opinions of Some Ancient Philosophers," in Cavendish (1666), 27)

19 For a discussion of Cavendish's reasons for thinking that bodies think, see Cunning (2016) Chapter 2. She argues for example that because minds and bodies interact, and because our minds travel with our bodies, and only bodies partake of motion, minds must be material.

20 Cavendish (1664), 514.

explained in terms of the other. The position is certainly available to him. We could grant Descartes the assumption that the modifications of a substance always need to be understood through a principal attribute, and we could grant him the assumption that modifications of thinking are not explicable in terms of extension and vice versa, but with Cavendish we could reject his conclusion that minds are immaterial substances.[21]

Descartes does not say much about why substances are restricted to just one principal attribute. One thing that he does say however is that an entity with just one principal attribute is a complete thing. He writes for example that

> the idea of a substance with extension and shape is a complete idea, because I can conceive it entirely on its own, and deny of it everything else of which I have an idea. Now it seems to me very clear that the idea which I have of a thinking substance is complete in this sense.[22]

> though a triangle can perhaps be taken concretely as a substance having a triangular shape, it is certain that the property of having the square on the hypotenuse equal to the squares on the other sides is not a substance. So neither the triangle nor the property can be understood as a complete thing in the way in which the mind and body can be so understood.... [T]he notion of a substance is just this – that it can exist by itself, without the aid of any other substance.[23]

The mention of a triangular shape is elucidating, if a shape is something that requires the existence of a substance and a principal attribute through which it can be understood. But a shape and a substance with the principal attribute of extension are a complete

---

21 Note that another figure who proceeds along the lines of Cavendish is Spinoza – arguing that there exists a single substance that has (in effect) the principal attribute of thought and the principal attribute of extension. See Spinoza (1677), Part II, Propositions I and II, 245.

22 "To Gibieuf, 19 January 1642," AT 3:475, CSMK 202.

23 *Fourth Replies*, AT 7:224–226, CSM 2:158–159.

thing – or so Descartes is intuiting. Perhaps he then identifies things with a single attribute as complete because (he supposes) they do not depend on any other creaturely reality, but if they did have a second (or third) principal attribute, they would depend on it for their existence. Perhaps that is what he is thinking, but if so, he is being a bit selective and ad hoc in his understanding of substances as entities that are ontologically independent. A substance with two principal attributes would still be ontologically independent in the sense that it – the entity with its two attributes – would not depend on any *other* creaturely reality for its existence. Still, Descartes focuses on (what he takes to be) the datum that having just one principal attribute is sufficient for an entity to be a complete thing:

> Now the mind can be perceived distinctly and completely (that is, sufficiently for it to be considered as a complete thing) without any of the forms or attributes by which we recognize that body is a substance.... And similarly a body can be understood distinctly and as a complete thing, without any of the attributes which belong to the mind.
>
> (AT 7:223, CSM 2:157)

Here he says that having just one principal attribute is sufficient to meet the threshold for being a substance. But again that would not mean that a thing could not have two principal attributes. Things that are way beyond that threshold – for example, substances with the principal attribute of extension and the principal attribute of thought – would presumably be substances also, in something like the way that an individual who plays a single sport is an athlete and an individual who plays two more sports is an athlete as well. Descartes does not say exactly what he means by the language of "complete things," but it is not clear how that language helps him to rule out that mentality is a feature of a substance with two principal attributes or that modifications like ideas and volitions and sizes and shapes are modifications of the same single substance.

Another reason why Descartes might hold that created substances have just one principal attribute is from his theory of conceptual distinction. If he holds that what it is for a substance and its principal attribute to be conceptually distinct is for the substance and its attributes to be identical outside of thought, then a substance would never have both the principal attribute of thought and the principal attribute of extension. If it did, the substance would be identical to its thought and identical to its extension, which is to say that its thought and extension would be identical, but our idea of thought and our idea of extension expose that thought and extension are not identical: there is not "any other pair of ideas in the whole of nature which are as different from each other as these two" (AT 3:421, CSMK 188).[24] However, I do not think that it is Descartes' theory of conceptual distinction that is driving his view that a substance has only one principal attribute. In Chapter 3, I argued that Descartes does not hold that we are in a position to make a clean demarcation between the claim that a substance and its principal attribute are inseparable and the claim that a substance and its principal attribute are identical.[25] He struggles to make such a demarcation himself and supposes that in the end, it is not in the cards for us to uncover. I also think that it is noteworthy that Descartes does not say anywhere that the reason why a substance has only one principal attribute is that a substance and its attributes are conceptually distinct. He holds that there is just a small number of metaphysical results that are within our reach, and if the ground of one of those results is that a substance and principal attribute are identical, it is surprising that he nowhere identifies it as such. I would propose instead that the reason why Descartes holds that a substance has only one principal attribute is that he takes the principal attribute of a substance to be the nature of the substance – a nature that the substance has ubiquitously and in such a way that every bit of the substance is able to have modifications that are explicable in terms of that nature. What Descartes says in *Principles* I.53 is that "each substance has one principal property which *constitutes* its nature and essence" (AT 8A:25, CSM 1:210, emphasis added). A substance would have thought as a principal attribute and extension as a principal attribute only if

---

24 Some commentators have argued that it is Descartes' theory of conceptual distinction that generates his view that a substance has only one principal attribute. See Dutton (2003) and Rozemond (2016), 838–846.

25 See Chapter 3, pp. 97–103.

thought constituted the essence of the substance on its own and extension constituted the essence of the substance on its own. In that case, thought and extension would be identical,[26] but Descartes is clear that they are not.

Descartes holds that each substance has just one principal attribute. There is a famous passage however in which he speaks as though there exists a substance that has more than one principal attribute. In an exchange with Regius, he suggests that the mind-body union of a human being is a kind of substance. Prior to the exchange, Regius had made very public his anti-Aristotelian view that minds and bodies are substances and that their union is not, and Regius also presented himself publicly as a Cartesian.[27] Descartes was extremely protective of his reputation and of the reception of his philosophy, as we have seen, and he preferred to avoid controversy when possible. He thus communicates to Regius that there is better language to use in describing mind-body union. First, he speaks in the same breath of substances and entities that have a substantial form as one of their components:

> It is inconceivable that a substance should come into existence without being created de novo by God; but we see every day that many so-called substantial forms come into existence; and yet the people who think they are substances do not believe that they are created by God; so their view is mistaken.[28]

Then he identifies the human soul as the substantial form of the human being, suggesting that mind-body union is a substance in its own right. He continues: "This is confirmed by the example of the soul, which is the true substantial form of man" (ibid.).

---

26 Note that Della Rocca (1996) argues that Spinoza is happy to accept that on their own mind and body each constitutes the essence of the one substance that exists (God). According to Della Rocca, Spinoza concludes that "the mind and the body are one and the same thing [but] expressed in two ways or conceived in two ways" (128). Not so for Descartes.

27 See the discussion in Chapter 2, pp. 63–67.

28 "To Regius, January 1642," AT 3:505, CSMK 208.

He concludes that the composite that is the mind-body union is something more than just its two parts:

> if a human being is considered in himself as a whole, we say of course that he is a single *ens per se*, and not *per accidens*; because the union which joins a human body and soul to each other is not accidental to a human being, but essential....
>
> (AT 3:508, CSMK 209)

Perhaps the 1642 Regius letter is evidence that Descartes held that mind-body union is a substance, but as evidence, it is pretty thin. The reason that Descartes offers to explain why mind-body union is essential to a human being is that "a human being without it is not a human being" (ibid.). However, that is not to say that a human being is a substance; it is just to say that if something is before us that is not a mind-body union, it is not a human being. Nor are there any systematic reasons that require Descartes to posit mind-body union as a third kind of substance. Some commentators have suggested that Descartes holds that mind-body union is a substance and that there is a (single) principal attribute that constitutes its nature and through which its modifications are explicable – the nature of the union of mind and body.[29] For example, we might suppose that there is no way to explain sensations and similar perceptions through the principal attribute of extension or the principal attribute of thought. If so, there would need to be another principal attribute through which those would be explained, and it would be the principal attribute of a third substance. But Descartes is clear in *Principles* I.68 that sensations are modifications of mind, even if a mind only has them as a result of its union with a body.[30] He does not posit a third kind of substance to explain sensations, or passions, and his descrip-

---

29 See for example Gueroult (1968), 134; Broughton and Mattern (1978), 23–32; Cottingham (1985); Hoffman (1986); Hoffman (2009), Chapters 5 and 7; and Embry (2020).

30 I have to admit that I do not understand the motivation behind the view that Descartes holds that sensations are modifications of a third substance. He is clear that sensations are modifications of finite mind (*Principles* I.68, AT 8A:33, CSM 1:217). They are modifications of finite mind that are occasioned by

tion of mind-body union as an *ens per se* would appear to be more a tactical maneuver than anything else. He had seen what happens to intellectuals who depart from Aristotelian orthodoxy. If his attempt at a paradigm shift in scientific and philosophical thinking was going to fail, it would not be due to the unvetted proclamations of a disciple.

The argument from language use

The third argument that Descartes offers for the view that minds are immaterial substances is from the contention that there are linguistic and other capacities that are had by substances but not by material substances. In *Discourse on the Method* Part V, Descartes carefully unpacks the ability of finite minds to deploy language. He allows that non-minded creatures sometimes *simulate* language use – for example, "we see that magpies and parrots can utter words as we do, and yet they cannot speak as we do" (AT 6:57, CSM 1:140). Non-minded creatures utter words, and the grottoes that Descartes admired at the Royal Gardens in St. Germain simulated language-use as well.[31] In all such cases,

> it is nature which acts in them according to the disposition of their organs. In the same way a clock, consisting only of wheels and springs, can count the hours and measure time more accurately than we can with all our wisdom.
>
> (AT 6:59, CSM 1:141)

But non-minded creatures do not "speak as we do." Descartes is hereby presupposing a view of what counts as language-use and what falls short. He holds that as a matter of fact non-human animals do not string together words in the way that a human being is able to do – "even the stupidest child" (AT 6:58, CSM 1:140) or the "dullest of men" (AT 6:57, CSM 1:140). We could create a robot that

---

material bodies (the Sixth Meditation, AT 7:79–80, CSM 2:55). See also Rozemond (1998), 189.

31 *Treatise on Man*, AT 11:130–131, CSM 1:100. See also Chapter 2, p. 47–48.

strung together far more words than a parrot or magpie, and that produced its noises in a reliable and consistent order, and Descartes would insist that we still do not have before us a language-user. That is because part of what it is to be a language-user is to "act... through understanding" (ibid.). – and as per *Principles* I.53, any act of understanding presupposes the principal attribute of thought and hence the existence of mental substance. Descartes does not go of his way to flesh out the role of the understanding in the use of language, but he does gesture at it. He says that "reason is a universal instrument which can be used in all kinds of situations" (ibid.); it is clearly operative at moments in which a creature utters a word that is appropriate or fitting but that its material and mechanical dispositions are not equipped to produce.[32] Some of the words of a language-user might be rote and mechanical – if Descartes is right that "the thoughts of almost all people are more concerned with words than with things; and as a result people very often give their assent to words they do not understand."[33] But not all. Part of what it is to deploy language is to recognize certain terms to be fitting, and to utter them. Language-users exist, and hence, there exists such a thing as understanding, and there exist modifications that are explained not in terms of the principal attribute of extension but in terms of the principal attribute of thought.

Descartes does not rule out once and for all that non-human animals possess immaterial minds.[34] He does say in *Discourse* Part V that "it would be incredible... if [animal] souls were not completely different in nature from ours" (AT 6:58, CSM 1:140, emphasis added). But he is a bit more circumspect in his November 1646 letter to William Cavendish: "since the organs of [animal] bodies are not very different from ours, it may be conjectured that there is attached to these organs some thought such as we experience in

---

32 As Descartes writes, "it is for all practical purposes impossible for a machine to have enough different organs to make it act in all the contingencies of life in the way in which our reason makes us act" (ibid.).

33 *Principles* I.74, AT 8A:37, CSM 1:220.

34 See also the discussions in Cottingham (1978), Boyle and Massey (1999), and Thomas (2020).

ourselves, but of a very much less perfect kind."[35] Descartes does not employ the argument from language-use to establish definitively that non-human animals lack (immaterial) minds. He employs it as additional evidence that human beings *do* have minds. Animals utter words but strictly speaking they are not language-users, Descartes supposes, and their utterance of words is the sort of behavior that we would expect from a wholly material thing. But if a creature *is* a language-user, it has a mind. The argumentation here is difficult to dismiss if Descartes is correct that language-users exist and that a creature does not meet the threshold of being a language-user unless it possesses and exhibits understanding. I myself do not agree that "it is for all practical purposes impossible for a machine to have enough different organs to make" us react to the "contingencies of life" in all of the functional and creative ways that we do. The human brain is just one organ, but it is pretty remarkable. Still, I don't have a knock-down argument – just an animist (and Cavendishean) view of matter and a different sense (than Descartes) of the unbound-edness of reason. We might also take issue with the argument from language-use insofar as it depends on the argument from the explicability of modifications in terms of principal attributes. But the latter argument would appear to be a level of ground-floor machinery for Descartes, and it is quite compelling if his opponent has to insist that thought emerges from body more or less by magic.

The argument from doubt

There is a fourth argument that Descartes offers for the conclusion that minds are immaterial substances, and it has been widely panned. This is the argument from doubt. On the surface, the argument is this: we can posit the existence of mental substance while not being certain of the existence of any material substance; therefore, minds are immaterial substances. The argument (as stated) is extremely problematic.[36] For example, we might posit the existence of Clark Kent, while not being certain of the existence of Superman;

---

35 "To The Marquess of Newcastle, 23 November 1646," AT 4:576, CSMK 304.
36 See for example Cottingham (1992).

we might then conclude that Clark Kent is not Superman.[37] Or we might posit the existence of the Morning Star, while not being certain of the existence of the Evening Star, and we might conclude that the one is not the other. More generally, we might argue that so long as we can posit the existence of X while being uncertain of the existence of Y, X is not Y. But that would be ridiculous. Perhaps X exists and is Y, and we just do not realize it. Or perhaps X exists and is Y, and the reason why we are not certain that Y exists is because we do not know what Y is. If Descartes were to argue that X is not Y because we can posit the existence of X while doubting the existence of Y, he would be operating at the height of inanity. If he is operating at the height of inanity, a number of further questions would arise, and one would be about us and why we have held him up as a figure to be interpreted and taught and critiqued. But Descartes does not argue that minds are immaterial because we can posit the existence of mind while being uncertain of the existence of body. A closer look at the texts reveals that he is doing something quite different.

One text in which the argument from doubt appears is Part 4 of *Discourse on the Method*. There (in 1637) Descartes echoes the language and argumentation that we find later in the (1641) *Meditations*. For example, he says (in the *Discourse*) that after "resolv[ing] to pretend that all the things that had ever entered my mind were no more true than the illusions of my dreams" (AT 6:32, CSM 1:127), he still cannot call into question the existence of his thinking mind: "this truth 'I am thinking, therefore I exist' was so firm and sure that all of the most extravagant suppositions of the sceptics were incapable of shaking it" (ibid.). He then concludes that his mind is an immaterial thinking substance:

> Next I examined attentively what I was. I saw that while I could pretend that I had no body and that there was no world and no place for me to be in, I could not for all that pretend that I did not exist. I saw on the contrary that from the mere fact that I thought of doubting the truth of other things, it followed

---

37 The literature still contains reconstructions of Descartes' argumentation along these lines, for example in Frankish and Kasmirli (2009).

quite evidently and certainly that I existed.... From this I knew
that I was a substance whose sole essence or nature is simply to
think, and which does not require any place, or depend on any
material thing, in order to exist.

(AT 6:32–33, CSM 1:127)

In the Discourse, Descartes is conceiving and grasping that his mind is
an immaterial substance. He confirms as much later in the "Preface
to the Reader" of the Meditations. He says that "[i]n the Discourse I asked
anyone who found anything worth criticizing in what I had written
to be kind enough to point it out to me" (AT 7:7, CSM 2:7), and
he then proceeds to address the objection that he is not entitled to
conclude in the Discourse that his mind is an immaterial substance.
He continues,

> The first objection is this. From the fact that the human mind,
> when directed towards itself, does not perceive itself to be any-
> thing other than a thinking thing, it does not follow that its
> nature or essence consists only in its being a thinking thing,
> where the word 'only' excludes everything else that could be
> said to belong to the nature of the soul.

Here Descartes is repeating an objection. He responds to the objection by asserting that in the Discourse, he was indeed conceiving and
grasping his mind to be an immaterial substance. He just wasn't
arguing (yet) that his conceptions conform to reality:

> My answer to this objection is that in that passage it was not my
> intention to make those exclusions in an order corresponding
> to the actual truth of the matter (which I was not dealing with
> at that stage) but merely in an order corresponding to my own
> perception.

(AT 7:8, CSM 2:7)

Descartes says here that in the Discourse, he was excluding body from
mind: he was conceiving of mind as immaterial. He was excluding
body from mind, "but merely in an order corresponding to [his]
perception." That is to say – he is grasping that mind is immaterial,

but he is not going so far as to conclude that what he grasps to be the case is in *fact* the case. In other passages, he speaks of a very different mental act in which he conceives of mind in abstraction from body: he has a clear and distinct idea of mind but does not compare it to an idea of body.[38] In the Second Meditation, he thinks of mind in abstraction from body. He has a clear and distinct idea of mind, but he is not in a position to compare it to a clear and distinct idea of body. He does not work up to a clear and distinct idea of body until later in the Meditation – in the discussion of wax.

In the *Discourse* passage, Descartes is conceiving of mind as immaterial. He grasps that mind is immaterial, but he does not take up the question of whether or not things are as he grasps them to be.

Note another thing that he does not do in the *Discourse*. He does not argue that his mind is immaterial because he is certain of the existence of his mind while being uncertain of the existence of bodies. In the *Discourse* passage, he is not in a state of *uncertainty* about the existence of material things. He is in a different but related mental state: that of pretending or supposing that nothing material exists. He supposes for the sake of argument that nothing material exists, and then he asks whether he is still able to posit the existence of his thinking mind. He insists that he is able to answer in the affirmative. We might then return to the Superman – Clark Kent variation on the argument. We posit that Superman exists, and we suppose that Clark Kent does not exist. Then we ask whether we are still able to posit that Superman exists even if Clark Kent does not. If we do not know whether Clark Kent is Superman, we would not be able to posit that Superman exists and deny the existence of Clark Kent. Instead, what we would say (if we were being careful) is that we do not know if

---

38 For example, in "To [Mesland], 2 May 1640," AT 4:120, CSMK 236. He writes, There is a great difference between *abstraction* and *exclusion*. If I said simply that the idea that I have of my soul does not represent it to me as being dependent on the body and identified with it, this would be merely an abstraction, from which I could form only a negative argument which would be unsound. But I say that this idea represents it to me as a substance which can exist even though everything belonging to the body be excluded from it; from which I form a positive argument....

we can posit the existence of Superman while denying the existence of Clark Kent, as the two might be identical, and the non-existence of the second might entail the non-existence of the first. However, if we deny the existence of Clark Kent and we *are* still able to posit the existence of Superman, then Superman is not Clark Kent – end of story.

Perhaps a better analogy is in terms of the essential and non-essential ingredients of a cake. Ice cream is (presumably) an essential ingredient in an ice-cream cake. We might suppose for the moment that ice cream does not exist, and then ask if we are able to posit the existence of ice-cream cake. We are not. The situation is different however if we deny the existence of plastic and ask if we are able to posit the existence of ice-cream cake. We are, and that is because ice-cream cakes do not consist of plastic. We do not need to run a chemical analysis of ice-cream cakes to determine whether or not plastic is an essential ingredient of them. In positing the existence of ice-cream cake, we are positing a collection of ingredients in advance – the minimum ingredients that are sufficient to make up such a cake. If we are able to posit the existence of ice-cream cake while denying the existence of plastic, that is a sure sign that plastic is not an ingredient of ice-cream cake, even though the plastic figure of a married couple might be attached to the cake as an extra. In a very different scenario, if we posit that plastic does not exist and are uncertain whether ice-cream cakes can still be posited, that is a sign that we do not know whether plastic is an ingredient of ice-cream cake. Instead of positing that ice-cream cakes exist, we would say that we do not know whether they exist and that we would need more information.

In the autobiographical *Discourse*, Descartes is in a fairly advanced epistemic position and is cognizant of some things that a Second Meditation meditator is not. Descartes concludes in the *Discourse* that his mind is a substance, and that it is an immaterial substance. That is to say, he understands what it is for something to be a substance, and he understands what it is for something to be material. He posits the existence of some thinking, and he concludes that it is the thinking of a substance. He then asks whether or not he can posit the existence of that thinking substance even if nothing material exists. If he is uncertain whether or not thinking is material, he cannot posit the existence of thinking substance and deny the existence of body: to deny the existence of the one might be to deny the existence of the other. He finds however that he is able to deny the existence of body while positing the existence of thinking substance. In the *Discourse*, he does not get into detail about why exactly he is able to do this. Presumably it is because he is delimiting the object of his thinking in advance: he has in mind a substance, and in particular a substance with the principal attribute of thought, along with any modifications that are understood through that attribute. That is all that he is thinking, and he recognizes that it is enough to constitute a substance. He then asks whether he can posit the existence of that substance while denying the existence of body. He checks his idea of body against his idea of thought and notices that there is no "other pair of ideas in the whole of nature which are as different from each other as these two." The principal attribute of thought does not coincide with any materiality; nor do the mental modifications that are understood in terms of that principal attribute. Descartes notices that what it is to think is different from what it is to be extended, and he concludes that thinking substance can still be posited even if nothing material exists at all.[39]

---

39 I am disagreeing with Christofidou (2001), who argues that in *Discourse* Part 4, Descartes is not drawing the metaphysical conclusion that minds are immaterial substances (219–228); instead, he is just reporting the epistemological conclusion that all that he is aware to pertain to his mind is thinking. Christifidou is attempting to be charitable and to read *Discourse* Part 4 as parallel to the Second Meditation discussion in which Descartes is clearly drawing only the epistemological conclusion. But Descartes is clear in the more autobiographical *Discourse* that "this "I" – that is, the soul by which I am what I am – is entirely distinct from the body" (AT 6:33, CSM 1:127). In the *Discourse*, Descartes grasps and perceives that mind excludes body, but he does not argue in addition that what he perceives to be the case is in fact that case. So I agree with Christofidou that Descartes is only arriving at an epistemological result in the *Discourse*, but that is not to say (with Christofidou) that all that he notices to pertain to his mind (in the *Discourse*) is that it thinks. He also perceives that it is immaterial, but he does not in addition argue that the "order corresponding to [his] perception" is the order that corresponds to reality. For example, it is easy to imagine a situation in which all that an individual is aware of in a room is a table, and in which there might be other things that are in the room. A very different situation is one in

Of course, if Descartes is thinking all that, the *Discourse* version of the "argument from doubt" is just a more drawn-out version of the argument from inexplicability. But that is a much better interpretive outcome than to say that he concludes that minds are immaterial because he is certain that his mind exists while being uncertain of the existence of any bodies.

A charitable reading of the *Discourse* argument would attribute to Descartes reasoning that delivers the conclusion that minds are immaterial thinking substances, so long as that reasoning is available to him. Here I have attempted to provide such a reading. To even think the conclusion that minds are immaterial substances, Descartes would have to understand a number of things: what it is for something to be a substance, what it is for something to think, and what it is for something to be material. I am supposing that he takes himself to understand all of these in the lead-up to his conclusion that minds are immaterial substances.

The reasoning of the Second Meditation is of course very different. Descartes does not conclude in the Second Meditation that minds are immaterial substances. He does conclude (in the first half of the Second Meditation) that his thinking exists, but that is all. For example, he does not yet know what body is, and so he does not conclude that his thinking is immaterial (AT 7:27, CSM 2:18).[40] The relatively amateur thinking of a Second Meditation meditator is not the same as the thinking that is transcribed in the more autobiographical *Discourse*. The *Meditations* is written with an eye to a variety of minds and to minds that are confused and in need of emendation. Descartes accordingly refrains from concluding in the Second Meditation that minds are immaterial substances – for at least three reasons. First, he has not yet meditated to a clear understanding of what body is. Since he does not have a clear and distinct idea of body, he does not have the resources to inspect whether or not his thinking answers to that idea. He adds in *Second Replies* that there is an analytic order to the presentation of the views and arguments

---

which the person is aware that all that there is in the room is the table, but they do not trust that their awareness of things is veridical.

40 See also Chapter 6, pp. 252–253.

in the *Meditations* and that "my adherence to it was the reason for my dealing with the distinction between mind and body only at the end, in the Sixth Meditation, rather than in the Second" (AT 7:155, CSM 2:110). He says the same thing in *Third Replies* as well (AT 7:175, CSM 2:123).[41] Descartes would be reckless to conclude that his thinking is immaterial before he (or his meditator) has an understanding of what it is for something to *be* material. In the first half of the Second Meditation, he has a clear and distinct perception of the existence of his thinking, but not a clear and distinct perception that it is immaterial.

Nor does he have a clear understanding of what it is for something to be a substance. In the *Discourse*, he concludes that his mind is an immaterial thinking substance, but in the Second Meditation, he concludes neither that his thinking is immaterial nor that it is substantial. He does not introduce the concept of substance until his Third Meditation discussion of the one entity that is wholly independent and is truly a substance: "By the word 'God' I understand a substance that is infinite, <eternal, immutable, >, independent..." (AT 7:45, CSM 2:31). He says that the notion of a substance is the notion of a thing that is "capable of existing independently" (AT 7:44, CSM 2:30), and he then begins to apply the notion to mind and body. He says – "I also think that I am a substance" (ibid.) – and he adds that although minds and bodies would seem to "differ enormously[,]... they seem to agree with respect to the classification 'substance'" (ibid.). The earlier discussion of wax no doubt helped in terms of generating clarity on what it is for an entity to persist through change, but the notion of substance is not explicitly unpacked until the Third Meditation. The discussion of wax also comes at the *end* of the Second Meditation; it does not provide insight as to whether the I of "I am, I exist" (AT 7:27, CSM 2:18) is substantial. Descartes even qualifies the result "I am, I exist" as soon as he presents it. He says: "I am, I exist – that is certain. But for how long? For as long as I am thinking" (ibid.). He has not yet analyzed

---

41 And in "Synopsis of the following six Meditations," AT 7:13, CSM 2:9, and the
   Fourth Meditation, AT 7:59, CSM 2:41.

the notion of substance in the Second Meditation, and he does not assert that his mind is a persisting entity.[42]

Part 4 of the *Discourse* is a very different text from the *Meditations*. In the *Discourse* argument for the immateriality and substantiality of mind, Descartes is equipped with concepts that have not yet been clarified in the corresponding text of the Second Meditation, and as we have seen the *Discourse* omits hyperbolic doubt entirely.[43] What Descartes is doing in the *Meditations* is still related to what he does in the *Discourse* – for example, he is doubting the existence of material things and concluding that his thinking exists. He even says in the Second Meditation (like in the *Discourse*) that he is not just *uncertain* of the existence of material things: instead, he turns his will "in completely the opposite direction" and "pretend[s] for a time that these former opinions are utterly false and imaginary" (AT 7:22, CSM 2:15). But in the Second Meditation, he does not yet have a clear sense of what it is that he is pretending does not exist. He just doubts the existence of anything that is sensible – as a way of arriving at a non-sensory idea of mind.

In the *Meditations*, Descartes waits until the Sixth Meditation to conclude that minds are immaterial substances. All that he is in an epistemic position to do in the Second Meditation is to conclude that his thinking exists. He does not *exclude* his idea of body from his idea of mind in the Second Meditation, but just abstracts an idea of mind from the confused and composite idea of "mind" that a meditator would likely have at the start of inquiry. He thinks of thinking in isolation from the ideas to which it has long been attached. He writes,

> I said in one place that while the soul is in doubt about the existence of all things, it knows itself *praecise tantum* – 'in the strict sense only' – as an immaterial substance; and seven or eight

---

42 A third reason why Descartes does not present an argument for the view that minds are immaterial substances in the Second Meditation is that until he neutralizes the hyperbolic doubt of the First Meditation, any argument that he offers will be subject (and victim) to it. (See *Fourth Replies*, AT 7:226, CSM 2:159.) He very appropriately decides *not* to argue that minds are immaterial substances in the Second Meditation. Instead, he waits until Meditation Six.

43 See Chapter 4, pp. 124–127.

lines further down I showed that by the words 'in the strict sense only' I do not at all mean an entire exclusion or negation, but only an abstraction from material things, for I said that in spite of this we are not sure that there is nothing corporeal in the soul, even though we do not recognize anything corporeal in it. Here my critic is so unfair to me as to try to persuade the reader that when I used the phrase 'in the strict sense only' I meant to exclude the body, and thus that I contradicted myself afterwards when I said that I did not mean to exclude it.[44]

Descartes does not conclude that thinking is immaterial in the Second Meditation. He does not yet have a clear and distinct idea of body with which to compare his idea of thinking, and so he waits to run the comparison until later (in the Sixth Meditation). In a sense, Descartes *does* have a clear and distinct idea of body in the Second Meditation; he had a clear and distinct idea of body way back in the *Discourse* in 1637.[45] He has a clear and distinct idea of body in the Second Meditation in the same sense that Spinoza has his larger system in mind at the start of Part I of *Ethics*. However, the analytic structure of the *Meditations* is such that Descartes does not assume that in the early stages of inquiry, his readers have all the same clear and distinct ideas that he does. We arrive at a better understanding of what mind and body are, and a better understanding of what it is for something to be a substance, but only after "[p]rotracted and repeated" meditation.[46]

The argument from a clear and distinct perception of mind without body

Descartes' fifth and final argument for the immateriality and substantiality of mind appears most prominently in the Sixth Meditation – in

---

44 *Appendix to Fifth Objections and Replies*, AT 9A: 215, CSM 2:276.
45 It appears that Descartes had all of the conceptual resources in hand to argue that minds are immaterial substances before the *Discourse* even – way back in *Rules for the Direction of the Mind*. See Dika (2020).
46 *Second Replies*, AT 7:131, CSM 2:94.

the paragraph that ends with the conclusion that mind can exist apart from body (AT 7:78).[47]

An initial bit of background to the argument is that Descartes supposes that the attempt to register that minds are immaterial substances is often accompanied by great difficulty. Each of our minds is part of an intimate mind-body union, and our vivid experience of the unity of that union can interfere with our ability to grasp that minds and bodies have wholly opposite natures.[48] We might even conclude on the basis of our awareness of mind-body union that the conclusion that minds are immaterial substances is absurd.[49] If we call into doubt our clear and distinct perception that minds are immaterial substances – or even just suspect that it

---

47 Here I focus on the Sixth Meditation, but see also the parallel argumentation later in *Principles* I.60.

48 Descartes writes,

> the fact that the mind is closely conjoined with the body, which we experience constantly through our senses, does result in our not being aware of the real distinction between mind and body unless we meditate attentively on the subject.
>
> (*Fourth Replies*, AT 7:228–229, CSM 2:160)

The discussions in Chamberlain (2019b) and Simmons (2017) are very instructive here.

49 Descartes writes,

> It does not seem to me that the human mind is capable of forming a very distinct conception of both the distinction between the soul and the body and their union; for to do this it is necessary to conceive them as a single thing and at the same time to conceive them as two things, and this is absurd.
>
> ("To Princess Elizabeth, 28 June 1643," AT 3:693, CSMK 227)

In another letter, he writes,

> There are two facts about the human soul on which depend all the knowledge we can have of its nature. The first is that it thinks, the second is that, being united to the body, it can act and be acted upon along with it. About the second I have said hardly anything; I have tried only to make the first well understood. For my principal aim was to prove the distinction between the soul and the body, and to this end only the first was useful, and the second might have been *harmful*.
>
> ("To Princess Elizabeth, 21 May 1643;" AT 3:664–665, CSMK 217–218, emphasis added)

See also the discussion in Gombay (2007), 112–113.

is unlikely – Descartes will remind us that our clear and distinct perceptions are veridical and that God has the power to have made things just so:

> You agree that thought is an attribute of a substance which contains no extension, and conversely that extension is an attribute of a substance that contains no thought. So you must also agree that a thinking substance is distinct from an extended substance. For the only criterion we have enabling us to know that one substance differs from another is that we understand one without [absque] the other. And God can surely bring about whatever we can clearly understand… But we can clearly understand a thinking substance that is not extended, and an extended substance that does not think, as you agree.[50]

As we will see, Descartes holds that we clearly and distinctly perceive mind absque body. Mind is without body, which is to say that it is without any materiality. If we are tempted to make the hasty judgment that it is impossible for mind to be without body at the same time that it is united with body, Descartes will remind us that God has the power to bring about whatever we clearly and distinctly perceive.

Descartes begins the Sixth Meditation argument with a reminder that clear and distinct perceptions are true and that God has enough power to have made reality to be exactly as we clearly and distinctly perceive it. He writes,

> First, I know that everything which I clearly and distinctly understand is capable of being created by God so as to correspond exactly with my understanding of it.
>
> (AT 7:78, CSM 2:54)

---

50 "To Regius, June 1642," AT 3:567, CSMK 214. I use the CSMK translation, except that I translate "absque" as "without." That is the primary definition of "absque" in Lewis and Short (1879), and as we will see, utilizing that definition makes better sense of Descartes' claim that we understand that mind is absque body even when it is united to a body.

We have seen this kind of reminder before. In *Principles* I:41, Descartes says that we clearly and distinctly perceive that God has preordained all events for eternity and that He has enough power to have created a universe in which all events are preordained for eternity – come what may. He offers a similar reminder in *Second Replies* that "it is quite irrational to cast doubt on the clear and distinct perceptions of the pure intellect merely because of preconceived opinions based on the senses, or because of mere hypotheses which contain an element of the unknown" (AT 7:164, CSM 2:116). In the AT 7:78 passage of the Sixth Meditation, Descartes is anticipating that we are primed to reject the result that minds are immaterial substances. Perhaps we will reject it because we have a vivid experience of mind-body union, and we suppose that it is impossible for minds and bodies to be united unless minds interface with bodies at a shared (and material) point of contact. Or perhaps we will reject it because of the tight and homogenous intermingling of mind and body: we suppose that the intermingling is so tight that the mind will no longer enjoy its status as an ontologically independent substance when it comes out the other side. Descartes accordingly reminds us that however unlikely it might seem that an immaterial substance would be united to a material body, we clearly and distinctly understand minds to be immaterial substances, and God has enough power to have made reality to be exactly as we clearly and distinctly understand it.

The topic of mind-body union is indeed insinuated throughout the entire AT 7:78 paragraph that posits the immateriality and substantiality of mind. Descartes begins the paragraph with the preemptive reminder that every clear and distinct perception is true. He is looking ahead to our clear and distinct perception of the immateriality and substantiality of mind and to doubts that we might raise about it. In the middle of the paragraph, he highlights that

> It is true that I may have (or, to anticipate, that I certainly have) a body that is very closely joined to me.
>
> (AT 7:78, CSM 2:54)

He then says that "Nevertheless" his clear and distinct perception of mind as an immaterial substance is veridical. That clear and distinct perception is veridical come what may, and what Descartes is expecting will come is not only an intimate awareness of mind-body union but also a corresponding judgment that it is impossible (or at least unlikely) for minds to be immaterial substances if they are so tightly intermingled with bodies. Mind-body union is front and center in the AT 7:78 discussion of the immateriality of mind. Descartes brings it up – in part because he expects that we (or his meditator) will bring it up, as embodiment is an unceasing fixture of day-to-day existence. And when we do bring it up we will be thrown. He frontloads the AT 7:78 argument for the immateriality and substantiality of mind with the reminder that God has enough power to have made reality to be exactly as we clearly and distinctly perceive it. We are not going to call into question the fact of mind-body union. Descartes goes to great lengths to make sure that we do not call into question the immateriality and substantiality of mind either.

The first sentence of the AT 7:78 paragraph is divided into two sentences in the CSM translation actually,[51] and the CSM translation overlooks some of the nuances in the appeal that Descartes makes to God's power, so I will now switch to the translation in Heffernan (1992), which better captures the subtlety in Descartes' language I think. In the first sentence of the AT 7:78 paragraph, Descartes writes,

> And, first, because I know that all the things that I clearly and distinctly understand can be made by God just as such as I understand them, it is enough that I could clearly and distinctly understand one thing without [absque] another in order that I might be certain that one is different from the other: because it can – at least by God – be posited separately.[52]

In the first part of the sentence, before the colon, Descartes uses the word "absque," which in the context of veridical clear and distinct perceptions is better translated as "without" and not as "apart" (which is featured in the CSM translation). A finite mind is a substance that is in many cases united to a body, and when it is without body but not apart from body. It is without body, or as Descartes

---

51 This is at CSM 2:54, AT 7:78.
52 Heffernan (1992), 76.

explains in *Fourth Replies* – mind is a substance "without [absque] any of the forms or attributes by which we recognize that body is a substance" (AT 7:223, CSM 2:157). We understand mind to be a substance without any (trace of) body in it, which is to say that it is true that mind is a substance without any body in it. It is an immaterial substance – and is without materiality – even when it is united to a body. That may seem unlikely if not impossible, but God can bring about whatever we clearly and distinctly perceive, and we clearly and distinctly perceive minds to be immaterial substances.

Descartes writes in the very next sentence of the Sixth Meditation that his reference to the power of God is meant to help us to think of mind and body as different:

> And it does not matter by which power it would happen that the things be thought as being different.[53]

Here Descartes is indicating that the mention of God's power in the argument for the immateriality of mind is a device to assist us in thinking of mind and body as different. He is attempting to put before his mind the thought that mind and body are substances with nothing in common, but the tight and homogenous intermingling of mind and body makes that attempt very difficult. In particular, we are likely to judge that there is no way that minds are immaterial substances *and* are united to bodies. Descartes thus encourages us to think of God's ability to make things to be exactly as we clearly and distinctly perceive them. But the reference to the power of God is not a formal step in the argumentation. Descartes says that "it does not matter" by which power we think of mind and body as different: a sophisticated cognizer might keep steady the thought of mind and body as different substances by imagining the decomposition of the brain and the immaterial thinking substance that is left over.[54] But for some (and arguably most), it is the thought of God's power that facilitates a sustained separation of the idea of thinking substance and the idea of corporeal substance.

---

53 Here and for the remainder of the AT 7:78 passage, I am using the translation in Heffernan (1992), 76.

54 See also *Second Replies*, AT 7:170, CSM 2:120.

Descartes then continues in the Sixth Meditation:

> And, therefore, from thence itself that I were to know that I
> exist, and that meanwhile I were to notice that nothing else at all
> belongs to my nature or essence except this alone – that I were a
> cogitating thing – I [would] correctly conclude that my essence
> consists in this one thing: that I be a cogitating thing.
>
> (76)

Here Descartes announces that he is about to move well beyond the
conclusion that he draws in the Second Meditation. He is arguing
in the Sixth Meditation not just that he is a thing that thinks; he
is arguing that he is only a thing that thinks and that his thinking
admits of no trace of extension. He is able to make that further step
because he understands what it is for something to be extended and
what it is for something to be substantial.

In the next sentence, he offers the aside that it is true that he
is conjoined to a body, but that nevertheless his thinking mind is
not extended. Then he recognizes that extension does not pertain to
thinking:

> because I have – on the one hand – a clear and distinct idea of
> me myself, in so far as I am only a cogitating thing and not an
> extended one, and because I have – on the other hand – a dis-
> tinct idea of [the] body, in so far as it is only an extended thing
> and not a cogitating one, it is still certain that I am really and
> truly distinct from my body....
>
> (ibid.)

Here Descartes recognizes the truth that his mind is a substance
that thinks and admits of no trace of extension, and so he asserts
that his mind is a substance that thinks and admits of no trace of
extension. He does not have to survey the entirety of his mind to
check it for any extension.[55] Instead, he delimits the object of his

---

55 He admits that this would not even be possible (*Fourth Replies*, AT 7:219–220,
   CSM 2:154–155).

thought in advance: he posits the existence of a substance with mental modifications and the principal attribute through which those modifications are explicable, and he notices that the principal attribute of thought and the principal attribute of extension have nothing in common.[56] The modifications of a thinking substance and the modifications of an extended substance would not coincide either.

The last (and very long) sentence of the AT 7:78 paragraph says that although his mind is united to a body, it is really distinct from that body and "can exist without [absque] it." Here Descartes has turned the tables with respect to the use of the term absque. He is not reflecting the datum that mind is without materiality; he is instead reflecting the datum that it can exist in separation from body. That is to say, he is explicitly contrasting the union of mind and body with the separation of mind and body. The language is more than a little awkward, given that earlier in the paragraph he was using "absque" to reference the without-ness of mind and body. But now he is highlighting "that the decay of the body does not imply the destruction of the mind, and [is] hence enough to give mortals the hope of an after-life."[57] Or as he puts it in Discourse on the Method Part V – he is arguing that "our soul is of a nature entirely independent of the body, and consequently that it is not bound to die with it" (AT 6:59, CSM 1:141). Perhaps the awkwardness in language is inevitable, given that in the Sixth Meditation, Descartes is talking about embodied minds – that is, minds that are without body (in the sense of being immaterial) but that are with body (in the sense of being part of a mind-body union). Mind is without body, Descartes supposes, but there is also a sense in which intermingled minds and bodies are

---

56 But Descartes does not use the language of principal attributes in the Sixth Meditation. He appears to suppose that we will pick up (or converge upon) the relevant concepts elsewhere in the Meditations, for example in the Second Meditation discussion of the relation between the nature of wax and sensible qualities like color. See also First Replies, AT 7:120, CSM 2:85, and Fourth Replies, AT 7:220–224, CSM 2:155–158.

57 "Synopsis of the following six Meditations," AT 7:13, CSM 2:10. But Descartes holds that there is no guarantee of an afterlife because strictly speaking, there is no guarantee that God will continue to preserve our minds in existence. See also "To Hyperaspistes, August 1641," AT 3:429 CSMK 193.

not without each other.[58] He defines a real distinction as a relation between two substances when they are without each other:

> Strictly speaking, a real distinction exists only between two or more substances; and we can perceive that two substances are really distinct simply from the fact that we can clearly and distinctly understand one without [absque] the other.[59]

In making the further claim that mind and body can exist without each other, Descartes is pointing out that the destruction of the one does not entail the destruction of the other. A finite mind continues to exist even after it is separated from the body to which it has been united, so long of course as God does not cease to keep it in existence.

Descartes holds that God wills the entire series of creaturely reality by a single volition that is immutable and eternal. In addition, he supposes that God contains absolutely no potentiality, and so there is not in God an alternative volition by which He might have willed a different series immutably and for eternity.[60] In some passages, Descartes uses language that is suggestive of a different view – the view that God is waiting in the wings to intervene in creaturely affairs, and in particular that He reserves the right to separate a given mind from a given body any time that He pleases. For example, he writes:

---

58 Descartes might have made things a lot less confusing if he had used one expression to track the way in which mind is *without* body – whether it is united to a body or not – and a different expression to track the separation of mind and body. For example, in *Fourth Replies*, he uses "sine" to reflect that mind is without materiality (AT 7:223). It would have been nice if he had used "sine" exclusively for the one purpose and "absque" for the other, but he does not. In fact he alternates the terms – using "absque" not only to track the separation of mind and body (AT 7:78) but also to reflect that mind is without materiality (AT 7:219), and "sine" to track the separation of mind and body (AT 7:170) and to reflect that mind is without materiality (AT 7:223). He also uses "absque" and "sine" interchangeably throughout *Principles* I.61.

59 *Principles* I.61, AT 8A:28, CSM 1:213. Here I am using the CSM translation, but again with the minor change that I translate "absque" as "without."

60 See the discussion in Chapter 5, pp. 192–203.

we can clearly understand a thinking substance that is not extended and an extended substance that does not think, as you agree. So even if God conjoins and unites them as much as he can, he cannot thereby divest himself of his omnipotence and lay down his power of separating them; and hence they remain distinct....[61]

even if we suppose that God has joined some corporeal substance to such a thinking substance so closely that they cannot be more closely conjoined, thus compounding them into a unity, they nonetheless remain really distinct. For no matter how closely God may have united them, the power which he previously had of separating them, or keeping one in being without the other, is something he could not lay aside; and things which God has the power to separate, or to keep in being separately, are really distinct.[62]

the mind can, at least through the power of God, exist without the body; and similarly the body can exist apart from the mind.[63]

It is certainly possible to read these passages as saying that mind and body can exist apart in the counterfactual sense that God always retains the option of separating a mind from the body to which it is united, but I propose that we read the passages in line with Descartes' view that all exercises of divine power are already included in the single act that is God's eternal and immutable volition.[64] If so, Descartes holds that mind and body can exist apart in the same sense that he holds that it is possible for bodies to admit of all the configurations that they ultimately exhibit.[65] Descartes is attempting to "prove the existence... of our souls when they are separate from the body."[66]

---

61 "To Regius, June 1642," AT 3:567, CSMK 214.

62 Principles I.60, AT 8A:29, CSM 1:213.

63 Second Replies, AT 7:170, CSM 2:119.

64 For example in Principles I.23, AT 8A:14, CSM 1:201.

65 Principles III.47, AT 8A:103, CSM 1:258. Here I am disagreeing with Rozemond (2011), 243, and also Christofidou (2001), 223, 234–237, who argue that for Descartes, the real distinction between mind and body entails that there exists the possibility of the separation of mind and body.

66 "To Mersenne, 25 November 1630," AT 1:182, CSMK 29, emphasis added. In the letter, Descartes is referencing the "little treatise on metaphysics" that he has begun to draft and that he will complete later.

He holds that God wills all of creaturely reality immutably and for eternity, including the union and separation of particular minds.

Descartes takes the reasoning of the AT 7:78 passage to be obvious to anyone who is paying attention:

> we clearly perceive the mind, that is, a thinking substance, without the body, that is, without an extended substance. ... And conversely we can clearly perceive the body without the mind (as everyone readily admits).[67]
>
> we can clearly and distinctly perceive the mind without the body and the body without the mind.[68]

Perhaps that is why the argument is so quick. It would appear to be more an intuition than an argument, and as we will see it is an intuition that sets up another argument – the argument for the existence of material things. After arriving at the non-sensory result "I am, I exist" in the Second Meditation, the meditator craved a return to thoughts of more sensible and tangible items, and Descartes mercifully entered into the digression on wax. We would expect the meditator to be even more starved for sensible and tangible objects by the time of the Sixth Meditation. There has been a significant amount of highly abstract thinking in the interim, and a human being can ward off the inducements of the body for only so long.

Further reading

There is a large literature on Descartes on the dualism of mind and body. A cross-section includes:

Lilli Alanen, *Descartes's Concept of Mind*, Cambridge, MA: Harvard UP (2003).
Galen Barry, "Cartesian Modes and the Simplicity of Mind," *Pacific Philosophical Quarterly* 96 (2015), 54–76.
Andrea Christofidou, "Descartes' Dualism: Correcting some Misconceptions," *Journal of the History of Philosophy* 39 (2001), 215–238.
Desmond M. Clarke, *Descartes's Theory of Mind*, New York and Oxford: Oxford UP (2003).

---

67 *Second Replies*, AT 7:169–170, CSM 2:119. As usual I have slightly modified the translation, substituting "without" for "apart."
68 *Fourth Replies*, AT 7:225, CSM 2:158.

John Cottingham, "Cartesian Trialism," Mind 94 (1985), 218–230.

Tarek R. Dika, "The Origins of Cartesian Dualism," The Journal of the American Philosophical Association 6 (2020), 335–352.

Blake Dutton, "Descartes's Dualism and the One Principal Attribute Rule," British Journal for the History of Philosophy 11(2003), 395–415.

Lynda Gaudemard, "Descartes's Conception of Mind Through the Prism of Imagination: Cartesian Substance Dualism Questioned," Archiv für Geschichte der Philosophie 100 (2018), 146–171.

Geoffrey Gorham, "Mind-Body Dualism and the Harvey-Descartes Controversy," Journal of the History of Ideas 55 (1994), 211–234.

Paul Hoffman, "Descartes's Theory of Distinction," Philosophy and Phenomenological Research 64 (2002), 57–78.

Jean-Luc Marion, On Descartes' Passive Thought: The Myth of Cartesian Dualism, trans. Christina Gschwandtner, Chicago and London: Chicago UP (2018).

Gonzalo Rodríguez Pereyra, "Descartes's Substance Dualism and His Independence Conception of Substance," Journal of the History of Philosophy 46 (2008), 69–89.

Amélie Oksenberg Rorty, "Descartes on Thinking with the Body," in The Cambridge Companion to Descartes, ed. John Cottingham, Cambridge and New York: Cambridge UP (1992), 371–392.

Marleen Rozemond, Descartes's Dualism, Cambridge, MA: Harvard UP (1998).

Marleen Rozemond, "The Faces of Simplicity in Descartes's Soul," in Partitioning the Soul: Debates from Plato to Leibniz, ed. Klaus Corcilius and Dominik Perler, Berlin and New York: W. de Gruyter (2014), 219–244.

Stephen J. Wagner, "Descartes's Arguments for Mind-Body Distinctness," Philosophy and Phenomenological Research 43 (1983), 499–517.

Margaret Wilson, Descartes, New York: Routledge (1978), 177–184.

Eugenio E. Zaldivar, "Descartes's Theory of Substance: Why He was not a Trialist," British Journal for the History of Philosophy 19 (2011), 395–418.

There is also a literature on Descartes and (non-human) animal thinking. A cross-section includes:

Deborah A. Boyle and Gerald J. Massey, "Descartes's Tests for (Animal) Mind," Philosophical Topics 27 (1999), 87–146.

John Cottingham, "'A Brute to the Brutes?' Descartes' Treatment of Animals," Philosophy 53 (1978), 551–559.

Gary Hatfield, "Animals," in A Companion to Descartes, ed. Janet Broughton and John Carriero, Oxford: Blackwell (2008), 404–425.

Evan Thomas, "Descartes on the Animal Within, and the Animals Without," Canadian Journal of Philosophy 50 (2020), 999–1014.

Janice Thomas, "Does Descartes Deny Consciousness to Animals?" Ratio 19 (2006), 336–363.

Eight

External bodies and sufficient certainty for application to ordinary life

In "Synopsis of the following six Meditations," Descartes makes a striking admission: he says that his argumentation for the existence of sensible particulars is not as solid as his argumentation for the existence of God and finite mind. He writes that in the Sixth Meditation,

> there is a presentation of all the arguments which enable the existence of material things to be inferred. The great benefit of these arguments is not, in my view, that they prove what they establish – namely that there really is a world, and that human beings have bodies, and so on – since no sane person has ever seriously doubted these things. The point is that in considering these arguments we come to realize that they are not as solid or transparent as the arguments which lead us to knowledge of our own minds and of God....
>
> (AT 7:15–16, CSM 2:11)

In the First Meditation, he had pledged to "demolish everything completely and start again right from the foundations" (AT 7:17, CSM 2:12). He then proceeds in search of better support – if not unimpeachable support – for the beliefs that he has called into question. In the Sixth Meditation, he secures the result that material things exist "at least [insofar as] they possess all the properties which I clearly and distinctly understand, that is, all those which, viewed in general terms, are comprised within the subject matter

DOI: 10.4324/9781351210522-8

of pure mathematics" (AT 7:80, CSM 2:55). He secures that result with the highest level of certainty.[1] But demonstrations of the existence of particulars – for example, "that there really is a world" and "that human beings have bodies" – are not as solid or transparent. As we have seen, Descartes is clear that our ideas of familiar sensible objects are compounds of ideas that individually conform to reality but that collectively do not.[2] If we were transported in the middle of the night to the universe of material bodies that Descartes takes to exist – with no sensible color or sound, and no empty space – we would not know where we were, and our surroundings would be almost unrecognizable.

In the Sixth Meditation, Descartes argues that material things exist insofar as they possess geometrical properties. But sensible particulars admit of a "high degree of doubt and uncertainty" (AT 7:80, CSM 2:55). The verdict is similar in the 1637 *Discourse*:

> if there are still people who are not sufficiently convinced of the existence of God and of their soul by the arguments I have proposed, I would have them know that everything else of which they may think themselves more sure – such as their having a body, there being stars and an earth, and the like – is less certain.
> (AT 6:37–38, CSM 1:129–30)

Descartes proceeds to state (in the *Discourse*) that our perceptions of sensible particulars have some truth in them (AT 6:38–39, CSM 1:130) – just as he does in the Sixth Meditation (AT 7:80, CSM 2:56).[3] But the argumentation for the existence of these is not "as solid or transparent" as the argumentation for the existence of

---

1 See the *Principles* IV.206 claim that "the knowledge that material things exist" involves absolute certainty and that "the same goes for all evident reasoning about material things" (AT 8A:328, CSM 1:290).

2 For example, an idea of a sensation of redness conforms to the mind-dependent sensation of redness, and an idea of extension conforms to extension, but a composite of the two ideas – which is to say, an idea of a red body – does not conform to anything. See the discussion in Chapter 4, pp. 112–114, and Chapter 3, pp. 77–78.

3 More on this below.

God and finite mind. Descartes allows that we achieve *moral certainty* about the details and existence of sensible particulars – or "sufficient certainty for application to ordinary life"[4] – even if our beliefs about such particulars "may be uncertain in relation to the absolute power of God" (AT 8A:327, CSM 1:290). We might expect that Descartes would be devastated upon concluding that we do not clearly and distinctly perceive the demarcations that individuate particular bodies. We might expect that he would express disappointment at the conclusion that for all we know the demarcations that we perceive are no more consequential than the many boundaries that we fail to notice. But he is not. He supposes that our metaphysical and epistemological tether reaches only so far, and he is content to settle for the sort of cognition that our finite minds are in a position to secure. We grasp enough about material particulars to navigate our surroundings and to take full advantage of the embodiment that is our nature.

The structure of the Sixth Meditation argument for the existence of material things

The first premise of the Sixth Meditation argument for the existence of material things is the result that minds are immaterial thinking substances.[5] That is to say, an individual mind is a complete thing whose boundary starts and stops at its immaterial thinking. The second premise – a corollary to the first – is that modifications of mind are such that "an intellectual [and immaterial] act is included in their essential definition; and hence... the distinction between them and myself corresponds to the distinction between the modes of a thing and the thing itself" (AT 7:7:78, CSM 2:54). The modifications of a substance are intelligible in terms of the principal

---

4 *Principles* IV.205, AT 8A:327, CSM 1:289-290.

5 Descartes presents it as such at AT 7:77–78, CSM 2:54. He says that now that he is "beginning to achieve a better knowledge of [him]self and the author of [his] being," he can consider again the beliefs that he "ha[s] acquired from the senses" and ask anew what "should be called into doubt." Then he says – "First," – and he offers the argument that mind is an immaterial substance. Then he proceeds to the other steps of the argument for the existence of material things.

attribute of that substance, and modifications of mind presuppose the principal attribute of thinking. The third premise is that the sensory perceptions of a mind have a cause – what Descartes calls "an active faculty, either in me or in something else, which produce[s] or br[ings] about" each sensory perception (AT 7:79, CSM 2:55). The fourth premise is that the active faculty that brings about a sensory perception is not a faculty of mind: "this faculty cannot be in me, since clearly it presupposes no intellectual act on my part, and the ideas in question are produced without my cooperation and often even against my will" (ibid.). We would know if the active faculty was in our mind because the line at which our mind starts and stops is our (conscious) thinking, but we are never aware of any such faculty. Descartes then argues that once we rule out that the active faculty that brings about a sensory perception is in our mind, the conclusion that material things exist follows almost straightaway.[6] But before we consider the final steps to that conclusion, we might address any additional support that Descartes provides for its fourth premise. The first premise is defended at AT 7:78; the second premise falls out of Descartes' understanding of the relation between a substance and its modes;[7] the third premise he takes to be obvious, presumably because it is an application of the principle that something cannot come from nothing.[8] The fourth premise is motivated in part by the claim that any active faculty of mind would be a mental modification, and in part by the assumption that if our minds possessed such a faculty, we would be aware of it.[9] But we are not. The Sixth Meditation does not provide additional support for this latter assumption, but Descartes does elaborate on it in other texts.

---

6 He argues that we have an extremely strong inclination to believe that material things produce our sensory perceptions and that God would be a deceiver if we had that level of inclination and material things were not their (existent) cause.

7 *Principles* I.53, AT 8A:25, CSM 1:210–211.

8 See for example *Principles* I.49, AT 8A:23, CSM 1:209.

9 Here I am largely following Newman (1994). I think that his reconstruction of Descartes' argument (for the existence of material things) is largely correct, but that that argument is not particularly strong – for reasons internal and external to Descartes' system. In the end, I propose a slightly different argument that is readily available to Descartes and that is much more plausible (I think).

The transparency of the mental

As we have seen, in *Fourth Replies* Descartes makes a very bold claim to the effect that we are aware of each and every one of our mental states (AT 7:246, CSM 2:171). If there is a state of which we are not aware, it is not a modification of our mind. So perhaps what he is thinking in the Sixth Meditation is that if his mind had a faculty for producing sensory perceptions, he would recognize it, but he does not recognize it, and so it is not there. He cannot be proceeding along *exactly* those lines, however. As we have seen, he holds that a mind is not always in a position to accurately describe the mental entities of which it has awareness.[10] He does say (in the *Fourth Replies* passage) that there is nothing in a mind of which it is not aware, but he is not thereby committed to the view that a mind is always in a position to describe accurately the object of its awareness.[11] He is committed to the view that minds have some awareness or other of their modifications. However, in the Sixth Meditation argument for the existence of material things, he is not limiting himself to the (weak) assumption that there is nothing in a finite mind of which it is not in some way aware. That assumption would not allow him to conclude that he would be aware of his mind as the cause of his sensory perceptions if it was the cause of his sensory perceptions.

In an earlier passage in *Fourth Replies*, Descartes makes an assertion about the transparency of the mental that is more careful and modest, even if it is still pretty bold. He clarifies his view that there can be nothing in the mind of which we are not aware: he adds that he takes the view to "refer to the operations of the mind" (AT 7:232, CSM 2:162). If so, what he is arguing in the Sixth Meditation is that we are aware of any operations or activities that are modifications of

---

10 He speaks for example of the individual who thinks the letters "God" and reports that they are thinking of God ("To Mersenne, 6 May 1630," AT 1:150, CSMK 24–25), or the individual who reports that they have "certainty of their own existence," but their idea of self is an idea of a material body, for example, their limbs, or a wind or fire (*Principles* I.12, AT 8A:9, CSM 1:196). See also Chapter 4, pp. 112–116.

11 See also the discussions in Hatfield (2011), 366; Simmons (2012); and Gorham (1994).

our mind and that since we are not aware of any activity by which we produce our sensory perceptions, we are not their cause. In addition, for the Sixth Meditation argument to work, Descartes would need to assume something stronger than that any operations of mind are within our field of awareness; he would need to assume that we are aware of them *as* activities. If he were allowing that our awareness of our mind's activity could be extremely confused to the point that we could be aware of it without being aware of it as activity, then our lack of explicit awareness that we do not produce our sensory perceptions would not do the argumentative work that is being asked of it.

Descartes takes to be self-evident that there is no activity that takes place in a mind such that the mind is not aware of it as an activity. An objection that a number of Descartes' contemporaries would pose is that there are states of mind that are active but that are not conscious. For example, Margaret Cavendish argued that much of human behavior is guided by unconscious thought – for example, when we generate the appropriate string of words in a conversation. She writes,

> we do not always think of our words we speak, for most commonly words flow out of the mouth, rather customarily then premeditatedly, just like actions of our walking, for we go by custome, force and strength, without a constant notice or observation; for though we designe our wayes, yet we do not ordinarily think of our pace, nor take notice of every several step; just so, most commonly we talk, for we seldomly think of our words we speak, nor many times the sense they tend to.[12]

Cavendish also highlights the way in which ideas often just come to us – for example, in the coherent order that is a train of thought. To use her language, there are background causes that "in order

---

12 Cavendish (1655), unnumbered page between pp. 26 and 27. Cavendish might add that when we do pay conscious attention to the words that we might utter in a conversation, our thinking often will stumble: we have interrupted the impactful but unconscious work that is taking place behind the scenes, and to our own detriment.

set" our thoughts.[13] Often (if not always) we are unaware of these background workings; we are just their beneficiary,[14] and lucky for us thoughts do not come to us in an order that is random. We might also consider the case of Henry More. He argued that there exists ubiquitously in nature a kind of thinking that is purposive and intelligent, but wholly unconscious. He writes,

> The Spirit of Nature therefore, according to that notion I have of it, is, a substance incorporeal, but without Sense and Animadversion, pervading the whole Matter of the Universe, and exercising a Plastical Power therein according to the sundry dispositions in the parts it works upon, raising such Phaenomena in the World, by directing the parts of the Matter and their Motion, as cannot be resolved into mere Mechanical powers.[15]

More is thinking in part of the orderly behavior of bodies that scientists and philosophers document again and again in the period.[16] Such order could not result from corporeal properties alone – for example, size, shape, and motion – because (More assumes) there needs to be something mental that guides the orderly behavior of bodies and keeps them on the rails. More's colleague Ralph Cudworth posited a similar unconscious intelligence that is pervasive in the natural world – what he called *plastick nature*. This is a being that "hath no Animal-Sense or Consciousness."[17] Or we might consider Leibniz, who famously argued that finite minds perceive the entirety of the universe, though he did not suppose that we are thereby conscious of all that transpires. There is much that we perceive very confusedly and there is much of which we are not aware at all – for example, the many states that are the necessary and sufficient cause

---

13 Cavendish (1653), 162. See also Cavendish (1664), 500–501. For the fuller discussion, see Cunning (2023).

14 A more recognized kind of example is that of the "eureka moment" and the cognitive processes that work behind the scenes to present us with exactly the idea that we need at the exact moment that we need it. See Hume (1739), I.i.7, 24.

15 More (1659), 169.

16 For example, Kepler's law on the elliptical motions of the planets, Galileo's law of gravitation, and Snell's law of refraction, to name just a few.

17 Cudworth (1678), 679.

of any occurrent idea or decision, even if (from the point-of-view of conscious awareness) an idea or decision often appears to have no cause at all.[18] Spinoza also held that there is much in a finite mind that is unconscious. He writes for example that

> men believe that they are free, precisely because they are conscious of their volitions and desires, yet concerning the [mental] causes that have determined them to desire and will they do not think, do not even dream about, because they are ignorant of them.[19]

Spinoza also holds that "[w]hatever happens in the object of the idea constituting the human mind is bound to be perceived by the human mind"[20] and that the object of the idea that constitutes the human mind is the human body and all of its constituents.[21] However, we are not consciously aware of all of our bodily states. The view that there are operations and states of mind of which we not conscious was seen as obvious by many philosophers of the Cartesian era, and there are plenty of contemporary philosophers who hold that there is a distinction between cognition, on the one hand, and consciousness of cognition, on the other.[22]

Now we return to the Sixth Meditation argument for the existence of material things.

In order for that argument to work, Descartes needs to be able to assume that there are no operations in his mind of which he is not aware. More specifically, he needs to be able to make the assumption

---

18 Leibniz (1714), Section 18, p. 215; Sections 20–24, pp. 215–216; Section 36, p. 217; and Section 56, p. 220.

19 Appendix to *Ethics* Part I, in Spinoza (1677), 239. Note that Spinoza holds that volitions and desires would have mental causes only. See Spinoza (1677), Part II, Proposition 6, pp. 246–247.

20 Spinoza (1677), Part II, Proposition 12, p. 251.

21 Spinoza (1677), Part II, Proposition 12–13, pp. 251–253, and Proposition 22, pp. 259–260. Garrett (2008) has argued that according to Spinoza all the ideas in a finite mind are conscious, but that many are extremely confused. If that is right, Spinoza is employing the notion of consciousness in a way that is very much non-standard when he says that we are conscious of all of the states of our body and that our awareness of those states is just confused.

22 See for example the discussion in Churchland and Suhler (2014).

that if his mind were the cause of his sensory perceptions, he would be aware that his mind was the cause of his sensory perceptions. He does make the assumption, but it would seem to be controversial at best. We might worry that he is not entitled to the assumption – if we sympathize with Cavendish and many of her contemporaries – but what is even more worrisome is that Descartes appears to retreat from the assumption himself. He says in a 1641 letter to Regius that

> strictly speaking, understanding is the passivity of the mind and willing is its activity; but... we do not easily distinguish in this matter passivity from activity.[23]

Here Descartes appears to concede that we are not always in a position to identify the activity of a mind while it is active.[24] If so, we might wonder why he concludes in the Sixth Meditation that if he is not aware of himself as the (active) cause of his sensory perceptions, he is not their cause in fact. There is also the 1648 letter to Arnauld in which Descartes says that there are aspects of our mental activity that we do not notice:

> we are not conscious of the manner in which our mind sends the animal spirits into particular nerves; for that depends not on the mind alone but on the union of the mind with the body.[25]

Descartes insists that the mind is aware of the more general "inclination of the will toward a particular movement of the body" (AT 5:222, CSMK 357), but he is leaving open that there is a (more granular) kind of activity by which the will moves the specific animal spirits and of which the mind is not aware. In the same letter, he makes a distinction between direct thought and reflective thought – which is apparently a distinction between thought and awareness of thought.[26] He writes,

---

23 "To Regius, May 1641," AT 3:372, CSMK 182.
24 See also Wee (2001), 126–127.
25 "For [Arnauld], 29 July 1648," AT 5:221–222, CSMK 357.
26 See also the discussions in Hatfield (2011) and Simmons (2012).

we make a distinction between direct and reflective thoughts corresponding to the distinction we make between direct and reflective vision. ...I call the first and simple thoughts of infants *direct* and not reflective – for instance the pain they feel when some wind distends their intestines, or the pleasure they feel when nourished by sweet blood. But when an adult feels something, and simultaneously perceives that he has not felt it before, I call this second perception *reflection*, and attribute it to the intellect alone, in spite of its being so linked to sensation that the two occur together and appear to be indistinguishable from each other.

(AT 5:220–21, CSMK 357)

Here Descartes calls to mind the letter (to William Cavendish) in which he says that perhaps animals possess "some thought such as we experience in ourselves...."[27] If Descartes does hold that there is a difference between mental activity and awareness of mental activity, and if in the end he allows that there might be activities of mind of which we are not aware, the Sixth Meditation argument for the existence of material things is in trouble straight out of the gate.

Additional worries and concerns

After positing that nothing else belongs to his nature or essence except that he is a thinking thing, Descartes takes inventory of the modifications of which he has ideas – some of which cannot be understood "without an intellectual substance to inhere in" (CSM 2:54, AT 7:78), and some of which "must be in a corporeal or extended substance" (CSM 2:55, AT 7:79) if they in fact exist. Perhaps the cause of his sensory perceptions is a substance with one of these two kinds of modification, or perhaps it is something else entirely. His sensory perceptions must have *some* cause, he supposes, but thus far he has not been able to say what. He quickly eliminates

---

27 "To The Marquess of Newcastle, 23 November 1646," AT 4:576, CSMK 304. See also *Passions* I.50, where Descartes says that animals "lack reason, and perhaps even thought" (AT 11:369, CSM 1:348, emphasis added).

the possibility that his mind possesses a faculty for producing sense perceptions: he has no awareness of any such (active) faculty, and so it does not exist. The faculty that produces his sense perceptions is not a modification of his mind, but perhaps it is a modification of a body, or perhaps it is a modification of some other finite substance – either another finite mind, or a substance of a different kind altogether. Or perhaps the cause of sensory perceptions is not a creature at all, but is God. Descartes puts the options in a way that is quite confusing actually:

> the only alternative is that it is in another substance distinct from me – a substance which contains either formally or eminently all the reality which exists objectively in the ideas produced by this faculty (as I have just noted). This substance is either a body, that is, a corporeal nature, in which case it will contain formally <and in fact> everything which is to be found objectively <or representatively> in the ideas; or else it is God, or some creature more noble than a body, in which case it will contain eminently whatever is to be found in the ideas.
>
> (AT 7:79, CSM 2:55)

Descartes cannot possibly mean to be applying his Third Meditation causal principle in the Sixth Meditation argument for the existence of material things. In the Third Meditation, he notices that his mind has an (infinite) idea of God, and he asks how the idea ever got there. He asks what it is that created the idea and placed it in his mind; he concludes that it is a being that has infinite power along with the rest of the divine attributes.[28] In the Sixth Meditation, he is doing something very different. He is asking what it is that prompts or activates his sensory perceptions of material objects. These perceptions include

> sensations of... hardness and heat, and of the other tactile qualities, ... [and] sensations of light, colours, smells, tastes and

---

28 He says at the end of the Third Meditation, "it is no surprise that God, in creating me, should have placed this idea in me to be, as it were, the mark of the craftsmen stamped on his work" (AT 7:51, CSM 2:35).

sounds, the variety of which enabled me to distinguish the sky, the earth, the seas, and all other bodies, one from another,

(AT 7:75, CSM 2:52)

and also those aspects of a body – its extension, flexibility, and changeability – that are "a case not of vision or touch or imagination... but of purely mental scrutiny" (AT 7:7:31, CSM 2:21).

Descartes could not be more clear that our idea of the extension of a body is underdetermined by the inputs of the senses and is not "from the senses or through the senses" (AT 7:18, CSM 2:12). Instead, it is part of the "treasure house of my mind" (AT 7:67, CSM 2:46). In the Sixth Meditation, he is not asking what creates that idea or places it into our mind. Nor is he asking what transfers a sensation from outside our thought into our awareness: he holds that sensations are modes of thinking and that they do not "reach... our mind from external objects."[29] In the Sixth Meditation argument for the existence of material things, Descartes is inquiring into what prompts or elicits ideas and sensations that are latent in our minds already.[30]

Descartes is therefore extremely misleading in the Sixth Meditation when he uses the language of the Third Meditation according to which the cause of an idea must have at least as much formal reality as the idea has objective reality. In the Third Meditation, he is talking about the creation of ideas and their placement into the mind; in the Sixth Meditation, he is talking about something very different. A (somewhat) charitable reading is that in the Sixth Meditation, Descartes is using the language of objective reality as a way of being

---

29 *Comments on a Certain Broadsheet*, AT 8B:359, CSM 1:304. See also Gorham (2002).

30 I think that the best account of Descartes' view on the occasioning of sense perceptions is in O'Neill (2013). She identifies the view in the work of Galen and Van Helmont and then traces it all the way to Descartes (and also Cavendish). For Descartes, the cause of a sensory perception is no more than a prompt or occasion that activates modifications of mind that the mind already houses. Note that other philosophers in the period spoke commonly of causes whose efficacy is a matter of activating latent dispositions – most famously Leibniz and Locke. See for example Leibniz (1765), 78–80, and Locke (1689), II.8, 132–142. See also Jolley (1988).

extremely precise in his identification of the range of candidates that might be the cause (or prompt) of our sense perceptions. One possible candidate is body – or a substance that has the same exact amount of formal reality as an idea of body has objective reality. Another possible candidate is a finite substance that is more noble than a body and so has more formal reality than the idea of body has objective reality. Another possible candidate is God. If that is all that Descartes is doing – using the language of formal and objective reality to delineate the entities that might be the cause of our sensory perceptions – he might have let us know.[31]

In the Sixth Meditation, Descartes supposes that his mind does not possess a faculty for producing sense perceptions – on the assumption that he would be aware of any such faculty if it existed (but he is not). He also has no inkling whatsoever that a different substance is the cause of his sensory perceptions – a substance that is more noble than a body, for example, other minds or God. What he says explicitly is that "God has given me no faculty at all for recognizing any [other] source for these ideas" (AT 7:79–80, CSM 2:55). What he *does* have is an extremely strong belief that bodies are their cause: "on the contrary, he has given me a great propensity to believe that they are produced by material things" (ibid.). We have been constructed in such a way that we have zero awareness of *any* active faculties that might be the cause of our sense perceptions, but instead we find ourselves with an extremely strong belief that they are caused by material things.[32] God would be a deceiver if we had that belief and material things did not exist, and so "It follows that corporeal things exist" (AT 7:80, CSM 2:55). Here Descartes is employing as a premise that God is not a deceiver. He is applying that premise to the claim that we have a strong inclination to affirm that material things exist as the cause of our sense perceptions. He is not applying the premise to the claim that we have an irresistible

---

31 In the *Principles* II.1 version of the argument for the existence of material things (AT 8A:40–41, CSM 1:223), Descartes makes no reference to the Third Meditation causal principle – perhaps because he realized that the reference in the Sixth Mediation was not very helpful. There is a discussion of the *Principles* II.1 argument below.

32 See also the discussion in Mehl (2018), 63–64.

belief – a clear and distinct perception – that material things exist as the cause of our sense perceptions. As we have seen, he holds that in cases of clear and distinct perception, we recognize a truth, and then any appeal to divine veracity comes afterward in the form of a dismissal of the incoherent defeater that we might be mistaken about matters that are utterly evident to us.[33] In the Sixth Meditation argument for the existence of material things, Descartes is proceeding differently. He is appealing to divine veracity as a premise. We have a strong inclination to affirm that material thing exist, and God would be a deceiver if we had that inclination and material things did not exist. So they do.

Before we proceed to further critique the argument, we might take note of some of its merits. In theory, a being – presumably a non-human or maybe Berkeley – could have sensory perceptions but not have an extremely strong inclination to affirm that material things are their cause. Descartes is pointing out that we are different. We have a given sense perception, and then we all of a sudden find ourselves affirming – without any reason and almost out of nowhere – that material things exist and are the cause of that perception. We do not have an irresistible inclination to believe that material things exist – just a strong propensity to believe that they exist, Descartes supposes – and he concludes that God would be a deceiver if we had that propensity and material things did not exist in fact. Human beings do have a very strong belief that material things exist – Descartes is right about that.[34]

We might also register that Descartes is not being arbitrary in his rejection of the view (in Cavendish and Spinoza and Leibniz and Hume) that unconscious states are sometimes the cause of the states of which we are aware. For example, he does not have to say that the order that is exhibited in a conscious train of thought has an unconscious mental cause, and he does not have to say that it has no cause. He can say instead that the reason why we sometimes have one thought rather than another is due to the work of memory traces in the brain and other (sophisticated) corporeal causes. His

---

33 See Chapter 4, pp. 138–142.
34 See also the related discussion in Hume (1748), Section 12, 200–202.

argument for the existence of material things does not crumble on either count, and indeed if Descartes is right that God exists and is not a deceiver, and if he is right that the strength of our inclination to believe that material things exist is such that God would be a deceiver if material things did not exist, his argumentation is impeccable.

But Descartes nowhere defends a view on how compelling a faulty inclination has to be before God counts as a deceiver in allowing us to have it. He nowhere provides (or defends) a threshold. Nor does he anywhere defend the view (or really the axiom) that finite minds are always aware of their own active faculties. Furthermore, what is odd is that he does not appear to *require* that axiom to draw the conclusion that material things exist. Descartes could allow that our active faculties are not fully transparent to us and that "we do not easily distinguish... passivity from activity," but then argue on different grounds – and grounds that are available to him – that our minds are not the cause of our sense perceptions. His reason for concluding that no *other* substance is the cause of our sense perceptions is that God has given us no way to "recogniz[e] any [other] source for these ideas." However, if the fact is that God has created us such that we are not aware of all of our active faculties – and in some passages, Descartes appears to admit that we have been created just so – then we do not have a way to check to see whether or not *we* are the cause of our sense perceptions either. In that case, Descartes might have just highlighted our extremely strong inclination to affirm that bodies produce our sense perceptions and our inability to tell if anything else is their cause – not other minds, not some other non-bodily creature that is more noble than a body, not our *own* mind. He might have argued from both of these to the conclusion that material things exist. He might have bypassed the highly questionable premise that if our minds had a faculty for producing sense perceptions, we would be aware of it.[35]

---

35 So I am supposing that there is a better argument that Descartes might have offered in the Sixth Meditation, but I do agree with Newman (1994) on how the actual argument runs. Wee (2001) argues that Newman's reconstruction cannot be correct because it attributes to Descartes premises that Descartes rejects elsewhere in his corpus. I think that Wee's critique is largely unsuccessful.

The Principles II.1 argument for the existence of material things

In *Principles of Philosophy*, Descartes offers an argument for the existence of material things that differs slightly from the Sixth Meditation argument. First, he repeats that our minds are not the prompt or occasion of our sense perceptions:

> all our sensations undoubtedly come to us from something that is distinct from our mind. For it is not in our power to make ourselves have one sensation rather than another; this is obviously dependent on the thing that is acting on our senses.
>
> (AT 8A:40, CSM 1:223)

Something else must be the occasion of our sense perceptions, and so Descartes inquires into what that might be. He says that upon having a sense perception we have a clear and distinct idea of matter

---

For example, she points out that in the Third Meditation, Descartes reports that he would know if his mind possessed the power to keep itself in existence – he says that "if there were such a power in me, I should undoubtedly be aware of it. But I experience no such power..." (AT 7:49, CSM 2:34). Wee (127–128) argues that before the Sixth Meditation Descartes is already appealing to the principle that we are always aware of the active faculties of our mind, and so (contra Newman) the Sixth Meditation argument for the immateriality of mind is not required to generate that principle. But contra Wee, in the Third Meditation, Descartes is not necessarily appealing to the principle. He is presumably arguing that a being that has the power to keep itself in existence would be omnipotent, and that since an omnipotent being would have all of the other divine attributes, it would be omniscient with respect to all of its powers. Another problem for Wee's critique is that in the Sixth Meditation, Descartes is actually offering the argument that Newman attributes to him, whether or not there are passages in Descartes' corpus that are in tension with his argumentation. For example, Descartes clearly appeals to the principle that we are always aware of the active faculties of our mind. He does the same in the *Principles* II.1 version of the argument. Wee is right (127) that the principle is in conflict with Descartes' claim that "we do not easily distinguish... passivity from activity," but that does not mean that Newman's reconstruction is mistaken, and Descartes is very clear in the Sixth Meditation that we do not fail to notice a faculty of our mind when it is operative.

that is extended in length, breadth, and depth; he adds that God would be a deceiver if He created us such a way as to have that idea (in the course of a sense perception) and material things did not exist. Descartes presumably does not suppose that all minds have a clear and distinct idea of body in the course of having a sense perception, for he is on record as holding that finite minds are largely confused. But perhaps he has in mind an advanced meditator – a mind that is asking about the cause of sense perception while having a sense perception, and a mind to whom a clear and distinct idea of body comes fairly easily. To such a mind, the regular occurrence of a clear and distinct idea of body in the course of sense perception would be a glaring hint or signal that body extended in length, breadth, and depth is the occasion of sense perception. Descartes writes,

> we have sensory awareness of, or rather as a result of sensory stimulation we have a clear and distinct perception of, some kind of matter, which is extended in length, breadth and depth... [I]f God were himself immediately producing in our mind the idea of such extended matter, or even if he were causing the idea to be produced by something which lacked extension, shape and motion, there would be no way of avoiding the conclusion that he should be regarded as a deceiver.
>
> (AT 8A:40–41, CSM 1:223)[36]

If the *Principles* II.1 argument is anything like the argument of the Sixth Meditation, Descartes is saying here that upon having a sense perception and inquiring into its cause, we find ourselves with an extremely strong inclination to believe that that cause is material things. We inquire into the cause of our sense perceptions, and we encounter the analogue of a flashing neon sign that reads: *body which is extended in length, breadth, and depth.* We immediately form the belief that the cause is body. God would be a deceiver if we were hit over the

---

36 The elided language is very important and will be discussed below. The CSM translation makes that language confusing, however, and so I am breaking the passage into parts.

head with such explicit signage and there did not exist "something extended in length, breadth and depth and possessing all the properties which we clearly perceive to belong to an extended thing" (AT 8A:41, CSM 1:223). So as in the Sixth Meditation, material things exist insofar as they possess all the properties "which, viewed in general terms, are comprised within the subject-matter of pure mathematics" (AT 7:80, CSM 2:55).

The Principles II.1 passage might appear to run differently if we take into account the text that I have elided from the CSM translation. The extended passage (in the CSM translation) is as follows:

> we have sensory awareness of, or rather as a result of sensory stimulation we have a clear and distinct perception of, some kind of matter, which is extended in length, breadth and depth, and has various differently shaped parts and variously moving parts which give rise to our various sensations of colours, smells, pains and so on. And if God were himself immediately producing in our mind the idea of such extended matter, or even if he were causing the idea to be produced by something which lacked extension, shape and motion, there would be no way of avoiding the conclusion that he should be regarded as a deceiver.

Here Descartes would appear to be saying that when we have a sense perception we have a clear and distinct idea of body whose content includes not just that it is extended in length, breadth, and depth but that it "give[s] rise" to sense perceptions. He would then appear to be saying that since God is not a deceiver, that idea is truth-conducive, and so matter is what gives rise to sense perceptions, and bodies therefore exist. But with all due respect, the CSM translation is failing us here. It misleads us into thinking that upon inspection, the content of a clear and distinct idea of body includes that body gives rise to sense perceptions, but Descartes does not say that in Principles II.1, and he does not say (or suggest) it anywhere else in his corpus. A clear and distinct idea of body tells us that body is flexible and changeable, and that it is extended in length, breadth, and depth, but it does not include as part of its content that body is the cause of sense perception.

The *Principles* II.1 text is no evidence to the contrary.[37] The CSM translation presents the feature – "give[s] rise to our various sensations of colours, smells, pains and so on" – as falling out of the concept of body. The mis-translation is a matter of trading a colon for a period and adding an occurrence of the word "And" to begin the putative new sentence. In addition, CSM leaves untranslated the word "quia" – but that is an important word indeed. The Latin is this:

> Sed *quia* sentimus, sive potiùs à sensu impulsi clarè ac distinctè percipimus, materiam quandam extensam in longum, latum & profundum, cujus variae partes variis figuris praeditae sunt, ac variis motibus cientur, ac etiam efficiunt ut varios sensus habeamus colorum, odorum, doloris, &c: *si Deus immediatè per se ipsum istius materiae extensae ideam menti nostrae exhiberet, vel tantùm si efficeret ut exhiberetur à re aliquâ, in quâ nihil esset extensionis, nec figurée, nec motûs: nulla ratio potest excogitari, cur non deceptor esset putandus.*
>
> (AT 8A:40–41, emphasis added)

I want to suggest an alternative translation that does justice to the occurrence of the word "quia" and that does not attribute to Descartes the view that the content of our idea of body includes that body is the cause of our sense perceptions. The alternative translation is this:

> But because we have sensory awareness of, or as a result of sensory impact we have a clear and distinct perception of matter that is extended in length, breadth, and depth, whose various parts are endowed with various figures and are stirred by various motions, and furthermore they produce the various sensations we have of color, smell, pain, and so on: if God were himself immediately producing in our mind the idea of such extended matter, or even if he were causing the idea to be produced by something which lacked extension, shape and motion, there would be no way of avoiding the conclusion that he should be regarded as a deceiver.

---

37 Here I am disagreeing with Vinci (1998), 104–105.

Here Descartes is not suggesting that "ac etiam efficiunt ut varios sensus habeamus colorum, odorum, doloris, &c" is part of the content of a clear and distinct idea of body. He is saying that "materiam quandam extensam in longum, latum & profundum" is part of the content of a clear and distinct idea of body and then drawing the conclusion that body causes our sense perceptions in virtue of the various figures, sizes, and motions that it possesses as extended matter. He draws the conclusion that bodies are the cause of our sense perceptions, and then immediately after the colon, he states the additional reason that brings the conclusion home: that God is not a deceiver. That is all to say – we conclude that bodies are the cause of our sense perceptions because we have a clear and distinct idea of body upon having a sense perception and because God would be a deceiver if we had that idea upon having a sense perception and God did not exist. The CSM translation leaves out the colon and the occurrence of the term "quia," and it mispresents Descartes as holding that the non-deceiverhood of God guarantees the truth of a clear and distinct idea of body that includes in its content that body is the cause of sense perceptions.

The Sixth Meditation argument and the Principles II.1 argument both conclude that material things are the cause of sensory perceptions, but they do not conclude that material things *as we sense them* are the cause of sensory perceptions. After concluding that material things exist in Principles II.1, Descartes writes,

> The unavoidable conclusion, then, is that there exists something extended in length, breadth and depth and possessing all the properties which we clearly and distinctly perceive to belong to an extended thing.
>
> (AT 8A:41, CSM 1:223)

Descartes does not conclude in Principles II.1 or the Sixth Meditation that material things exist as we sense them. A compound idea that is composed of an idea of extension and ideas of sensible qualities does not conform to an existent, and Descartes does not anywhere conclude that it conforms to an existent. Clear and distinct ideas of material things – insofar as they possess geometrical and mathematical properties – are different. The second half of the Sixth Meditation is then a discussion of the truth that is involved in the case of ideas (of material things) that are extremely confused.

Material particulars – a high degree of doubt and uncertainty

After concluding in the Sixth Meditation that material things exist and possess geometrical properties, Descartes sends up a flare in reporting that our ideas of sensory particulars are "less clearly understood" and involve a "high degree of doubt and uncertainty" (AT 7:80, CSM 2:55). The language that Descartes uses to describe our knowledge of the details of particular material bodies – above and beyond what we know of them via pure mathematics – is telling. But we should not be surprised given what he says in much of the rest of his corpus – for example, in the Second Meditation. In the wax experiment, we entertain the idea of a sensible piece of wax and strip the idea of what we do not clearly and distinctly perceive in it. What remains is an idea of extension, flexibility, and changeability (AT 7:31, CSM 2:20). We then find out in separate argumentation that the sensible color, taste, and sound of a body are not among its actual features and that a clear and distinct grasp of those features exposes them to be sensations that are modifications of mind.[38] Sensations are modifications of mind, according to Descartes, and not modifications of body, and so an idea of a thing that is extended *and* has a feature like color is going to be very confused. It is like any idea of a thing that attributes to the thing a feature that it does not possess.

Sensory perceptions of particulars are confused, Descartes thinks, but they do enable us to make distinctions by which to navigate the world and to register information that is relevant to our survival as embodied beings. He says in the Sixth Meditation that our perceptions of color, etc., are what allow us to discriminate between objects.[39] It is clear what he has in mind. The smaller bodies that compose an individual – for example, a tree – produce in us

---

38 *Principles* I:68; CSM 1:217, AT 7:33. See also the discussion in Chapter 1, pp. 10–13.

39 AT 7:75, CSM 2:52. See also *Optics*, AT 6:133, CSM 1:168.

perceptions of brown and green regions that together constitute the tree, and more generally, there are regions of extended substance that surround us and exhibit patterns of motion that result in our perception of discrete objects, with the bodies in-between and around those regions exhibiting patterns of motion as well.[40] Our sensory perception of objects is extremely felicitous. For example, if we did not see color, but in some other way registered the patterns of motion in the regions that constitute a tree, we might not respond to the patterns with the requisite sort of immediacy. The example of a bear (as opposed to a tree) is perhaps more elucidating. We see sharp white teeth; we hear a roar; we flee. It is not clear that we would react in a way that is maximally conducive to our survival if we just tracked the motions of the bodies that form the mouth and arms and legs of the bear. Arguably, we would not live to find out. We know how we react in analogous cases of hunger and pain and thirst: our body needs food, but if we are wholly absorbed in a project, we might fail to feel the force of the sensation of hunger, and we will not make a priority of eating just because we remember (or because a loved one tells us) that nourishment is in order. What motivates us much better is a vivid sensation. The same applies in the case of damage to our body and we experience a sensation of pain rather than a report that our body is under threat. Fortunately for us we are human beings, and we are constructed in such a way that the signals that we receive are attention-getting (if very confused).

Descartes accordingly spends the remainder of the Sixth Meditation— after the AT 7:80 argument for the existence of material things – arguing that sensory perception is not a faculty for uncovering the truth about the details of external bodies but a faculty for helping us pragmatically to survive. He writes,

> the proper purpose of the sensory perceptions given me by nature is simply to inform the mind of what is beneficial for the composite of which the mind is a part; and to this extent they are sufficiently clear and distinct. But I misuse them by treating them as reliable touchstones for immediate judgments about the

---

40 See also Simmons (2008).

essential nature of the bodies located outside us; this is an area where they provide only very obscure information.

(AT 7:83, CSM 2:57–58)

Here Descartes is contrasting the sensory perceptions that we have as a result of being a mind-body composite with the purely intellectual perceptions that we have of abstract metaphysical truths about mind, body, and God. The latter are not his focus in the second half of the Sixth Meditation:

> In this context I am taking nature to be something more limited than the totality of things bestowed on me by God. For this includes many things that belong to the mind alone – for example my perception that what is done cannot be undone, and all other things that are known by the natural light; but at this stage I *am not speaking of these matters*. It also includes much that relates to the body alone, like the tendency to move in a downward direction, and so on; but I *am not speaking of these matters either*.
>
> (AT 7:82, CSM 2:57, emphasis added)

Descartes is focusing instead on our nature as a mind-body composite and on the epistemological relevance of the sensory perceptions that we have in virtue of being a composite. He continues,

> My sole concern here is what God has bestowed on me as a combination of mind and body. My nature, then, in this limited sense, does indeed teach me to avoid what induces a feeling of pain and to seek out what induces feelings of pleasure, and so on. But it does not appear to teach us to draw any conclusions from these sensory perceptions about things located outside us without waiting until the intellect has examined the matter. For knowledge of the truth about such things seems to belong *to the mind alone*, not to the combination of mind and body.
>
> (AT 7:82–3, CSM 2:57, emphasis added)

A sensory perception is not on a par with a clear and distinct perception that what is done cannot be undone or a clear and distinct perception of the non-sensory features of body. Both of the latter sorts of perception are clear and distinct, but sensory perceptions are not.[41] Still, we have been built in such a way that such perceptions are extremely compelling, and the being that built us would be a deceiver if those perceptions were not truth-conducive in some way.

Descartes holds that the perceptions that nudge us to preserve the health of our mind-body union are confused and provide only obscure information about the essential nature of the bodies that surround us. Still, he supposes that those perceptions are the handiwork of a cognitive system that is extremely sophisticated. He continues in the Sixth Meditation:

> when the nerves in the foot are set in motion in a violent and unusual manner, this motion, by way of the spinal cord, reaches the inner parts of the brain, and then gives the mind its signal for having a certain sensation, namely the sensation of a pain as occurring in the foot. This stimulates the mind to do its best to get rid of the cause of the pain, which it takes to be harmful to the foot. It is true that God could have made the nature of man such that this particular motion in the brain indicated something else to the mind; it might, for example, have made the mind aware of the actual motion occurring in the brain, or in the foot, or in any of the intermediate regions; or it might have indicated something else entirely. But there is nothing else which would have been so conducive to the continued well-being of the body. ...And so it is in the other cases.
>
> (CSM 2:60–61, AT 7:88)

Descartes does not lay out a formal argument for the conclusion that sensations provide us with information by which to track benefits and harms to the body, but it can be reconstructed from what he does say. We might start by focusing on the sensation of pain, and then generalize to an argument that applies to all sensations. One step in the argument is that sensations of pain impel us to eradicate their apparent cause reflexively and immediately. Descartes takes this step

---

41 See Chapter 1, pp. 6–10.

to be obvious. The second step of the argument is that God created us and is not a deceiver. Descartes states this premise up front:

> Despite the high degree of doubt and uncertainty here, the very fact that God is not a deceiver... offers me a sure hope that I can attain the truth even in these matters.
>
> (AT 7:80, CSM 2:55–56)

The third step is that if God created us and is not a deceiver, then He would not have constructed us to have pain sensations that impel us to eradicate their cause immediately and reflexively unless those sensations were informing us of harm to our bodies. Sensory perceptions do not inform us of the essential nature of extended bodies; that is clear. Instead, they inform us of benefits and threats to our continued existence as a mind-body union.

We might expect that Descartes would conclude that since God is not a deceiver, we should be able to trust all cases in which our sensations impel us to pursue and avoid. He proceeded along these lines at the very beginning of the Fourth Meditation when he supposed that it is impossible that the products of a divine being would err ever. He then thinks things through a bit (in the Fourth Meditation) and concludes that it is wholly consistent with the perfection of a supreme entity that we err on occasion. He draws the same conclusion in the Sixth Meditation as well. He supposes that just as human error is consistent with divine perfection, it is consistent with divine perfection that God created us with bodies that sometimes send us faulty signals about what is and is not of benefit to our well-being and survival. Each of us has a body with a nervous system, and in most cases, our nerves communicate a signal to our mind that is accurate. But in rare cases, the signal is not accurate. A person might have dropsy and feel very thirsty even though water is the last thing that they need for their health, or they might have a phantom limb. Bodies are divisible, Descartes argues (CSM 2:59, AT 7:86), and sometimes there is a disruption in the causal chain through which the nerves of the body send a signal to the mind. In such a case, all local (and distant) bodies still exhibit a perfect and exceptionless order, but part of what it is to adhere to that order – as in the case of a broken clock – is to communicate information that is unreliable.[42] Descartes then supposes that God would be a deceiver if our inclinations to pursue and avoid objects were as strong as they were, but they did not in most cases track benefits and harms to our body. He concludes, accordingly, that in most cases they do. He does not provide an exact ratio of the percentage of inclinations that we can trust, but presumably it approximates the ratio of the strength of those inclinations to the full will-compellingness of a clear and distinct perception.[43]

Descartes supposes that sensory perceptions provide mostly accurate information about threats and benefits to the well-being of a mind-body composite. He also appears to hold that the senses are revelatory in that the boundaries that we perceive between objects are (at least roughly) tracked by actual boundaries in the objects them-selves. We have perceptions of colored objects with a particular size, shape, and motion, and for each of these perceptions, there is pre-sumably a region of bodies that exist in a similar configuration and that produce in us our perceptions of them. For example, in the Sixth Meditation, Descartes describes the limbs of a human body in a way that supposes that our sensory perceptions of them pretty closely track the configurations of the bodies that compose the limbs themselves:

> For example, in a cord ABCD, if one end D is pulled so that the other end A moves, the exact same movement could have been brought about if one of the intermediate points B or C had been pulled, and D had not moved at all. In similar fashion, when I feel a pain in my foot, physiology tells me that this happens by means of nerves distributed throughout the foot, and that these nerves are like cords which go from the foot right up to the brain. When the nerves are pulled in the foot, they in turn pull on inner parts of the brain to which they are attached, and produce a certain motion in them; and nature has laid it down that this motion should produce in the mind a sensation of pain, as occurring in the foot.
>
> (AT 7:86–87, CSM 2:60)

---

42 See Chapter 2, pp. 54–56, and also Patterson (2016), 91–92.
43 This is also suggested in Patterson (2013), 256–257.

Here Descartes is offering an explanation of phantom-limb cases and, in so doing, he assumes that a human body has nerves, and a brain. He assumes that there are nerves and brains and that these exist in basically the configurations that we sense them to have. He uses similar language in his discussion of dropsy, and in his reference to the pineal gland that he takes to be the interface at which the mind meets the brain (CSM 2:59, AT 7:86). That would seem to be utterly reasonable. We distinguish bodies from each other by the "empty space" that separates them and by the different colors, sounds, smells, and tastes that we sense. And the regions that those sensory features delineate presumably have the sizes and shapes that we sense them to have. For example, a bear is composed of a large number of smaller bodies, and those bodies engage in motions that produce in us the perception of brown fur, black claws, and white teeth – with each region of (smaller) bodies behaving in a way that corresponds to the different perceptions that we have of the parts of the bear.[44] The region of the bear that is its eyes is different from the region that is its teeth – if the sensory perceptions that those regions of body produce are different – and the motions of the other regions of the bear that we sense are different as well. The same then entails that there is a significant difference in the motions of the bodies that surround the outer perimeter of the bear: the motions of those bodies are different because they produce in us the perception of what we regard as empty space (or perhaps water if the bear is in a pond or lake). Descartes does not talk about bears and trees in the Sixth Meditation, or about their lines of individuation, but he does seem to have in mind that our perceptions of color and

---

44 For a very different interpretation – according to which Descartes holds that the motion (and individuation) of bodies is merely phenomenal – see Lennon (1993), 191–210, and Sowaal (2004). It is certainly right to say that Descartes holds that the motions and boundaries that we register in bodies are due in large part to our cognitive constitution and our perspective, but that is not to say that he holds that individual bodies do not have some motions and boundaries or other. If Descartes held that motion was merely phenomenal, and that the single extended substance that composes the material universe lacked motion, he would have no way to explain how different sensory perceptions are produced in us across time. See also Cunning (2010), 184–186.

other sensory qualities at least roughly track the boundaries between objects (and parts of objects).

For Descartes the material universe is a plenum, and we do not notice all of the things that surround us. We do not notice all of the bodies that constitute what we regard as empty space, and we do not notice everything about the objects that we *do* perceive with our senses. We notice what is relevant to our survival as mind-body composites, and we also notice much of the macroscopic world, but there is quite a lot that we miss. Presumably what we do notice is actually there in the same configurations that we sense, but there are two important caveats that Descartes would highlight.

One is that we tend to sense things in a way that is relative to our interests and concerns.[45] The features that we notice about an object are relevant to the preservation of our mind-body union, and given how little we actually observe of the surrounding plenum, the features of an object that are relevant to us might constitute only a small fraction of it. A number of examples might be illustrative. One is poison ivy. We might suppose that its entire identity consists in the danger that it poses to our skin, but when it is growing in the woods with all the other plants, its danger to us is of no consequence. One hundred percent of what we take it to be is perhaps 1% of what it is in fact. It might even be an elixir to some other species of creature – and to many other species of creature – but we simply do not care, or we do not care to take the time to find out, and our concept of poison ivy makes no mention of that at all. Another example is the occurrence of rain. We might drive into town, and upon hearing the patter of droplets on our windshield, we have the thought that "it has started to rain." Upon reflection we recognize that it did not *start* raining, but that we drove into a region in which it was raining already. Or we might consider the analogy of a paint-by-numbers exercise in a coloring book. When we first look at the page, nothing jumps out at us except for lines and squiggles, along with numbers that signal what colors to shade and where. Then as certain regions of the page take on a particular color, for example brown or blue, a determinate figure begins to

---

45 See also Simmons (2003), Simmons (2014), and Chamberlain (2016).

emerge, and the spaces in-between might take a color that serves as a background (for example, of yellow or black or white). But some of the entities in those spaces might be extremely relevant to non-human creatures, and on Descartes' view, there are further and further lines and demarcations still. No doubt we can overcome our parochial perspective, in some cases more easily than others, but Descartes holds that we are constructed in such a way that we have a default stance of near oblivion toward entities that we do not detect to be relevant to our interests and concerns. As he puts it in Principles I.71, we often suppose that they are nothing at all (AT 8A:36, CSM 1:219). With respect to the picture of reality that forms in our mind, what we do notice closes in on what we do not, and what is left is a representation that is radically incomplete. That default stance has some survival advantages, but part of Descartes' effort to turn us away from the senses is to get us to notice that there is a perspective that is much more informed. That perspective is more informed, and it is more conducive to the longer and more pleasant kind of survival to which the fruits of the tree of philosophy – medicine, mechanics, and morals – are directed.

A second important caveat that Descartes would highlight is that we cannot rule out that the world of external bodies exists in a different configuration from the one that we sense. We do not have clear and distinct perceptions of particulars, he thinks, and he nowhere supposes that we achieve the same kind of confidence about the details of the bodies that cause our perceptions as we do about the existence of material entities insofar as they "possess all the properties which... viewed in general terms, are comprised within the subject-matter of pure mathematics." He had said way back in the First Meditation that "[w]hatever I have up till now accepted as most true I have acquired either from the senses or through the senses" (AT 7:18, CSM 2:12), and he said in the Second Meditation that "general perceptions are apt to be somewhat more confused" than perceptions of particulars (AT 7:30, CSM 2:20). However, by the time he has engaged the rigorous exercises of subsequent Meditations, he comes around to the entirely opposite view. As early as the end of the Second Meditation – after he notices that the nature of wax is not perceived by the imagination but by the mind alone – he reports, "I am speaking of this particular piece of wax; [but]

the point is even clearer with regard to wax in general" (AT 7:31, CSM 2:21). By the time of the Sixth Meditation, he says of his sensory perception of particulars that "there is a high degree of doubt and uncertainty involved here" (AT 7:80, CSM 2:55). Later in *Second Replies*, he says that if there is any certainty to be had, it occurs in the clear perceptions of the intellect and nowhere else (AT 7:145, CSM 2:104).[46] There are no clear and distinct perceptions of material particulars, for Descartes. When we do break down our idea of a particular into its clear and distinct elements, we have an idea of extension and ideas of sensations that are modifications of mind.

Descartes expresses much the same view in the concluding passages of *Principles of Philosophy*. He has just spent pages and pages laying out a picture of the workings of the material universe, but in the end, he concedes that our knowledge of the details of material bodies does not rise to the level of clear and distinct perception. He writes,

> Just as the same craftsman could make two clocks which tell the time equally well and look completely alike from the outside but have completely different assemblies of wheels inside, so the supreme craftsman of the real world could have produced all that we see in several different ways. I am very happy to admit this; and I shall think I have achieved enough provided only that what I have written is such as to correspond accurately with all of the phenomena of nature.
>
> (*Principles* IV.204; AT 8A:327, CSM 1:289)

Here Descartes is echoing the language of the Sixth Meditation – noting that sensory perceptions do not expose to us the truth about the configurations of external bodies, and suggesting instead that they have pragmatic value in helping us to navigate our environs. He concludes in the Sixth Meditation that material things exist and are the occasion of sensory perceptions, but what exists (aside from minds) are material things insofar as they possess the properties that are the subject-matter of pure mathematics. The truth that we

---

46 See also Chapter 1, pp. 6–10.

uncover via sensory perception is not about the exact configurations of bodies but about benefits and threats to our existence as mind-body composites. He continues in this same vein in *Principles* IV.205:

> It would be disingenuous, however, not to point out that some things are considered as morally certain, that is, as having sufficient certainty for application to ordinary life, even though they may be uncertain in relation to the absolute power of God.... Suppose for example that someone wants to read a letter written in Latin but encoded so that the letters of the alphabet do not have their proper value, and he guesses that the letter B should be read whenever A appears, and C when B appears, i.e. that each letter should be replaced by the one immediately following it. If, by using this key, he can make up Latin words from the letters, he will be in no doubt that the true meaning of the letter is contained in these words. It is true that his knowledge is based merely on a conjecture, and it is conceivable that the writer did not replace the original letters with their immediate successors in the alphabet, but with others, thus encoding quite a different message; but this possibility is so unlikely... that it does not seem credible.
>
> (AT 8A:327–328, CSM 1:289–290)

To return to the example of a bear, we presume that our sensory perceptions of its teeth and claws and legs are produced by bodies that are arranged in the configurations of teeth and claws and legs. Strictly speaking, however, our perceptions of particulars are confused, and they do not become unconfused until they are broken down to the point that they are perceptions of material things insofar as they possess the properties that are the subject-matter of pure mathematics. We are in a position to say that material things exist *in that sense*. Descartes accordingly writes in *Principles* IV.206:

> Besides, there are some matters, even in relation to the things in nature, which we regard as absolutely, and more than just morally, certain. <Absolute certainty arises when we believe that it is wholly impossible that something should be otherwise than we judge it to be>. ...Mathematical demonstrations have this kind

of certainty, as does the knowledge that material things exist, and the same goes for all evident reasoning about material things.

(AT 8A:328, CSM 1:290)

In other passages, he adds to the list of matters that involve more than moral certainty – the existence of the thinking self and the real distinction between mind and body.[47] But sensory perceptions fall short. We utilize them to discriminate between the objects that surround us and to make inferences about the configurations and boundaries of those objects, but sensory perceptions "provide only very obscure information" about these. We might be correct in our judgments about the configurations of sensory particulars, but for all we know we are not:

sensory perceptions are related exclusively to this combination of the human body and mind. They normally tell us of the benefit or harm that external bodies may do to this combination, and do not, except occasionally and accidentally, show us what external bodies are like in themselves.

(Principles II.3; CSM 1:224, AT 8A:41–42)

In this section of Principles of Philosophy, Descartes allows that for all we know the configurations of external bodies are largely as we perceive them – minus sensory features like color and taste of course. But for all we know they are not.[48] He titles the section: "Sensory perception does not show us what really exists in things, but merely shows us what is beneficial or harmful to man's composite nature" (AT 8A:41, CSM 1:224). He is registering that if we are correct in our assumption that bodies exist in the configurations that we sense, "it is by pure chance that [we] arrive at the truth" (CSM 2:41, AT 7:60), and not on the basis of the evidence of our cognition. The current-day theoretical physicist might remind us that what is really out there is fields and particles and waves – and that these are dramatically different from the things that appear in the sensory manifold. Descartes is suggesting much the same view almost 400 years earlier.

---

47 For example, in "Synopsis of the following six Meditations," AT 7:16, CSM 2:11.
48 See also Shepherd (1827), 188–189.

The resolution of dream doubt

The resolution of dream doubt that Descartes presents at the end of the Sixth Meditation accordingly does not appeal to clear and distinct sensory perceptions that mark the difference between waking and dreaming. Descartes does not think that we have at our disposal *any* tools for making a distinction between sensory perceptions that are clear and distinct and sensory perceptions that are not. No such distinction is in the cards, but we do have at our argumentative disposal the extremely strong inclinations that incline us to pursue and avoid objects. Descartes prefaces his resolution of dream doubt by saying that

> I know that in matters regarding the well-being of the body, all my senses report the truth much more frequently than not. Also, I can almost always make use of more than one sense to investigate the same thing; and in addition, I can use both my memory, which connects present experiences with preceding ones, and my intellect, which has by now examined all the causes of error.
> (CSM 2:61, AT 7:89)

Here Descartes is flagging that he will not overcome dream doubt by positing that we have clear and distinct sensory perceptions of material particulars – for example, of a bear that is actually present (when we are awake) versus a bear that we are only dreaming. He does not do an about-face and abandon the result that "knowledge of the truth about such things" does not belong "to the combination of mind and body" or that sensory perceptions "provide only very obscure information" about "the essential nature of bodies located outside us." Instead, he builds on the theme of the second half of the Sixth Meditation – that sensory perceptions provide information about what is beneficial or harmful to our mind-body union. His attempt to refute dream doubt occurs at the very end of the Meditation, and almost in passing, as if he has already done all of the argumentative legwork to set it up. He has just spent a number of pages emphasizing the respects in which sensory perceptions provide information that helps to preserve our mind-body union. Then at the very end of the Meditation, he notices that if we could not tell the difference between waking perceptions and dream perceptions, sensory perceptions would not be able to provide information that helps us to preserve mind-body union. But they do. Therefore, there is a distinction between waking perception and dreams, and a distinction that we are in a position to decipher. The difference between a single dream perception and a single waking perception may not be very much in terms of its lucidity and vivacity, but there is another difference between waking perceptions and dreams. There has to be. Descartes explores the terrain and notices that many sensory perceptions are linked by continuity with prior stretches of perception, and others – no matter how internally coherent – are not so linked. He uses actually that language – "I now notice that there is a vast difference between the two" (CSM 2:61, AT 7:89, emphasis added) – as if he was not in a position to notice that difference when he was looking for a different kind of difference, for example, that between sensory perceptions that are clear and distinct and sensory perceptions that are confused.[49] But all sensory perceptions are confused, and no such difference is to be found.

Descartes then appeals to the premise that God is not a deceiver to delineate which of our sensory perceptions are providing us with information for navigating our environment and which are not. He writes,

> when I see distinctly where things come from and where and when they come to me, and when I can connect my perceptions of them with the whole of the rest of my life without a break, then I am quite certain that when I encounter these things I am not asleep but awake. And I ought not to have even the slightest doubt of their reality if, after calling upon all the senses as well as my memory and my intellect in order to check them, I receive no conflicting reports from any of these sources. For from the fact that God is not a deceiver it follows that in cases like these I am completely free from error.
>
> (CSM 2:62, AT 7:90)

---

49 See also Cunning (2010), 181–190, Chynoweth (2010), 166–175, and the related discussion in Dellsén (2017). The latter discussion is more specifically about Descartes' view that scientific explanations are always uncertain and speculative.

Unless he is contradicting himself, Descartes is not suggesting here that we reach an epistemic point at which we are completely free from error in all respects. For example, he is on the record as holding that we will inevitably err in phantom-limb, dropsy, and similar cases.[50] What he is saying instead is that we never have (and never will have) a sensory perception that coheres with our past history of perception but does not provide information about benefits and harms to the composite that is our mind and body. We "see distinctly where things come from," but that is not to say that we have distinct waking sensory perceptions of material particulars. We see distinctly that there is a difference between sensory perceptions that are internally coherent and cohere with our past history and sensory perception that do not. The former are due to entities that bear on the well-being of our mind-body union; they have to be occasioned by such entities, otherwise God is a deceiver. Some of our sensory perceptions are thus rightly ignored as irrelevant. We dismiss dream perceptions, but not because they fail to be clear and distinct. If that were our reason, we would dismiss waking sensory perceptions as well. We dismiss dream perceptions because they do not provide pragmatic information for navigating our environment.

In the Sixth Meditation, Descartes concludes that material things exist insofar as they possess the properties that are the subject-matter of pure mathematics. His mathematical idea of body is clear and distinct, and so body (as the subject-matter of pure mathematics) is at least a candidate for existence. He then points to his extremely strong propensity to affirm that geometrical bodies are the occasion of sensory perceptions and concludes that, since God is not a deceiver, material things exist in fact. He offers a parallel argument in *Principles of Philosophy* II.1. In neither text does he conclude that material bodies exist in the configurations that we sense them to have, and indeed he leaves open that for all we know they do not. In addition, we might highlight the worry that for all we know we are brains in a vat: the features in material objects that correspond to our sensory perceptions of their size and shape might not have those sizes or

---

50 See also *Passions* II.142. Descartes speaks of "the affairs of everyday life, where we cannot avoid the risk of being mistaken" (AT 11:435, CSM 1:378).

shapes at all – even if there exist material vats and brains. Descartes recognizes the worry and thinks that we have no way to overcome it.[51] His reaction to our predicament is singular. He is not alarmed; he does not fret. He proposes that we use the deliverances of the senses to navigate our surroundings and do the best that we can to get by. He harnesses the very small amount of knowledge that he thinks is within our reach, and he applies it in service of the question of how to live.

Further reading

There is a large literature on Descartes' argument for the existence of material things. A cross-section includes:

Brad Chynoweth, "Descartes' Resolution of the Dreaming Doubt," *Pacific Philosophical Quarterly* 91 (2010), 153–179.

Desmond M. Clarke, "Descartes' Proof of the Existence of Matter," in *The Blackwell Guide to Descartes' Meditations*, ed. Stephen Gaukroger, Malden, MA: Blackwell (2006), 160–178.

John Cottingham, "Descartes' Sixth Meditation: The External World, 'Nature' and Human Experience," *Royal Institute of Philosophy Supplements* 20 (1986), 73–89.

James M. Humber, "Descartes' Dream Argument and Doubt of the Material World," *The Modern Schoolman* 69 (1991), 17–32.

Lex Newman, "Descartes on Unknown Faculties and Our Knowledge of the External World," *The Philosophical Review* 103 (1994), 489–531.

Emanuela Scribano, "Science contra the Meditations: The Existence of Material Things," *The European Legacy* 27 (2022), 348–360.

James D. Stuart, "Descartes' Proof of the External World," *History of Philosophy Quarterly* 3 (1986), 19–28.

Cecilia Wee, "Descartes's Two Proofs of the External World," *Australasian Journal of Philosophy* 80 (2002), 487–501.

---

51 But he would add that if we *are* brains in a vat, each of our brains is surrounded by further body, which is also surrounded by further body, *ad indefinitum*. Brains and vats also have no sensory qualities. In addition, a vat would not be the only thing that plays a role in the occasioning of our sense perceptions, as the surrounding bodies of the plenum would make a difference as well. On Descartes' view, the brain-in-a-vat scenario is different from the scenario that we take ourselves to inhabit, but not as different as we might think.

There is also a substantial literature on Descartes and "the proper purpose of the sensory perceptions given me by nature." A cross-section includes:

Lilli Alanen, "Descartes' Mind-Body Composites, Psychology and Naturalism," Inquiry 51 (2008), 464–484.

Deborah Brown, "The Sixth Meditation: Descartes and the Embodied Self," in The Cambridge Companion to Descartes' Meditations, ed. David Cunning, Cambridge and New York: Cambridge UP (2014), 240–257.

Brian Embry, "Cartesian Composites and the True Mode of Union," Australasian Journal of Philosophy 98 (2020), 629–645.

Lisa Shapiro, "Princess Elizabeth and Descartes: The Union of Soul and Body and the Practice of Philosophy," British Journal for the History of Philosophy 7 (1999), 503–520.

Alison Simmons, "Sensible Ends: Latent Teleology in Descartes' Account of Sensation," Journal of the History of Philosophy 39 (2001), 49–75.

Alison Simmons, "Descartes on the Cognitive Structure of Sensory Experience," Philosophy and Phenomenological Research 67 (2003), 549–579.

Alison Simmons, "Mind-Body Union and the Limits of Cartesian Metaphysics," Philosophers' Imprint 17 (2017), 1–36.

Nine

How best to live

Descartes secures just a small number of metaphysical results. One is that finite minds are immaterial substances. Another is that material things exist and possess extensive qualities like size, shape, and motion, but not sensory qualities like color, taste, or heat. There is also no empty space, according to Descartes, but instead there is a plenum of contiguous bodies to which minds are united. He also arrives at the result that God exists and that supreme perfection is to be identified with God. We are already similar to God with respect to our immateriality and in particular with respect to our will. No creature is perfect, but there is a spectrum of perfection from non-being to God, and finite minds are within reach of an approximation of the immutability, unflappability, independence, and omniscience that characterize perfection at its highest end. Finite bodies also admit of perfections, and with the right kind of perspective we benefit from incorporating these into our everyday routine. But Descartes supposes that there is much that we do not understand and that the appropriate life for a human being is not a life of understanding.[1] The metaphysical and epistemological questions of the *Meditations* and other texts – these are to be addressed "once in the course of… life" (AT 7:17, CSM 2:12), with limited returns, and thereafter we are to incorporate them into our behavior in a way that is sustainable for creatures to whom clear and distinct perception does not come easily. The result that God exists and constitutes the standard of perfection is perhaps the most important metaphysical result for

---

1 See the discussion in Chapter 3.

DOI: 10.4324/9781351210522-9

us to register and apply.[2] Finite minds move further in the direction of the good when we acquire more knowledge and information: we become more independent and more immutable.[3] We buffer our will from the many forces that encumber it, and we experience incomparable grades of activity and joy. We unite ourselves to regions of God's creation – we acquire more being, and we associate more tightly with entities that participate in higher degrees of perfection themselves. We calibrate our activity with an eye to the small number of metaphysical truths that are within our reach, and we flourish and thrive.

To approach Descartes' view on how best to live, we must first unpack a series of notions that are operative in the background. These notions help to flesh out what it is to want something, what it is to pursue something, what it is to become frustrated in the pursuit of something, and the like. There is a sense in which we would already have to understand the notions if we were going to understand the definitions of them, but an initial discussion is helpful for purposes of clarity.

---

2 I will be disagreeing with commentators who hold that according to Descartes God wills standards of goodness arbitrarily (see Chapter 1, note 76), and I will also be disagreeing with commentators who hold that Descartes' conception of the good is circular in that emphasizes the exercise of freedom for the sake of exercising freedom itself. See for example Brown (2006), 196–197, and Rutherford (2019). I am arguing that the proper exercise of freedom is to emulate perfection as much as is possible for a finite being. I am also disagreeing with Gombay (2003), who offers a sociological explanation of Descartes' account of the good and argues that it is heavily influenced by changes in the educational systems of the West in the Seventeenth Century (240–244, 257–258). Note that I agree with Brown on many of the important details of Descartes' view on how to live, even if I disagree with her about the metaphysical underpinnings of that view. There are further references to the work of Brown below.

3 See the initial discussion in Chapter 1, pp. 26–30. Descartes holds that among the supreme perfections are independence (First Replies, AT 7:108–117, CSM 2:76–83), immutability (Principles II.36, AT 8A:61, CSM 1:240; Passions III.152, AT 11:445, CSM 1:384), and the possession of knowledge ("To Chanut, 1 February 1647," AT 4:608, CSMK 309).

Desire and motivation

Descartes defines *desire* as a modification of the soul in which it "wish[es], in the future, for the things it represents to itself as agreeable."[4] The definition here is not particularly elucidatory, of course, given that a wish is basically a desire, but to be fair to Descartes it is not clear how such a basic notion would be defined, or how it could be accurately articulated without some reference to synonymous notions that are presumed to be understood already. Note also that Descartes defines a desire as a wish for things that we represent to ourselves as agreeable, but a desire is not always for a thing that is in fact agreeable. He allows for example that there are cases in which we desire an object that actually harms us – for example, when we have dropsy and a thirst for water, but water is the last thing that we need. There are also cases in which the things that we take to be goods are in fact goods, but we have an exaggerated sense of their value. Our attachments to material things tend to fall into this category. As Descartes had described in *Principles* I.70–I.73, we focus attention in our earliest years on the bodies that most overtly benefit or threaten the composite that is our mind-body union (AT 8A:34–37, CSM 1:218–220). We notice (and desire) the food that we need to secure; we notice (and desire to avoid) macroscopic sensible objects that constitute a danger and cause us pain. We are strongly motivated to pursue or avoid such objects and to pay attention to them. In the Sixth Meditation, Descartes highlights the uncontroversial datum that we would not tend to the needs of our body as urgently if we were provided with a neutral and non-exclamatory report of its states, and so we are instead provided with vivid sensations (AT 7:81–88, CSM 2:56–61). In the same vein, we are built to have desires that err on the side of motivating us to act:

> all our passions represent to us the goods to whose pursuit they impel us as being much greater than they really are....[5]

---

4 *Passions* II.86, AT 11:392, CSM 1:358.
5 "To Princess Elizabeth, 15 September 1645," AT 4:294–295, CSMK 267.

Amplified desires assist us by providing a sense of urgency that would otherwise be absent in our motivation set, in part because we are not always (or often) having clear perceptions of the good.[6]

When we *are* having a clear perception of a good, Descartes supposes, we desire it and are compelled to pursue it. He says in a letter to Mesland,

> it seems to me certain that a great light in the intellect is followed by a great inclination in the will; so that if we see very clearly that a thing is good for us, it is very difficult – and, on my view, impossible, as long as one continues in the same thought – to stop the course of our desire.[7]

However, as embodied beings, most of us have nothing but confused perceptions our entire lives.[8] Descartes thus makes sure to add in the very next sentence of the letter to Mesland: "But the nature of our soul is such that it hardly attends for more than a moment to a single thing." We have seen the same cognitive skirmish referenced across much of Descartes' corpus: our bodies are bombarded with sense perceptions almost constantly, and in addition there are happenings in the nervous system that have an impact on our attention whether we are in a position to identify them or not.[9] So long as we perceive a good clearly, we are drawn to it, but we are often distracted, and we will not be motivated to pursue a good continuously and seamlessly unless we experience some additional motivation. Passions like desire do that work and more:

---

6 See also Shapiro (2003), 46–51, Radner (2003), Beyssade (2003), 139–143, Greenberg (2007), and Jayasekera (2020).

7 "To [Mesland], 2 May 1644," AT 4:116, CSMK 233. Descartes then adds in the next couple of sentences that so long as what is before the intellect is a clear and distinct idea, it is impossible for the will to not affirm, but if a different idea comes before the intellect, the will might affirm differently. See also *Second Replies*, AT 7:166, CSM 2:117; the Fifth Meditation, AT 7:69, CSM 2:48; and *Principles* I.43, AT 8A:21, CSM 1:207.

8 *Principles* I.73, AT 8A:37, CSM 1:220.

9 See for example *Passions* II.93–94, AT 11:398–399, CSM 1:361–362.

The function of all the passions consists solely in this, that they dispose our soul to want the things which nature deems useful for us, and to persist in this volition.[10]

Descartes provides a helpful example of the case in which an individual persists in their desire to stand firm in the face of danger. If the individual keeps their mental eye on the value of confronting the danger, they will be motivated to stand up to it, but our mental eye tends to waver. For example, we need to focus on things like the sensory particulars of the danger and how best to avoid it. With our attention shifted, the motivation to act will have to come from elsewhere. Descartes hence describes a case in which

nerves... serve to move the hands in self-defense and... agitate the blood and drive it towards the heart in the manner required to produce spirits appropriate for continuing this defense and for maintaining the will to do so.[11]

Even in the case of what Descartes will identify as the highest good for a human being – acting from virtue – supplemental motivation is extremely helpful. In the heat of the moment, it is unlikely that an embodied mind would have a sustained clear and distinct perception of the value of virtue, but other sources of motivation are operative instead. Descartes writes,

Suppose there is a prize for hitting a bull's-eye: you can make people want to hit the bull's-eye by showing them the prize, but they cannot win the prize if they do not see the bull's-eye; conversely, those who see the bull's-eye are not thereby induced to fire at it if they do not know there is a prize to be won. So too virtue, which is the bull's-eye, does not come to be strongly desired when it is seen all on its own, and contentment, like the prize, cannot be gained unless it is pursued.[12]

---

10 *Passions* II.52, AT 11:372, CSM 1:349.
11 *Passions* I.39, AT 11:358–359, CSM 1:343.
12 "To Princess Elizabeth, 18 August 1645," AT 4:277, CSMK 262.

A sustained clear and distinct perception of the good is not especially helpful in navigating sensory particulars, and at the moment of action it would be inexpedient and counterproductive. We are built with supplementary motivational structure to help make up the difference.

The desires of a mind-body composite incline it to pursue items that are good, at least for the most part, but there are also items that are better.[13] We will not notice these if we continue in the habit of judging that things are real to the extent that they are sensible, or if we do not notice the value of increased knowledge, immutability, and independence. The paradigm of goodness is divine perfection, for Descartes, but if we are clueless about that perfection, we fail to notice the near ubiquity of its finite incarnations, and we do not have an eye to developing it in ourselves. Instead, we proceed as before – approaching situations (and what we notice of them) with a parochial and narcissistic perspective.[14] Most of what surrounds us will fail to register, and almost nothing will register for all that it is. We will not have a properly calibrated sense of the value of the immutable order of bodies or a properly calibrated sense of the value of studying and cognizing it. We will not have a properly calibrated sense of the value of our own independence, or a properly calibrated sense of what that independence even is. We will not understand our relationship to omniscience and other perfections, and we will not be in a position to live finite approximations of these.[15] Nor will we understand the value and import of other mind-body composites and the activity and perfection that are within their reach. With effort, we move from a common and precarious level of pleasure to a state in which "we are capable of enjoying the sweetest

---

13 Or as Descartes puts it, there are not only unimportant pursuits but also "serious pursuits" and things that are "worthier" ("To Beeckman, 23 April 1619," AT 10:163, CSMK 4).

14 See also Chapter 8, pp. 325–326.

15 I take it that in Descartes the individual who achieves finite approximations of independence and omniscience is an anticipation of the "free man" of Spinoza's *Ethics* Parts IV and V. The individual is an approximation of substantiality and independence, but of course is not God. Nor does it possess libertarian freedom.

pleasures of this life."[16] A mind-body union that is emended is still a mind-body union, but Descartes supposes that a radically different kind of existence is in store if we spend a small amount of time uncovering the principles of metaphysics and a large amount of time insinuating them into practice.

Levels of joy and levels of sadness

Descartes defines desire as a wish for things that we take to be agreeable,[17] and he also provides a definition of the passion that comes with the satisfaction of desire. He writes that "joy results from the belief that we possess some good"[18] and that joy is a "pleasant emotion which the soul has when it enjoys a good which impressions in the brain represent to it as its own."[19] There is a spectrum of goodness from non-being to perfection, and joy still accompanies the acquisition of material goods, but "our soul... is much nobler than the body...," which is to say that material things are less noble than minds.[20] The miser might believe that he is in possession of a good, for example, but "money is not worth the trouble of such safeguarding,"[21] and his joy is of a different order than that of an individual whose stance toward material things is better informed. Descartes accordingly says that the passions of attraction

---

16 *Passions* IV. 212, AT 11:488, CSM 1:404. The current chapter includes a further defense of the claims that I make in this paragraph.

17 Descartes says that a desire is a wish to possess what we take to be good, but there are passages in which he says that desires incline us to pursue what is actually good, suggesting that desires do not just track what we take to be good. See for example *Passions* II.91, AT 11:396, CSM 1:360. He holds also that there are cases in which we cannot quite tell what is causing a passion, and thus that there are cases in which a good is causing a passion in us but we are not in a position to fully or accurately identify it. He says for example that "it often happens that we often feel sad or joyful without being able to observe so distinctly the good or evil which causes this feeling" (*Passions* II.93, AT 11:398, CSM 1:361).

18 *Passions* II.93, AT 11:398, CSM 1:361.

19 *Passions* II.91, AT 11:396, CSM 1:360.

20 "To Princess Elizabeth, 15 September 1645," AT 4:292, CSMK 265.

21 *Passions* III.169, AT 11:458, CSM 1:390.

and repulsion as they apply to the objects of the senses "usually contain less truth" and "are the most deceptive of all the passions, and the ones against which we must guard ourselves most carefully."[22] Some things are just more good than others, Descartes supposes, even if we are sometimes drawn to entities that are low on the scale of perfection and that have a historical track record of meeting the basic needs of embodiment. We will not be drawn to higher goods unless we recognize them as such and unless our desires are adjusted accordingly. Luckily for us, desires are malleable:

> It is useful to note here... that although nature seems to have joined every movement of the gland to certain of our thoughts from the beginning of our life, yet we may join them to others through habit. Experience shows this in the case of language. Words produced in the gland movements which are ordained by nature to represent to the soul only the sounds of their syllables when they are spoken or the shape of their letters when they are written, because we have acquired the habit of thinking of this meaning when we hear them spoken or see them written. It is also useful to note that although the movements (both of the gland and of the spirits and the brain) which represent certain objects to the soul are naturally joined to the movements which produce certain passions in it, yet through habit the former can be separated from the latter and joined to others which are very different.[23]

There are biological reasons why we desire and are motivated to seek after sensible material objects, and we do experience at least some joy at their acquisition. But there is such a thing as retraining the mind so that it desires what is more desirable. We do not update our desires just by willing that they be different. Descartes offers the analogy of attempting to enlarge our pupils by a mere act of will: "if we think only of enlarging the pupils, we may indeed have such a volition, but we do not thereby enlarge them."[24] Instead, we pro-

---

22 *Passions* II.85, AT 11:392, CSM 1:358.
23 *Passions* I.50, AT 11:368–369, CSM 1:348.
24 *Passions* I.44, AT 11:362, CSM 1:344.

ceed indirectly: we have a volition to look at a distant object, or if we want our pupils to contract we have a volition to look at an object that is close up. We do not change our desires by a mere act of will either, but we execute other volitions instead: "the will, lacking the power to produce the passions directly, ... is compelled to make an effort to consider a series of different things."[25] For example, we might remind ourselves of the reasons for thinking that minds are more noble than body – like that minds are "somehow made in his [God's] image and likeness" (CSM 2:35, AT 7:51) and that "our soul's nature resembles his sufficiently for us to believe that it is an emanation of his supreme intelligence, a 'breath of divine spirit'" (AT 4:608, CSMK 309).[26] Or we might remind ourselves that independence is a supreme perfection and that there is a level of independence that is within reach for a finite mind. We might also recall the immutable order that is exhibited in the behavior of the creatures that surround us, if we would just look for it, and then achieve an occasional and approximate sense of what things are like from a detached and non-narcissistic perspective. We align with perfection, and our motivations begin to fall into line. Then we rinse and repeat.[27]

Another passion that is had by embodied minds is sadness. Roughly the opposite of joy, "[s]adness is an unpleasant listlessness which affects the soul when it suffers discomfort from an evil or deficiency which impressions in the brain represent to it as its own."[28] Just as "joy results from the belief that we possess some good, ... sadness [results] from the belief that we have some evil or deficiency."[29] Descartes does not provide many examples to illustrate the passion of sadness – perhaps taking it to be something

---

25 Passions I.47, AT 11:365–366, CSM 1:346.

26 See also the treatment in Gombay (2007), 98–100.

27 Here I am agreeing with Frierson (2002) that Descartes has in mind a gradual evolution from an egoistic and narcissistic perspective to a perspective that is more altruistic. But the latter perspective ends up involving so much pleasure that it is hard to know exactly how to describe it (as egoistic or not).

28 Passions II.92, AT 11:397, CSM 1:361.

29 Passions II.93, AT 11:398, CSM 1:361. See also the helpful discussion in Brassfield (2012).

that is sufficiently familiar – but instead he focuses on its physio-logical underpinnings.[30] He does give as an example the feeling that we have "when it has happened that the body has lacked nourish-ment," speculating that we first experienced sadness through our earliest desire for food and its very unwelcome absence.[31] There are numerous other instances of sadness of course – the hope that a situ-ation turns out a certain way, together with the recognition that it does not; our separation from an individual to whom we have a strong attachment; the loss of a good the possession of which has brought us joy; among others. Descartes also recognizes the complications that come with attempting to identify specific instances of sadness (and other passions), given that it often occurs simultaneously with other states. We experience (and are aware of) sadness upon the loss of a good, but there is much that is happening in our body at any given moment, and we might be feeling sadness, hatred, love, and remorse all at once.[32] In the example that Descartes provides, an infant feels sadness due to a lack of food, but presumably also feels hunger. Descartes does not provide the cleanest definitions or examples of each passion, but to his credit, he recognizes that the phenomenology of the passions is very messy.

A central pillar of Descartes' metaphysics is that God exists and is perfect. But that is not to say but that there exists a standard of per-fection that is independent of God and that God meets. Nor is it to say that there exists a standard of perfection that God has decreed arbitrarily and that He meets immediately afterward. God is the standard of perfection, which is to say that what is perfect is what God is – omniscient, eternal, immutable, and independent, just to start.[33] Finite embodied minds are not God, but Descartes supposes that we are made in the image of God and are in some way an eman-ation of His perfection. We are not actually omniscient or eternal or immutable or independent; nor do we become any of these. Still, we

---

30 For example in *Passions* II.116–117, AT 11:414–415, CSM 1:368–369; and *Passions* II.131, AT 11:425, CSM 1:374.

31 *Passions* II.110, AT 11:410, CSM 1:367.

32 See for example *Passions* III.211, AT 11:486–487, CSM 1:403; *Passions* III.178, AT 11:464–465, CSM 1:393; and *Passions* I.31, AT 11:352, CSM 1:340.

33 Again see Chapter 1 above, pp. 25–30.

are on the spectrum of non-being to perfection, and we have plenty of room to grow.

In the letter to Chanut in which Descartes contends that finite minds are a breath of divine spirit, Descartes proceeds to reflect on omniscience in particular. We are not omniscient ourselves, but the attribute of omniscience does serve as a regulative ideal through which a human being is able to increase its perfection. Descartes identifies knowledge as a good to be sought and acquired, but not just because he happens to be a philosopher. Nor (in the Cartesian framework) is knowledge a good automatically. It is good because God is an omniscient mind that is the exemplar of perfection. That is the only standard of perfection that exists and has any reality. Descartes identifies the acquisition of knowledge as a good in numerous passages, for example in the list of provisional moral codes that he advances in *Discourse on the Method*: "[I will] devote my whole life to cultivating my reason and advancing as far as I c[an] in the knowledge of the truth" (AT 6:27, CSM 1:124). That part of his provisional code is then confirmed in later work – in the identification of God and perfection. Descartes does not thereby suppose that the appropriate goal for a human being is to have clear and distinct perceptions at all times. Those are the perceptions that we would have if we were not embodied,[34] but we are embodied, and the knowledge that it is appropriate (and sustainable) for us to seek is of a different order. We benefit from arriving at clear and distinct perceptions, but for an embodied being clear and distinct perceptions are few and far between, and in addition there is only so far that our metaphysical tether is able to reach. In addition, bodies exhibit perfection and are a worthy object of attention, as are finite minds. The appropriate goal for us is therefore to secure the small number of metaphysical results that are within our reach and to use them as a leverage point to revolutionize our orientation toward the creatures that surround us. We will achieve very little *scientia*, but there is also moral certainty, which is "sufficient certainty for application to ordinary life" (AT 8A:327, CSM 1: 289–290).[35] The increase in knowledge that elevates a mind on the scale of perfection is not just due to an increase in clear and

---

34 See Chapter 3, pp. 77–78.
35 See also Chapter 8, pp. 318–329.

distinct perceptions; in the case of an embodied being, there are not enough of those to get us very far. The increase in perfection will instead be in terms of how we incorporate the results of clear and distinct perception into practice.

Wonder

Descartes supposes that we are created in the image of God to a significant degree, and he also holds that God has constructed us in such a way as to be motivated to become more perfect. In the case of the project of moving in the direction of omniscience, God has created us so as to experience the passion of wonder when we are inquiring into subjects that are new or unfamiliar.[36] The passion of wonder helps us to focus our attention on objects in which we might otherwise lose interest. He writes,

> Wonder is a sudden surprise of the soul which brings it to consider with attention the objects that seem to it unusual and extraordinary. It has two causes: first, an impression in the brain, which represents the object as something unusual and consequently worthy of special consideration; and secondly, a movement of the spirits, which the impression disposes both to flow with great force to the place in the brain where it is located so as to strengthen and preserve it there, and also to pass into

---

36 A worry might arise as to whether Descartes allows that we can speak to God's purposes given that he says in the Fourth Meditation that "the customary search for final causes [is] totally useless in physics" (AT 7:55, CSM 2:39). Descartes does hold that the search for final causes is useless in physics, but he does not think that it is useless in other contexts, especially in contexts where we grasp what God has willed and created and we inquire into how and where it fits on the scale of perfection. For example, he writes in *Fifth Replies* that "in ethics, then, where we may often legitimately employ conjectures, it may admittedly be pious on occasion to try to guess what purpose God may have had in mind in his direction of the universe" (AT 7:375, CSM 2:258). In the Sixth Meditation, he goes even farther – he draws the definitive conclusion that God has produced "the best system that could be devised" in constructing us to have sensations that inform us of benefits and harms to our body (AT 7:87, CSM 2:60).

the muscles which serve to keep the sense organs fixed in the same orientation so that they will continue to maintain the same impression....[37]

Descartes is speaking here of objects that are unusual and beyond the ordinary but that in the absence of the passion of wonder would only keep our attention for so long. Presumably, he has in mind objects that are not an immediate threat to our survival or that (as far as we can tell) do not bear on our well-being. Objects that are an immediate threat for the most part do get and keep our attention, due to the operation of passions that are different from wonder – for example, fear.[38] But in the case of the passion of wonder, we are often motivated to dwell on a thought in a more-or-less disinterested manner, as when we "seek out rarities simply in order to wonder at them and not in order to know them."[39] The passion of wonder is pleasant enough that it motivates us to seek out new knowledge, and Descartes indeed supposes that "it is good to be born with some inclination to wonder, since it makes us disposed to acquire scientific knowledge."[40] Without the passion of wonder, we would still be inclined to learn about the objects that bear immediately on our well-being, but those are a very select subset of the things that are actually relevant to our well-being. There are also things that merit our attention more generally – for example, music, parahelia, vision, acoustics, light, lenses, anatomy, barometric pressure, tides, and rainbows.[41] Without the passion of wonder, we might register only the features of objects that are most salient to us at first glance. With wonder, we are more curious. There is such a thing as too much wonder, however, and Descartes supposes that human beings would be wise to calibrate the passion so that we move on to other things. He says that the best remedy for "excessive wonder" is not to squash the passion but to spread it around – "to acquire the knowledge of many things and to practice examining all those which may

37 *Passions* II.70, AT 11:380–381, CSM 1:353.
38 *Passions* I.36–48, AT 11:356–367, CSM 1:342–347.
39 *Passions* II.78, AT 11:386, CSM 1:356.
40 *Passions* II.76, AT 11:385, CSM 1:355.
41 See also the discussion in Chapter 2, pp. 45–57.

seem most unusual and strange" (ibid.). It goes without saying that well-calibrated wonder would be a boon in terms of moving in the direction of increased confidence about matters that have "application to ordinary life."

Firm and determinate judgments

Descartes also supposes that we move in the direction of supreme perfection when we become more independent. He argues that one way for us to increase our independence is to act on the basis of firm and resolute judgments. The passion of wonder will help us to acquire the knowledge that informs those judgments, and adherence to the judgments will keep us from being at the mercy of passions like sadness, irresolution, remorse, and hatred.[42] Descartes writes,

> happiness consists solely in contentment of mind – that is to say, in contentment in general. For although some contentment depends on the body, and some does not, there is none anywhere but in the mind. But in order to achieve a contentment which is solid, we need to pursue virtue – that is to say, to maintain a firm and constant will to bring about everything that we judge to be the best, and to use all the power of our intellect in judging well.[43]

The language here is a bit open-ended – we become virtuous (and then happy) so long as we judge well and do not waver from our (good) judgment.[44] But we can see what Descartes has in mind. As finite beings, we will never possess all the information that is relevant to a given situation, and so that cannot be our goal. Nor will

---

42 See also Shapiro (2003b) and Brown (2006), 170. Note that a specific discussion of the passion of hatred will come later in the chapter.

43 "To Princess Elizabeth, 18 August 1645," AT 4:277, CSMK 262.

44 Viljanen (2021, 65–67) argues that strictly speaking Descartes holds that a third condition must be met in order to achieve happiness – a condition that is above and beyond the two conditions that are necessary for virtue. A person will not be fully happy if they have met those conditions but they do not also have a meta-level awareness of meeting them.

we ever act in the light of information that is not available to us. We might come across such information later, and we might recognize (in the light of it) that there is something that would have been better for us to have done instead, but that does not mean that the information was available to us at the time that we acted. Descartes considers for example a case in which we might feel the passion of repentance. He writes,

> there is nothing to repent of when we have done what we judged best at the time when we had to decide to act, even though later, thinking it over at our leisure, we judge that we made a mistake. ...[I]t does not belong to human nature to be omniscient, or always to judge as well on the spur of the moment as when there is plenty of time to deliberate.[45]

It is not in our nature to be omniscient, but we increase our perfection when we move in the direction of omniscience, and one of the rules that Descartes recommends is that each person "try to employ his mind as well as he can to discover what he should or should not do in all the circumstances of life."[46] He does not recommend that we do that just once in the course of life,[47] but that we do it regularly. He then advances a second rule: that each person "have a firm and constant resolution to carry out whatever reason recommends without being diverted by his passions or appetites" (AT 4:265, CSMK 257–258). We develop informed resolutions to which we adhere in action, but still operating in line with the first rule, we work to acquire new information and then update our resolutions as we go. For example, we might judge on the basis of our past experience that it is good to extend a handshake when meeting another human being. Perhaps our experience up to that point has been that individuals interpret the offer as

---

45 "To Princess Elizabeth, 6 October 1645," AT 4:307, CSMK 269.

46 "To Princess Elizabeth, 4 August 1645," AT 4:265, CSMK 257.

47 The First Meditation, AT 7:17, CSM:12. He recommends that once in the course of life we engage in the detached and abstract project that is metaphysical inquiry, where "the task... in hand does not involve action but merely the acquisition of knowledge" (AT 7:22, CSM 2:15). But otherwise we act and in a way that is informed by that knowledge.

a sign of respect.[48] If it turns out that on a given occasion we are meeting an individual who finds physical contact objectionable, we might reach out our hand and offend them. But that is not a reason to tear into ourselves. If we are meeting the person and we had no reason to think that they were an outlier, we did all that we could on the basis of the information that we had. We acquire some *new* information, which might be prompted by the passion of wonder – where we take pleasure in thinking about why a particular case might be an outlier or about how and why the more standard cases run exactly as they do. We experience pleasure rather than frustration. We are active rather than passive. We might even notice a cue by which to identify a significant percentage of outlier cases in advance and then update our maxim accordingly. But if that new information is not yet available to us, there is no way for us to take it into account.

Nor would we benefit from abandoning the effort to formulate firm and resolute judgments, just because we get things wrong every once in a while. A very different and much less functional approach to our failure would be to roll the dice in the practice of handshakes and offer our hand at some times and not others. In that case, we would not be "us[ing] all the power of our intellect [to] judg[e] well," but in addition we would increase the number of instances in which we cause offense. If we follow Descartes' prescription, we will make firm and constant judgments on the basis of increasingly updated information, and instances of failure will provide a wondrous opportunity to update those judgments in the future. For example, we might do research on the different cultural backgrounds of the individuals in our vicinity, or we might adopt a maxim by which we tentatively hold back a handshake if and when we suspect that it would not be welcome. The passions of irresolution and repentance would be experienced rarely by an individual who has formulated firm and constant judgments on the basis of extensive (but not exhaustive) information:

> Irresolution is also a kind of anxiety. ...[T]his anxiety is so common and so strong in some people that although they have

---

48 Or perhaps we have simply registered a custom of our local environment (as per *Discourse* Part 3, AT 6:23–24, CSM 1:122–123).

no need to make a choice and they see only one thing to be taken or left, the anxiety often holds them back and makes them pause to search in vain for something else. ...[T]he remedy against such excess is to become accustomed to form certain and determinate judgements regarding everything that comes before us, and to believe that we always do our duty when we do what we judge to be best, even though our judgment may perhaps be a very bad one.[49]

We will not feel the unsettling and discombobulating passion of irresolution if we act on the basis of unwavering judgments that take into account the information that we have worked to acquire prior to the time of action. We will also prevent the passions of regret and remorse after the fact, for "nothing causes regret and remorse except irresolution."[50] Instead of revisiting earlier judgments that misfired and stewing over all the ways that we might have been better informed, we recognize that we were as informed as were and that one of our maxims is almost certainly in need of emendation. Remorse and regret are no doubt useful in some contexts – "[t]he function of this passion [remorse] is to make us inquire whether the object of our doubt is good or not, and to prevent our doing it another time"[51] – just as there is value in making the habitual judgment that things are real to the extent that they are sensed. But there is a perspective on remorse that is more perfect still:

> it would be better never to have occasion to feel it; and we may prevent it by the same means by which we can free ourselves from irresolution.

> (ibid.)

The more perfect stance is one in which we approximate the independence and unflappability of a mind that sees all that happens and its connection to what happened the moment before. Emotionally speaking, we would be almost invincible. We would

---

49 *Passions* III.170, AT 11:459–460, CSM 1:390–391.
50 "To Princess Elizabeth, 15 September 1645," AT 4:295, CSMK 267.
51 *Passions* III.177, AT 11:464, CSM 1:392.

still feel things – for example, joy – and we would even have bouts of frustration and remorse, but in short order, our experience of these would change from passive to active.[52] We become more independent, and that "renders us in a certain way like God by making us masters of ourselves."[53]

Descartes offers his own example of a case in which an individual benefits from assembling information into the form of a firm and determinate maxim and applies it without wavering. He writes,

> [S]uppose we have business in some place to which we might travel by two different routes, one usually much safer than the other. And suppose Providence decrees that if we go by the route we regard as safer we shall not avoid being robbed, whereas we may travel by the other route without any danger. ...Reason insists that we choose the route which is usually the safer, and our desire in this case must be fulfilled when we have followed this route, whatever evil may befall us; for, since any such evil was inevitable from our point of view, we had no reason to wish to be exempt from it: we had reason only to do the best that our intellect was able to recognize....[54]

Here Descartes is saying that what matters most in cases of human behavior is not the outcome of that behavior but the extent to which it is the product of informed and resolute judgments. Outcomes still have *some* importance, insofar as they reflect a position on the spectrum of non-being to perfection. More important though are the maxims on which our activity is based. So long as we do well on the latter count, "our desire in this case must be fulfilled." If we turn out to be right, we experience the pleasure of having pieced together the reality of the situation that confronted us, and if we turn out to

---

52 In *Passions* III.187, Descartes accordingly speaks of a difference in perspective that we can take on our passions in which we view them in the way that we view the unfolding of events in play on a stage (AT 11:469–470). Williston (2003) calls this a "transcendental move" (320–323) in Descartes, borrowing from the argumentation in Schmitter (1994).

53 *Passions* III.152, AT 11:445, CSM 1:384.

54 *Passions* II.146, AT 11:439–440, CSM 1:380–381.

be mistaken we have approximated perfection as well. We exhibit an increase in activity if we are right, and we exhibit an increase in activity if we are mistaken and our reaction to the situation is due to us (and our adherence to maxims) and not to the vicissitudes of the situation itself.[55] Our behavior is more active and free in the sense that it is due to us and our maxims.

If we are mistaken, we also have the opportunity to update our judgment and have "[o]ur knowledge... grow by degrees to[ward] infinity." If a route that we have experienced to be safe comes to show that it was not nearly as safe as we thought, or that it was once safe but is safe no longer, we make a new and more informed judgment. Descartes provides the example of a person who is deciding between one of two routes. We might consider a similar but more complicated example – that of a driver who sometimes gets stuck at a train crossing and becomes frustrated as a result. Let us suppose that the route that includes the train crossing is the shortest for reaching the driver's desired destination. Let us suppose also that the destination reflects the driver's understanding of what is (and what is not) higher on the scale of perfection – and that their destination is perhaps a knowledge-enhancer like a library, or an archeological dig, or a lab or observatory; or perhaps it is some other venue in which patterns might be observed in the series of creatures that has been willed immutably and for eternity.[56] Or even better – the destination is a venue at which the driver is able to interface with other finite minds.[57] First, the driver might consider the measures

---

55 Waldow (2017, 309–316) argues that one of the aims of the First Meditation dream argument is to prompt the mind to engage in a level of activity that becomes more and more pronounced as the *Meditations* unfolds – a level of activity that builds and spirals on itself and from which there is little chance of return. A similar view is in Boehm (2014), with a focus on the connection between the assertion of existence in the Second Meditation and the experience of freedom and activity. Boehm argues that the Second Meditation meditator even secures a version of the Cartesian virtue of generosity in the Second Meditation (713–722), but that is going much too far I think. See also Parvizian 2016, 229–241.

56 With the right shift in perspective the latter venue could be almost anywhere.

57 More on that below.

that are available to lessen his inconvenience. For example, he might try to beat the train just before it actually crosses; but that would be unwise. Or, he might yell and curse at the train; but that would not help him to arrive at his destination any sooner, and he would be exposing the depth of his ignorance of the variables that led the train to arrive exactly when and where it did. He would also be expecting an event to transpire that was simply never going to happen. An alternate measure would be for the driver to attempt to become omniscient and know when the train will pass the crossing each and every day. No finite being will ever become omniscient, however; the driver will never come to know everything about everything, and he will not come to acquire every bit of information about the particular train crossing that is his albatross. The driver would have to abandon many if not all of his other (perfection-enhancing) projects in the effort to secure such information, and still he would get things wrong, at least from time to time.

Another step that the driver might take is to follow Descartes' advice and tap the passion of wonder to generate an informed but fallible maxim that applies to train crossings in general and to the local crossing in particular. For example, the driver might notice that there are two traffic lanes that intersect the crossing, and that the lane on the left regularly features a large number of cars that turn (left) into the middle school up ahead. The cars that turn left have to wait for a pause in oncoming traffic, which is heavy at certain times of day due to the drop-off and pick-up routine at the school. The cars in the left lane are more likely to get stuck at the train crossing, the driver realizes, but cars in the right lane tend to move at a steady pace. The driver might then form the maxim that it is better to use the right lane in the early morning and mid-afternoon – given the school's bell schedule – and he would be right to do so. But he might still be out of luck on occasion. On a random day, the school might have a walking field trip, where a long stretch of returning students inhabit a crosswalk that blocks a line of cars from turning right. The driver does not get angry or frustrated in that circumstance, recognizing that there is a limit to the amount of fine-tuning that is sustainable in the formation of maxims, but instead he appreciates how most of the time his maxim helps to get things right. The driver also appreciates that of course there are going to be field trips sometimes – even if it is not sustainable for anyone but a school administrator to know all the dates and times on which they will occur.[58] If there are occasions in which the driver absolutely has to be at their destination on time – perhaps for a meeting that bears on an item that is high on the scale of perfection – he might take a route that is longer in terms of distance but that includes a train overpass. The driver would set aside extra time on those occasions and leave a little early, acting from a different (and more informed) maxim. Whatever the outcome in the *actual world*, the driver would feel a tremendous amount of satisfaction. Most often he would use the right lane to pass the train crossing and arrive at his destination in due time. He might even feel some additional satisfaction on an occasion in which he just misses the train as it passes behind him. There might arise a few occasions in which it is cars in the right lane that are held up, or instances in which the driver takes the (longer) route that has the overpass, and he comes to learn that no train went through town that day. With a developed sense of wonder, he might take a small amount of time to look into why. Descartes supposes that "those with a weak and abject spirit are guided by chance alone" (*Passions* III.159, AT 11:450, CSM 1:386). He is suggesting that a much better approach would be to achieve a cognitive position in which we experience satisfaction and contentment whether the (proverbial) train comes or not. We move in the direction of omniscience and independence, and we *feel* better too.[59]

---

58 The driver might also feel joy at the thought that the students have taken part in an activity that enhances the perfection of region of the plenum, or he might contact the school about important field-trip opportunities in the local community that the school might not recognize.

59 Note that in *Discourse on the Method* Descartes includes as the first maxim of a provisional moral code that he will

obey the laws and customs of my country, holding constantly to the religion in which by God's grace I had been instructed from my childhood, and governing myself in all other matters according to the most moderate and least extreme opinions.

(AT 6:23, CSM 1:122)

But he will not obey the laws and customs of his country because he has a proof that they are right, and he adds that "there may be men as sensible among the

The increased independence of finite will

A related respect in which a finite mind increases its perfection is by taking steps to have its will be less encumbered. Descartes says in some passages that finite wills are already similar to the divine will, for example in the Fourth Meditation (AT 7:57, CSM 2:40), but a finite will also has a significant amount of room to develop, especially in terms of its independence. Descartes makes very clear that a common circumstance for a finite will is for its activity to be at the mercy of bodily and other forces. He says about the passions that sometimes they "jostle the will in opposite ways[,]... render[ing] the soul enslaved and miserable."[60] He also provides the straightforward example of the individual who is in the grip of fear and who is unable to think calmly or clearly:

> fear or terror... [is] a disturbance or astonishment of the soul which deprives it of the power to resist the evils which it thinks lie close at hand.[61]

Persians or Chinese as among ourselves" (ibid.). (See also the discussion in Chapter 2, pp. 33-36.) The reason that he will obey the laws and customs of his country is that he "thought it would be most useful for me to be guided by those with whom I should have to live." That is, he recognizes that the laws and customs of one's community are a fact on the ground that one needs to take into account in amassing the information on the basis of which firm and informed judgments are generated. For a further discussion of the provisional morality of the *Discourse*, see Marshall (2003). The other three maxims of Descartes' provisional morality are (1) "to be as firm and decisive in my actions as I could" (AT 6:24, CSM 1:123), (2)"to master myself rather than fortune, and change my desires rather than the order of the world" AT 6:25, CSM 1:123), and (3) "to review the various occupations which men have in this life, in order to try to choose the best" (AT 6:27, CSM 1:124). The first and second of these are confirmed (and made non-provisional) in Descartes' later correspondence and in *The Passions of the Soul* – after he has unpacked the relationship between God, supreme perfection, and the good. The occupation he selects is that of a philosopher and natural scientist who works to understand the interdependence of creatures and the ways in which minds and bodies might be reconfigured to result in increased perfection.

60 *Passions* I.48, AT 11:367, CSM 1:347.
61 *Passions* III.174, AT 11:462, CSM 1:392.

The will is not wholly independent in such cases, and part of the program of *The Passions of the Soul* is to provide guidance on how a finite mind might take steps to create a buffer between its will and the influences that adulterate its behavior. In another passage he writes that the condition of our body is a factor that constrains the activity of our will:

> although when thriving in an adult and healthy body the mind enjoys some liberty to think of other things than those presented by the senses, we know there is not the same liberty in those who are sick or asleep or very young; and the younger they are, the less liberty they have.[62]

Here Descartes is echoing the language that we have already seen in Sections 71–74 of Part I of *Principles of Philosophy*. At a very young age, our attention focuses almost exclusively on material bodies that might be a benefit or threat to our existence. But we continue to focus on our embodiment even when we are older and have more security – and more time and space for reflection. He had said in *Principles* I.73 that our embodied nature is such that it is very difficult to attend to what is not perceived through the senses and that we tire easily if we attempt to think too much (AT 8A:37, CSM 1:220). And again he holds that we are

> so constituted that our mind needs much relaxation if it is to be able to spend usefully a few moments in the search for truth. Too great application to study does not refine the mind, but wears it down.[63]

A finite will is free on its own and "by its nature,"[64] but when it is half of a mind-body union it is often constrained by external bodies and other influences. Still, independence of finite will is a desideratum, and there are steps by which to make it free from forces that weigh it down.

---

62 "To Hyperaspistes, August 1641," AT 3:424, CSMK 190. Descartes says here not just that we sometimes have a reduced liberty to act, but a reduced liberty to think.

63 "To Princess Elizabeth, 6 October 1645," AT 4:307, CSMK 268–269.

64 *Passions* I.41, AT 11:359, CSM 1:343.

Descartes does not hold that the freedom of a finite will consists in a libertarian two-way ability to do otherwise. Instead, what it is for a finite will to be free is for its activity to be unencumbered.[65] Freedom of will is thus a state that we need to engender and is not a feature that a will (or an embodied will) has automatically. As a will becomes more independent, fewer and fewer causes act on it, and its activity is entirely its own. It is therefore to be praised and blamed when it acts freely; then and only then is it the source of the activity in virtue of which praise and blame are attributed.[66] A mind is a mind whether it is attached to a body or not – and the will of a mind is free by its nature whether that mind is attached to a body or not – but when a mind is attached to a body it is subject to many influences. Until a will is entirely free and independent of these, it is not free and independent: a will is sometimes jostled in opposite directions; passions like fear and terror deprive it of the power to resist evils that are close at hand. What it means for a will to be free is not for it to exercise a libertarian two-way ability to do otherwise but for it to have its encumbrances removed. Descartes is then supposing that there are steps that a mind might take to lessen its dependence on the body to which it is attached so that its states are not due to anything other than its own unobstructed activity. That free and unobstructed activity is a finite approximation of supreme perfection and as such has extremely high value. Descartes thus says that activities that depend on us are an appropriate target of desire:

> the error we commit most commonly with respect to our desires is failure to distinguish adequately the things which depend wholly on us from those which do not depend on us at all. Regarding those which depend only on us – that is, on our free will – our knowledge of their goodness ensures that we cannot desire them with too much ardour....[67]

---

65 See also the discussion in Chapter 6, pp. 229–230.
66 See Chapter 6, pp. 223–228, and *Principles* I.37, AT 8A:18–19, CSM 1:205. In the latter, Descartes says that when a person is the source of his own activity he is "the author of his actions and [is] deserving of praise for what he does."
67 *Passions* II.144, AT 11:436–437, CSM 1:379.

In recommending that we engage in activities that depend on us and our free will, Descartes is not encouraging us to employ our will with more intensity to force conditions to be as we want them to be. Quite the opposite. He is suggesting that we narrow down our activities to those that are more a product of volitional activity and understanding.[68] In the case of the train example, he would not suggest that we take steps to force an adjustment to the local commerce schedule, and the commerce schedule of the next town and the next; nor would he suggest that we engage an effort to have school start and end a few hours later each day. To do either would be to engage in behavior in which the outcome does not depend wholly (or even largely) on us. We would benefit instead from having an ever larger percentage of our activity be the product of us – which is to say, a product of firm and determinate maxims that we have generated. If we act by a maxim that is informed by our increased understanding of trains, and schools, more of our activity is due to us as its cause. The larger outcome of our activity – whether or not we make it to our important meeting, but more importantly whether or not we are frustrated or satisfied, or joyful or sad – will depend more on us and our adherence to informed and resolute maxims. We will be more independent, and our activity will be more often due to a free and unencumbered will. We will experience joy and contentment, and we will possess a kind of cognitive armor by which to move in the direction of further perfection still.

Descartes touts the benefits of a state in which our activity is free and independent and is the product of firm and determinate

---

68 Brown (2006) notes that this might be Descartes' view on the freedom of finite will, and she points to historical predecessors like Boethius who held that free acts are those that have internal mental causes only – for example judgments and processes of deliberation (173–76) – whether they are necessitated or not. But Brown argues that in the end "Descartes' own position with regard to determinism and free will is nothing short of obscure" (174). I hope that I have argued successfully in Chapter 6 that Descartes subscribes to a compatibilist view of freedom. I also hope that I argued successfully in Chapter 5 that Descartes holds more generally that in no case does there exist the possibility that things be other than they are.

judgments that are updated and informed through the quest for increased knowledge. He calls this state *generosity*:

> I believe that true generosity, which causes a person's self-esteem to be as great as it may legitimately be, has only two components. The first consists in knowing that nothing truly belongs to him but this freedom to dispose his volitions, and that he ought to be praised or blamed for no other reason than using his freedom well or badly. The second consists in his feeling within himself a firm and constant resolution to use it well – that is, never to lack the will to undertake and carry out whatever he judges to be best. To do that is to pursue virtue in a perfect manner.[69]

The state of mind that Descartes defines as generosity would appear to be somewhat removed from the everyday notion of generosity – the other-directed notion that is more about helping others to acquire goods that they lack and about being charitable and understanding in the interpretation of their behavior. But as we will see, the generous individual (as Descartes understands him or her) does stand toward others in a way that is reflective of the more standard notion. In recognizing our freedom and acting from it, we no doubt become happy and content ourselves: we "acquire the habit of governing our desires so that their fulfillment depends only on us, making it possible for them always to give us complete satisfaction."[70] However, we also recognize the value of the freedom and activity of others – and the place of independent and unencumbered minds on the scale of perfection – and we act accordingly. Generosity is in part a matter of appreciating the value of the will that we possess – a will that is free and independent and an approximation of perfection, so long as it is excavated from influences that hinder its activity. But we recognize that other minds are also diamonds in the rough, and we treat them as such. We focus on the diamond and what it would be were not for the crust.[71] Arguably, that is generosity at its core.

---

69 *Passions* III.153, AT 11:445–446, CSM 1:384.

70 *Passions* II.146; AT 11:440, CSM 1:381.

71 Descartes writes for example that "there is no person so imperfect that we could not have for him a very perfect friendship, given that we believe

Creaturely perfection

Descartes supposes that there are a number of goods among the creation. He holds that minds are more noble than bodies, for example, and that human minds are especially noble if they achieve a buffer from bodily influences and the bulk of their activity is the self-guided product of informed and resolute judgments. He also says that bodies admit of perfection, though on the spectrum of non-being to perfection they are lower than a mind.[72] There are also passages in which he speaks of a more fine-grained ability to distinguish good from bad, for example:

> we must use experience and reason in order to distinguish good from evil and know their true value, so as not to take the one for the other or rush into anything immoderately.[73]
>
> The right use of reason..., by giving a true knowledge of the good, prevents virtue from being false.[74]

In some passages, he then identifies particular goods – for example, health and beauty.[75] However, he nowhere offers an analysis of the nature of goodness that is on a par with the analysis that he provides of other natures – for example, those of mind and body in the Second Meditation. He identifies supreme perfection with God, and he holds that God creates a universe that exhibits perfection on a spectrum. But he does not locate clear and distinct perceptions that tell us where things are on the spectrum exactly: he just identifies some things as good and less good, making a few comparative judgments here and there. He does say that our earliest assessments of things as "good" or "bad" do not automatically reflect their position on the scale. In many cases, they reflect a perspective that is selfish and narcissistic

---

ourselves loved by him and that we have a truly noble and generous soul" (*Passions* II.83, AT 11:390, CSM 1:357).

72 See Chapter 1, p. 28, and Chapter 2, pp. 46–57.

73 *Passions* II.138, AT 11:431, CSM 1:377.

74 "To Princess Elizabeth, 4 August 1645;" AT 4:267, CSMK 258.

75 "To Chanut, 6 June 1647," AT 5:55, CSMK 321; *Passions* III.154, AT 11:446, CSM 1:384.

and in need of emendation. Our final assessments of finite value are bound to be imprecise, but Descartes offers a number of guidelines and parameters by which to achieve distance from non-being.

Descartes supposes that all of creation participates in value and that there is reason to associate with it: "there is nothing real which does not have some goodness in it."[76] Finite minds have value, as we are created in the image of God and exhibit a significant degree of perfection. We are thus well-advised to focus our attention on our own mentality and the mentality of others. But material things still have some value as well:

> Because the pleasures of the body are minor, it can be said in general that it is possible to make oneself happy without them. However, I do not think that they should be altogether despised, or even that one should free oneself altogether from the passions.[77]

In the same letter, he speaks of "the value of all of the perfections, both of the body and of the soul" (AT 4:4:286–287, CSMK 265, emphasis). All of creation has at least some value, Descartes says, and although he does not provide many examples of the goods of the body, he does provide a few. He says for example that the things that "can give us supreme contentment can be divided into two classes: those which depend on us…, and those which do not, like honors, riches and health."[78] He grants that one who has riches and health is better off than one who does not, so long as "the two are equally wise and virtuous" (ibid.). A person who is not wise or virtuous will be worse off than a person who is wise and virtuous and materially destitute, but Descartes is granting the obvious fact that one who has modest riches and good health is better able to avoid the illness and stress that interfere with higher goods – for example, increased knowledge and independence. Such a person would also be in a better position to demarcate a quiet and non-chaotic space

---

76 *Passions* II.140, AT 11:433, CSM 1:378.
77 "To Princess Elizabeth, 1 September 1645," AT 4:287, CSMK 265.
78 "To Princess Elizabeth, 4 August 1645," AT 4:264, CSMK 257.

for themselves, and they would have more opportunities to practice the calibration of their passions. Material wealth might also provide us with more and better venues for interfacing with finite minds.

Descartes supposes that there are other aspects of materiality that have value as well. He says for example that the larger universe has value – that even though every creature is relatively minor, "we must weigh our smallness against the greatness of the created universe, observing how all created things depend on God, and regarding them in a manner proper to his omnipotence."[79] He says similarly in the Fourth Meditation that each and every creature has a significance that might go unnoticed if we ignore its place in the larger whole (AT 7:56–57, CSM 2:39). He goes on to provide a specific example in the Sixth Meditation. He points out that "a clock constructed with wheels and weights observes all the laws of its nature just as closely when it is badly made and tells the wrong time" (CSM 2:58, AT 7:84). In Principles II.36, he infers from the supreme perfection of God that all bodies follow an immutable order (AT 8A:61, CSM 1:240); like a broken clock, they exhibit that order exactly, even if they sometimes behave in a way that runs counter to our expectations and interests. Bodies exist somewhere on the scale of non-being to perfection, and some aspects of materiality are higher on the scale than others. There are the orderly patterns exhibited in music, parahelia, snowflakes, barometric pressure, rainbows, the planets of the solar system, the occurrence of the passions, the physiology of the human body, and the winds and the rain. The whole material nature is also a single substance[80]; it approaches a level of independence that its modifications do not.

Descartes also speaks of a kind of union that we might achieve with other creatures – material things included. He writes,

> when we... unite ourselves willingly to all the things he has created, then the more great, noble and perfect we reckon them, the more highly we esteem ourselves as being parts of a more perfect whole....[81]

---

79 "To Chanut, 1 February 1647," AT 4:609, CSMK 309.
80 See Chapter 1, pp. 13–18.
81 "To Chanut, 6 June 1647," AT 5:56, CSMK 322.

Here Descartes references a union that we can achieve with creatures –
minds and bodies both. He writes in *Passions* II.83,

> We may, I think, more reasonably distinguish kinds of love
> according to the esteem which we have for the object we love,
> as compared with ourselves. For when we have less esteem for it
> than for ourselves, we have only a simple affection for it; when
> we esteem it equally with ourselves, that is called 'friendship';
> and when we have more esteem for it, our passion may be called
> 'devotion'. Thus, we may have affection for a flower, a bird, or
> a horse; but unless our mind is very disordered, we can have
> friendship only for persons.
>
> (AT 11:390, CSM 1:357)

We may have affection for a flower, bird, or horse, as these exhibit
perfection, and with them, we are parts of a more perfect whole.
Descartes does not say exactly what it is in which our union with
a flower or bird or horse would consist. Perhaps we recognize that
each is eventually contiguous with our body in the plenum or perhaps we register that in concert with our body each exhibits an
immutable and exceptionless order. Or perhaps Descartes has in
mind an analogue of the intimate union that a mind achieves with
its body, where the less perfect is subordinated to the more perfect.
We might consider the case of the chef who becomes so good at
cooking that the instruments of the kitchen become an extension of
their body. The chef maneuvers a spoon or pan almost as seamlessly
as they maneuver the fingers that are grasping it. Or we might consider the pianist who is one with the piano that they are playing, or
the dancer who is one with their (equally perfect) partner. Descartes
does not suppose that forming a union with another creature would
be a matter of achieving a theoretical understanding of how a mind
and body unite; that is not in the cards. Nor does he have to say that
the unions that we form with other creatures are as durable or long-
lasting as those that our minds have with our bodies: the expert chef
is not always in the kitchen, but its instruments are ready-at-hand.
Descartes does not offer specific examples of what it would be for a
mind-body composite to unite with additional bodies in a way that
recognizes and incorporates the perfection of those bodies and that

increases our activity in going with the grain of their behavior.[82] But it is easy to imagine cases that are in line with the kind of union that he does highlight – mind-body union – and it is easy to see how these would be a matter of increased independence and knowledge.[83] Anyone would agree who has trained to ride a horse, or who is an expert bird-watcher or botanist.

Descartes is also thinking that we unite to bodies and other creatures when we do not have an eye to what we *want* them to do, but we observe them from a perspective that is disinterested, and we coordinate our own behavior accordingly. In that vein he speaks of the love of God or the love of supreme perfection. Descartes appears to hold that one way to love God is to attempt to align with the immutable series of creatures that God has willed for all eternity. He writes,

> Joining himself willingly entirely to God, he [the person who has meditated properly] loves him so perfectly that he desires nothing at all except that his will should be done. Henceforth, because he knows that nothing can befall him which God has not decreed, he no longer fears death, pain or disgrace. He so loves this divine decree, deems it so just and so necessary, and knows that he must be so completely subject to it that even when he expects it to bring death or some other evil, he would not will to change it even if, *per impossible*, he could do so.[84]

Here Descartes is suggesting that one way to love God is to embrace the products of His will as they unfold, and not to resist them.[85] All that exists (apart from God) is what He wills immutably and for eternity, and that is what is good, and so it makes no sense either to desire or expect anything else. A hard pill to swallow, Descartes is in effect asking us to undertake a significant revision of our sense of the good. He would add however that we are more than compensated

---

82 But see the discussion in Garrett (2018), in which environmentalist implications of Descartes' view on union with the plenum are explored.

83 See also the discussion in Brown and Normore (2019), Chapter 7.

84 "To Chanut, 1 February 1647," AT 4:609, CSMK 309–310.

85 See also Brown (2006), 178–182, and Chukurian (2018), 386–391.

by the realistic attitude that we develop and by the corresponding evolution of our passions. God authors all of creaturely reality by a single immutable and eternal act, and there does not exist the possibility that His will be otherwise. Whatever happens has to happen exactly as it does – reflecting an immutable order of creatures that exhibit varying levels of perfection. If we register and understand as much, we will never be frustrated or upset. In a passage that merits (partial) re-citing, Descartes writes,

> we should reflect upon the fact that nothing can possibly happen other than as Providence has determined from all eternity. Providence is, so to speak, a fate or immutable necessity, which we must set against Fortune in order to expose the latter as a chimera which arises solely from an error of our intellect. For we can desire only what we consider in some way to be possible; and things which do not depend on us can be considered possible only in so far as they are thought to depend on Fortune – that is to say, in so far as we judge that they may happen and that similar things have happened at other times. But this opinion is based solely on our not knowing all the causes which contribute to each effect. For when a thing we considered to depend on Fortune does not happen, this indicates that one of the causes necessary for its production was absent, and consequently that it was absolutely impossible and that no similar thing has ever happened, i.e. nothing for the production of which a similar cause was also absent. Had we not been ignorant of this beforehand, we should never have considered it possible and consequently we should never have desired it.[86]

Here Descartes is highlighting his doctrine of the divine preordination of all events, and he is pairing it with the Third Meditation view that all creaturely reality has a sufficient cause for every aspect of its existence (AT 7:41, CSM 2:28–29; AT 7:135, CSM 2:97) and the Sixth Meditation and *Principles* II.36 view that the same cause always brings about the same effect (AT 7:87–88, CSM 2:60; AT 8A:61–62,

---

86 *Passions* II.145, AT 11:438, CSM 1:380.

CSM 1:240).[87] We sometimes encounter situations in which all the same causes seem to be in place, but different effects ensue, and we easily conclude that the difference in effects is due to chance. For example, we might look at the clouds on a given day and see that they are in the same arrangement as yesterday, and that the temperature is exactly the same, but today we encounter rain. Or we might interact with a colleague at the same time every day just prior to their class, and they are always calm and cheerful, but today they snap at us in anger. We might conclude that their reaction is random, but Descartes is arguing that because the effects are different, the causes had to be different as well. Perhaps our colleague had a really bad class earlier in the week, and they are nervous about returning. Or perhaps they received extremely bad news the day before and have not slept, and they are not in their usual psychological place. Descartes does not suppose that any finite mind would ever be able to piece together all of the reasons why and how things happen as they do, but we are in a position to come up with firm and resolute maxims that are informed by the best information that we have at our disposal.[88] To recognize that everything has to happen exactly as it does is a start. We unite with God – in a way – by making judgments that are in line with his immutable and eternal decree, or at the very least we make the judgment that everything that happens is the consequence of that decree.

Descartes says that nothing can possibly happen other than Providence has determined for all eternity. He also says that a finite mind could not have the slightest mental modification without

---

87 For the latter, see also *Conversation with Burman*, AT 5:164, CSMK 346.

88 Nor does Descartes anywhere suggest that a human being would be wise to attempt to figure out what is and is not possible and then limit their desires and expectations accordingly. No human being is ever in a position to do either, but we proceed on the basis of the information that we have at the moment of action. See also Brown (2006), 179–180. Descartes echoes Epictetus (1983), but not the view that the wise person "has kept off all desire from himself" or that "His impulses toward everything are diminished" (Section 48, p. 27). Instead, Descartes would agree with the language in Section 27 of the *Handbook* according to which it is appropriate to have enthusiastic desires and goals, so long as we adhere to firm and informed maxims in our pursuit of them.

God having willed immutably and for all eternity that we have that mental modification, and he adds that the immutable divine volition that decrees all events for eternity reaches down to the particular actions of finite minds.[89] He allows that it is a mystery why we would (sometimes) have an experience of utter independence if God has preordained all events for eternity, and a mystery indeed it is.[90] He also says that in everyday action there is no demand that we regard our mental modifications as having been decided immutably from eternity. In the face of our experience of independence, that is not in the cards.[91] Apart from our own mental activity, we are wise to regard everything else to be necessitated:

> As for the rest, although we must consider their outcome to be wholly fated and immutable, so as to prevent our desire from occupying itself with them, yet we must not fail to consider the reasons which make them more or less predictable, so as to use these reasons in governing our actions.
>
> (AT 11:439, CSM 1:380)

Descartes says that "nothing can befall [us] which God has not decreed" (AT 4:609, CSMK 310) – including the behavior of others. He does not subscribe to a libertarian view of freedom that exempts the modifications of finite minds from the eternal and immutable decree of God. Instead, he supposes that we can use our knowledge of what is possible and what is not to inform our expectations of the behavior of other creatures – finite minds included. We can also use it to inform our reactions to that behavior in retrospect.

Hate and contempt

One of the benefits of regarding everything (else) as necessitated is not just that we will have a perspective that is more realistic and truthful. We will also never (or rarely) experience discombobulating passions like hate or anger or contempt. Descartes writes,

---

89　"To Princess Elizabeth, 6 October 1645," AT 4:314–15, CSMK 272–273. See also Chapter 6 above, pp. 214–223.

90　*Principles* I.41, AT 8A:20, CSM 1:206. See also Chapter 6, pp. 216–217, 219–220.

91　See Chapter 6 above, pp. 219–222.

[S]uch people never have contempt for anyone. Although they often see that others do wrong in ways that show up their weakness, they are nevertheless more inclined to excuse than to blame them and to regard such wrong-doing as due rather to lack of knowledge rather than lack of a virtuous will.[92]

When there is information that a person does not have – and it is not anywhere reflected in their mental modifications – it is not available to the person and cannot serve as part of the reason for their action. The person might be acting in the light of a confused or incomplete understanding of the good or a confused or incomplete understanding of their immediate environment. If we knew that in advance of our interaction with the person, we would never have expected that they might act differently, and we would not feel hatred: "Had we not been ignorant of this beforehand, we should never have considered it [an alternative outcome] possible and consequently we should never have desired it." Or perhaps we only come to appreciate their cognitive situation after the fact, if we come to appreciate it at all. Or perhaps their cognitive situation is entirely off-limits to us. If so, we would at best register that some cognitive variables or others led them to see and act as they did, and our reaction would adjust accordingly. We would confront the situation armed with a firm and determinate maxim; our reaction to the person's behavior would be the product of activity.

The case of incomplete information is quite revealing in the context of Descartes' understanding of self-activity and increased perfection. A generous person attempts to acquire as much information as they are able in the formation of their firm and resolute maxims, but there are always things that the person will miss. Descartes admits that; he says that in the case of any given action all that we are able to do is "the best that our intellect was able to recognize" (AT 11:440, CSM 1:381).[93] We are only able to act in the light of the information that we possess, and instead of feeling frustration or sadness at an unanticipated outcome, we feel joy. We recognize that we did all that we could given the information that we had been able to amass, and we approximate the perfection of immutability and independence in

---

92 *Passions* III.153, AT 11:446, CSM 1:384.
93 See also "To Princess Elizabeth, 6 October 1645," AT 4:307, CSMK 269.

not becoming discombobulated. We update our maxims further still, and we move closer to a finite approximation of omniscience. We are then wise to take a similar perspective on the behavior of others, Descartes supposes, as the actions of others can only be the product of modifications that are actually present in their thinking.[94] Instead of being angry or frustrated or contemptuous toward a person who acts in a way that we dislike, there is an entirely different reaction that is more perfect – a reaction that is a product of our own states and, more precisely, of firm and informed maxims that have as their object the behavior of human minds. If others are only able to act on the basis of the information that they actually possess, it is to be expected that they would make mistakes. Or, they might have a timidity that makes them less able to endure misfortune with forbearance. Or, they might be subject to a fear that deprives them of the power to resist an evil. Or, they might have a skewed sense of the relative quality of things and where those things stand on the spectrum of perfection: for example, a person might choose riches over a connection to another mind. Descartes accordingly holds that "vice usually proceeds from ignorance,"[95] though he also allows that passions like timidity and fear misdirect the will as well. A finite will is on its own and by its nature free and has value. A will that is encrusted with a body is also a diamond, even if it is still in the rough. The appropriate stance toward such an entity is never to hate it: "hatred… should be rejected by the soul."[96] We might instead be generous toward them, and have good will, even if there are pragmatic reasons for keeping our distance in the short term.

Descartes accordingly writes that

> Hatred… cannot be so mild as to be harmless, and it is never devoid of sadness. I say it cannot be too mild because, however much the hatred of an evil moves us to an action, we could always be moved to it even more effectively by love of the contrary good.[97]

---

94 See also Williston (2003), 324.

95 *Passions* III.160, AT 11:452, CSM 1:387.

96 *Passions* II.142, AT 11:434, CSM 1:378.

97 *Passions* II.140, AT 11:433, CSM 1:377. See also Tate (2017), 345–348.

There is no sense to hating another human being if Descartes is right. An individual who acts from a lack of information might have acted differently if they had had the relevant information, but they did not have it, and so it did not guide their behavior. Or, we might hate a person because they pursue something that is very low on the scale of perfection, but Descartes would point out that there is something that they fail to recognize and that we recognize much better. We might hate the person; or, we might experience a more effective level of motivation by loving the contrary good of their coming to have more knowledge. On the basis of our clearer vision, we might judge that the mind of the person is high on the scale of perfection and with assistance could be even higher:

> wealth or humour, or even… more intelligence, knowledge or beauty… seem to them to be very unimportant, by contrast with the virtuous will for which alone they esteem themselves, and which they suppose also to be present, or at least capable of being present, in every other person.[98]

It is therefore inappropriate to hate a creature that has a mind and a will or to abandon them to their confusion:

> those who are the most generous and strong-minded, in that they fear no evil for themselves and hold themselves to be beyond the power of fortune, are not free from compassion when they see the infirmities of other men and hear their complaints. For it is part of generosity to have good will towards everyone.[99]

Descartes adds that it is also not inappropriate to pity an individual with infirmities, so long as we focus on their limitations and what they preclude. The object of the pity of the greatest individuals is not weak individuals themselves, but their weakness, and their inability

---

98 Passions III.154, AT 11:446–447, CSM 1:384.
99 Passions III.187, AT 11:469–470, CSM 1:395.

to endure misfortune with forbearance.[100] Toward the individuals themselves a different stance is appropriate:

> I say that this love is extremely good because by joining real goods to us it makes us to that extent more perfect. I say also that it cannot be too great, for all that the most excessive love can do is to join us so perfectly to these goods that the love we have especially for ourselves must apply to them as well as to us, and this, I believe, can never be bad. And it is necessarily followed by joy, because it represents to us what we love as a good thing belonging to us.[101]

We might desire that a person act differently, but as soon as we recognize that that is not possible, our desire dissipates, and we instead act from the good will that we have toward others and a desire to increase their perfection. We experience joy in developing our own independence of will, but we experience joy upon witnessing the increased perfection of others as well. They will generate their own maxims, hopefully, and they will appreciate the order in the reality that surrounds them. Instead of coveting bodies, they might covet an understanding of bodies, and they might compare notes in an effort to make their knowledge more comprehensive, more public, and more impactful. Instead of feeling hatred at the loss of an object that might have been taken from us – an object that can only be possessed by a few[102] – we recognize that there was no loss and that instead there might be a gain.

Descartes thus emphasizes the value of a kind of union with other minds. He says that because minds are more valuable than bodies, they merit more attention:

> It is the nature of love to make one consider oneself and the object loved as a single whole of which one is but a part; and to transfer the care one previously took of oneself to the preservation of this whole. One keeps for oneself only a part of one's

---

100 Ibid., AT 11:470, CSM 1:395.
101 *Passions* II.139, AT 11:432, CSM 1:377.
102 "To Chanut, 6 June 1647," AT 5:55, CSMK 321.

care, a part which is great or little in proportion to whether one thinks oneself a larger or smaller part of the whole to which one has given one's affection. So if we are joined willingly to an object which we regard as less than ourselves – for instance, if we love a flower, a bird, a building or some such thing – the highest perfection which this love can properly reach cannot make us put our life at any risk for the preservation of such things. For they are not among the nobler parts of the whole which we and they constitute any more than our nails or our hair are among the nobler parts of our body....[103]

In this passage, Descartes is applying his view that goodness is exhibited on a spectrum from non-being to perfection and arguing that it is appropriate for us to prioritize creatures that have minds over creatures that do not.[104] He says that we might become part of a larger whole with such minds – for example, by developing friendships that downplay our own self-interest and emphasize instead the union of which we are a part (ibid.). It is difficult to think that Descartes is not appealing here to a couple of views that are in the background of his thought – the view that individual minds are united with regions of body and the view that the material universe is a single substance with pockets of mentality throughout.[105] He says in another letter that

though each of us is a person distinct from others, whose interests are accordingly in some way different from those of the rest of the world, we ought still to think that none of us could subsist alone and that each one of us is really one of the many parts of the universe, and more particularly a part of the earth, the state, the society and family to which we belong by our domicile....[106]

---

103 "To Chanut, 1 February 1647;" 4:611–612, CSMK 311.
104 He also reinforces the view that our bodies have perfections when he says that "our nails and our hair" are not among the "nobler parts of our body," in contrast to the parts of the body (like presumably the eyes and the heart) that are especially sophisticated. See the discussion in Chapter 2 above, pp. 48–56.
105 See the discussion in Chapter 1, pp. 13–19.
106 "To Princess Elizabeth, 15 September 1645;" AT 4:293, CSMK 266.

No human being could subsist alone, for example, as we all need food, water, sunlight, and other items on which we depend, and we are influenced by the bodies that surround us. We are regularly bombarded with sense perceptions, and if our own neural states can make our mind enslaved to a passion, the behavior of others can contribute to the occurrence of a passion as well. We benefit from becoming more independent, Descartes supposes, but others still have an influence on us in the process, and that influence might as well be positive – especially in the course of the effort to become more perfect. Descartes therefore adds that part of what it is to love others is to connect with them in such a way that the boundary that demarcates our self is more aligned with the metaphysical fact that there are no true borders in nature: "if someone considers himself part of the community, he delights in doing good to everyone" (ibid.). We become a larger being, in effect, and just like we care about the heart and liver in our own individual body, we care about the other minds that are affixed to the matter that surrounds us and that constitutes a more homogeneous whole. Descartes then adds another strike against hatred: "In the case of hatred, we consider ourselves alone as a whole entirely separated from the thing for which we have an aversion."[107] The passion of hatred betrays the truth that creatures together constitute a whole whose internal boundaries are more fluid than is usually thought.

An active recognition of our limits

For all his optimism, Descartes allows that no human being ever becomes fully independent. He recognizes that we are attached to bodies and that events take place in our bodies that sometimes divert our attention and get the best of us. In many of his discussions about a particular passion, he speaks of the large number of bodily processes that occur on their own and without our knowledge, but that still affect our psychological states. He says for example that sometimes we can find ourselves feeling the passion of sadness even if we do not know why:

---

107 *Passions* II.80, 11:387, CSM 1:356.

[W]hen we are in good health and things are calmer than usual, we feel in ourselves a cheerfulness which results not from any operation of the understanding but solely from impressions formed in the brain by the movement of the spirits. And we feel sad in the same way when our body is indisposed even though we do not know that it is.[108]

Here Descartes is describing a fairly common experience, in which we experience a mood but we cannot quite put our finger on why we are in the mood. Descartes does not have the resources to offer a complete account of the physiology of the nerves in such cases. The descriptions that he provides might seem very quaint, but he is not offering them so that we know the detailed causes of every one of our psychological states. He is offering them to make sure that it registers just how much is happening in the body at all times. In the same way that we are constantly bombarded with sense perceptions, there is constant activity on the inside of our body as well. There is the spleen and the heart and the liver, and the intestines, kidneys, and lungs. There are also brain traces that have registered previous events in our past, along with passions that might be activated by an unexpected or unnoticed prompt. We thus find ourselves experiencing passions of sadness and cheerfulness, and also hatred, even if we are not sure why. Descartes writes,

Sometimes, on the other hand, there came to the heart a juice of an alien nature.... This caused the spirits rising from the heart to the brain to produce the passion of hatred in the soul. At the same time these spirits went from the brain to nerves capable of driving blood from the spleen and the minute veins of the liver to the heart so as to prevent this harmful juice from entering it; and they also went to nerves capable of driving this juice back to the intestines and stomach, or capable sometimes of making the stomach regurgitate it. As a result these same movements usually accompany the passion of hatred.[109]

---

108 *Passions* II.94, AT 11:398–399, CSM 1:361.
109 *Passions* II.108, AT 11:408, CSM 1:366.

Descartes has to know that the identification of something as an alien juice is not especially helpful in terms of carving nature at the joints or enabling us to understand the inner workings of the body. What he does emphasize accurately is how much activity there is in the body and nervous system at a given moment, and how such activity bears on the tranquility and immutability of its mind. He is offering guidance to enable us to become more and more independent of bodily processes over which we have little say. We are not independent already, and we will never be fully independent, but independence is a state for us to keep in mind and a state to which it would be wise for us to aspire.

Sometimes there is very little that we are able to do to neutralize an unwelcome passion. We get upset and worked up in some instances, and we just need to let our discombobulation sort itself out. If our thoughts are being pulled in all manner of directions, then realistically speaking the best thing to do is to wait to calm down. Descartes writes,

> [T]hose who are strongly inclined by nature to the emotions of joy, pity, fear and anger, cannot prevent themselves from fainting, weeping, or trembling, or from having their blood all in turmoil just as if they had a fever, when their imagination is strongly affected by the object of one of those passions. But there is something we can always do on such occasions, which I think I can put forward here as the most general, and most readily applicable remedy against all excesses of the passions. When we feel our blood agitated in this way, we should take heed, and recollect that everything presented to the imagination tends to mislead the soul and make the reasons for pursuing the object of its passion appear much stronger than they are, and the reasons for not pursuing this object much weaker. When the passion urges us to pursue ends whose attainment involves some delay, we must refrain from making any immediate judgement about them, and distract ourselves by other thoughts until time and repose have completely calmed down the disturbance in our blood.[110]

---

110 *Passions* III.211, AT 11:486–487, CSM 1:403.

In such a case, we wait until our body calms down so that we can think independently and clearly. We consider reasons that help our body to calm down and think more clearly still. If we are too upset to do even that, we will look back later and appreciate that it wasn't in the cards for us to do any different.

Descartes holds that part of what is it to love another is to transfer to another the care that we take toward ourselves, and he says that to love is to embrace "the interests of that which one loves" (AT 4:611, CSMK 311). There is also our own interest, of course, but for Descartes self-interest and other interest to a significant degree coincide. What is in our self-interest is to become more perfect – for example, to become more independent, but we become more independent in a context in which we are already interdependent. We work on our own and with others to acquire more knowledge, to become active and free, to secure material objects to the extent that they promote our health and well-being, to recognize the immutable order in all that transpires, to experience the passions that are among the sweetest pleasures of human life, and to brace ourselves with cognitive armor that neutralizes passions that are discombobulating and unwelcome. As finite minds, we are relatively high on the scale of perfection, even if we are united to a body that limits our freedom. There are steps that we can take however to increase our perfection, and if we take these steps, we secure a lock on contentment, and we are more or less invincible. We arrive at knowledge of a small number of metaphysical principles – once in the course of life, with very occasional check-ups – and we apply them to the everyday situations that we confront. That finite minds are immaterial substances is an abstract metaphysical result, but it also carries along practical fruit. Knowledge of the existence of God is important for overcoming hyperbolic doubt – which is inane and incoherent – but it is critical for unpacking perfection in terms of independence, immutability, activity, and increased knowledge. It is also critical for arriving at non-sensory ideas and zeroing in on an accurate picture of the kinds of things that there are and the kinds of modifications they possess. Then we navigate particulars and generate maxims for how to live.

Two final comments merit emphasis. One is that Descartes is not in any way contradicting himself in offering a compatibilist view of freedom in conjunction with a view on how best to live.[111] God wills the entire series of creaturely reality by a single immutable volition – all the way down to the modifications of finite minds – and there does not exist the possibility that things happen other than they do. That recognition does not automatically entail that there will exist an attitude of quietism or despair across human minds, especially if that attitude is not a constituent of the series. We sometimes have a vivid experience of freedom, and we deliberate in the light of the reasons that are made available to us. We adhere to maxims that are grounded in ever-increasing knowledge, and we experience joy at the outcome of our actions, no matter what that outcome is. Or, if we experience passions like frustration or anger, we step back and recognize the causes that give rise to those, and we are active yet again. Perhaps on occasion, we also step back and notice that even that episode of reflection had to happen just as it did, and we are active yet again. We take something like a transcendental perspective[112] – one that might be laced with humor – but like all other creatures our volitions do not circumvent divine preordination. Or finally, we might reflect on the worry that libertarian freedom would not appear to give us any added control over our modifications, and arguably it would give us less.[113] If it turns out that we end up rather low on the spectrum of perfection, the fact remains (Descartes would say) that we are some-where on that spectrum and "there is nothing real which does not have some goodness in it" (AT 11:433, CSM 1:378).

A second comment is that Descartes' stoic ethics is not an intellectualist refuge for the elite. He is not telling impoverished and destitute individuals that they are to be content with the small amount that they have and that their energies are to be directed at securing immutability and knowledge. If anything, he is attempting to re-position those of us who do have resources. He is arguing that we do not need them in abundance and that a proper re-calibration of our desires – and a proper sensitivity to the standard of supreme

---

111 For example, Brown (2006) writes, "What room is there for virtue, we might ask, when everything, right down to our acts of assent, is governed by an immutable necessity" (182)?

112 Again see Williston (2003).

113 See the discussion in Chapter 6, pp. 248–249.

perfection – will motivate us to seek after very different things. We will seek after increased union with other minds. We will appreciate and study the order in the material universe that surrounds us, and we will make advances in medicine, mechanics, and morals. Descartes speaks against spending a lot time on abstract metaphysical matters – except to clear the ground – and says that "[t]he preservation of health has always been the principal end of my studies...."[114]. If we do what he is suggesting – namely, live well – then people of means will covet fewer material items, and issues of wealth and destitution will begin to fall by the wayside.[115] To the extent that material goods *do* facilitate increased perfection, they will be far more available. We unite with the material and intellectual substance that surrounds us and become a more substantial and less vulnerable individual. We become an approximation of immutability, omniscience, and independence. We are happy, and we thrive.

Further reading

There is a large literature that engages Descartes' work on the relationship between the passions and question of how best to live. A cross-section includes:

Shoshana Brassfield, "Never Let the Passions Be Your Guide: Descartes and the Role of the Passions," British Journal for the History of Philosophy 21 (2012), 459–477.

Deborah Brown, *Descartes and the Passionate Mind*, Cambridge and New York: Cambridge UP (2009).

Deborah Brown and Calvin Normore, *Descartes and the Ontology of Everyday Life*, New York and Oxford: Oxford UP (2019).

Ryan Garrett, "A Cartesian Approach to Environmental Ethics," Environmental Ethics 40 (2018), 261–268.

Sean Greenberg, "Descartes on the Passions. Function, Representation, and Motivation," Noûs 41 (2007), 714–734.

Marie Jayasekera, "'All in Their Nature Good': Descartes on the Passions of the Soul," Journal of the History of Philosophy 58 (2020), 71–92.

---

114 "To [The Marquess of Newcastle], October 1645;" AT 4:329, CSMK 275.

115 Here it is hard not to agree with Marquardt (2015), who argues (70–81) that although Descartes does not offer anything close to a view on how society is best structured, such a view can be assembled from his discussion of generosity and of the kinds of things that (after taking a very long road) are more fulfilling than the appropriation of bodies.

Sarah Marquardt, "The Long Road to Peace: Descartes' Modernization of Generosity in the Passions of the Soul (1649)," *History of Political Thought* 36 (2015), 53–83.

John Marshall, *Descartes's Moral Theory*, Ithaca, NY: Cornell UP (1998).

Daisie Radner, "The Function of the Passions," in *Passion and Virtue in Descartes*, ed. Byron Williston and André Gombay, Amherst, NY: Humanity Books (2003), 175–187.

Donald Rutherford, "Descartes' Ethics," in *The Stanford Encyclopedia of Philosophy* (Winter 2019 Edition), ed. Edward N. Zalta. https://plato.stanford.edu/archives/win2019/entries/descartes-ethics/.

Amy M. Schmitter, "Representation, Self-Representation, and the Passions in Descartes," *Review of Metaphysics* 48 (1994), 331–357.

Amy M. Schmitter, "How to Engineer a Human Being: Passions and Functional Explanation in Descartes," in *A Companion to Descartes*, ed. Janet Broughton and John Carriero, Oxford: Blackwell (2008), 426–444.

Lisa Shapiro, "Cartesian Generosity," *Acta Philosophica Fennica* 64 (1999), 249–275.

Lisa Shapiro, "Descartes on Human Nature and the Human Good," in *The Rationalists: Between Tradition and Innovation*, ed. Carlos Fraenkel, Dario Perinetti and Justin E.H. Smith, New York: Springer Publishing (2011), 13–26.

Cecilia Wee, "Self, Other, and Community in Cartesian Ethics," *History of Philosophy Quarterly* 19 (2002), 255–273.

Byron Williston and André Gombay (eds.), *Passion and Virtue in Descartes*, Amherst, NY: Humanity Books (2003).

Ten
Conclusion

Descartes writes that the whole of philosophy is like a tree with metaphysics as the roots, physics as the trunk, and medicine, mechanics, and morals as the branches.[1] The roots of a tree lie mostly invisible below the ground, and once they are in place they do not need much tending. It is the branches of the tree that bear fruit. But of course the roots are absolutely critical – they give shape to the particulars that emerge from the branches, and the fruits of one tree will often differ greatly from the fruits of another. Descartes thinks that the same applies in the case of the tree of philosophy. We arrive at a small number of metaphysical results: for example, that God exists and is the standard of perfection; that finite minds are immaterial substances; and that material things exhibit an order and sophistication that is not immediately apparent from a perspective that puts a lot of credence in the senses. We arrive at these metaphysical results – "once in the course of... life" (AT 7:17 CSM 2:12) and with occasional refreshers – but for the rest of our time, we own and express our embodiment. We proceed in a way that is informed by the roots of the tree of philosophy. We see and inhabit a different world, and we live and act accordingly.

Descartes is well-known for his skeptical arguments. He is also well-known for his turn inward toward non-sensory ideas that help to yield abstract metaphysical results. But his skeptical arguments are epistemic garbage, and that is one of the reasons that he holds that it is so easy to dislodge them. Their sole purpose is to enable us to identify

---

1 Preface to the French edition of *Principles of Philosophy*, AT 9B:14, CSM 1:186.

DOI: 10.4324/9781351210522-10

axioms and premises that are unimpeachable and that expose the premises of skeptical (and most other) arguments to be amateurish by comparison. We then arrive at metaphysical results, but we are not especially built for metaphysics, and the results at which we arrive are few and far between. For an embodied mind, there are occasional peaks of clear and distinct perception, but we spend the bulk of our time in the valleys of perception that is confused.

The results at which we arrive are nonetheless transformative. We recognize perfections in the beings that surround us, and we recognize that we ourselves have room to grow. We free our will of influences that encumber it. We not only cultivate but also modify and adjust our passions. For example, we target our wonder at matters of science, community, and human well-being. We also calibrate – and mitigate – our wonder about matters of metaphysical inquiry. To the extent that is possible for a human being, we become more independent, more wise, more agentic, and more free. I do have to admit that I struggle to make sense of my own agency on the assumption that I "could [not] ever do anything which was not already preordained by" God (AT 8A:20, CSM 1:206). That is not an objection to Descartes; he recognizes that our experience of independence and freedom is puzzling to say the least. Nor does there come any relief in noting that much of his picture of reality depends on the not-further-defended assumption that we have an idea of a supremely perfect being. But in at least one passage Descartes identifies God with "nature... in its general aspect" (AT 7:80, CSM 2:56), and that clearly exists. God is not a bearded man on a cloud: He is the insensible and wholly active source of all creaturely reality – uncaused, immutable, and eternal. Presumably there is *something* that is uncaused, and once it brings into being the things that are not uncaused, it is difficult to understand how the "slightest thought could enter into a person's mind" (AT 4:314, CSMK 272) without it being the result of some non-random causal process or other. Descartes appears to hold that we just cannot help regarding ourselves as free and independent – at least much of the time – and he is certainly right about that. He also appears to hold that we become more active and energized when we register and test applications of the non-sensory picture of reality that he has presented to us. He is certainly right about that as well.

Glossary

Note that here I am omitting terms whose definition is especially controversial in the Descartes literature, for example *divine freedom*. I just do not want to proceed as though my own definition of any such term is accepted as standard. But please reference the index for the page numbers of the book in which I lay out my attempt to capture Descartes' understanding of terms that I have left out below.

Note also that there are two outstanding resources that offer definitions of key terms that Descartes utilizes throughout his corpus. These are *A Descartes Dictionary* by John Cottingham, Oxford: Blackwell (1993) and *The Cambridge Descartes Lexicon* by Lawrence Nolan (ed.), Cambridge UP (2016).

abstraction: a cognitive operation in which a finite mind considers an idea in isolation and without considering (or comparing it to) a different idea.

analytic method: a method of discovery by which a finite mind uncovers a true idea – usually as a result of thinking through analogies that are confused and imprecise but that expose by comparison the clarity of the true idea itself.

animal spirits: the nerves of a human or animal body.

attribute: an unchanging feature of a substance.

clear and distinct perception: a non-sensory and utterly will-compelling grasp of a truth.

common notion: a non-sensory axiom or premise that is self-evident upon reflection.

conceptual distinction: the distinction between features of a thing that are inseparable from the thing to the point that they are nothing other than the thing.

confused idea: an idea that is a composite of true ideas and that attributes to the object of the idea features that do not pertain to it.

constant creation: the divine activity by which creatures are maintained in existence from moment to moment.

contingent existence: the kind of existence that had by entities that do not exist unless they are brought into existence by another entity.

embodied self: a thinking mind insofar as it is united to a body.

eminent reality: being that is sufficiently exalted that it can serve as a stand-in for an entity that has a lesser degree of reality.

empty space: being that is identical to extended substance but that we confusedly regard as nothingness.

error: the mismatch between the affirmation of an idea and reality.

essence (or nature): a feature of a thing that cannot be denied of it, or alternately the idea of such a feature.

eternal truth: a common notion that has no existence outside of a finite mind.

exclusion: a cognitive operation by which a finite mind considers an idea of some entity (X) and recognizes that a second idea (of Y) does not overlap with it in any way.

extension: material substance, or alternately the principal attribute of material substance.

finite intellect: the faculty by which a finite mind considers ideas that are the subject of possible judgments.

finite will: the faculty by which a finite mind affirms an idea.

finitude: a delimitation of infinitude.

force (of creatures): the power by which a finite creature is able to impact other creatures.

force (of God): the power by which God impacts creatures.

formal falsity: the mismatch between the affirmation of an idea and reality.

formal reality: the reality that is had by an object when it is the entity to which a true idea of the object conforms; alternately, it is the entity to which the true idea would conform if the idea existed.

freedom (of creatures): a finite mind's lack of encumbrance by material or other hindrances.

generosity: the recognition of the value of the independence of a finite will, paired with a commitment to steer the will by self-generated maxims that are firm and determinate and highly informed.

idea: a mental item by which entities are represented.

imagination: a corporeal faculty by which a finite mind pictures an image.

indefiniteness: the lack of a known limit or endpoint.

infinite intellect: the mind of God, in which willing, understanding, and creating are all identical.

infinite will: the mind of God, in which understanding, willing, and creating are all identical.

infinitude: being that has absolutely no limits.

judgment: the affirmation of an idea.

material falsity: confusion in an idea that provides the subject-matter for error, ensuring that affirmations of the idea will not conform to reality.

memory: a corporeal faculty of finite minds by which images record thoughts and perceptions.

metaphysics: the area of inquiry in which non-sensory ideas provide information about insensible objects.

mind: thinking substance.

modification: an impermanent feature or way of being of a substance.

moral certainty: a level of cognition that is sufficient for everyday purposes but that falls short of clear and distinct perception.

morality: a set of rules by which to guide our behavior.

motion: the change of position of a body with respect to the bodies that surround it.

natural light: the intellect of a finite mind insofar as it grasps a true idea.

necessary existence: the wholly independent existence of a being that exists by its own power.

negation: an absence that is not a deficiency.

objective being: the being that is had by an entity insofar as the entity exists in a finite mind.

objective reality: the representational reality or content of an idea in a finite mind.

passion: an affective state that is occasioned in a finite mind and is not experienced as a state of external bodies.

pineal gland: the region of the body at which the mind and body are united.

plenum: the stretch of contiguous and continuous bodies that is the material universe.

preservation: the divine activity by which creatures are maintained in existence from moment to moment, and the same activity by which God creates.

primitive notion: an idea that is part of the basic furniture of a finite mind, and an idea from which many other ideas follow.

principal attribute: the attribute of a substance through which all of the modifications of the substance are explicable and intelligible.

privation: an absence that is a deficiency.

real distinction: the distinction between two substances insofar as they are ontologically independent entities.

scientia: a fully evident cognition that admits of no possible doubt.

self: the thinking mind.

sensation: a mind-dependent entity that is occasioned by material bodies and that is experienced as inhering bodies, but that bodies do not possess.

sensory perception: a set of mental items – sensations and an idea of body – that are occasioned by external bodies.

substance: an entity that is ontologically independent and that (in the case of creatures) possesses attributes and modifications.

supreme perfection: being, eternality, immutability, independence, immutability, independence, omnipotence, omniscience, truth.

synthetic method: a method through which true conclusions are derived from true premises.

true and immutable nature: the nature of an entity insofar as the entity exists in reality.

truth: the conformity of an idea with its object.

voluntary: of the will, and not due to any other influences.

wonder: an attitude toward an object that a finite mind experiences to be new and unfamiliar.

Bibliography

John Edward Abbruzzese, "The Structure of Descartes's Ontological Proof," British Journal for the History of Philosophy 15 (2007), 253–282.

Igor Agostini, "Descartes and More on the Infinity of the World," British Journal for the History of Philosophy 25 (2017), 878–896.

Lilli Alanen, "Descartes's Dualism and the Philosophy of Mind," Revue de Metaphysique et de Morale 94 (1989), 391–413.

Lilli Alanen, "Descartes, Conceivability, and Logical Modality," in Thought Experiments in Science and Philosophy, ed. Tamara Horowitz, Savage, MD: Rowman and Littlefield (1991), 65–84.

Lilli Alanen, Descartes's Concept of Mind, Cambridge, MA: Harvard UP (2003).

Dan Arbib, "Note sur une maxime cartésienne «A nosse ad esse valet consequentia», AT, VII, 520, 5," Revue philosophique de Louvain 111 (2013), 491–512.

Antoine Arnauld, Fourth Objections, in The Philosophical Writings of Descartes, Volume II, ed. and trans. John Cottingham, Robert Stoothoff, and Dugald Murdoch, Cambridge and New York: Cambridge UP (1985), 138–153.

Mary Astell (1694/1697), A Serious Proposal to the Ladies, Parts I and II, ed. P. Springborg, Ontario: Broadview Literary Texts (2002).

Paul Audi, "Primitive Causal Relations and The Pairing Problem," Ratio 24 (2011), 1–16.

Annette Baier, "The Meditations and Descartes' considered conception of God," in Cunning (2014), 299–305.

Fabrizio Baldassarri, "The Mechanical Life of Plants: Descartes on Botany," British Society for the History of Science 52 (2019), 41–63.

Blandine Barret-Kriegel, "Politique-(s) de Descartes?," Archives de Philosophie 53 (1990), 371–388.

Galen Barry, "Cartesian Modes and the Simplicity of Mind," Pacific Philosophical Quarterly 96 (2015), 54–76.

Jonathan Bennett, "Descartes's Theory of Modality," The Philosophical Review 103 (1994), 639–667.

Jose Luis Bermudez, "Levels of Skepticism in the First Meditation," British Journal of the History of Philosophy 6 (1998), 237–245.

Jean-Marie Beyssade, "On Sensory-Motor Mechanisms in Descartes: Wonder Versus Reflex," in Williston and Gombay (2003), 129–152.

Omri Boehm, "Freedom and the Cogito," British Journal for the History of Philosophy 22 (2014), 704–724.

Martha Bolton, "Obscure and Confused Ideas of Sense," in Rorty (1986), 389–404.

Hélène Bouchilloux, "Le cogito de la Seconde Méditation: Une protestation contre le Malin genie," Revue Philosophique de la France et de l'Etranger 205 (2015), 3–16.

Deborah A. Boyle and Gerald J. Massey, "Descartes's Tests for (Animal) Mind," Philosophical Topics 27 (1999), 87–146.

Shoshana Brassfield, "Never Let the Passions Be Your Guide: Descartes and the Role of the Passions," British Journal for the History of Philosophy 21 (2012), 459–477.

Janet Broughton, Descartes's Method of Doubt, Princeton, NJ: Princeton UP (2002).

Janet Broughton and Ruth Mattern, "Reinterpreting Descartes on the Notion of the Union of Mind and Body," Journal of the History of Philosophy 16 (1978), 23–32.

Deborah Brown, Descartes and the Passionate Mind, Cambridge and New York: Cambridge UP (2006).

Deborah Brown, "The Sixth Meditation: Descartes and the Embodied Self," in Cunning (2014), 240–257.

Deborah Brown and Calvin Normore, Descartes and the Ontology of Everyday Life, New York and Oxford: Oxford UP (2019).

Panayot Butchvarov, "Faith without Theology," unpublished (2021).

John Carriero, Between Two Worlds: A Reading of Descartes's Meditations, Princeton, NJ: Princeton UP (2009).

Margaret Cavendish, Poems, and Fancies Written by the Right Honourable, the Lady Margaret Newcastle, London: Printed by T.R. for J. Martin, and J. Allestrye (1653).

Margaret Cavendish, Worlds Olio Written by the Right Honourable, the Lady Margaret Newcastle, London: Printed for J. Martin and J. Allestrye (1655).

Margaret Cavendish, Philosophical Letters, London (1664).

Margaret Cavendish, "Observations Upon the Opinions of Some Ancient Philosophers," in Observations Upon Experimental Philosophy, ed. Margaret Cavendish, Printed by A. Maxwell (1666).

Colin Chamberlain, "A Bodily Sense of Self in Descartes and Malebranche," in Subjectivity and Selfhood in Medieval and Early Modern Philosophy, ed. Jari Kaukua and Tomas Ekenberg, New York: Springer International Publishing (2016), 219–234.

Colin Chamberlain, "Color in a Material World: Margaret Cavendish against the Early Modern Mechanists," Philosophical Review 128 (2019), 293–336.

Colin Chamberlain, "The Body I Call 'Mine': A Sense of Bodily Ownership in Descartes," European Journal of Philosophy 27 (2019), 3–24. In the text this is Chamberlain (2019b).

Colin Chamberlain, "What Am I? Descartes's Various Conceptions of Self," Journal of Modern Philosophy 2 (2020), https://jmphil.org/articles/10.32881/jomp.30/.

Pierre Charron (1601), "On Wisdom," in *Descartes' Meditations: Background Source Materials*, ed. and trans. Roger Ariew, John Cottingham, and Tom Sorrell, Cambridge and New York: Cambridge UP (1998), 52–67.

Andrea Christofidou, "Descartes' Dualism: Correcting Some Misconceptions," *Journal of the History of Philosophy* 39 (2001), 215–238.

Andrea Christofidou, "Descartes on Freedom, Truth, and Goodness," *Noûs* (2009), 633–655.

Andrea Christofidou, "Descartes: A Metaphysical Solution to the Mind–Body Relation and the Intellect's Clear and Distinct Conception of the Union," *Philosophy* 94 (2019), 87–114.

Aurélien Chukurian, "L'approche cartésienne des attributs divins. L'indifférence du Dieu infini et providentiel suscitant une relation d'amour," *Revue de Theologie et de Philosophie* 150 (2018), 373–392.

Patricia S. Churchland and Christopher Suhler, "Agency and Control: The Subcortical Role in Good Decisions," in *Moral Psychology, Volume 4: Free Will and Responsibility*, ed. Walter Sinott-Armstrong, Cambridge, MA: MIT Press (2014), 309–326.

Brad Chynoweth, "Descartes' Resolution of the Dreaming Doubt," *Pacific Philosophical Quarterly* 91 (2010) 153–179.

Desmond M. Clarke, *Descartes: A Biography*, Cambridge and New York: Cambridge UP (2006).

David Clemenson, *Descartes' Theory of Ideas*, London: Continuum (2007).

David Clemenson, "The Scholastic Background," in *The Routledge Companion to Seventeenth Century Philosophy*, ed. Dan Kaufman, London: Routledge (2018), 3–32.

Harold J. Cook, *The Young Descartes*, Chicago and London: Chicago UP (2018).

John Cottingham, "'A Brute to the Brutes?': Descartes' Treatment of Animals," *Philosophy* 53 (1978), 551–559.

John Cottingham, "Cartesian Trialism," *Mind* 94 (1985), 218–230.

John Cottingham, *Descartes*, London: Blackwell (1986).

John Cottingham, "Cartesian Dualism: Theology, Metaphysics, and Science," in *The Cambridge Companion to Descartes*, ed. John Cottingham, Cambridge and New York: Cambridge UP (1992), 236–257.

John Cottingham, "Descartes and the Problem of Consciousness," in *Consciousness and the Great Philosophers*, ed. Stephen Leach and James Tartaglia, Abingdon and New York: Routledge (2017), 63–72.

John Cottingham, "The Passions and Religious Belief," *Royal Institute of Philosophy Supplement* 85 (2019), 57–74.

Ralph Cudworth (1678), *The True Intellectual System of the Universe*, Stuttgart-Bad Cannstatt: F. Fromann Verlag (1964).

David Cunning, "True and Immutable Natures and Epistemic Progress in Descartes's *Meditations*," *British Journal for the History of Philosophy* 11 (2003), 235–248.

David Cunning, "Systematic Divergences in Malebranche and Cudworth," *Journal of the History of Philosophy* 41 (2003), 343–363. In the text this is Cunning (2003b).

David Cunning, "Descartes on the Dubitability of the Existence of Self," *Philosophy and Phenomenological Research* 74 (2007), 111–131.

David Cunning, "Malebranche and Occasional Causes," *Philosophy Compass* 3 (2008), 1–20.

David Cunning, *Argument and Persuasion in Descartes' Meditations*, New York and Oxford: Oxford UP (2010).

David Cunning, *The Cambridge Companion to Descartes' Meditations*, Cambridge and New York: Cambridge UP (2014).

David Cunning, *Cavendish*, in the series *The Arguments of the Philosophers*, London: Routledge (2016).

David Cunning, "Hyperbolic Doubt, Cognitive Garbage, and the Regulae," *Revue Internationale De Philosophie* 290 (2019), 449–467.

David Cunning, "Cavendish and Strawson on Emergence, Mind, and Self," *Oxford Studies in Philosophy of Mind* 4 (2023), 369–398.

E.M. Curley, *Spinoza's Metaphysics*, Cambridge, MA: Harvard UP (1969).

E.M. Curley, "Descartes on the Creation of the Eternal Truths," *The Philosophical Review*, 93 (1984), 569–597.

E.M. Curley, "Analysis in the *Meditations*: The Quest for Clear and Distinct Ideas," in Rorty (1986), 153–176.

Edwin Curley, *Behind the Geometrical Method: A Reading of Spinoza's Ethics*, Princeton, NJ: Princeton UP (1988).

Jack Davidson, "Omnipotence: The Real Power Behind Descartes' Proofs of God's Existence," *The Modern Schoolman* 81 (2004), 275–294.

François-Xavier De Peretti, "L'ego cartésian à l'image de Dieu," *Laval Theologique et Philosophique* 71 (2015), 219–231.

François-Xaiver De Peretti, "Des idées aux choses chez Descartes. Sommes-nous capables d'idées adéquates?," *Revue Philosophique de Louvain* 114 (2016), 193–220.

Rafaella De Rosa, "Descartes on Sensory Misrepresentation: The Case of Materially False Ideas," *History of Philosophy Quarterly* 21 (2004), 261–280.

Raffaella De Rosa, "Rethinking the Ontology of Cartesian Essences," *British Journal for the History of Philosophy* 19 (2011), 605–622.

Rafaella De Rosa, "Descartes and the Curious Case of the Origin of Sensory Ideas," *Philosophy and Phenomenological Research* 97 (2018), 704–723.

Michael Della Rocca, *Representation and the Mind-Body Problem in Spinoza*, New York and Oxford: Oxford UP (1996).

Michael Della Rocca, "Descartes, the Cartesian Circle, and Epistemology Without God," *Philosophy and Phenomenological Research* 70 (2005), 1–33.

Michael Della Rocca, "Spinoza and the Metaphysics of Scepticism," *Mind* 116 (2007), 851–74.

Finnur Dellsén, "Certainty and Explanation in Descartes's Philosophy of Science," *HOPOS: The Journal of the International Society for the History of Philosophy of Science* 7 (2017), 302–327.

Daniel Dennett, *Intuition Pumps and Other Tools for Thinking*, New York: W.W. Norton & Company (2013).

Dennis Des Chene, *Physiologia: Natural Philosophy in Late Aristotelian and Cartesian Thought*, Ithaca, NY: Cornell UP (1996).

Dennis Des Chene, *Spirits and Clocks: Machine and Organism in Descartes*, Ithaca, NY: Cornell UP (2000).

Karen Detlefsen (ed.), *Descartes' Meditations: A Critical Guide*, Cambridge and New York: Cambridge UP (2012).

Georges Dicker, *Descartes: An Analytical and Historical Introduction*, New York and Oxford: Oxford UP (1993).

Tarek R. Dika, "The Origins of Cartesian Dualism," *The Journal of the American Philosophical Association* 6 (2020), 335–352.

Lisa Downing, "Sensible Qualities and Material Bodies in Descartes and Boyle," in Nolan (2011), 109–135.

Blake Dutton, "Descartes's Dualism and the One Principal Attribute Rule," *British Journal for the History of Philosophy* 11 (2003), 395–415.

Patricia Easton, "Robert Desgabets: A Cartesian?," in *A Companion to Early Modern Philosophy*, ed. Steven Nadler, Hoboken, NJ: Wiley-Blackwell (2002), 197–209.

Princess Elisabeth, "Princess Elisabeth of Bohemia to Rene Descartes, 16 May 1643," in *The Princess and the Philosopher*, ed. Andrea Nye, New York: Roman and Littlefield (1999), 9–10.

Brian Embry, "Cartesian Composites and the True Mode of Union," *Australasian Journal of Philosophy* 98 (2020), 629–645.

Epictetus, *The Handbook*, ed. and trans. Nicholas White, Indianapolis, IN: Hackett (1983).

Matthew C. Eshleman, "The Cartesian Unconscious," *History of Philosophy Quarterly* 24 (2007), 297–315.

Paul Feyerabend, *Against Method*, London: Verso (1975).

Carrie Figdor, *Pieces of Mind: The Proper Domain of Psychological Predicates*, New York and Oxford: Oxford UP (2018).

Gail Fine, "Plato and Aristotle on Form and Substance," *Proceedings of the Cambridge Philological Society* 29 (1983), 23–47.

Gail Fine, "Descartes and Ancient Skepticism: Reheated Cabbage?," *The Philosophical Review* 109 (2000), 195–234.

Harry Frankfurt, "Descartes on the Creation of the Eternal Truths," *The Philosophical Review* 86 (1977), 36–57.

Keith Frankish and Maria Kasmirli, "Mind and Consciousness," in *Central Issues in Philosophy*, ed. John Strand, Hoboken, NJ: Wiley-Blackwell (2009), 107–120.

Patrick Frierson, "Learning to love: From egoism to generosity in Descartes," *Journal of the History of Philosophy* 40 (2002), 313–338.

Galileo Galilei (1615), "Letter to the Grand Duchess Christina," in *Discoveries and Opinions of Galileo*, ed. and trans. Stillman Drake, Garden City, NY: DoubleDay Anchor Books (1957), 175–216.

Daniel Garber, "*Semel in Vita*: The Scientific Background to Descartes' *Meditations*," in Rorty (1986), 81–116.

Daniel Garber, *Descartes' Metaphysical Physics*, Chicago and London: Chicago UP (1992).

Daniel Garber, "Leibniz: Physics and Philosophy," in *The Cambridge Companion to Leibniz*, ed. Nicholas Jolley, Cambridge and New York: Cambridge UP (1994), 270–352.

Daniel Garber, *Descartes Embodied: Reading Cartesian Philosophy through Cartesian Science*, Cambridge and New York: Cambridge UP (2000).

Daniel Garber, "Descartes against the Materialists," in Detlefsen (2012), 45–63.

Daniel Garber and Roger Ariew (eds. and trans.), *Leibniz: Philosophical Essays*, Indianapolis, IN: Hackett Publishing (1989).

Don Garrett, "Representation and Consciousness in Spinoza's Naturalistic Theory of the Imagination," in *Interpreting Spinoza: Critical Essays, ed. Charles Huenemann*, Cambridge and New York: Cambridge UP (2008), 4–25.

Ryan Garrett, "A Cartesian Approach to Environmental Ethics," *Environmental Ethics* 40 (2018), 261–268.

Pierre Gassendi (1641), "Fifth Objections," in *The Philosophical Writings of Descartes, Volume II*, ed. and trans. John Cottingham, Robert Stoothoff, and Dugald Murdoch, Cambridge and New York: Cambridge UP (1985), 179–239.

Lynda Gaudemard, "Descartes's Conception of Mind Through the Prism of Imagination: Cartesian Substance Dualism Questioned," *Archiv für Geschichte der Philosophie* 100 (2018), 146–171.

Stephen Gaukroger, *Descartes: An Intellectual Biography*, London: Clarendon Press (1995).

Stephen Gaukroger, *Cartesian Logic: An Essay on Descartes's Conception of Inference*, New York and Oxford: Oxford UP (2002).

Christopher Gilbert, "Freedom and Enslavement: Descartes on Passions and the Will," *History of Philosophy Quarterly* 15 (1998), 177–190.

André Gombay, "Careerist Emotions," in Williston and Gombay (2003), 239–259.

André Gombay, *Descartes*, Hoboken, NJ: Wiley-Blackwell (2007).

Geoffrey Gorham, "Mind-Body Dualism and the Harvey-Descartes Controversy," *Journal of the History of Ideas* 55 (1994), 211–234.

Geoffrey Gorham, "Descartes on the Innateness of All Ideas," *Canadian Journal of Philosophy* 32 (2002), 355–388.

Geoffrey Gorham, "Descartes on God's Relation to Time," *Religious Studies* 44 (2008), 412–431.

Allan Gotthelf, "Aristotle's Conception of Final Causality," *Review of Metaphysics* 30 (1976), 226–254.

Sean Greenberg, "Descartes on the Passions. Function, Representation, and Motivation," *Noûs* 41 (2007), 714–734.

Amber L. Griffioen, "Doing Public Philosophy in the Middle Ages? On the Philosophical Potential of Medieval Devotional Texts," *Res Philosophica* 99 (2022), 241–274.

Laura Benitez Grobet, "Is Descartes a Materialist? The Descartes-More Controversy about the Universe as Indefinite," *Dialogue* 49 (2010), 517–526.

Martial Gueroult, *Descartes selon l'ordre des raisons, I: L'Ame et Dieu*, Paris: Aubier (1953).

Martial Gueroult, *Spinoza, I: Dieu*, Hildesheim: G. Olms (1968).

Glenn A. Hartz and Patrick K. Lewtas, "Is Descartes' Theological Voluntarism Compatible with His Philosophy?," in *Hypotheses and Perspectives in the History and*

Philosophy of Science: Homage to Alexandre Koyré 1892–1964, eds. Raffaele Pisano, Joseph Agassi, and Daria Drozdova, New York: Springer Academic Publishing (2017), 189–203.

Gary Hatfield, "Force (God) in Descartes' Physics," *Studies in History and Philosophy of Science Part A* 10 (1979), 113–140.

Gary Hatfield, "The Senses and the Fleshless Eye: The Meditations as Cognitive Exercises," in Rorty (1986), 45–80.

Gary Hatfield, "Transparency of Mind: The Contributions of Descartes, Leibniz, and Berkeley to the Genesis of the Modern Subject," in *Departure for Modern Europe: A Handbook of Early Modern Philosophy (1400–1700)*, ed. Hubertus Busche, Hamburg: Felix Meiner Verlag (2011), 361–375.

Gary Hatfield, "Descartes on Sensory Representation, Objective Reality, and Material Falsity," in Detlefsen (2012), 127–150.

Gary Hatfield, "Natural Geometry in Descartes and Kepler," *Res Philosophica* 92 (2015), 117–148.

Gary Hatfield, "Descartes: New Thoughts on the Senses," *British Journal for the History of Philosophy* 25 (2017), 443–464.

George Heffernan (trans.), *Meditations on First Philosophy*, South Bend, IN: Notre Dame UP (1992).

Jaakko Hintikka, "Cogito, Ergo Sum: Inference or Performance?," *The Philosophical Review* 71 (1962), 3–32.

Thomas Hobbes (1668), *Leviathan*, ed. Edwin Curley, Indianapolis, IN: Hackett (1994).

P.H.J. Hoenen, "Descartes's Mechanicism," in Willis Doney (ed.), *Descartes: A Collection of Critical Essays*, Garden City, NY: Doubleday (1967), 353–368.

Paul Hoffman, "The Unity of Descartes's Man," *Philosophical Review* 95 (1986), 339–70.

Paul Hoffman, "Descartes's Theory of Distinction," *Philosophy and Phenomenological Research* 64 (2002), 57–78.

Paul Hoffman, *Essays on Descartes*, New York and Oxford: Oxford UP (2009).

David Hume (1739), *A Treatise of Human Nature*, ed. P.H. Nidditch, Oxford: Clarendon Press (1978).

David Hume (1748), *An Enquiry Concerning Human Nature*, ed. Tom L. Beauchamp, New York and Oxford: Oxford UP (1999).

Marie Jayasekera, "'All in Their Nature Good': Descartes on the Passions of the Soul," *Journal of the History of Philosophy* 58 (2020), 71–92.

Renée Jeffery, "The Origins of the Modern Emotions: Princess Elisabeth of Bohemia and the Embodied Mind," *History of European Ideas* 43 (2017), 547–559.

Nicholas Jolley, "Leibniz and Malebranche on Innate Ideas," *The Philosophical Review* 97 (1988), 71–91.

Nicholas Jolley, *The Light of the Soul: Theories of Ideas in Leibniz, Malebranche, and Descartes*, New York and Oxford: Oxford UP (1990).

Richard Joyce, "Cartesian Memory," *Journal of the History of Philosophy* 35 (1997), 375–393.

Immanuel Kant (1781), *A Critique of Pure Reason*, ed. and trans. Norman Kemp Smith, Boston, MA and New York: Bedford/St. Martins (1965).

Dan Kaufman, "Descartes' Creation Doctrine and Modality," *Australasian Journal of Philosophy* 80 (2002), 24–41.

Dan Kaufman, "God's Immutability and the Necessity of Descartes's Eternal Truths," *Journal of the History of Philosophy* 43 (2005), 1–19.

Dan Kaufman, "Cartesian Substances, Individual Bodies, and Corruptibility," *Res Philosophica* 91 (2014), 71–102.

S.V. Keeling, *Descartes*, New York and Oxford: Oxford UP (1968).

Norman Kemp Smith, *Studies in the Cartesian Philosophy*, New York: Russell and Russell (1962).

Anthony Kenny, *Descartes: A Study of His Philosophy*, Bristol: Thoemmes Press (1968).

Anthony Kenny, "The Cartesian Circle and the Eternal Truths," *Journal of Philosophy* 67 (1970), 685–700.

Julie Klein, "Memory and the Extension of Thinking in Descartes's *Regulae*," *International Philosophical Quarterly* 42 (2002), 23–40.

Joshua Knobe and Shaun Nichols (ed.), *Experimental Philosophy*, New York and Oxford: Oxford UP (2008).

Alexandre Koyré, *From the Closed World to the Infinite Universe*, New York: Harper (1958).

David Landy, "Descartes' Compositional Theory of Mental Representation," *Pacific Philosophical Quarterly* 92 (2011) 214–231.

Jean Laporte, "La Finalité chez Descartes," *Review d'Histoire de la Philosophie* 2 (1928), 366–396.

Charles Larmore, "The First Meditation: Skeptical Doubt and Certainty," in Cunning (2014), 48–67.

Michael J. Latzer, "Descartes's Theodicy of Error," in *The Problem of Evil in Early Modern Philosophy*, ed. Elmar Kremer, Toronto: Toronto UP (2001), 35–48.

G.W. Leibniz (1686), *Discourse on Metaphysics*, in Garber and Ariew (1989), 35–68.

G.W. Leibniz (1686b), "Remarks on Arnauld's Letter about My Proposition That the Individual Notion of Each Person Includes Once and for All Everything That Will Ever Happen to Him," in Garber and Ariew (1989), 69–77.

G.W. Leibniz (1714), *Monadology*, in Garber and Ariew (1989), 213–224.

G.W. Leibniz (1765), *New Essays on Human Understanding*, trans. Peter Remnant and Jonathan Bennett, Cambridge and New York: Cambridge UP (1981).

Thomas M. Lennon, *The Battle of the Gods and Giants: The Legacy of Descartes and Gassendi*, Princeton, NJ: Princeton UP (1993).

Thomas M. Lennon, "Pandora; Or, Essence and Reference: Gassendi's Nominalist Objection and Descartes's Realist Reply," in *Descartes and His Contemporaries: Meditations, Objections, and Replies*, ed. Roger Ariew and Marjorie Greene, London and Chicago: Chicago UP (1995) 159–81.

Thomas M. Lennon, "Descartes's Supposed Libertarianism: Letter to Mesland or Memorandum concerning Petau?," *Journal of the History of Philosophy* 51 (2013), 223–248.

Thomas M. Lennon, "The Fourth Meditation: Descartes' theodicy *avant la lettre*," in Cunning (2014), 168–185.

Thomas M. Lennon and Michael W. Hickson, "The Skepticism of the First Meditation," in Detlefsen (2012), 9–24.

Thomas M. Lennon and Robert J. Stainton (eds.), *The Achilles of Rational Psychology*, New York: Springer Verlag (2008).

David Lewis, *Counterfactuals*, Oxford: Blackwell Publishing (1973).

David Lewis, *On the Plurality of Worlds*, New York and Oxford: Oxford UP (1986).

Charleton T. Lewis and Charles Short, *A Latin Dictionary*. Oxford: Clarendon Press (1879).

John Locke (1689), *An Essay Concerning Human Understanding*, ed. P.H. Nidditch, New York and Oxford: Oxford UP (1979).

Louis Loeb, "Is There Radical Dissimulation in Descartes' *Meditations*?," in Rorty (1986), 243–270.

Louis Loeb, "The Cartesian Circle," in *The Cambridge Companion to Descartes*, ed. John Cottingham, Cambridge and New York: Cambridge UP (1992), 200–235.

Gert-Jan Lokhorst, "Descartes and the Pineal Gland," *The Stanford Encyclopedia of Philosophy* (Winter 2021 Edition), Edward N. Zalta (ed.), https://plato.stanford.edu/archives/win2021/entries/pineal-gland/.

Ann MacKenzie, "The Reconfiguration of Sensory Experience," in *Reason, Will, and Sensation*, ed. John Cottingham, Oxford: Clarendon Press (1994), 251–272.

Daniel Malacara, *Color Vision and Colorimetry: Theory and Applications*, Second Edition, SPIE Press, Bellingham, WA (2011).

Nicolas Malebranche (1674), *The Search After Truth*, ed. and trans. Thomas M. Lennon and Paul J. Olscamp, Cambridge and New York: Cambridge UP (1997).

Nicolas Malebranche (1688), *Dialogues on Metaphysics and on Religion*, trans. David Scott and ed. Nicholas Jolley, Cambridge and New York: Cambridge UP (1997).

John Byron Manchak, "On Force in Cartesian Physics," *Philosophy of Science* 76 (2009), 295–306.

Pascal Marignac, "Descartes et ses concepts de la substance," *Revue Métaphysique et de Morale* 85 (1980), 298–314.

Jean-Luc Marion, *On Descartes' Metaphysical Prism*, trans. Jeffrey L. Kosky, Chicago and London: Chicago UP (1999).

Jean-Luc Marion, *On Descartes' Passive Thought: The Myth of Cartesian Dualism*, trans. Christina Gschwandtner, Chicago and London: Chicago UP (2018).

Sarah Marquardt, "The Long Road to Peace: Descartes' Modernization of Generosity in the Passions of the Soul (1649)," *History of Political Thought* 36 (2015), 53–83.

John Marshall, "Descartes's *Morale par Provision*," in Williston and Gombay (2003), 191–238.

Édouard Mehl, "Descartes ou la philosophie des (re)commencements," *Archives de Philosophie* 81 (2018), 49–67.

Christia Mercer, "The Methodology of the *Meditations*: Tradition and Innovation," in Cunning (2014), 23–47.

Christia Mercer, "Descartes' Debt to Teresa of Ávila, or Why We Should Work on Women in the History of Philosophy," Philosophical Studies 174 (2017), 2539–2555.

Murray Miles, "Connaissance de Dieu et conscience de soi chez Descartes," Dialogue: Canadian Philosophical Review 49 (2010), 1–24.

Michel Montaigne (1575–1576/1578–1580), "Apology for Raymond Sebond," in The Complete Essays of Montaigne, ed. and trans. Donald M. Frame, Redwood City, CA: Stanford UP (1957), 318–457.

Henry More (1659), "The Immortality of the Soul," in Philosophical Writings of Henry More, ed. Flora Isabel Mackinnon, Oxford: Oxford UP (1925), 55–180.

Georges J.D. Moyal, "L'arrière-plan aristotélicien du cogito," Studia Leibnitiana: Zeitschrift fuer Geschichte der Philosophie und der Wissenschaften 48 (2016), 89–105.

Anna Ortín Nadal, "Descartes on the Distinction between Primary and Secondary Qualities," British Journal for the History of Philosophy 27 (2019), 1113–1134.

Steven Nadler, Spinoza's Ethics: An Introduction, Cambridge and New York: Cambridge UP (2006).

Alan Nelson, "The Falsity in Sensory Ideas: Descartes and Arnauld," in Interpreting Arnauld, ed. Elmar J. Kremer, Toronto: Toronto UP (1996), 13–32.

Alan Nelson, "Descartes's Ontology of Thought," Topoi 16 (1997), 163–178.

Alan Nelson, "How Many Worlds?," British Journal for the History of Philosophy 19 (2011), 1201–1212.

Alan Nelson, "Conceptual Distinctions and the Concept of Substance in Descartes," ProtoSociology 30 (2013), 192–205.

Alan Nelson, "The Structure of Cartesian Sensations," Analytic Philosophy 54 (2013), 107–116. In the text this is Nelson (2013b).

Alan Nelson, "Modality in Descartes's Philosophy," in The Routledge Handbook of Modality, eds. Otávio Bueno, Scott A. Shalkowski, London: Routledge (2020), 355–363.

Alan Nelson and David Cunning, "Modality and Cognition in Descartes," Acta Philosophica Fennica 64 (1999), 137–153.

Lex Newman, "Descartes on Unknown Faculties and Our Knowledge of the External World," The Philosophical Review 103 (1994), 489–531.

Lex Newman, "The Fourth Meditation," Philosophy and Phenomenological Research 59 (1999), 559–591.

Lex Newman and Alan Nelson, "Circumventing Cartesian Circles," Noûs 33 (1999), 370–404.

Lawrence Nolan, "The Ontological Status of Cartesian Natures," Pacific Philosophical Quarterly 78 (1997), 169–194.

Lawrence Nolan, "Reductionism and Nominalism in Descartes's Theory of Attributes," Topoi 16 (1997), 129–140. In the text this is Nolan (1997b).

Lawrence Nolan, "Descartes' Theory of Universals," Philosophical Studies 89 (1998), 161–180.

Lawrence Nolan, "The Ontological Argument as an Exercise in Cartesian Therapy," Canadian Journal of Philosophy 35 (2005), 521–562.

Lawrence Nolan, "The Role of Imagination in Rationalist Philosophies of Mathematics," in *A Companion to Rationalism*, ed. Alan Nelson, Hoboken, NJ: Wiley-Blackwell (2005), 224–249. This is Nolan (2005b).

Lawrence Nolan, "Descartes on 'What We Call Color'," in *Primary and Secondary Qualities: The Historical and Ongoing Debate*, ed. Lawrence Nolan, New York and Oxford: Oxford UP (2011), 83–108.

Lawrence Nolan, "The Third Meditation: causal arguments for God's existence," in Cunning (2014), 127–148.

Lawrence Nolan and Alan Nelson, "Proofs for the Existence of God," in *The Blackwell Companion to Descartes' Meditations*, ed. Stephen Gaukroger, Hoboken, NJ: Blackwell (2006), 104–121.

Calvin Normore, "Meaning and Objective Being: Descartes and His Sources," in Rorty (1986), 223–242.

Calvin Normore, "Descartes's Possibilities," in *Rene Descartes: Critical Assessments*, Volume 1, ed. G.J.D. Moyal, London: Routledge (1991), 68–84.

Tammy Nyden and Mihnea Dobre (eds.), *Cartesian Empiricisms*, in the series *Studies in History and Philosophy of Science*, Dordrecht: Springer (2013).

Paul J. Olscamp (trans. and ed.), *Rene Descartes: Discourse on Method, Optics, Geometry, and Meterology*, Indianapolis, IN: Hackett (2001).

Mark A. Olson, "Descartes' First Meditation: Mathematics and the Laws of Logic," *Journal of the History of Philosophy* 26 (1988), 407–438.

Eileen O'Neill, "Margaret Cavendish, Stoic Antecedent Causes, and Early Modern Occasional Causes," *Revue Philosophique de la France Et de l'Etranger* 138 (2013), 311–326.

Margaret J. Osler, "Laws of Nature: The Theological Foundations of Descartes' Philosophy of Nature," *Journal of the History of Ideas* 46 (1985), 349–362.

David Owen, *Hume's Reason*, New York and Oxford: Oxford UP (2002).

Saja Parvizian, "Generosity, the Cogito, and the Fourth Meditation," *Res Philosophica* 93 (2016), 219–243.

Sarah Patterson, "Descartes on Nature, Habit and the Corporeal World," *Proceedings of the Aristotelian Society*, Supplementary Volumes, 87 (2013), 235–258.

Sarah Patterson, "Descartes on the Errors of the Senses," *Royal Institute of Philosophy Supplement* 78 (2016), 73–108.

Elliot Samuel Paul, "Descartes's Anti-Transparency and the Need for Radical Doubt," *Ergo* 5 (2018), 1083–1129.

Elliot Samuel Paul, "Cartesian Clarity," *Philosophers' Imprint* 20 (2020), 1–28.

Marie-Fréderique Pellegrin, "Cartesianism and Feminism," in *The Oxford Handbook of Descartes and Cartesianism*, ed. Steven Nadler, Tad M. Schmaltz, and Delphine Antoine-Mahut, New York and Oxford: Oxford UP (2019), 564–579.

Arnaud Pelletier, "Leibniz's Anti-scepticism," in *Scepticism in the Eighteenth Century: Enlightenment, Lumières, Aufklärung*, ed. Sébastien Charles and Plínio J. Smith, Dordrecht: Springer Academic Publishing (2013), 45–61.

Andrew Pessin, "Malebranche's Natural Theodicy and the Incompleteness of God's Volitions," *Religious Studies* 36 (2000), 47–63.

Andrew Pessin, "Malebranche's Doctrine of Freedom/Consent and the Incompleteness of God's Volitions," *British Journal for the History of Philosophy* 8 (2000), 21–53. In the text this is Pessin (2000b).

Andrew Pessin, "Divine Simplicity and the Eternal Truths: Descartes and the Scholastics," *Philosophia* 38 (2010), 69–105.

Lucian Petrescu, "Cartesian Meteors and Scholastic Meteors: Descartes against the School in 1637," *Journal of the History of Ideas* 76 (2015), 25–45.

Kristopher Gordon Phillips, *Cartesian Modality: God's Nature and the Creation of Eternal and Contingent Truth*, U Iowa PhD dissertation, ProQuest Publishing (2014), 3638421.

Plato, "Phaedo," in *Five Dialogues*, ed. and trans. G.M.A. Grube, revised by John M. Cooper, Indianapolis, IN: Hackett (2002), 93–154.

Andrew R. Platt, "Divine Activity and Motive Power in Descartes's Physics: Part I," *British Journal for the History of Philosophy* 19 (2011), 623–646.

Andrew R. Platt, "Divine Activity and Motive Power in Descartes's Physics: Part II," *British Journal for the History of Philosophy* 19 (2011), 849–871. In the text this is Platt (2011b).

Hilary Putnam, "Meaning and Reference," *The Journal of Philosophy* 70 (1973), 699–711.

Quintilian, *Institutio Oratio*, trans. H.E. Butler, London: Loeb Classical Library (1920–1922), volume II.

Daisie Radner, "The Function of the Passions," in Williston and Gombay (2003), 175–187.

C.P. Ragland, "Descartes on Divine Providence and Human Freedom," *Archiv für Geschichte der Philosophie* 87 (2005), 159–188.

C.P. Ragland, "Descartes on the Principle of Alternative Possibilities," *Journal of the History of Philosophy* 44 (2006), 377–394.

C.P. Ragland, "Descartes's Theodicy," *Religious Studies* 43 (2007), 125–144.

C.P. Ragland, *The Will to Reason: Theodicy and Freedom in Descartes*, New York and Oxford: Oxford UP (2016).

C.P. Ragland and Everett Fulmer, "The Fourth Meditation and Cartesian Circles," *Philosophical Annals: Special Issue on Descartes' Epistemology* 68 (2020), 119–138.

Jasper Reid, "Descartes and the Individuation of Bodies," *Archiv für Geschichte der Philosophie* 96 (2014), 38–70.

Laurence Renault, "Causa sui et substantialité: La réforme de la notion de substance, de Descartes à Spinoza," *Educação E Filosofia* 29 (2015), 123–146.

Marina Reuter, "Freedom of the Will as a Basis of Equality: Descartes, Princess Elisabeth and Poullain de la Barre," in *Freedom and the Construction of Europe*, Volume I, ed. Quentin Skinner and Martin van Gelderen, Cambridge and New York: Cambridge UP (2010), 65–83.

C. Riek, D.V. Seletskiy, A.S. Moskalenko, J.F. Schmidt, P. Krauspe, S. Eckhart, S. Eggert, G. Burkard, and A. Leitenstorfer, "Direct Sampling of Electric-Field Vacuum Fluctuations," *Science* 350 (2015), 420–423.

Camille Riquier, "Descartes, Spinoza et la preuve ontologique," *Archives de Philosophie* 83 (2020), 21–35.

Geneviève Rodis-Lewis, *Descartes: His Life and Thought*, trans. Jane Marie Todd, Ithaca, NY: Cornell UP (1998).

Richard Rorty, *Philosophy and the Mirror of Nature*, Princeton, NJ: Princeton UP (1981).

Amélie Oksenberg Rorty, *Essays on Descartes's* Meditations, Berkeley and Los Angeles: California UP (1986).

Marleen Rozemond, "The First Meditation and the Senses," *The British Journal of the History of Philosophy* 4 (1996), 21–52.

Marleen Rozemond, *Descartes's Dualism*, Cambridge, MA: Harvard UP (1998).

Marleen Rozemond, "Real Distinction, Separability, and Corporeal Substance in Descartes," *Midwest Studies in Philosophy* 35 (2011), 240–258.

Marleen Rozemond, "The Faces of Simplicity in Descartes's Soul," in *Partitioning the Soul: Debates from Plato to Leibniz*, ed. Klaus Corcilius and Dominik Perler, Berlin & New York: W. de Gruyter (2014), 219–244.

Marleen Rozemond, "Descartes, Malebranche and Leibniz: Conceptions of Substance in Arguments for the Immateriality of the Soul," *British Journal for the History of Philosophy* 24 (2016), 836–857.

Bertrand Russell, "The Philosophy of Logical Atomism," in *Logic and Knowledge*, ed. R.C. Marsh, London: Allen and Unwin (1956), 178–281.

Donald Rutherford, "Descartes' Ethics," in *The Stanford Encyclopedia of Philosophy* (Winter 2019 Edition), ed. Edward N. Zalta, https://plato.stanford.edu/archives/win2019/entries/descartes-ethics/.

Anat Schechtman, "Descartes' Argument for the Existence of the Idea of an Infinite Being," *Journal of the History of Philosophy* 52 (2014), 487–517.

Anat Schechtman, "Substance and Independence in Descartes," *Philosophical Review* 125 (2016), 155–204.

Anat Schechtman, "The Allegedly Cartesian Roots of Spinoza's Metaphysics," *Philosophers' Imprint* 18 (2018), 1–23.

Dániel Schmal, "Intellectual Memory and Consciousness in Descartes's Philosophy of Mind," *Society and Politics* 12 (2018), 28–49.

Tad M. Schmaltz, "Platonism and Descartes' View of Immutable Essences," *Archiv für Geschichte der Philosophie* 73 (1991), 129–170.

Tad M. Schmaltz, *Radical Cartesianism*, Cambridge and New York: Cambridge UP (2002).

Tad M. Schmaltz, *Descartes on Causation*, New York and Oxford: Oxford UP (2007).

Tad M. Schmaltz, "Descartes on the Extensions of Space and Time," *Analytica* 13 (2009), 113–147.

Tad M. Schmaltz, "The Metaphysics of Rest in Descartes and Malebranche," *Res Philosophica* 92 (2015), 21–40.

Tad M. Schmaltz, "Descartes on the Metaphysics of the Material World," *Philosophical Review* 127 (2018), 1–40.

Amy Morgan Schmitter, "Representation, Self-Representation, and the Passions in Descartes," *Review of Metaphysics* 48 (1994), 331–357.

Amy Schmitter, "The Third Meditation on objective being: representation and intentional content," in Cunning (2014), 149–167.

Rudolf Schüssler, "Descartes' Doxastic Voluntarism," *Archiv für Geschichte der Philosophie* 95 (2013), 148–177.

Jorge Secada, "God and Meditation," in Detlefsen (2012), 200–225.

Dennis L. Sepper, "Imagination, Phantasm, and the Making of Hobbesian and Cartesian Science," *The Monist* 71 (1988), 526–542.

Dennis Sepper, "Animal Spirits," in *The Cambridge Descartes Lexicon*, ed. Lawrence Nolan, Cambridge and New York: Cambridge UP (2015), 26–28.

Dennis Sepper, "Descartes," in *The Routledge Handbook of Philosophy of Imagination*, ed. Amy Kind, London: Routledge (2016), 27–39.

Lisa Shapiro, "Cartesian Generosity," *Acta Philosophica Fennica* 64 (1999), 249–275.

Lisa Shapiro, "The Structure of *The Passions of the Soul* and the Soul-Body Union," in Williston and Gombay (2003), 31–79.

Lisa Shapiro, "Descartes' Passions of the Soul and the Union of Mind and Body," *Archiv für Geschichte der Philosophie* 85 (2003), 211–248.

Lisa Shapiro, "Descartes on Human Nature and the Human Good," in *The Rationalists: Between Tradition and Innovation*, ed. Carlos Fraenkel, Dario Perinetti, and Justin E.H. Smith, New York: Springer Publishing (2011), 13–26.

Lady Mary Shepherd (1827), "Essays on the Perception of an External Universe," in *Mary Shepherd: Selected Writings*, the Library of Scottish Philosophy Series, ed. Deborah Boyle, Exeter: Imprint Academic (2018), 93–199.

Samuel Shirley (trans.) and Michael L. Morgan (ed.), *Spinoza: Complete Works*, Indianapolis, IN: Hackett Publishing (2002).

Alison Simmons, "Sensible Ends: Latent Teleology in Descartes' Account of Sensation," *Journal of the History of Philosophy* 39 (2001), 49–75.

Alison Simmons, "Descartes on the Cognitive Structure of Sensory Experience," *Philosophy and Phenomenological Research* 67 (2003), 549–579.

Alison Simmons, "Guarding the Body: A Cartesian Phenomenology of Perception," in *Contemporary Perspectives on Early Modern Philosophy: Essays in Honor of Vere Chappell*, ed. Paul Hoffman and Gideon Yaffe, Guelph, ON: Broadview Press (2008), 81–113.

Alison Simmons, "Re-Humanizing Descartes," *Philosophic Exchange* 1 (2010), 53–71.

Alison Simmons, "Cartesian Consciousness Reconsidered," *Philosophers' Imprint* 12 (2012), 1–21.

Alison Simmons, "Sensory Perception of Bodies: Meditation 6.5," in Cunning (2014), 258–276.

Alison Simmons, "Mind-Body Union and the Limits of Cartesian Metaphysics," *Philosophers' Imprint* 17 (2017), 1–36.

David Skrbina, *Pansychism in the West*, Cambridge, MA: The MIT Press (2005).

Edward Slowik, "Descartes' Physics," *The Stanford Encyclopedia of Philosophy*, ed. Edward N. Zalta (2021), https://plato.stanford.edu/entries/descartes-physics/.

Kurt Smith, "A General Theory of Cartesian Clarity and Distinctness Based on the Theory of Enumeration in the Rules," *Dialogue: Canadian Philosophical Review* 40 (2002), 279–309.

Kurt Smith, *Matter Matters*, New York and Oxford: Oxford UP (2010).

Alice Sowaal, "Cartesian Bodies," *Canadian Journal of Philosophy* 34 (2004), 217–240.

Alice Sowaal, "Descartes's Reply to Gassendi: How We Can Know All of God, All at Once, but Still Have More to Learn about Him," *British Journal for the History of Philosophy* 19 (2011), 419–449.

Alice Sowaal, "The Emerging Picture of Mary Astell's Views," in *Feminist Interpretations of Mary Astell*, ed. Alice Sowaal and Penny A. Weiss, University Park, PA: Penn State UP (2015), 188–206.

Baruch Spinoza (1677), *Ethics*, in Shirley and Morgan (2002), 213–382.

Baruch Spinoza (1660), *Treatise on the Emendation of the Intellect*, in Shirley and Morgan (2002), 1–30.

Baruch Spinoza (1662), *Short Treatise on God, Man, and His Well-Being*, in Shirley and Morgan (2002), 31–107.

Galen Strawson, "Realistic Monism: Why Physicalism Entails Panpsychism," in *Real Materialism and Other Essays*, ed. Galen Strawson, New York and Oxford: Oxford UP (2008), 53–74.

Galen Strawson, "Consciousness, Free Will, and Determinism," in *Real Materialism and Other Essays*, ed. Galen Strawson, New York and Oxford: Oxford UP (2008), 337–358. This is abbreviated as Strawson (2008b).

Galen Strawson, "Real Materialism," in *Real Materialism and other essays*, ed. Galen Strawson (Oxford UP, 2008), 19–51. In the text this is Strawson (2008c).

Galen Strawson, *Selves*, New York and Oxford: Oxford UP (2009).

Leopold Stubenberg, "Neutral Monism", *The Stanford Encyclopedia of Philosophy*, ed. Edward N. Zalta (2018), https://plato.stanford.edu/archives/fall2018/entries/neutral-monism/.

Joshua Stuchlik, "Circling to Scientia: Reading Descartes in Light of the Debate between Stoic Dogmatists and Academic Skeptics," *Journal of the History of Philosophy* 55 (2017), 55–81.

Eleonore Stump and Normal Kretzmann, "Being and Goodness," in *Being and Goodness: The Concept of the Good in Metaphysics and Philosophical Theology*, ed. Scott MacDonald, Ithaca, NY: Cornell UP (1991), 98–128.

Francisco Suarez (1597), *On Creation, Conservation, and Concurrence: Metaphysical Disputations 20–22*, trans. and ed. Alfred J. Freddoso, South Bend, IN: St. Augustine's Press (2002).

Melanie Tate, "Descartes on Hatred," *The Southern Journal of Philosophy* 55 (2017), 336–349.

Evan Thomas, "Descartes on the Animal Within, and the Animals Without," *Canadian Journal of Philosophy* 50 (2020), 999–1014.

Amie Thomasson, "Truthmakers and Easy Ontology," *Oxford Studies in Metaphysics* 12 (2021), 3–34.

Mihai-Dragos Vadana, "La Meditatio Quinta de Descartes est-elle une méditation métaphysique? Sur la méditation métaphysique de l'attention," *Revue Roumaine de Philosophie* 61 (2017), 157–172.

James Van Cleve, "Descartes and the Destruction of the Eternal Truths," *Ratio* 7 (1994), 58–62.

Peter Van Inwagen, *An Essay on Free Will*, Oxford: Clarendon Press (1983).

David Vander Laan, "Creation and Conservation," *The Stanford Encyclopedia of Philosophy* (Winter 2017 Edition), ed. Edward N. Zalta, https://plato.stanford.edu/archives/win2017/entries/creation-conservation/.

Valtteri Viljanen, "Why Virtue Is not Quite Enough: Descartes on Attaining Happiness," *Archiv für Geschichte der Philosophie* 103 (2021), 54–69.

Jean-Baptiste Jeangène Vilmer, "Argumentation cartésienne: Logos, Ethos, Pathos," *Revue philosophique de Louvain* 106 (2008), 459–494.

Jean-Baptiste Jeangène Vilmer, "Le paradoxe de l'infini cartésien," *Archives de Philosophie* 72 (2009), 497–521.

Jean-Baptiste Jeangène Vilmer, "Descartes et les bornes de l'univers: l'indéfini physique," *Philosophiques* 37 (2010), 299–323.

Thomas C. Vinci, *Cartesian Truth*, New York and Oxford: Oxford UP (1998).

Stephen J. Wagner, "Descartes's Arguments for Mind-Body Distinctness," *Philosophy and Phenomenological Research* 43 (1983), 499–517.

Anik Waldow, "Activating the Mind: Descartes' Dreams and the Awakening of the Human Animal Machine," *Philosophy and Phenomenological Research* 94 (2017), 299–325.

Richard Watson, "Descartes Knows Nothing," *History of Philosophy Quarterly* 1 (1984), 399–411.

Richard Watson, *Cogito Ergo Sum: The Life of Descartes*, Jaffrey, NH: David R Godine Publishing (2002).

Mark Webb, "Natural Theology and the Concept of Perfection in Descartes, Spinoza and Leibniz," *Religious Studies* 25 (1989), 459–475.

Cecilia Wee, "Newman and the Proof of the External World in Descartes's *Meditations*," *British Journal for the History of Philosophy* 9 (2001), 123–130.

Cecilia Wee, "Self, Other, and Community in Cartesian Ethics," *History of Philosophy Quarterly* 19 (2002), 255–273.

Cecilia Wee, "Descartes and Leibniz on Human Free-Will and the Ability to Do Otherwise," *Canadian Journal of Philosophy* 36 (2006), 387–414.

Cecilia Wee, "Descartes's Ontological Proof of God's Existence," *British Journal for the History of Philosophy* 20 (2012), 23–40.

Cecilia Wee, "The Fourth Meditation: Descartes and Libertarian Freedom," in Cunning (2014), 186–204.

Bernard Williams, *Descartes: The Project of Pure Enquiry*, London: Routledge (1978).

Byron Williston and André Gombay (eds.), *Passion and Virtue in Descartes*, Amherst, NY: Humanity Books (2003).

Byron Williston, "The Cartesian Sage and the Problem of Evil," in Williston and Gombay (2003), 301–331.

Margaret Wilson, *Descartes*, in the series *The Arguments of the Philosophers*, New York: Routledge and Kegan Paul (1978).

Margaret Wilson, "History of Philosophy in Philosophy Today; and the Case of the Sensible Qualities," *The Philosophical Review* 101 (1992), 191–243.

Margaret Wilson, *Ideas and Mechanism: Essays on Early Modern Philosophy*, Princeton, NJ: Princeton UP (1999).

Celia Wolf-Devine, *Descartes on Seeing: Epistemology and Visual Perception*, Carbondale: Southern Illinois University Press (1993).

Eugenio E. Zaldivar, "Descartes's Theory of Substance: Why He Was Not a Trialist," *British Journal for the History of Philosophy* 19 (2011), 395–418.

Index

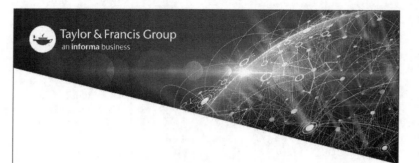